A Defense of Abortion

David Boonin has written the most thorough and detailed case for the moral permissibility of abortion yet published. Critically examining a wide range of arguments that attempt to prove that every human fetus has a right to life, he shows that each of these arguments fails on its own terms. He then explains how even if the fetus does have a right to life, abortion can still be shown to be morally permissible on the critic of abortion's own terms. Finally, he considers several arguments against abortion that do not depend on the claim that the fetus has a right to life – arguments based on the golden rule, on principles of uncertainty, or on various feminist theories – and concludes that these, too, are ultimately unsuccessful.

This major book will be especially helpful to those teaching applied ethics and bioethics whether in philosophy departments or professional schools of law and medicine. It will also interest students of women's studies as well as all general readers for whom abortion remains a high-profile and complex issue.

David Boonin is Associate Professor of Philosophy at the University of Colorado at Boulder.

Cambridge Studies in Philosophy and Public Policy

General editor: Douglas MacLean, *University of Maryland, Baltimore County*

A Defense of Abortion

DAVID BOONIN

University of Colorado, Boulder

CAMBRIDGE
UNIVERSITY PRESS

CAMBRIDGE UNIVERSITY PRESS
Cambridge, New York, Melbourne, Madrid, Cape Town, Singapore, São Paulo

Cambridge University Press
The Edinburgh Building, Cambridge CB2 2RU, UK

Published in the United States of America by Cambridge University Press, New York

www.cambridge.org
Information on this title: www.cambridge.org/9780521817011

First published 2003

A catalogue record for this publication is available from the British Library

Library of Congress Cataloguing in Publication data
Boonin, David.
A defense of abortion/David Boonin.
p. cm – (Cambridge studies in philosophy and public policy)
Includes bibliographical references and index.
ISBN 0-521-81701-3 – ISBN 0-521-52035-5 (pbk.)
1. Abortion – Moral and ethical aspects. I. Title. II. Series.
HQ767.15 .B66 2002
179.7'6–dc21   2002022282

ISBN-13 978-0-521-81701-1 hardback
ISBN-10 0-521-81701-3 hardback

ISBN-13 978-0-521-52035-5 paperback
ISBN-10 0-521-52035-5 paperback

Transferred to digital printing 2005

For my students

Contents

Contents

Contents

Preface

This was a difficult book to write for two reasons. One is that the subject with which it is concerned raises a number of philosophical questions that have no simple answers. In this sense, writing the book was intellectually difficult. It is, of course, a commonplace to observe that the moral problem of abortion is a difficult one. But it is a platitude that nonetheless merits repeating: Even though people say it all the time, relatively few people seem actually to believe it. Opponents of abortion typically seem to believe that the matter is fairly clear-cut: The fetus is a human being, killing human beings is morally wrong, abortion causes the death of the fetus, therefore abortion is morally wrong. And supporters of abortion often seem to treat the matter as equally simple: It's the woman's body, so it's her choice. This book grew out of a course on the ethics of abortion that I first offered at Tulane University in the fall of 1995, and if there is one thing that I learned from teaching that course, it is that the moral problem of abortion is every bit as complicated as the platitude would suggest.

The other reason that this book was difficult to write is more personal. On the desk in my office where most of this book was written and revised, there are several pictures of my son, Eli. In one, he is gleefully dancing on the sand along the Gulf of Mexico, the cool ocean breeze wreaking havoc with his wispy hair. In a second, he is tentatively seated in the grass in his grandparents' backyard, still working to master the feat of sitting up on his own. In a third, he is only a few weeks old, clinging firmly to the arms that are holding him and still wearing the tiny hat for preserving body heat that he wore home from the hospital. Through all of the remarkable changes that these pictures preserve, he remains unmistakably the same little boy.

In the top drawer of my desk, I keep another picture of Eli. This picture was taken on September 7, 1993, 24 weeks before he was born. The sonogram image is murky, but it reveals clearly enough a small head tilted back slightly, and an arm raised up and bent, with the hand pointing back toward the face and the thumb extended out toward the mouth. There is no doubt in my mind that this picture, too, shows the same little boy at a very early stage in his physical development. And there is no question that the position I defend in this book entails that it would have been morally permissible to end his life at this point.

Perhaps it will be thought distasteful of me to mention this fact. I find, on the contrary, that what is distasteful is to think of abortion as a purely theoretical issue, an intriguing philosophical problem that should be grappled with only in abstract and impersonal terms. It is true that abortion poses an intriguing philosophical problem, and it is true that it is necessary to apply abstract and general categories of thought to it in order to make progress in its resolution. That is what I have attempted to do in this book. But the moral problem of abortion is not like other intellectual puzzles where little is at stake beyond the mere display of philosophical acumen, and it is objectionable to think of it as if it were. It gives me no pleasure to confess that there were times when I was working on this book when I was tempted to lose sight of this important fact, even though it is precisely the practical gravity of the problem that drew me to this research project in the first place. On those occasions, when to my dismay I found myself becoming more concerned with being clever than with being right, when I was tempted to complacently embrace an unconvincing response to a cogent objection to my position rather than to seriously confront the possibility that my position stood in need of revision, I often pulled that picture out of my drawer. That picture prevented me from giving in to such inclinations. It forced me to ask myself directly and honestly not whether I believed that the words that I had thus far written were impressive, or whether they might convince others, or whether they might be good enough to be published, but simply whether I believed that they were true. In doing so, the picture in my desk drawer made my task far more challenging and, at times, emotionally burdensome. My hope is that, in the end, it also helped me to do justice to a difficult and important subject.

Acknowledgments

This book began as a series of lecture notes for a course on the ethics of abortion, a course that I first taught at Tulane University in the fall of 1995. My first and most important debt is therefore to my students, both at Tulane and later at the University of Colorado. Virtually every decision that I made about how to organize, present, clarify, analyze, and revise the material in this book was shaped by the questions and comments that arose through my teaching of the issues that the book covers in a variety of courses over a period of several years. It is possible that I could have written a book about abortion without the countless contributions that my students made to my thinking and my writing on this subject, but I could not have written *this* book. I am therefore pleased to acknowledge how much this book owes to the many students who studied the problem of abortion with me over the last several years and to dedicate the final result to them.

As my sketchy lecture notes gradually began to be transformed into readable paragraphs, arguments, and chapters, I benefited enormously from a further pool of talented critics. Some of these were colleagues, first at Tulane and then, as I came closer to a final draft, at the University of Colorado. Of these, I would especially like to thank Bruce Brower, Graeme Forbes, and Eric Mack at Tulane and Luc Bovens, Claudia Mills, Jim Nickel, Graham Oddie, and Michael Tooley at Colorado. Claudia and Michael, in particular, deserve special thanks for meticulously poring over the entire penultimate draft of the book and providing extremely clear and detailed suggestions for further revisions. Although I cannot say that I was happy to see how much more work they found for me to do at a time when I thought I was very close to being finished, I can now honestly say that I am grateful that they prodded me into doing it.

Acknowledgments

I also received valuable suggestions and feedback on this project from a number of friends from my graduate school days. Of these, I would especially like to acknowledge Alisa Carse, Jon Mandle, Alec Walen, and Sara Worley. Other fellow philosophers contributed valuable insights throughout the course of my work on this project, including Marcia Baron, Michael Burke, Sara Buss, Michael Davis, Todd Furman, Jeff McMahan, Christian Perring, and Bonnie Steinbock. I also received a great deal of useful advice and criticism at a number of stages from my series editor, Douglas MacLean. My father, Len Boonin, earned the perhaps dubious distinction of being the only person to comment on complete drafts of both this book and my previous work on Thomas Hobbes. And I am deeply indebted to four forceful critics of abortion whose works I grappled with at numerous points in my research and who all generously shared their time and insights with me: Patrick Lee, by mail and e-mail; Don Marquis, in writing and in person; Steven Schwarz, in several long and productive telephone conversations; and, especially, Jim Stone, in numerous rewarding and challenging conversations during my four years in New Orleans.

In addition to the intellectual support that I depended on during the writing of this book, I would also like briefly to acknowledge three further sources of assistance. One is financial: I am grateful to the Senate Committee on Research at Tulane University for a grant that supported research during the summer of 1995 and to the University of Colorado for a grant that supported further work in the summer of 1999. The second is editorial: I would like to thank Terry Moore, my editor at Cambridge University Press, for all of his work on behalf of this project, and to apologize belatedly for neglecting to thank him in the acknowledgments to my previous book for the equally valuable assistance he provided me with then. My final debt is personal: I am profoundly grateful to my friends and family for their love and support. Without their support, finishing this book would not have been possible. Without their love, finishing it would not have been worthwhile.

Chapter 1

Framing the Debate

The moral problem of abortion is difficult because it is unusual. It is unusual both because the human fetus is so unlike other individuals and because the relationship between fetus and pregnant woman is so unlike other relationships. Its unusualness makes it difficult because we are accustomed to settling particular moral disputes by appealing to general moral principles, a procedure that presupposes a substantial degree of similarity between the question we wish to answer and other questions we feel we have, at least tentatively, resolved. As a result, people who find themselves substantially in agreement about what their moral duties to each other are often find themselves not only sharply divided over the problem of abortion, but uncertain about how to bridge the divide.

This feature of the abortion debate can give rise to the impression that the problem cannot be resolved rationally. If what is meant by this claim is that reasonable people will continue to disagree about abortion, then the claim is surely true. But the claim that the abortion controversy cannot be settled rationally is often taken to mean more than this. It is often taken to mean, as one writer has put it, that "each side of the abortion debate has an internally coherent and mutually shared view of the world that is...completely at odds with the world view held by their opponents," and that "the two sides share almost no common premises" (Luker 1984: 159, 2). On this view, the question of the moral status of abortion is so far removed from any other moral question about which the two sides agree that neither side's position can be shown to be more reasonable than the other's on terms that the other side can accept. The debate about the morality of abortion, then, boils down

1

to a mere exchange of conflicting normative assertions or to a clash of fundamental, and incommensurable, values.

If this is what is meant by the claim that the moral problem of abortion cannot be resolved rationally, then I believe that the claim is false. Most arguments against abortion rest on claims that defenders of abortion are unlikely to reject, such as the claim that killing people like you and me is wrong and the claim that the zygotes that are formed by the fusion of a sperm and an egg at conception eventually develop into people like you and me. If one or more of these arguments is successful, then critics of abortion can justifiably claim that their position has been shown to be more reasonable than the other's on terms that the other side can accept. And if none of these arguments are successful, then defenders of abortion can justifiably claim that they have successfully defended abortion from the challenge that its critics have mounted against it. I believe that many such arguments against abortion are substantially stronger than they are typically recognized to be, and that many people who argue in defense of abortion have failed to respond to them adequately. But I also believe that these arguments against abortion, although at times quite powerful, are ultimately unsuccessful. Indeed, it is the central thesis of this book that the moral case against abortion can be shown to be unsuccessful on terms that critics of abortion can, and already do, accept. I attempt to defend this thesis in the chapters that follow.

Before turning to this task, however, I must first say something about how a discussion of abortion must be framed in order to argue on terms that the critic of abortion accepts. Doing so is the purpose of this brief, introductory chapter. In Section 1.1, I specify what it means to call a practice morally permissible, and I explain why a defense of abortion that seeks to address critics of abortion on their own terms should focus on defending the claim that abortion, at least in typical cases, is permissible in this sense. In Section 1.2, I briefly describe the method of moral reasoning that I make use of in this work and attempt to show why it is not only a reasonable approach to addressing moral problems in general but, more importantly, why it is especially well suited to a discussion of abortion that attempts to engage critics of abortion on their own terms. In Section 1.3, I distinguish between two kinds of arguments that critics of abortion have offered, those that are based on the claim that the fetus has a right to life and those that are not, and emphasize that a satisfactory defense of abortion must address both.

In Chapters 2 and 3, I take up the central claim made by the first, rights-based, kind of argument against abortion: the claim that the fetus has a right to life. In Chapter 2, I consider those arguments that have been offered in defense of the claim that the fetus acquires this right at the moment of its conception, and argue that none of them are successful. In Chapter 3, I examine arguments that have been offered in defense of the claim that the fetus acquires this right at various points after its conception, and argue that, by the abortion critic's own standards, the most reasonable view is the one in which the fetus acquires this right when its brain reaches a certain level of maturity. Since it turns out that the vast majority of abortions occur well before this point, the result of the discussion in Chapters 2 and 3 is that the central claim needed to sustain the rights-based argument against abortion must be rejected on the abortion critic's own terms.

In Chapter 4, I turn to the second claim needed to sustain the rights-based argument against abortion: the claim that if the fetus does have a right to life, then abortion is morally impermissible. I present an argument, first proposed by Judith Jarvis Thomson, that attempts to demonstrate that this claim is false. The argument compares a woman with an unwanted pregnancy to one who may permissibly refuse to perform an act of good samaritanship that is needed to keep an innocent person alive. Although the argument has been subject to a number of important objections, I argue that all of these objections ultimately fail on the abortion critic's own terms. The result of Chapter 4, then, is that even if my analysis in Chapters 2 and 3 is rejected, the rights-based argument against abortion must still be deemed unsuccessful for most (but not all) cases of abortion. Finally, in Chapter 5, I turn to those arguments against abortion that do not fit the model of the rights-based argument, including those that appeal to some version of the golden rule or to claims about our lack of certainty about the morality of abortion, as well as those that underlie the position that has come to be known as pro-life feminism. These arguments do not rely on either claim made by the rights-based argument, and so are not undermined by anything said in Chapters 2–4. I argue, however, that these arguments, too, can be shown to be unsuccessful on the abortion critic's own terms.

1.1. THE QUESTION

1.1.1. Framing the Question

There are two different kinds of questions about which critics and defenders of abortion disagree: "Is abortion moral or immoral?" and

"Should abortion be legal or illegal?" In principle, these are importantly distinct questions. There are actions, such as jaywalking, which we may think to be justifiably illegal and yet not immoral, and there are actions, such as adultery, which we may think to be immoral and yet not justifiably illegal. Still, as a practical matter, it is difficult to avoid the conclusion that, at least in the case of abortion, the moral question is the more fundamental. If almost everyone believed that abortion was perfectly moral, it is unlikely that there would be much public demand for laws criminalizing abortion or that such laws would be effectively enforced if they were passed.[1] And if almost everyone believed that abortion was morally on a par with murder, it is unlikely that women wishing to have abortions would find that they were easily available, even if they were technically legal.[2] Since the moral question of abortion is the more fundamental in this respect, an inquiry into the subject should begin with it. And since the moral question of abortion is a difficult enough question on its own, I will limit my focus in this book to it alone.

To refer to *the* moral question of abortion, however, is misleading. There is more than one moral question that can be asked. One can ask "Is abortion morally impermissible?" and "Is abortion morally criticizable?" Like many distinctions in ethics, this one is easier to recognize when it is seen than to characterize adequately in general, formal terms. So let me begin with an example: Consider an imaginary billionaire named Donald who has just unexpectedly won a million dollars from a one-dollar lottery ticket. He is trying to decide what to do with the money and has limited himself to the following options: (1) donating the money to several worthy charities, (2) putting it in his savings account, (3) buying a gold-plated Rolls Royce, (4) putting up billboards across the country that read "I hate Ivana," and (5) hiring a hitman to kill Ivana. One thing we are likely to say about this list is that there is a morally relevant sense in which the choices become progressively worse. We would be entitled to aim more moral criticism at Donald for choosing (4), for example, than for choosing (3). This is what I mean by calling an action morally criticizable. But most of us will be inclined

---

[1] For evidence that abortion remained widespread in many communities in the United States when it was illegal, see Reagan (1997: esp. Chap. 2).

[2] Indeed, legalized abortion does not ensure availability of abortion even where moral opposition is far short of unanimous. Although abortion is legal in the United States, 83 percent of all counties in the United States have no abortion providers (cited by Hadley [1996: 15]).

to say something more than this: It isn't just that (5) is worse than (4), which is worse than (3), which is worse than (2), which is worse than (1); it is that there is a difference in kind between (5) and the others. The difference might be put like this: Even though it is his money, and so there is some sense in which he is entitled to spend it in any way he wants, still he is not entitled to spend it in *that* way. This is the distinction I have in mind in saying that (5) is impermissible while (1)–(4) are permissible. I am not at all confident that I can provide a fully satisfactory formal account of this distinction, but for the purposes of this book, the following should suffice: To say that an action of mine is morally permissible is to say that no one has a valid claim against my doing it, that doing it violates nobody's moral rights. And in the case of (5), we presumably believe that there is someone, namely Ivana, who has such a claim against Donald's using his money in this way.

The question that this book addresses concerns the moral permissibility of abortion, not its moral criticizability. In claiming that it constitutes a defense of abortion, I mean that it offers a defense of the claim that abortion, at least in typical cases, is morally permissible, that, morally speaking, a woman's having an abortion violates no rights. The reason for this focus is simple: Virtually everyone who is morally opposed to abortion claims that abortion is morally impermissible in this sense, that it does violate rights, not merely that it is morally criticizable. Suppose that a woman is pregnant, does not wish to carry her pregnancy to term, and knows a couple who want very much to adopt and provide a secure, loving home for her child. Then the claim of such critics is not that her having an abortion rather than bringing her unwanted pregnancy to term is like Donald's buying a gold-plated car rather than contributing his winnings to charity; it is that it is like his hiring a hitman to kill his ex-wife. Since the claim that abortion is morally impermissible is clearly the central claim made by critics of abortion, and since calling a practice morally impermissible is qualitatively stronger than calling it morally criticizable, this is the claim that the defender of abortion must attempt to rebut. Since not all critics of abortion maintain that abortion is morally impermissible in all cases, the claim that the defender of abortion must attempt to rebut is the claim that abortion is morally impermissible at least in typical cases. And since critics of abortion attempt to press their case by appealing to claims that defenders of abortion are likely to accept, the defender of abortion must attempt to construct this rebuttal by appealing to considerations that critics of abortion can and do accept. Doing so is the central task of this book.

1.1.2. Three Objections

Three objections, however, might be raised against framing the moral question of abortion in this way. One is that in defining the moral problem of abortion in terms of its permissibility and then defining the permissibility of an action in terms of someone's having a valid claim against its being done, it may seem that the deck has been stacked in favor of the defender of abortion. The fetus, after all, is in no position to stake a claim against anyone, and if the claim that abortion is a wrong against the fetus is ruled out ahead of time, then how can an argument against the permissibility of abortion be expected to get off the ground? This objection rests on a confusion between having a valid claim and making a valid claim. If Donald died and left all of his money to his six-week-old niece, then she would have a valid claim to the money even if she was not capable of demanding that the claim be respected. If the money was legitimately Donald's and was transferred to his niece in an appropriate manner, these facts would provide sufficient grounds for a third party or custodian to make the claim on her behalf, and this would be enough to warrant the conclusion that depriving her of the money would be morally impermissible. Similarly, if there is something about the act of aborting a human fetus that deprives the fetus of something to which the fetus is entitled, then the critic of abortion can use this to establish that the fetus has a valid claim against the abortion's taking place without having to maintain that the fetus itself is capable of making this claim, and this will suffice for establishing that the abortion would be morally impermissible.

A second concern that might be raised is that this formulation of the question blurs the distinction between abortion as a moral problem and abortion as a legal problem, a distinction that I said should remain in principle clear. If someone does have a valid claim against an abortion's being performed, after all, doesn't that simply amount to saying that the law should prevent it from taking place? And if no one has a valid claim against its being performed, then what grounds could there be for criminalizing it? But this objection is also misguided. The conclusion that no one has a valid claim against an abortion's being performed would undermine one kind of argument in favor of laws against abortion. But other sorts of considerations would remain open. Arguments can be made for laws restricting such forms of behavior as gambling, pornography, and drug use and for laws requiring such forms of behavior as jury duty or military service even if no one has a valid moral claim against one's engaging in (or refraining from engaging in) such activities. And the conclusion that someone (presumably the fetus) does have a valid moral claim against an abortion's being performed need not entail that abortion should be illegal. Not every valid moral claim is one we would wish to see enforced by the law. If I promise to help you move next week, or not to see anyone else while we are dating, then this provides you with a legitimate moral claim against me, but we may nonetheless think there is good reason not to treat it as one that the courts may enforce. My formulation of the moral question is thus compatible with acknowledging that although an argument against the moral permissibility of abortion may provide sufficient reasons for believing that abortion should be illegal, it need not do so, and that although an argument in defense of the moral permissibility of abortion may provide sufficient reasons for believing that abortion should be legal, it need not do so.

Finally, it may be complained that to limit the moral problem of abortion to the question of its moral permissibility renders the discussion unacceptably narrow. Indeed, at least one writer has gone so far as to insist that even if we grant that it is morally permissible for a woman to have an abortion, if we agree, that is, that her having an abortion is within her moral rights, "*nothing* follows from this supposition about the morality of abortion, . . . once it is noted . . . that in exercising a moral right I can do something cruel, or callous, or selfish, light-minded, self-righteous, stupid, inconsiderate, disloyal, dishonest – that is, act viciously" (Hursthouse 1991: 235). And if this objection is sustained, then even if the defense of abortion offered in this book is successful, it will do relatively little to vindicate the moral record of those who have and who perform abortions.

I believe that in one important respect this objection must be accepted, and for two reasons. The first is that it follows from the way that I have framed and analyzed the question that the claim that an action is permissible does not justify the conclusion that it should be performed. So even if we conclude that it is morally permissible for a woman to have an abortion, it will not follow that having an abortion is what she ought to do. The second is that it also follows from my analysis that the claim that an action is permissible does not justify the conclusion that it is not morally criticizable. To say that an action is permissible is not to say that there are no moral reasons against doing the action, but only

7

that it is a candidate from which one is morally permitted to choose. In then choosing from the set of permissible possibilities, there may well be moral reasons to refrain from doing the act. The reasons may include such considerations as that doing the act would produce less overall happiness or social equality than some alternative, or would disappoint someone, or leave someone worse off, and so on. If you choose to do the action, no one will be able to say that they (or anyone else) had a legitimate claim against your doing it, or that you had violated their (or anyone else's) rights, but they may be entitled to aim moral criticism at you nonetheless.[3] To say that an action is impermissible, on the other hand, is to say that it is not one of the eligible candidates for consideration. If torturing an innocent person is impermissible, for example, then even in cases where torturing someone would be ranked higher than not torturing him by such standards as promoting overall happiness, still you must not choose to torture him.

The moves from "I have the right to do it" to "It is right for me to do it" or to "I cannot be morally criticized for doing it" are simply invalid. This is an elementary point, but one that is frequently overlooked in popular discussions of moral issues. It is all too common to hear people defend their decision to do something by insisting that they had the right to do it: the right to broadcast their sleazy shows, to take advantage of their neighbors' misfortunes, to exclude women from their private clubs, and so on, as if their having the right to do something ensures that their doing it is not only permissible but immune to moral criticism.[4] But establishing that an action would be morally permissible should represent only the beginning of one's moral deliberation, not the end it is too often taken to represent. And in this sense, the objection to focusing exclusively on the permissibility of abortion is an important one. Even if we end up

---

[3] Similarly, if Donald chooses (4), we may well be right to call him cruel, mean, nasty, vindictive, and hateful; and if he chooses (3), we may be right to call him selfish, insensitive, and vain, all of which are terms of moral criticism.

[4] Relatedly, when critics of abortion complain about those who want abortion to be "safe, available, and rare," they proceed as if those who believe that abortion is permissible must also believe that it is never a bad thing that an abortion occur. How, they ask, can you think that abortion should be rare if you think it is morally defensible? If a practice is morally defensible, then one shouldn't care how often it occurs. But this, too, is to overlook the distinction between an act's being permissible and its being criticizable. It is perfectly consistent to believe that abortion (or prostitution, or pornography, and so on) should be safely available because it is permissible, but rare because it is (or is often) criticizable (though one could, of course, also believe that it is not morally criticizable either, but should be rare merely because it is undesirable from a purely prudential point of view).

agreeing that abortion is morally permissible, much more would need to be said about when, if ever, abortion is the morally best course of action available and when, in those cases in which it is not, it is not only *not* the morally best course of action but a morally criticizable one as well.

But even though all of this is true, there is nonetheless good reason to focus in great detail on what is admittedly this relatively narrow question. For even if relatively little about the morality of abortion follows from concluding that it is permissible, something absolutely crucial about the morality of abortion would follow from concluding that it is impermissible. If a particular abortion would be impermissible, then it follows that a woman would have no moral right to choose to have it performed even if having the abortion would rank high by other morally relevant standards of evaluation such as promoting overall happiness or equality. It is the claim that abortion is impermissible in this sense that is advanced by virtually every critic of abortion, and, as we will see, attempting to respond to this claim on the abortion critic's own terms is a difficult enough task in itself.

1.2. THE METHOD

Let us now assume that we are clear about the question I pose in this book. How should we go about answering it? The method of moral argument I propose to employ is a version of the method made famous by John Rawls as "reflective equilibrium" (1971: 20ff.), which has since been embraced in one form or another by writers on both theoretical issues (e.g., Gowans 1994: Chap. 2) and such specific issues as the moral status of animals (e.g., Reagan 1983: 133ff.; Carruthers 1992: 6–8, 21–4), though it may differ from Rawls's approach in some ways that are not trivial. A detailed explanation and defense of this method must remain beyond the scope of this work, but in this section I will offer a brief account of reflective equilibrium, at least as I understand it, and will explain why it seems to be an appropriate method for addressing moral problems in general, and, more importantly, why it is particularly well suited to constructing a defense of abortion that seeks to address critics of abortion on their own terms.

1.2.1. Reflective Equilibrium

The method of reflective equilibrium, at least as I mean to be using this term, can be described roughly as follows: We begin by accepting, at

9

least provisionally, our moral intuitions about a variety of types of actions, giving more initial weight to those which seem especially clear or forceful. We then attempt to develop a credible moral theory that would serve to unify and underwrite these various judgments. We ask: What sort of more basic principle or set of principles would have to be true in order for these sorts of more particular judgments to prove to be correct? This procedure can appear to be circular, and in its most naive application it would be. For we could easily generate a basic principle that would match all of our judgments about more specific classes of actions by simply inventing a complex principle that endorsed the conjunction of all the particular judgments. And inventing such a convoluted principle would of course do nothing to provide support for those judgments. But the method of reflective equilibrium does not warrant such a move. In seeking principles to underwrite our considered moral judgments about particular types of actions, the method directs us to give preference to those principles that are more general and more fundamental and which more fully exemplify the general theoretical virtues. I cannot provide an exhaustive list of those virtues here, or present a formula for weighting them, but they would include, at the least, such factors as parsimony, salience, coherence, and explanatory power, and they would be constrained by an overriding requirement of logical consistency.

Of course, it is unlikely that a theory will be found that does perfectly well by all such standards while at the same time accommodating every single one of our initial moral judgments about the entire range of specific types of actions about which we have moral intuitions. So the process to this point produces only what we might think of as our first candidates for an acceptable moral position. We may identify moral principles that provide a better or worse fit, but not a perfect fit, with our initial judgments. And in those cases in which our theory fails to conform to our intuitions, the intuitions themselves will seem to constitute counterexamples to the theory. A theory that does a generally satisfactory job of accounting for our obligation to keep our promises, for example, might fail to justify an obligation to keep our promises to those who have since died; and to the extent that we think it is still wrong to break our promises in such cases, this will seem to demonstrate that the theory itself is flawed.

When confronted with an apparent counterexample of this sort, there are essentially two options, each of which can be thought of as providing some benefit in terms of rendering our system of thought as a whole more consistent and coherent, but at some cost. One option is to revise our proposed theory so that it produces the "correct" answers to some of the questions it initially got "wrong." This might be done by taking a general principle and adding some restrictions or exceptions to it. The cost here is in terms of making the theory as a whole less attractive in terms of simplicity, generality, salience, and so on. The more drastic the revisions are and the more difficult it is to motivate them in terms of the more basic principles of the theory, the more the resulting theory will seem to be arbitrary or ad hoc, or at least unparsimonious. The other option is to abandon or revise some of our initial judgments. The cost here is that in order to accept the theory as a whole, we will have to accept certain implications that, at least initially, seemed independently objectionable.

It is possible, of course, that in some cases the considerations that favor a given theory will at the same time change our initial intuitions, so that what at first seemed to be a counterintuitive implication will no longer seem counterintuitive. While it might at first seem, for example, that it is wrong to break a promise you made to someone even if that person is now dead, reflection on the best reasons for thinking that promise breaking in general is wrong might lead us to see promise breaking as permissible in such cases after all. In other cases, initial intuitions to the contrary might be dissolved in other ways. It might turn out, for example, that someone's belief in an obligation to keep promises to the dead was dependent upon a nonmoral belief to the effect that people have souls that survive the deaths of their bodies and which are then distressed by the knowledge that promises made to them during their earthly existence have since been broken. Moral intuitions that arise at least in part from nonmoral beliefs in this way can be uprooted by rebutting the nonmoral beliefs at their foundation, and when this is accomplished, the fact that one initially had a different moral reaction to a particular sort of case need no longer carry any moral weight. Finally, in at least some cases, one may find that the force of one's initial moral intuition can be effected by considering how one thinks one acquired the intuition in the first place, and how likely one thinks it is that one would have roughly the same belief if one had, for example, been raised in a different culture or by different parents. And so, in at least some cases, the fact that a theory conflicts with our initial judgments need not count against it. But there seems to be no guarantee that these sorts of considerations will be available in every case, and in cases in which they are not, accepting a theory will still seem objectionable to the extent that some of its implications continue to seem objectionable. In such cases, then, one must attempt to strike the most reasonable balance between the merits of the theory on the one hand and the drawbacks of its implications on the other.

Why should one attempt to answer substantive moral questions in the way that I have described? The answer is simple: There seems to be no plausible alternative. Perhaps someone can produce a deductively valid argument that settles the abortion debate as conclusively as formal proofs settle debates in mathematics and makes no use whatsoever of our moral intuitions about particular kinds of cases, but this is extremely difficult to believe. What could such an argument look like? Perhaps we can reach a satisfactory position on the subject simply by appealing to our particular intuitive responses on a case-by-case basis, but this, too, seems difficult to imagine. What could make such a position reasonable when the position itself leaves no room for appeals to reasons? Yet if it is difficult to imagine relying exclusively on either theoretical or intuitive considerations, it is even more difficult to picture doing entirely without either of them. What else, after all, is left? Playing the two sets of considerations off of each other until one arrives at the most satisfactory balance between them seems to be the only plausible way of making use of both, and this is what reflective equilibrium, at least as I am using the term, directs us to do. Indeed, to some extent the reason for accepting reflective equilibrium so understood is simply that this is what we do, and all that we can do, when we think about moral problems.

For many readers, this approach will seem natural and appropriate. If you are one such reader, then the methodological assumptions behind this work should pose no problems, and you need worry only about whether I have made use of this approach faithfully and effectively in the chapters that follow. For other readers, however, the method employed here may itself seem to provide a subject of concern. If you are one such reader, I would like to believe that you still have reason to read on. Perhaps you should think of the question posed by this book as a purely theoretical one: What position on abortion would it be more reasonable for you to accept if you began with the judgments about certain types of actions that I will attribute to you in what follows and you wanted your position on abortion to mesh most coherently with them? This is essentially how I view the book's project; though for me, of course, these are not purely theoretical concerns since the particular judgments I will attribute to you are my particular judgments as well, since it does matter to me that my view of abortion be brought into line with these judgments, and since I have found that doing so is no small task.

1.2.2. *Reflective Equilibrium and Abortion*

Even if you remain skeptical of the reflective equilibrium approach to ethics in general, however, there seems to me to be an additional and powerful reason to think it important to exploit it in an inquiry about the moral problem of abortion in particular, especially one that seeks to engage critics of abortion on their own terms. The reason is simply that reflective equilibrium, or something very much like it, has largely been adopted, at least implicitly, by those who argue against the moral permissibility of abortion. One of the most common argumentative strategies among critics of abortion, for example, is the attempt to demonstrate that arguments which purport to vindicate the moral permissibility of abortion would, if accepted, also entail that killing newborn infants is equally permissible. Another is the attempt to demonstrate that if we do not agree that the killing of the fetus is impermissible from the moment of conception on, there is no reason to draw the line at which killing it becomes impermissible at any one point rather than at any other. The appeal to such arguments presupposes not only that the claim that killing newborn infants is permissible violates extremely deep moral intuitions or that lines drawn without reasons are arbitrary, but that it is a legitimate requirement of a moral position both that it not yield results that are so strongly counterintuitive and that it not attempt to accommodate our moral intuitions simply by abandoning such theoretical virtues as salience, coherence, and parsimony. Critics of abortion, that is, are best understood as arguing that their position on the moral permissibility of abortion should be accepted because it better enables not only them but also their opponents to achieve an equilibrium between the general theoretical considerations and intuitive responses to certain types of actions that not only they but, more importantly, their opponents already accept.[5]

One could, of course, attempt to offer a defense of abortion that does not take place within the methodological framework that critics of abortion presuppose. One could, for example, offer an argument in defense

---

[5] That there is an important sense in which each side of the abortion controversy claims that its position best coheres with the values of the other has been recognized by a number of critics of abortion (e.g., Beckwith 1993: 27–8).

of abortion, agree that it implies that killing newborn infants is also permissible, agree that this implication is extremely counterintuitive, and simply deny that the existence of extremely counterintuitive implications should count as an objection to moral arguments. I have already registered my doubts about the plausibility of such an approach to moral argument in general. But even if such an approach could be sustained at a theoretical level, it would be a serious mistake for defenders of abortion to rely upon it in practice. A defense of abortion that proceeds on methodological terms that the critic of abortion rejects leaves the debate at a standstill. It reenforces the impression that the controversy over abortion arises from a simple clash of incommensurable viewpoints. It fails to address critics of abortion on their own terms. But a defense of abortion that succeeds on the critic of abortion's own methodological terms does none of these things. It justifies the claim that abortion, at least in typical cases, is morally permissible on terms that the critic of abortion can, indeed already does, accept. Only this kind of argument can contribute to resolving the abortion controversy, and it is this kind of defense of abortion that I propose to develop in the chapters that follow.

1.3. THE ARGUMENTS

In framing the question to be addressed in this book, and in selecting a methodology for evaluating the various arguments that purport to answer it, I have attempted as much as possible to allow the critic of abortion to frame the debate. The same should be done when it comes to determining which arguments merit consideration in attempting to apply this method to this question. A fully satisfactory defense of abortion must attempt to respond not only to those arguments against abortion that defenders of abortion may find particularly challenging, but to the entire range of arguments against abortion that critics of abortion have developed.

1.3.1. The Rights-Based Argument

The most familiar argument against abortion rests on the claim that the human fetus, or at least the typical human fetus, has a right to life. Conjoined with the assumption that if the fetus has such a right, then abortion, at least in typical circumstances, is morally impermissible, this claim generates the conclusion that the critic of abortion seeks to justify, that is, the claim that abortion, at least in typical circumstances, is morally impermissible. I will call this argument the rights-based argument:

P1: The (typical) human fetus has a right to life.
P2: If the (typical) human fetus has a right to life, then abortion (at least in typical circumstances) is morally impermissible.
C: Abortion (at least of a typical human fetus in typical circumstances) is morally impermissible.

This rights-based argument is sometimes presented in terms of the claims that the fetus is a person and that all persons have a right to life. Put in this way, the argument looks like this:

P1: The (typical) human fetus is a person.
P2: Every person has a right to life.
C1: The (typical) human fetus has a right to life.
P3: If the (typical) human fetus has a right to life, then abortion (at least in typical circumstances) is morally impermissible.
C2: Abortion (at least of a typical human fetus in typical circumstances) is morally impermissible.

But presenting the rights-based argument against abortion in terms of the claim that the fetus is a person is neither necessary nor illuminating. This is so because the term *person* is ambiguous. On the one hand, *person* can be used in a purely normative sense. So understood, the claim that the fetus is a person simply *means* that the fetus has a right to life. On this construal of the term, any reason for believing that the fetus is a person just is a reason for believing that the fetus has a right to life. The claim that the fetus is a person in this sense plays no substantive role in justifying the claim that it has a right to life, and so there is no reason to consider it as a distinct claim. On the other hand, *person* can be used in a purely descriptive sense that has no normative implications. So understood, for example, the claim that the fetus is a person may merely be a claim that it possesses certain biological features. On this construal of the term, any reason for believing that the fetus is a person will do nothing to justify the claim that the fetus has a right to life, since the claim that the fetus is a person in this sense will have no normative implications. So, again, there will be no reason to put the rights-based argument in terms of the claim that the fetus is a person.

It might be suggested, of course, that there is a third possibility: The term *person* might be used in some kind of intermediate way so that there could be one set of reasons for believing that the fetus is a person in this sense and then a second set of reasons for believing that every individual who is a person in this sense has a right to life. But even if *person* is construed in such a third way, its use is still superfluous. We can simply consider the conjunction of the two sets of reasons as a set of reasons for believing that the fetus has a right to life and then ask whether they are good reasons for believing this. There is again no reason to treat the claim that the fetus is a person as an independent claim warranting consideration.[6] Since the use of the term *person* as a means of explicating the rights-based argument against abortion is unnecessary and potentially confusing, I will generally avoid it. I will analyze the rights-based argument as the conjunction of the claim that the (typical) human fetus has a right to life and the claim that if the (typical) human fetus has a right to life, then abortion (at least in typical circumstances) is morally impermissible.

A defender of abortion could respond to the first claim made by the rights-based argument, the claim that the typical human fetus has a right to life, in a number of ways. He could, for example, deny that anyone has a right to life. If no one has a right to life, then fetuses, in particular, do not have a right to life, and the rights-based argument against abortion will fail for that reason. I do not want to insist that such a response to the rights-based argument cannot be sustained. Perhaps it can. But it would be a serious mistake for the defender of abortion to depend upon such a response. A defense of abortion will be more effective the more it can work from premises that critics of abortion accept, and surely most critics of abortion believe that you and I do have a right to life. In arguing against the first claim made by the rights-based argument in Chapters 2 and 3, I will therefore simply assume that you and I do, in fact, have a right to life. If this assumption proves to be mistaken, then the rights-based argument against abortion will fail for that reason. My concern is to demonstrate that

---

[6] This is not to say that there is never a good reason to break up a particular set of reasons given for believing that the fetus has a right to life into two distinct sets of reasons. For purposes of philosophical analysis, it may often be useful to do so. It may be helpful, for example, to break a particular argument down into such terms as "P1: The (typical) human fetus has a future-like-ours (or has a certain kind of potential, or is a member of a certain species, etc.). P2: If something has a future-like-ours (or has a certain kind of potential, or is a member of a certain species, etc.), then it has a right to life. C: The (typical) human fetus has a right to life." The point is simply that there is no reason to insist on using the term *person* in doing so, and, given the ambiguous and potentially misleading nature of the term, good reason not to.

even if the assumption is correct, the argument against abortion is still unsuccessful.

A defender of abortion could also offer a less extreme response to the first claim made by the rights-based argument. He could agree that you and I have a right to life but deny that newborn infants do. If newborn infants do not have a right to life, then it will again be a simple matter to establish that fetuses lack such a right, and the rights-based argument against abortion will again be defeated. This suggestion is likely to strike most readers as hardly more attractive than the first. In the popular debate about abortion, at least, to say that abortion is morally on a par with killing newborn babies is simply to say that abortion is morally impermissible. It is therefore worth emphasizing that within the philosophical literature on abortion, at least, there is less agreement on this subject. A number of philosophers, including such prominent figures as Peter Singer and Michael Tooley, have argued that human infants do not have a right to life. And these arguments deserve to be taken seriously on their own terms.

But they need not be taken seriously here. For the purposes of this book, arguments for the claim that human infants do not have a right to life can simply be set aside. If it turns out that one or more of these arguments can be sustained, then the claim that abortion is morally permissible in typical cases will follow easily enough. But a defense of abortion that attempts to engage critics of abortion on their own terms will again do best simply to accept this belief, even if only for the sake of the argument. In arguing against the first claim made by the rights-based argument against abortion, I will therefore also assume, at least for the sake of the argument, that newborn human infants have a right to life. The claim that I will argue for in Chapters 2 and 3, therefore, may best be understood as a conditional one: if the critic of abortion is correct in maintaining that you and I have a right to life and that newborn human infants do as well, then the moral theory that would best account for this assumption entails that it is not true that the typical human fetus has such a right.

The second claim made by the rights-based argument against abortion maintains that if the (typical) human fetus does have a right to life, then abortion (at least in typical circumstances) is morally impermissible. A defender of abortion could also respond to this claim in a number of ways. He could argue, for example, that there is not one right to life but many, ranging from the very strong right to life that you and I have to a much weaker version of this right that might be atttributed, for example, to some nonhuman animals. He could agree that if the fetus had a right to life in the strong sense that you and I have a right to life, then abortion (at least in typical cases) would be morally impermissible, but maintain that if the fetus has any right to life at all it has only the much weaker sort of right to life and that having this relatively weak right to life fails to render abortion morally impermissible. Or, he could maintain that even if the fetus does have the very same right to life that you and I have, there is some even more pressing moral consideration that justifies violating it in the case of abortion. He might argue, for example, that abortion is needed in order to prevent catastrophic overpopulation. Or he might argue that it is needed in order to ensure social, political, and economic equality for women. I will not argue against such claims in this work, but I will not rely on them either. A defense of abortion that depends on such claims will again do less to engage critics of abortion on their own terms than one that does not. In Chapter 4, I will argue against the claim that if the fetus has a right to life, then abortion is morally impermissible. But in doing so, I will therefore assume, at least for the sake of the argument, that if the fetus has a right to life, it has the very same right to life that you and I have, and that abortion is not needed in order to achieve such pressing goals as population control or sexual equality (or that if it is needed, that such goals do not justify violating the right to life). I will attempt to show that the second claim needed to sustain the rights-based argument against abortion can be shown to be unacceptable on terms that critics of abortion can and already do accept.

1.3.2. Non-Rights-Based Arguments

While the rights-based argument against abortion is almost certainly the most familiar argument, it is not the only one. Arguments that appeal to some version of the golden rule or to our uncertainty about the moral status of the fetus, as well as many of the arguments that are identified with the position known as pro-life feminism, are all capable of being sustained without appealing to the claim that the fetus has a right to life. Many critics of abortion believe that one or another of these arguments are successful, and thus even if the defender of abortion succeeds in undermining the rights-based argument, a defense of abortion that seeks to engage critics of abortion on their own terms must also address these arguments, and on terms that critics of abortion accept. Doing so will be the task of Chapter 5.

Chapter 2

The Conception Criterion

2.0. OVERVIEW

The first claim needed to sustain the rights-based argument against abortion maintains that the (typical) human fetus has a right to life. A number of distinct arguments can be made in defense of this claim, but all stem in one way or another from a common idea: that you and I have this right, and that we are related to human fetuses in important ways in which we are not related to dogs, trees, ecosystems, and other possible objects of moral concern. The challenge facing the proponent of this claim, then, is to identify specifically what the salient relationship is between the human fetus and us and to explain which fetuses it shows to have this right and how it shows this. This chapter will consider arguments of this form that attempt to show that the human fetus acquires the right to life at the moment of its conception, a claim that I will refer to as the conception criterion. I will argue that none of the arguments for the conception criterion that have thus far been proposed is satisfactory, and that this can be shown on terms that critics of abortion can and do accept.

Some of the arguments that have been proposed in favor of the conception criterion, particularly some of the arguments treated relatively early in this chapter, are not especially powerful, and I devote relatively little space to responding to them. But it would be a serious mistake to dismiss the conception criterion itself merely because some of the most commonly heard arguments in its favor are somewhat weak. This is a mistake that I fear some defenders of abortion have been willing to make, and in this sense the proponents of the rights-based argument against abortion have not been well served by the fact that there are so many different arguments that have been made in defense of the argument's crucial first premise. For even if some of the arguments in favor of the conception criterion do prove to be relatively easy to overcome, others do not. One such argument worth singling out for this reason is the argument best articulated in Donald Marquis's article, "Why Abortion Is Immoral" (1989), widely viewed by philosophers as containing the single most powerful argument against abortion.[1] What Marquis calls the "future-like-ours" argument is generally agreed to be extremely important, which is one of the reasons that I devote substantially more space to responding to it. But this is not the only reason. I also discuss the future-like-ours argument in more detail because, although I believe that in the end it fails to establish the conclusion it sets out to establish, I also believe that it is nonetheless on the right track. The objection that I end up defending against the future-like-ours argument, that is, provides a basis not so much for rejecting the argument outright as for revising it. The modified version of the future-like-ours argument that results from accepting my objection to Marquis's original formulation of it in turn forms the foundation for the positive proposal I go on to make in Chapter 3. Thus, while much of the purpose of this chapter is essentially negative in character, and while individual sections can be passed over by readers already inclined to reject the particular arguments under discussion, Section 2.8 on the future-like-ours argument is crucial not only as a major component of my case against the conception criterion, but also as the fundamental basis of the case for an alternative criterion that is then completed near the end of Chapter 3.

2.1. THE PARSIMONY ARGUMENT

Perhaps the most straightforward relation between you or me on the one hand and every human fetus from conception onward on the other is this: All are living members of the same species, *homo sapiens*. A human fetus, after all, is simply a human being at a very early stage in his or her development. A defender of abortion, of course, could reject this characterization of the human fetus. The fetus, it might be said, is not yet an individual, living organism, or is not yet a member of the human species. Perhaps it is only a potential human being. But a defense of

---

[1] However, as I note later, Marquis is not the only, or even the first, philosopher to have endorsed this sort of argument, and Marquis himself explicitly refrains from insisting that the argument establishes that the fetus has the same right to life as you or I immediately at the conclusion of fertilization.

abortion that depends on such a claim will again fail to address critics of abortion on their own terms. It is common, for example, for critics of abortion to cite scientific testimony such as that given before Congress in 1981 in hearings on the question of "when human life begins." In the course of those hearings, prominent scientists made such remarks as: "The fact that after fertilization has taken place, a new human has come into being, is no longer a matter of taste or of opinion. The human nature of the human being from conception to old age is not a metaphysical contention, it is plain experimental evidence." "In biology and in medicine, it is an accepted fact that the life of any individual organism reproducing by sexual reproduction begins at conception (fertilization)." "By all the criteria of modern molecular biology, life is present from the moment of conception." "Human life begins at the time of conception." "Human life begins when after the ovum is fertilized the new combined cell mass begins to divide." "The beginning of a single human life is from a biological point of view a simple and straightforward matter – the beginning is conception."[2] A defense of abortion that seeks to engage critics of abortion on their own terms must therefore take this assumption as a given.

Now the term *human being*, understood in the sense in which these scientists are using it, means something like "individual living member of the species *homo sapiens*" and not "individual with a right to life." And since these two meanings are clearly distinct, the claim that "If an individual is a human being, then that individual has a right to life" is not a claim that is true by definition. But this does not mean that it is not true. It simply means that it stands in need of justification. And in fact there are several ways in which critics of abortion have attempted to justify it. I will assume that the claim that a new human being comes to exist at the moment of conception is true. The question is whether this provides good reason to accept the claim that a human fetus has a right to life from the moment of its conception.

One reason for thinking that it does might arise from the following consideration: Suppose that I asked you to go out and round up ten different individuals whom both defenders and critics of abortion alike would generally recognize as uncontroversial examples of individuals with a right to life. There is little doubt that, although they might differ in many important respects, the ten individuals you would select would

---

[2] Jerome Lejeune, Micheline Matthews-Roth, Hymie Gordon, Alfred Bongiovanni, Jasper Williams, Watson A. Bowes, Jr., all quoted in Powell (1981: 70–4).

have at least this one property in common: All would be members of the species *homo sapiens*. Some people have argued that there are other individuals, such as nonhuman animals, who also have this right, but even if that claim is true, it is not uncontroversially true. So if you were forced to make your selection from among those individuals about whom people on both sides of the abortion debate would uncontroversially agree, it seems all but certain that all of your choices would be human beings.

The question then arises: in virtue of what property do these ten individuals have a right to life? And the simplest way to answer this question, the critic of abortion might maintain, is to note that what they all have in common is that they are all members of the species *homo sapiens*. It is difficult to believe that it would be mere coincidence that all of the uncontroversial cases were human beings. In addition, the property of being a member of the human species can plausibly be characterized as morally relevant, since the human species itself can plausibly be characterized as superior to other species in terms of a number of important properties, such as rationality, linguistic ability, and so on, that in turn can plausibly be characterized as morally relevant. If this is the most parsimonious way to account for the judgment that the ten individuals in question have a right to life, a judgment that we must surely accept if we wish to argue on terms that the critic of abortion accepts, then this suggests that an important principle implicit in the views that both sides of the debate hold most strongly is that being a member of the human species is a sufficient condition for having a right to life. Since every human fetus is a member of the human species, this would in turn imply that every human fetus acquires a right to life at the moment of its conception. Since this argument appeals to the claim that appealing to our humanity provides the most parsimonious explanation of why you and I have a right to life, I will refer to it as the parsimony argument.

The parsimony argument should be rejected because species membership in itself does not provide a satisfactory explanation for the consensus that both sides of the abortion debate will reach in the case of the ten individuals you would have selected. Suppose, for example, that it turned out that one of the people you brought back as an uncontroversial example of an individual with a right to life turned out not to be a human being after all. Although exactly like a human being in every other respect, he is in fact an alien from another planet whose DNA structure is slightly differerent from that of human beings. No matter what our views on abortion, it is extremely difficult to believe that this discovery would make us think it any more permissible to kill him. He has all of the same properties we thought he had before; he simply got them from alien parents instead of human ones. And suppose, on the other hand, that one of the people you identified as an uncontroversial example of an individual with a right to life was a human being who subsequently suffered the permanent destruction of the higher regions of his brain but who was nonetheless able to be kept alive on a life-support machine. There might prove to be some reason to think it morally criticizable to remove such a person from life support, but surely the claim that he would continue to have the same right to life as you or I would be extremely controversial at best. A defender of the claim that the typical human fetus has a right to life cannot appeal to an argument that entails that people in such conditions do as well. And so a critic of abortion cannot appeal to the parsimony argument. The fact that the only actual uncontroversial cases of individuals with a right to life are human beings provides no support for the claim that all human beings have a right to life.

2.2. THE SPECIES ESSENCE ARGUMENT

A second argument for the claim that being a human being is sufficient for having a right to life is suggested by Schwarz, who maintains that it is an error "to dismiss the category of human being as not (in itself) morally significant" (1990: 100). Schwarz presents this argument in terms of the language of personhood. He defines a person as "a being who has the basic inherent capacity to function as a person, regardless of how developed this capacity is, or whether or not it is blocked, as in severe senility" (1990: 101). As it stands, of course, this definition is circular, since it includes the term to be defined in the scope of the definition. But this defect can be remedied by attending to Schwarz's explanation that "Functioning as a person refers to all the activities proper to persons as persons, to thinking in the broadest sense" (1990: 89). This emendation would itself be circular were it not for the last six words, so I take it we can say that for Schwarz a person is "a being who has the basic inherent capacity for thinking in the broadest sense regardless of how developed or blocked it is." The basic idea is that while you are asleep or under anesthesia you cannot function as a person, but you retain the capacity for so functioning. Similarly, an infant may not yet be able to function as a person, but she has the capacity to become able to do so, and so is already a person in this sense. Schwarz then claims that "*Human* designates, in its most significant meaning, a type of being whose nature it is to be a person. . . . We respect and value human beings, . . . because it is the nature of a human being to be a person" (1990: 101).

Now, there is admittedly some ambiguity here. If Schwarz simply means that the term *human being* sometimes *means* something other than member of the species *homo sapiens*, then he is not giving an argument for the moral relevance of species membership. But I take it that he means more than this, that it is an essential property of every living member of the species *homo sapiens* that it has the capacity to function as a person. If this is so, and if the capacity to function as a person confers on one a right to life, then being a member of *homo sapiens* does ensure that one has a right to life. And since every human fetus is a member of *homo sapiens*, it follows that every human fetus has a right to life. I will call this the species essence argument.

There are two problems with this argument. The first is that the claim that every member of *homo sapiens* has the capacity to function as a person is false. There can, for example, be human fetuses with such severe deformities that they will never develop a brain capable of sustaining thought, or even any brain at all. These are human beings who have not even the capacity for functioning as a person and so are not persons on Schwarz's definition of the term. One could, I suppose, characterize such a fetus as a person whose capacity for thought simply happens to be "blocked" by a contingent fact about its head. But then it is difficult to see why we should not also call the spider crawling up my window a person. If he were able to develop a big enough brain, he too would be able to function as a person, so he is simply a person whose capacity is blocked by the fact that he will never have a large enough brain. Of course, this is true of all spiders and only of some human beings, but why should that fact make a difference? In addition, there are human beings who permanently lose their capacity for functioning as a person, such as those whose higher brain regions are irreparably destroyed. They do not have even the capacity to function as a person in Schwarz's sense. Of course, they once did, but that shows only that they were once persons in Schwarz's sense of the term, not that they are now. So even if being a person in Schwarz's sense, having the capacity to function as a person, does suffice for having a right to life, it is still not the case that being a human being, a member of the species *homo sapiens*, suffices for being a person in Schwarz's sense of the term. The defender of the conception criterion will therefore have to look to some other fetal property beyond its species membership.

One response might be made at this point. I have been treating the claim that having a certain property is a part of the essence of the human species as meaning or entailing that every human being has that property. So the fact that some human beings lack even the capacity for functioning as a person shows that having such a capacity is not a part of the essence of the human species. But one might object that this forces an uncharitable reading onto Schwarz's text, and that the argument is more forcefully construed as resting on the claim that having the property is (or is partly) definitive only of paradigmatic members of the species. So we might say about even the severely deformed fetus and even the severely brain-damaged adult that they are corrupt or imperfect instances of a species whose nature it is to have this capacity, while this is not true of my window-climbing spider. This much is certainly true. But if this is all that is meant by the claim that such a capacity is part of human nature, then its moral relevance is no longer clear even if one agrees that capacities themselves are morally relevant. Why should the fact that the deformed fetus is a corrupt instance of a rational species mean that we must treat it as if it were itself capable of reason?

There is, in addition, a more fundamental problem. The species essence argument rests at least in part on the claim that the fact that you now have the capacity to be able to do something later imposes moral limits on how we are permitted to treat you now. Even if we concede that every human being has this capacity (and, as I have already noted, this claim is surely false) we still need a defense of the moral significance of the fact that the fetus now has the potential to do the sorts of things later that you and I can do now. Now, an argument in defense of the moral relevance of such potentiality may well be forthcoming. I will consider a number of them in some of the sections that follow.[3] But even if such an argument succeeds, this will show that the fetus has a right to life because of facts about its capacities, not because of facts about its species membership. As an attempt to justify the moral relevance of species membership, the species essence argument must be rejected even if we later accept the conclusion that every human fetus has a right to life.

---

[3] Including some defended by Schwarz; I do not mean to be suggesting that the argument considered here constitutes his entire position.

2.3. THE KINDRED SPECIES ARGUMENT

Warnock reports that although the members of the commission on embryo research that she chaired disagreed on many points, they all agreed "that an embryo's being human placed it in a different category with regard to research from any other creature, embryonic or full-grown. Simply in virtue of being human, and consisting of human cells, even a two-cell embryo was subject to considerations different from those that would apply to a perfectly formed specimen of any other species." She then acknowledges the view that would label this speciesism, a form of prejudice akin to and as indefensible as racism and sexism, and responds that "We all believed, on the contrary, that it would require justification *not* to prefer one's own species to another. Those who thought that an argument was needed to explain why they would save a human rather than a dog or a fly would themselves be guilty of prejudice" (1987: 10).

The fact that this statement represents a consensus among an otherwise sharply divided panel suggests that its sentiment may be widespread. And the content of the statement suggests yet another way in which the fact that a human zygote is a member of the same species as you and I might be used to support the conception criterion. Here the idea is that you should respect the zygote not simply because it is a member of a species whose mature members have certain legitimate claims against you, but because it is a member of *your* species. And the form of this argument does have a certain kind of appeal, cohering well with other considered attitudes we are likely to share, such as that one ought to give preference to family over friends, friends over strangers, and so on. The argument, then, which I will call the kindred species argument, raises two questions: Is favoring the interests of one's own species over the interests of others morally justified? And, if it is, can this fact be used to ground the conception criterion?

A defender of abortion could attempt to respond to the kindred species argument by insisting that the answer to the first question is no. But a defense of abortion that depends on such a response is likely to prove contentious at best. Most critics of abortion are likely to believe that we are morally justified in favoring the interests of our own species over the interests of others. And so a defense of abortion that turns on denying this claim will fail to argue on terms that the critic of abortion accepts.

Such a defense is, in any event, unnecessary, because the answer to the second question is plainly no. Even if we are convinced that the relation between our obligations to human fetuses and our obligation to nonhuman animals is the same as the relation between our obligations to relatives and our obligations to friends, or the relation between our obligations to friends and our obligations to strangers, this will still fail to establish that a human fetus has a right to life. After all, even if I have greater duties to friends than to strangers, this does not show that my friends have a greater right to life than do strangers. The special duties we have to some others in virtue of the special relations in which we stand toward them need not correspond to any differences between their rights and the rights of others, and certainly need not correspond to any difference in terms of their right to life. And so the fact (if it is a fact) that I have greater duties to human fetuses than to mature pigs does not show that human fetuses have a greater right to life than do mature pigs, or, indeed, that they have any right to life at all.

2.4. THE SANCTITY OF HUMAN LIFE ARGUMENT

In considering whether we should accept the claim that the fetus's being a human being suffices to make it an individual with a right to life, I have been asking whether there is a reason that can be given for making species membership morally relevant, a reason that could be grounded in some other belief or set of beliefs that critics and defenders of abortion both are likely to share. I have argued that the answer to this question is no. But perhaps this is the wrong approach. For one could argue that no further reason needs to be given: Most of us, it might be urged, already agree that each individual human life is sacred. Although the term *sanctity of human life* is often associated with the popular movement opposed to abortion, it is often invoked in defense of other positions that critics and defenders of abortion alike typically share. And perhaps this is all of the foundation that the proponent of the conception criterion needs. If every human life is sacred, after all, and if each of us is an instance of human life from the moment of our conception, then there is an important kind of value that we all have from that moment on. And if it is in virtue of the sanctity of lives like yours and mine that we have the right to life that we have, then since all humans share this value from the moment of their conception, their comparable right to life must also be acknowledged. We might put the argument like this:

P1: The fetus is a human life from the moment of its conception.
P2: Every human life is sacred.
P3: If the life of an individual is sacred, then the individual has a right to life.
C: The fetus has a right to life from the moment of its conception.

Perhaps it is this argument, which we can call the sanctity of human life argument, that critics of abortion have in mind when they appeal to the fact that the fetus is a member of the human species.

This argument is plainly valid, and I am assuming that P1 is true. The question, then, comes down to P2 and P3. Since both employ the notion of sanctity, it may be useful to begin by noting that the term *sacred* has at least two importantly distinct meanings. In one sense, the term is essentially religious, referring to something that stands in a special relation to a deity. This is the sense, for example, in which one might believe that the Shroud of Turin is sacred. One would think of the artifact as sacred not because of facts about the fabric itself, its size, its color, or its composition, but rather because of some fact about the way in which it had been created by or used by a deity (or by one who in turn stood in a special relation to a deity). If one thought the shroud sacred in this sense because it had been used to cover the body of Jesus, for example, then if one later determined that the shroud had not been so used, one would no longer consider the shroud sacred even though none of one's beliefs about the properties of the shroud itself would have changed. But in another sense, the term is nontheological, meaning simply that something is worthy of reverence or awe. In this sense, one might believe that the few surviving ancient redwoods in a forest are sacred, not in virtue of their relation to something or someone holy, but simply because they are in and of themselves awe inspiring, such as to induce a sense of wonderment in a suitably sensitive person.

It is not difficult to see how an argument appealing to a claim about sanctity in the first of these senses might prove satisfactory. A 1987 Vatican pronouncement, for example, maintains that "Human life is sacred because from its beginning it involves 'the creative action of God' and it remains forever in a special relationship with the Creator, who is its sole end" (quoted by Coughlin 1988: 315). If one believes that God stands in a special relation to every human being from the moment of conception, then this might provide firm support for the conclusion that each life has the sort of value that makes ending it morally impermissible.

One might hold, for example, that each of our lives is a gift from God, so that it is God's place, and not ours, to decide when any life (including our own) should end.[4] Or one might believe that all humans were created in God's image, and that killing any human would thus amount to a kind of attack against God. Pope John Paul II puts it this way in *The Gospel of Life*: "God proclaims that he is absolute Lord of the life of man, who is formed in his image and likeness. Human life is thus given a sacred and inviolable character, which reflects the inviolability of the Creator himself" (1995: 95).[5] If sanctity is understood in this religious sense, then, there is good reason to suppose that someone who assents to P2 will also affirm P3.

If critics of abortion were willing to concede that their claim that abortion is morally impermissible is conditional on the truth of a particular set of religious assumptions, then the defender of abortion might have little choice but to acknowledge that, depending on the content of the religious assumptions, the critic's position so understood may well be sound. But few if any critics of abortion are willing to make this concession. Many critics of abortion are avowedly nonreligious. And even those critics of abortion who do believe in religious prohibitions against abortion do not believe that abortion is wrong *only* for reasons that are essentially religious in nature, any more than people who believe in religious prohibitions against theft and murder believe that these forms of behavior are wrong only for religious reasons.[6] The introduction to one collection of essays arguing against abortion, for example, opens with the important notice that "Not a single essay or paper among the nineteen is theological or programmatically religious.... The arguments against abortion as a public policy can be cogently stated without resort

---

[4] Kuhse (1987: 2) treats this view as almost synonymous with the view that human life is sacred (see also p. 17–20).

[5] Alternatively, he argues in a different passage as follows: "Man is called to a fullness of life which far exceeds the dimensions of his earthly existence, because it consists in sharing the very life of God. The loftiness of this supernatural vocation reveals the *greatness* and the *inestimable value* of human life even in its temporal phase" (Pope John Paul II 1995: 4).

[6] There may, of course, be some people who oppose abortion exclusively on religious grounds and who concede that no convincing argument against abortion can be made on nonreligious grounds. The arguments in this book do not directly address the concerns of such people, nor need they do so. This book represents a defense of abortion from those arguments that attempt to give reasons to oppose abortion to those who are not already opposed to it. Opposition to abortion that rests on one's already accepting a set of religious beliefs that includes opposition to abortion does not attempt to provide such reasons.

to religious, ecclesiastical, or theological sanctions," despite the fact that its author is himself a professor of divinity (Williams 1972: ix). A booklet published as a "Pro-Life Student's Abortion Debate Guide" offers the following advice: "Don't get trapped into making it a religious issue – it is not – it is a human rights issue; a social justice issue" (Hochderffer 1994: 5–6).[7] One of the most commonly cited figures in popular works opposed to abortion is Bernard N. Nathanson, a physician and opponent of abortion who was once a director of the largest abortion clinic in the world and a cofounder of the National Association for Repeal of Abortion Laws (now the National Abortion Rights Action League) and who identifies himself as a "convinced atheist" whose position on abortion has "never been influenced in the slightest by the empires of faith" (1979: 6).[8] And even the introduction to *The Gospel of Life* [*Evangelium Vitae*], Pope John Paul II's encyclical letter on abortion, euthanasia, and capital punishment, avows that the natural law that underwrites the Catholic Church's opposition to abortion is accessible to "every person sincerely open to truth and goodness" including "believer and non-believer alike," and the text itself maintains at several points that this law is "knowable by reason itself" (1995: 4–5, e.g., p. 113). If we are to engage critics of abortion on their own terms, then, we must reject any argument for the claim that abortion is impermissible whose validity depends on essentially religious assumptions. When the sanctity of human life argument is understood in this way, it does rest on an essentially religious assumption. And so understood in this way, the argument must be rejected.

This does not show, however, that the sanctity of human life argument itself should be rejected. For there remains an important sense in which many agnostics and atheists could be led to grant that human life is sacred. Precluding religious assumptions, therefore, need not undermine the general strategy of the sanctity of human life argument. The question, then, is what kind of argument might be given for P2, understood in a nontheistic sense.

One possibility would be to construct an argument parallel to the divine creation story but resting on a nonreligious account of human creation. Thus Dworkin has suggested that we might view human beings as the culmination of the long historical process of evolution, and so sacred

---

[7] For a forceful defense of the claim that religious assumptions are superfluous to the abortion debate, see also Newton (1978).

[8] Civil libertarian Nat Hentoff is a comparable figure.

(in the nontheistic sense) on that account. But as at least one critic of Dworkin's has pointed out, this suggestion rests on a deeply misguided understanding of what evolutionary theory maintains. That theory pictures us not as the supreme product of some naturally ordered force, but merely as the tentative result of minor random variations guided by natural selection (Rachels 1994: 272). In this respect, it is equally true of every species that it is the culmination of a long historical process of evolution. So there is no reason for our evolutionary history to confer a moral status on us that it does not confer equally on all species that have survived this process. Critics of abortion will reject the claim that all species are of equal moral status, and so critics of abortion cannot appeal to such considerations.

Perhaps the basic problem here is that it is just not clear how one goes about arguing for the claim that something is worthy of awe. If you can visit the redwood forest and not find it awesome, the temptation is to say that you simply lack the appropriate sensitivity to the awesome, and that there is nothing we can do to argue you into it. A defender of the sanctity of human life argument, however, might try to do more than this. He might, for example, attempt to cajole a person into viewing the human zygote with awe by presenting him with various facts about the zygote, about how quickly it develops, about how complex the various processes involved are, and so on. And this might well have some effect. It is difficult to read even a brief summary introduction to human embryology without coming away with the feeling of awe for the human zygote. But, then again, it may be equally difficult to come away without an equally strong feeling of awe for the sperm and egg, which, after all, have the power between them to produce such a zygote. And perusing a text on mammalian embryology in general might well leave one with a comparable feeling of awe for the zygotes of dogs, cats, rats, and so on. So if we rule out appeals to claims that are essentially theological in nature, the prospects for vindicating the claim that the human zygote is sacred without at the same time showing that dogs and cats, eggs and sperm are also, seem poor.

But let us nonetheless suppose that such a vindication is achieved. The problem now lies in P3. If "sacred" is used in the religious sense in P2, then, as I have suggested, P3 may well seem reasonable. But if we restrict our notion of sanctity to one that is nontheological, then it is much less clear that P3 is reasonable. Why should it follow from the fact that the zygote is amazing, astonishing, or awesome, that we are only permitted to kill it under the sort of extreme circumstances that would also justify killing individuals like you and me?[9] Surely this does not seem to follow in the case of the redwood. A person who holds the tree to be sacred would think, for example, that vandalizing a redwood tree is reprehensible in a way that vandalizing an ordinary tree is not. He would think that we are bound to make sacrifices to protect such a tree that we would not be bound to make to protect an ordinary tree. But he would not have to think that we are permitted to kill the tree only under the sorts of extreme circumstances that would justify killing individuals like you and me. Although some people might believe this, it is perfectly consistent with affirming the sanctity of the tree to maintain that it would be permissible to kill the tree if this were necessary to avoid suffering a major disruption of one's life, even though avoiding a comparable degree of disruption would not justify killing an individual like you or me.

And the same seems to go for the fetus from the moment of conception. To say that one should treat the fetus with reverence is not the same as saying that killing it is morally impermissible. It is to say that in one's deliberations one must not treat it as just another collection of cells. If P2 is true in the nontheological sense, for example, then it would be wrong to wantonly vandalize human embryos in a lab in a way that it would not be wrong to vandalize cancer cells. Perhaps this can be seen more clearly by looking at the other end of life. Picture an adult who has fallen into an irreversible coma and who can be kept alive on life support systems. This is still a living human being and so worthy of reverence if we have accepted P2. But this does not mean that he has a right to life. Reverence for him as a human being does impose certain constraints on us, but it does not mean that we can only kill him under the same sorts of extreme circumstances that might justify killing you or me. Even though he has permanently lost consciousness, for example, it would be inappropriate for us to simply toss him in a garbage can. And the same, at the least, can be said for human fetuses, on this view. But this is still importantly short of saying that they have a right to life. Indeed, I believe that the limitation of this approach is inadvertently recognized by Schwarz in the course of his attempt to use the notion of what he refers to as "reverence" for human life in support of the claim that abortion is impermissible. An attitude of reverence, Schwarz notes, can be understood as "an antithesis to using a person as a mere means, as in rape, enslavement, and other ways, and to the attitude of 'get rid

---

[9] Kuhse (1987: 15) presses this point effectively.

of it' so *often* displayed in the context of abortion" (1990: 112, emphasis added). The implicit concession here is that while raping a person is always incompatible with revering her, having an abortion is not always incompatible with revering the fetus. It is incompatible if the woman treats the fetus as a mere clump of cells. But she may have a suitable attitude of reverence for the fetus without being obligated to incur the significant burdens of an unwanted pregnancy, just as one might have a suitable attitude of reverence for the redwoods without being obligated to incur the significant burdens that might be involved in keeping them healthy. Finally, it is again worth noting that if the zygote is taken to be worthy of awe, it is extremely difficult to avoid the conclusion that a sperm and an egg are also. After all, they have the ability to produce a zygote, which is in turn worthy of awe. This suggests that this version of the sanctity of human life argument could succeed only by also showing contraception to be morally on a par with abortion. Since critics of abortion, even those who also oppose contraception, do not believe that contraception is morally on a par with abortion, this counts as a further reason to conclude that they cannot successfully appeal to this argument.

2.5. THE SLIPPERY SLOPE ARGUMENT

If the considerations marshalled thus far are correct, then the fact that a human fetus is a member of the same species as you and I cannot ground an argument conferring upon it the same right to life as you and I. Being a member of the same species, however, is not the only relation that obtains between the fetus and us and that might be thought to ground such an argument. Another such relation is this: The difference between a developing fetus at one moment and the fetus a moment later is always very small, but if you add enough such moments, you eventually get an individual just like you and me. I will refer to this as the relation of continuity. The fact that this relation obtains between a zygote and us is, of course, a function of the fact that a zygote is a living member of our species and the fact that it thus has the potential to develop into a human adult in a continuous, gradual manner. But it is important to note that the relation of continuity is nonetheless distinct from these other relations. I want to focus in this section on the sort of argument that appeals purely to the fact of continuity itself, without importing any possible significance that might attach to species membership or potentiality. I have already rejected the arguments from species membership, and so if the argument from continuity also fails, we will then have to consider whether any of the arguments from potentiality can succeed.

So why should the fact of continuity between the zygote and us be taken as support for the conclusion that if we have a right to life, then so does the zygote? The most familiar way of putting the answer to this question takes the form of a slippery slope argument, urging that in virtue of the continuity relation, we must attribute a right to life to the zygote in order to avoid starting down a path that leads inexorably to the denial of our own right to life. A preliminary statement of the argument runs as follows: Suppose that you deny that the conceptus immediately following conception has a right to life. Then since there is no significant difference between the conceptus at this moment and at the very next moment, you must conclude that the conceptus at the very next moment also lacks a right to life. But since you will continue to find no significant difference between the conceptus at each moment and the next, and since you will eventually reach an adult just like you and me, you will then have to conclude that the adult just like you and me also lacks a right to life. A defender of abortion, of course, could simply bite the bullet at this point and accept the conclusion that adult human beings do not have a right to life. But if we are to engage critics of abortion on their own terms as much as possible, we must surely concede that this conclusion is unacceptable. Since the conclusion that you and I lack a right to life must therefore be rejected, and since the slippery slope argument seems to show that the claim that a zygote lacks a right to life entails this conclusion, the slippery slope argument seems to show that the claim that a zygote lacks a right to life must also be rejected. As one advocate of the argument has put it, "My question to my pro-abortion friend who will not kill a newborn baby is this: 'Would you kill this infant a minute before he was born, or a minute before that, or a minute before that, or a minute before that?' " (Koop 1978: 9).[10] This slippery slope argument appeals to many people. Indeed, it is perhaps the single most common argument against abortion. How can a defender of abortion respond to it while arguing on terms that the critic of abortion must accept?

---

[10] See also, for example, Wertheimer (1971: 83): "Going back stage by stage from the infant to the zygote one will not find any differences between successive stages significant enough to bear the enormous moral burden of allowing wholesale slaughter at the earlier stage while categorically denying that permission at the next stage." The argument is also made by many others, including Benson (1990: 30) and Hochderffer (1994: 2–3).

One common response to the slippery slope argument is to insist that it embodies a simple logical fallacy. For one could apparently say precisely the same thing about the brightness of the sky at noon and the darkness of the sky at midnight. There is not a signficant difference between the amount of light at noon and at one second before noon, nor between then and one second before that, all the way to midnight. But surely this does not mean that we must conclude that midnight is as bright as noon or that we should treat it as if it is. From the fact that there is a continuous route of development from A to B it does not follow that A and B are not fundamentally different with respect to some property P, and since the slippery slope argument seems to rest precisely on the claim that this inference is legitimate, it seems to be invalid on this count. Indeed, even some of the strongest critics of abortion, such as Schwarz, are eager to disassociate themselves from the slippery slope argument for this very reason (1990: 14–15).

But this rebuttal, although tempting, goes by too quickly. We can account for the gradual transition from day to night because we recognize that being light is a property that comes in degrees, so that things can become gradually darker or gradually lighter. And the same is true of other examples which are standardly offered in response to the slippery slope argument, such as the difference between red and blue, hairy and bald, heavy and light. But if we rely on this analysis, then we can reject the slippery slope defense of the claim that the zygote has a right to life only by insisting upon the claim that the right to life, like darkness and baldness, is something that comes in degrees. The inference from the continuity between A and B to the conclusion that they are not fundamentally different, that is, is undermined only for those cases in which the property in virtue of which A and B differ greatly is one that can be acquired gradually, like extra hairs or shades of darkness, a little bit at a time. But surely most critics of abortion will reject this claim. They view the right to life as a categorical property: One either has it or one does not. If the defender of abortion wishes to challenge the critic on this point, then he may use this point of contention as a way to reject the slippery slope argument. But if we wish to argue as much as possible on terms that the critic of abortion accepts, then we cannot reject the slippery slope argument merely by appealing to such admittedly common counterexamples.

A second common objection to the slippery slope argument cannot as easily be dismissed. For if the relation of continuity forces us to continually push the point at which we first have an individual with a right to life back further and further, then why should it stop at the moment of conception? Why not take it that the sperm and egg must also be thought of as having this right? And since virtually no one on either side of the abortion debate will accept this implication, doesn't this count as a successful *reductio* on the argument itself? It is at this point that our initial formulation of the slippery slope argument must be amended. The argument thus far does nothing to preclude this backwards move, and if it is not blocked, the argument will indeed remain unacceptable. But there is a natural way to block it. Proponents of the slippery slope argument can, and at least the more careful among them do, include the claim that there is an important discontinuity at this point. So in moving back from the moral status of you today to that of you one second before and one second before that, there is no reason to stop until the moment of conception *and* there is reason to stop at that point.[11] Since this is the only place where there is a fundamental discontinuity in your developmental history, the argument maintains, it is the only place to draw a line between there being a right to life and there not being such a right that is not arbitrary. And surely morality demands that the distinctions it makes not be arbitrary. So we might spell out the entire argument more precisely as follows:

P1: The only radically discontinuous event in the developmental history of an individual like you and me is the forming of the zygote at the moment of conception.

P2: If the developmental history of an individual contains only one radically discontinuous event, then the only non-arbitrary place to draw a line along it is at the point of that event.

P3: Morality demands that the line between having a right to life and not having a right to life be a non-arbitrary one.

P4: Individuals like you and me have a right to life.

P5: Sperm and eggs do not have a right to life.

C: Morality demands that, in the case of the developmental history of individuals like you and me, the line between having a right to life and not having a right to life be drawn at the moment of conception.

This formulation seems to me to represent the strongest construal of the slippery slope argument, and it is subject to neither the night/day objection nor the sperm/egg objection. What, then, can be said against it?

---

[11] Note that this provides a second reason to reject the night and day counterexample as disanalagous: there is no comparable discontinuity at noon or at midnight.

One problem lies with P1. For while it is common to refer to the "moment" of conception, this is importantly misleading. Fertilization is itself a gradual process that typically takes about twenty-two hours from beginning to end. As such, it is no more instantaneous than other potentially important points in fetal development such as the point at which the fetus first becomes sentient or viable.[12] If the claim is that we should draw the line at conception because it is the only place to draw it precisely, while drawing it at, say, viability or brain activity emergence will leave an unacceptable gray area, then that claim seems to be false. We can't draw a precise line here either.[13] Proponents of the slippery slope argument often claim that there is a solution to this difficulty. Fertilization may be a process that takes time, as Joyce, for example, concedes, but "it has a definite conclusion. The moment at which this process terminates in the resulting zygote can be called conception" (1981: 350).[14] On this account, there truly is one instant about which we can say that there is a fundamental discontinuity between what lies on one side and what lies on the other.

This reply is tempting, but it is unsatisfactory. Indeed, it simply begs the question of when, exactly, the sperm and egg cease to exist as distinct individuals and the zygote begins to exist as one. To see why this is so, it is necessary to consider the process of fertilization in slightly more detail. It seems clear that we should consider the sperm and ovum as two distinct organisms even as the head of the sperm begins to penetrate the ovum's outer layer at the beginning stages of fertilization. Even though the two have become physically continuous (indeed, the plasma membranes of the sperm and the oocyte become fused, and the sperm leaves its behind as it continues toward the egg's center), and even though this contact prompts physical changes in each, we plainly have two distinct

---

[12] This point is pressed persuasively by Kuhse: "Fertilization is not a single, instantaneous event. It is a process and involves, amongst other things, the penetration of the outer shell of the egg...by a sperm, following which it takes a further 20–22 hours before the genetic material of the egg and of the sperm merges in a process known as syngamy. When, then, does an embryo come into existence, or when has fertilization occurred?" (1988: 335). See also, e.g., Tribe (1992: 123).

[13] Relatedly, there is a sense in which we can draw a precise line with respect to these other criteria. Given our current state of knowledge about the relationship between brain states and mental states, for example, we cannot *know* precisely when a fetus first has a certain kind of mental state or first has a certain kind of capacity, but we can still confidently say that there must *be* some specific moment when it first has them.

[14] This suggestion is also endorsed by Schwarz (1990: 76).

complex systems interacting with each other, rather than a single, individual organism. It even seems fairly clear that when the sperm initially completes its penetration and is entirely contained within the egg, we have one distinct organism operating inside of another. But what do we have at the point of time, say, one or two hours before fertilization is complete? At this stage, the male and female chromosomes have been released from their respective pronuclei and have begun to mingle. They are no longer physically segregated as they were before, but they are not yet physically connected as they will be once they successfully pair off. If the sperm and the egg still exist as distinct individual organisms at this point, then where are they? We can point to twenty-three of the chromosomes and say that they are the ones from the sperm, but they are no longer related to one another in the way they were before when it made sense to think of them as constitutive parts of a single pronucleus. And the same can be said of the female chromosomes. So there seems to be no good reason to insist that at this point we have one distinct organism. But if the sperm and the egg no longer exist as distinct individual organisms at this point, then when, precisely, did they cease to do so? The difference between what we have at this moment and what we had a moment before seems neither greater nor smaller than the difference between any two consecutive moments that occur throughout the process of fertilization. To stipulate that a fundamentally discontinuous event occurs at the "end" of the process of fertilization is simply to ignore the fact that the question of exactly when the end of the process occurs itself raises a slippery slope problem. So there really does not seem to be any one instant during the process of fertilization at which a fundamentally discontinuous event occurs. And for this reason, it seems to me that P1 of the slippery slope argument should be rejected.

But let us nonetheless assume that P1 is true. Since we are assuming that you and I have a right to life and that sperm and eggs do not, this leaves only P2 and P3 as possible sources of difficulty for the argument. Taken individually, both premises seem to be reasonable enough: given the truth of P1, any line other than one at conception would seem to be arbitrary – why draw it just *there* and not just a tiny bit to the left or to the right? – and if anything seems to be clear about moral distinctions it is that they cannot be drawn arbitrarily: the whole point of drawing such a distinction between A and B is to say that there is a *reason* to treat them differently, and arbitrary distinctions are, by their very nature, made without reason. Nonetheless, a crucial problem with the slippery slope argument emerges when these two premises are conjoined. The problem lies in an equivocation on what we mean when we call a distinction "arbitrary" and it is perhaps best introduced by means of an example.

So consider the old joke about the drunk who is crawling around under a street light late at night looking for his wallet. When asked if this is where he dropped his wallet, he replies no, he is pretty sure that he dropped it a few blocks away, but he's looking here because the light is better. In one sense, the spot under the light is a non-arbitrary one to pick. If it is the only working light around for several blocks, then it is noticeably different from every other point in the area; for any other place he might choose to look, one could always say: Why not a little to the left or the right? It is a non-arbitrary point in the sense that it, and only it, is conspicuously different from all the other points. Let us say that such a point is salient. But the fact that the spot under the light is salient, and so non-arbitrary in this sense, does not mean that it is a sensible place to look. Given the goal of choosing the action most likely to result in finding the wallet, it is of course true that one should not choose the spot to investigate arbitrarily. One should appeal to considerations that are relevant to the goal. But in this case, that will mean not choosing the point that is salient, even if it means then having to choose from among a range of other points no one of which is salient with respect to the others.[15] Applied back to the original argument, then, we can agree that P2 is true where "non-arbitrary" means "salient," but in this sense, P3 is false. Morality demands that the considerations that go into drawing the line between having a right to life and not having a right to life be morally relevant, but in doing this it does not insist that we must appeal to the point that is salient. Similarly, if by "non-arbitrary" we mean "relevant to the judgment being made," then P3 is plainly true. The line between having a right to life and not having a right to life must be drawn in a manner that is relevant to such rights attributions. But in this sense of "non-arbitrary," we do not yet have any reason to accept P2. P2, understood in this sense, maintains that the only radically discontinuous event in one's developmental history is morally relevant, but whether or not this is so is precisely what we are trying to determine. So the fact, if it is a fact, that conception is the only radical discontinuity in one's developmental history means that this is where

---

[15] And one cannot object that it is unreasonable to choose one point over another if neither is salient. As Williams has pointed out, this would imply that the reasonable thing for Buridan's ass to do is starve between the two equal piles of hay it can choose from (1986: 190; 1985: 133–4).

the line between having a right to life and not having a right to life can be drawn most clearly, but it does not mean that this is where it can be drawn most reasonably.

Finally, and I think most decisively, the slippery slope argument is subject to a commonly noted but not commonly appreciated rebuttal by *reductio ad absurdum*. As one writer has put it, the development from acorn to oak tree is equally continuous, but "it does not follow that acorns are oak trees, or that we had better say they are" (Thomson 1971: 131). Now defenders of the slippery slope argument often claim to have an answer to this objection: The two cases are disanalogous, they insist, because people are important in a way that oak trees are not. If we cared about oak trees as much as we care about people, they say, then the facts about oak development really would force us to conclude that acorns have the same sort of value as oaks. Philip E. Devine, for example, has complained about what he calls the "surprising persistence" of "the 'acorn' argument" in discussions of abortion on precisely these grounds: "Whatever may be the case with dormant acorns, a germinating acorn is, while not an oak *tree*, still a member of the appropriate species of oak. If oaks had a serious right to life in their own right, so would oak saplings and germinating acorns." (1990: 52). And the point is often cast in terms of the tree-loving Druid: "For the Druid, the life-force which exists in the oak tree and which makes it divine, also exists in the acorn" (Cooney 1991: 162). And so, on this account, the acorn objection to the slippery slope argument backfires and ends up reinforcing the position it is meant to undermine.

There is something right about this response to the acorn objection. It is misleading to compare the implications of the gradual development of human beings with the implications of the gradual development of oak trees if we don't take such trees themselves to be morally important. The fact that the slippery slope argument fails in a nonmoral context does not entail that it must fail in a moral context. But critics of the acorn objection such as Cooney and Devine are mistaken in claiming that once the analogy is suitably mended the slippery slope argument is rescued from the objection. For let us suppose that we do value oak trees morally in just the way that we value people morally: We think that they have just the same right to life that you and I have. What will follow from this about the moral status of acorns?

The answer depends entirely on what it is about oak trees that we think confers upon them this right in the first place. If we value oak trees, as in Cooney's example, because of their "life-force," then since this is a property they share with acorns it will follow that acorns have the same right to life as mature oaks. And if we confer a right to life on oak trees because they are members of an "appropriate species," as in Devine's example, then we will grant that right to acorns since they are members of the oak species as well. But notice that in either case our attributing a right to life to the acorn will do absolutely nothing to vindicate the slippery slope argument: We will be led to attribute a right to life to the acorn not because such a right follows from the conjunction of the claim that oak trees have a right to life and the claim that acorns develop gradually into oak trees, but rather because we agree that acorns themselves already possess a property (a certain kind of life force, membership in an appropriate species) that is itself sufficient to warrant such attribution.

And in the case of fetal development, of course, this will simply beg the question. The slippery slope argument was supposed to show that the claim that the fetus has a right to life from its conception follows from the conjunction of the fact that there is a relation of continuity between it and the adult it gradually develops into and the claim that the adult itself has a right to life. But the right to life of the acorn does not follow from the fact that there is a relation of continuity between it and the oak tree it gradually develops into even if we assume that oak trees have such a right. The acorn objection to the slippery slope argument therefore survives the objections that have been aimed at it. Its persistence is well earned.[16]

I suspect, in fact, that those who are tempted by the sort of objection pressed by Cooney and Devine are in part moved by the fact that many of us do attribute at least one kind of value to oak trees, but are then misled by a failure to distinguish between two importantly different

---

[16] Li suggests a further problem with Cooney's argument: that even if we accept it, it would at most show that acorns would have some value, but not as much as oaks. And this is not enough to establish that fetuses have the same rights had by you and me. From the fact that I value a gold ring and that it gradually emerges from a block of gold, to take Li's example, it may follow that I value the block of gold but not that I value it as much (1992: 236). As a criticism of Cooney's own example, this seems to fall short, since Cooney stipulates that what is of value in the oak is just what is in the acorn: If I value the ring only for its gold, then I would value the block of gold equally. But, of course, this is precisely because Cooney begs the question of what makes people like you and me valuable in the first place. If that question is not begged, then Li's point does seem to provide an additional objection to the attempt to overcome the acorn objection. Even if some of the properties that make me morally special emerge gradually, it does not follow that all of them do.

sorts of value an object might have. One is the sort of value that gives us reason to say that the object is a good thing, that the world is a better place if the object exists than if it does not exist. We might call this existence value. This is the sort of attitude that many people take toward endangered species, for example. And if an object has existence value, then this clearly provides at least some reason for thinking it morally wrong to destroy it. The other sort of value is neutral with respect to whether or not it is good that the object exists, but provides reason for thinking that given that the object exists it has a kind of integrity that merits some kind of respectful treatment. We might call this integrity value. Promises are in a sense like this. We do not think that promises are themselves a good thing, that there is some reason to go around making them, but we do think that if you have made a promise, the fact that it exists makes a morally powerful demand on you.

This distinction is important for a combination of two reasons. First, the value most people are willing to attribute to oak trees is existence value. They think that oak trees are a good thing, that a world with plentiful oaks is a better world than is one without. And this is why they believe, if they do believe, that it would be morally wrong to pointlessly destroy one. But the value that the critic of abortion attributes to people in believing that it is wrong to kill individuals like you or me is integrity value. The critic of abortion does not maintain that killing people like you and me is wrong because it reduces the number of good things in the world. He need not think that it would be better for there to be more people in the world and may even agree that it would be better if there were fewer. And he surely thinks it would be wrong to kill one innocent person in order to save two others even though killing one person in such cases would maximize the amount of people who would then exist. Rather, the claim that the critic of abortion appeals to, the claim that killing people like you and me is wrong, rests on the claim that it is wrong because it fails to respect the kind of integrity that people like you or I have, given that we do exist.[17] Most defenders of abortion believe this as well, of course, but the point here is simply that a defense of abortion that attempts to engage critics of abortion on their own terms as much as possible must accept that people like you and me have this kind of value.

[17] I do not mean to suggest here that people do not have existence value, only that it is not the existence value that they have that accounts for the wrongness of killing them.

The second reason the distinction between existence value and integrity value is important is this: while the slippery slope argument seems to work in the case of something that gradually develops into an object with existence value, it does not work in the case of something that gradually develops into something with integrity value. If what is wrong about destroying an oak at a certain point in time is that it prevents the world from having as many good things in it as it would otherwise have had, then it would also seem to be wrong to pointlessly destroy it at any previous point in time, including when it was a budding acorn, and for the same reason. Destroying the acorn and destroying the oak each deprive the world of a valuable oak that would otherwise have existed. But if what is wrong about destroying an object at a certain point in time is that it has integrity value, which destroying it fails to respect, then this counts as no reason against destroying it prior to that time if it is developing but does not yet have that value. If we do not especially care how many of those objects there are, then it is perfectly consistent to say that it will be wrong to destroy it once it has integrity value but not before that. As a result of these two distinctions, it follows that even if the slippery slope argument does show that if oaks have existence value, then so do acorns, it still fails to show that if you and I have integrity value, then so do human fetuses. It is the claim that you and I have integrity value that the critic of abortion attempts to exploit in proposing the slippery slope argument, and the claim that human fetuses have integrity value that he must vindicate in order to justify the first premise of the rights-based argument against abortion.

While the acorn example seems to me sufficient to bring out this defect of the slippery slope argument, I suspect that many people will continue to view the example with some suspicion. It is therefore worth noting that an even more powerful counterexample to the slippery slope argument emerges from the following consideration: The continuity relation could in principle obtain between us and a zygote even if zygotes were not members of our species and even if they had no potential to develop into beings like us.[18] For imagine a time-line representing the

---

[18] It should also be noted that the continuity relation could also fail to obtain between zygotes and us even given that zygotes were members of our species with the potential to develop into beings just like us. If fetal development occurred in quantum steps, in which a zygote lay dormant for a few months in the womb and then was instantly zapped into a sentient being, the argument from continuity would no longer apply even though arguments appealing to the zygote's species membership and potential would still apply.

development of a single human being from conception to adulthood. It consists of an extremely long sequence of pictures, with each one representing a tiny increase in development over the previous one, from one-celled zygote, to two-celled conceptus, and so on. For simplicity's sake, suppose that human beings develop one cell at a time, so that we have a sequence of pictures from a one-celled organism, to two-celled, to three-celled, to four-celled, to as many cells as you currently have in your body and of just the same kind. Now imagine that rather than representing the development of a single individual at different stages of his life, this same series of pictures instead represents a collection of *discrete individuals,* each of whom are members of a different and unrelated species at the point of maturity for their species. So instead of representing Alec the human being at the one-celled stage of his life and then Alec the human being at the two-celled stage of his life, the first picture represents Alice, a fully developed one-celled creature who will never be more than a one-celled creature, and the second represents Bob, a fully-developed two-celled creature who will never be more than a two-celled creature. On the first interpretation of this massive sequence of pictures, we are faced with the fact that there is virtually no difference between Alec at the one-celled stage of his life and Alec at the two-celled stage of his life, nor between Alec at the two-celled stage of his life and Alec at the three-celled stage of his life, nor between Alec at any stage of his life and Alec at the stage immediately before or after it, all the way up to the point at which Alec is a fully developed adult human being. In just the same way, on the second interpretation of the pictures, we are faced with the fact that there is virtually no difference between Alice the fully developed one-celled creature and Bob the fully developed two-celled creature, or between Bob the fully developed two-celled creature and Claudia the fully developed three-celled creature, or (imagining at each new step a fully developed creature with just a single cell more than the previous one) between Claudia and David, or David and Eli, all the way until we reach (after numerous runs through the alphabet), Yvonne and Zachary, where Zachary is someone just like you or me.

Now, the slippery slope argument maintains that the continuity relation that obtains between Alec the human being at the one-celled stage of his life and Alec as a fully developed adult suffices to demonstrate that since the fully developed Alec has a right to life, so therefore does the one-celled Alec. There is, after all, no non-arbitrary place to draw a line between the two. But the continuity relation that obtains between these two stages of Alec's life also obtains, and just as strongly, between Alice the fully developed one-celled creature and Zachary the fully developed adult human being. It is equally the case that there is no non-arbitrary place to draw a line between Alice and Zachary. Wherever the line is drawn, one could always ask: Why not draw it just a little bit to the left or to the right? And so if the continuity relation suffices to show that since fully developed adult Alec has a right to life, then so does Alec at the one-celled stage of his development, then it also suffices to show that since fully developed adult human being Zachary has a right to life, then so does one-celled Alice, a fully developed one-celled creature who will never be more than a one-celled creature. But surely the critic of abortion will not accept the claim that one-celled Alice has the same right to life as you and I merely in virtue of the fact that we cannot identify a clear line between a fully developed one-celled creature and a fully developed human being. And so the critic of abortion cannot appeal to the slippery slope argument as a way of justifying the conception criterion.

Of course, proponents of the claim that Alec, the human being at the one-celled stage of his development, has a right to life while Alice the fully developed one-celled creature does not, could appeal to the fact that one-celled Alec, but not one-celled Alice, has the potential to develop into an individual like us. And this difference between one-celled Alec and one-celled Alice could well prove to be a morally relevant one. But to appeal to the claim that this difference between the two cases is morally relevant would not be to rescue the slippery slope argument. It would simply be to abandon it and to appeal instead to an argument from potentiality. Abandoning the slippery slope argument does seem the right thing for the proponent of the conception criterion to do at this point. The question now is whether arguments from potentiality will prove to be more satisfactory.

2.6. THE POTENTIALITY ARGUMENT

I have thus far considered those arguments in favor of the conception criteria that are based on one of two distinct relations that hold between you and me on the one hand and a zygote on the other: the relation of common species membership and the relation of continuity. I have argued that arguments based on these relations are ultimately unsuccessful. A third relation that holds between you and me on the one hand and a zygote on the other is this: A zygote has the potential to develop into an individual just like us. It follows from this that, at the very least, the zygote is an individual with the potential to develop into an individual with a right to life. The question is what follows from this. There are several distinct arguments that attempt to show that what follows from this is that the zygote already has a right to life.

Perhaps the simplest argument from potentiality is one that rests on a general assumption of the following sort: Potential possession of a right entails actual possession of a right. If an individual is such that it is developing into a being that clearly has a given right, then this fact about it justifies conferring the right on it already. Call this the potentiality argument. This argument is common in the popular discourse on abortion and has been given a more philosophically sophisticated defense by Wilkins (1993). Wilkins notes that many philosophers view the argument as unsound on the grounds that its major assumption embodies a logical error. It certainly is not true of properties in general that if a given individual potentially has a given property, then the individual already has this property. Prunes have properties that plums do not have, wine has properties that grape juice does not have, and adults have properties that fetuses do not have. Perhaps a proponent of the potentiality argument could complain that these examples appeal exclusively to nonmoral properties. But the claim is equally unacceptable if it is limited to moral properties: Adults have moral responsibilities that children do not have, and older people cultivate moral virtues they did not have when they were younger. The question, then, is whether, given all this, there is any reason to think the assumption true of rights in general, or of the right to life in particular.

Wilkins attempts to defend the argument from this challenge by focusing on a counterexample proposed by Benn and later developed by Feinberg. When Jimmy Carter was six years old, he was a potential president of the United States, but even though the president of the United States has the right to command the armed forces, it does not follow that six-year-old Jimmy had even a very weak right to command the armed forces, let alone a right on a par with actual presidents. This example shows that potential rights do not entail actual rights, and that the assumption needed to ground the potentiality argument must be rejected.

As Wilkins points out, however, there are several problems with the analogy between potential president and potential fetus (1993: 126–7).

In the first place, to say that a fetus is a potential child is to say more than merely that it is possible that it will become one; it is to say that a child is something that the fetus is developing into. But all we can really say of Carter is that it was possible in 1930 that he would one day be elected president. Being president is not something one develops into; rather, becoming president is something that happens to one, as a result of the elective actions of others. Relatedly, the right to command the armed forces is one that is conferred on you by others, but the right to life is not. The former is conventional whereas the latter is natural. And there is a further problem that Wilkins does not notice: The right to command a given army is, by its very nature, a right that can only be possessed by one person at a time. We might call this an exclusive, as opposed to non-exclusive, right. If I have the right to command a given army at a given time, it follows that you do not. So long as there is an actual president in 1930, then, six-year-old Jimmy cannot have the right to command the armed forces at that time. But this is not so of moral rights in general, and certainly not of the right to life in particular. So the fact that an individual who will possibly be given a conventional, exclusive right in the future does not now possess this right does not show that an individual who is developing into the sort of individual who has a certain natural, non-exclusive right does not have it now.

These are indeed substantial disanalogies. But it is important to remember that the critic of the potentiality argument need not claim that such a person does not have this right now. She must claim merely that possession of this right is not *entailed* by potential possession of it. Feinberg's example still shows that rights are not in general entailed in this way, and this is still sufficient to defeat the argument that claims that the fetus has the right to life merely by appealing to its potential possession of it.[19] Still, the weakness of the analogy does suggest that if a case more like the fetus case yields the result that potential rights entail actual rights, then the argument could be revised to meet the objection. And this is precisely what Wilkins attempts to do by means of the following example:

Consider the case of a medical student who is surely a potential doctor in a strong and relevant sense, i.e., he is well on the way to becoming a doctor. Of course, he still may not become a doctor, but he is in training and is fairly close

---

[19] Reiman notes this in his critique of Wilkins (1993: 172–3).

to his goal. Such a student has the right to participate in a limited way in the diagnosis and treatment of some illnesses under the supervision of his teachers. The right in question is of course restricted, but it is not on that account a 'partial', 'quasi,' or 'weak' right. (1993: 127)

If this case is relevantly more like the case of the fetus, and if we accept Wilkins's analysis of it, then this may provide at least some support for the potentiality argument.

But there are several problems here. First, although it is less obvious here than in the case of six-year-old Jimmy, being a doctor and having the rights of a doctor are essentially conventional properties. Someone might know everything that a doctor knows and be every bit as good as a doctor is at diagnosing and treating illnesses, but if he did not graduate from medical school and receive the appropriate credentials, we call the person an imposter rather than a doctor and do not grant him the right to practice medicine that we grant to doctors. Thus, even if we agree that medical students have some of the rights that doctors have, this will not be an example of the sort of natural right that the potentiality argument seeks to ascribe to the fetus. It will only show that sometimes we extend conventional rights to those who potentially possess them while at other times we don't. Second, it is not at all clear that what we have here is a right of the students at all, since Wilkins adds the proviso "under the supervision of his teachers." We might equally say that medical school teachers have the right to extend to students the privilege of assisting them in diagnosing and treating illnesses. Third, even if this is a right possessed by these students, it seems far more plausible that it is a right they possess in virtue of their properties as actual medical students, rather than in virtue of their properties as potential doctors. Wilkins attempts to rebut this objection by noting that if such a student dropped out of school he would no longer have the right even though he would still have the knowledge and ability (1993: 127). But this fact is equally consistent with both explanations: He would no longer be a potential doctor, and he would also no longer be an actual medical student. Finally, even if the example is accepted and even if it is thought to be substantially like the fetus case, it would still, after all, be one example. And other examples that are at least as similar seem at least as clearly to point in the opposite direction. The fact that I now have the right to own property, or to watch anything I want on television, does not mean that I had the right when I was a small child. And a child is much more like an adult than a zygote is like a child. Wilkins's efforts notwithstanding, then, the potentiality argument is indeed unacceptable.

Finally, I should note a related defense of the potentiality argument that seems at least to be suggested by Donagan (1977: 171):

[I]f respect is owed to beings because they are in a certain state, it is owed to whatever, by its very nature, develops into that state. To reject this principle would be arbitrary, if indeed it would be intelligible. What could be made of somebody who professed to rate the state of rational agency as of supreme value, but who regarded as expendable any rational creature whose powers were as yet undeveloped?

Understood as an argument for the conception criterion, this argument embodies the same fallacy as the attempted rebuttal to the acorn objection to the slippery slope argument discussed in Section 2.5. There are two distinct senses in which we might value an individual in virtue of its being in a certain state: We might value it in the sense that we think it a good thing to have around, or we might value it in the sense that we think that it has a right not to be destroyed. Donagan's argument seems to work in the first sense: If we value adults in the sense that we think that having more of them is better than having fewer of them, then we should value fetuses for the same reason, given that they will eventually develop into such adults. But it does not work for the second: If we think an individual like you and me has a right not to be killed even if killing him would bring about a better state of affairs, it does not follow that we should think that individuals with the potential to become like us already have that right. It is in this second sense that critics of abortion maintain that individuals like you and me have a right not to be killed. And so they cannot successfully appeal to the potentiality argument as a way of showing that if we have this right, then so does the human fetus.

2.7. THE ESSENTIAL PROPERTY ARGUMENT

The potentiality argument represents one way to get from the claim that a zygote has the potential to develop into an individual like you or me to the conclusion that a zygote has the same right to life as you or me. I have argued that it also represents an unsuccessful way. A second and distinct argument based on the zygote's potential arises from the claim that, in a morally relevant sense, potentiality implies identity. To say that an adolescent is a potential adult, for example, is not to say that an adolescent has the potential to *produce* an adult. Rather, it is to say that he has the potential to *become* an adult. And to say that the adolescent can become an adult is to say that the adult he becomes and the adolescent he was are one and the same individual, that adulthood and adolescence are simply different phases in the life of one and the same living being. By parity of reasoning, then, the same should be true of the fact that a fetus is a potential adult. If the zygote simply *produced* a human adult, the resulting adult would be a new individual being, distinct from the being that the zygote was. But since the zygote eventually *becomes* a human adult, this human adult is the very same individual living being that the zygote was. It is simply that being at a later stage of its development. And this in turn seems to suggest that if the resulting being has a right to life, then the zygote has a right to life as well. Critics of abortion often develop this suggestion by asking the reader to consider it from the first personal perspective (e.g., Schwarz 1990: 83), and since the argument based upon this suggestion is typically presented in terms of the language of personhood, I will begin by formulating it in this way. So understood, a preliminary version of such an argument runs like this:

P1: I am the same individual living being as the zygote from which I developed.
P2: I am a person.
C: The zygote from which I developed was a person.

And since I am no different from anyone else in this respect, the conclusion generalizes to all human zygotes. All of them are persons.

There are two problems with this argument. One concerns the fact that the meaning of the term *person*, and thus the significance of the argument's conclusion, is potentially ambiguous. I will return to this problem later. But the more immediate problem with the argument is simply that it is invalid. It moves from a claim about the relation between you now and the zygote then and a substantive claim about you now to a further substantive conclusion about the zygote then. And this move is illegitimate unless there is some more general principle warranting it. What might that principle be? The argument would plainly succeed if we were to add to it something like this:

P3: If an individual living being has a property at one point in time, then it has that property at every point in its existence.

But P3 is plainly false. I have many properties now that I did not have when I was a zygote. I am now skeptical, ticklish, and hairy, but was none of these when I was a zygote. And there are many properties that I had when I was a zygote that I do not have now. I was single-celled and invisible to the naked eye, but am neither of these things now. So from the facts that personhood is a property of mine now and that I was once a zygote, it does not follow that the zygote from which I developed had the property of personhood then.

An argument that attempts to build from these facts, of course, need not appeal to P3 in order to license the inference from P1 and P2 to C. It could instead make a more restricted claim, one narrow enough to avoid these unacceptable implications, but broad enough to warrant the inference. There seems to be one kind of restriction, in particular, that might prove capable of doing both, and it is one that is appealed to, at least implicitly, by most of those who defend this sort of argument. The restriction turns on the distinction between essential and accidental properties, where a property is an essential property of an individual if the individual cannot lose the property without ceasing to exist and is an accidental property if it is not essential. Given this distinction, the proponent of the argument can plausibly hope to avoid the difficulties noted above by replacing P3 with what I will call

P3': If an individual living being has an *essential* property at one point in time, then it has that property at every point in its existence.

P3' is true by definition, and since its scope is sharply limited, it does not produce the unacceptable result that I have always been skeptical, hairy, and ticklish or am still single-celled and invisible to the naked eye. All of those properties are plainly accidental properties of me and so are excluded from the principle's reach.

If we replace P3 with P3', then all of the premises of the argument are true. But now the argument itself is rendered invalid all over again, since P2 says only that personhood is a property of me, not that it is an essential property. The argument can therefore succeed only if we also replace P2 with what I will call

P2': I am a person essentially.

It is clear that a number of proponents of this potentiality-based defense of the claim that the fetus has a right to life do mean to be making this claim. Joyce, for example, writes as follows: "No individual living body can 'become' a person unless it already is a person. No living being can become anything other than what it already *essentially* is" (1981: 351, emphasis added). Similarly, Humber maintains that "it is *essential* for me to be me that I be human" (1975: 288, emphasis added). And Paul Ramsey argues as follows:

[I]t might be said that in all *essential* respects the individual is whoever he is going to become from the moment of impregnation. He already is this while not knowing this or anything else. Thereafter, his subsequent development cannot be described as becoming something he is not now. It can only be described as a process of achieving, a process of becoming the one he already is. Genetics teaches us that we were from the beginning what we *essentially* still are in every cell and in every generally human attribute and in every individual attribute (1970: 66–7, emphases added).[20]

The result is what can be called the essential property argument:

P1: I am the same individual living being as the zygote from which I developed.

P2': I am a person essentially.

P3': If an individual living being has an essential property at one point in time, then it has that property at every point in its existence.

C: The zygote from which I developed was a person.

And now the question becomes: do we have reason to accept P2'?

This is the point at which the problem concerning the ambiguous nature of the term *person* arises. For whether or not we have reason to accept P2' depends largely on whether by *person* we mean something like "biological organism that is a member of the species *homo sapiens*" or something like "individual with the same right to life as you and I." If it is the former, then P2' is surely plausible. Aristotle, among others, held that the species membership of an individual is an essential property of the individual. To say that this is so is to say that you would cease to exist if you ceased being a member of *homo sapiens*, that there is no possible world in which you would be, or be transformed into, a member of some other species. It is certainly not obvious that this is true, but one might well feel entitled to believe it until given a sufficiently powerful reason to reject it. If this is what we mean by P2', however, then C will say only that the zygote is an individual member of the human species. And this conclusion is insufficient for the critic of abortion's purposes. The first claim needed to sustain the rights-based argument

---

[20] The same argument is made by, for example, Burtchaell, who argues that a human being is the same individual from conception on and that human rights must rest on grounds of identity (1982b: 84, 87). See also Benson (1990: 30), Ramsey (1968: 74).

against abortion maintains that the fetus has a right to life, not merely that the fetus is biologically human. And so understood in this way, the essential property argument fails on the critic of abortion's own terms.

Suppose, on the other hand, that *person* is being used in the moral sense in P2'. If this is the case, then the conclusion it seeks to support can be used to support the rights-based argument against abortion. So understood, P2' maintains not only that I have a right to life, but that the property of having a right to life is an essential property. I have had it for as long as I exist, and I will continue to have it for as long as I exist. But now it is no longer clear whether there is any reason to believe that P2' is true. The importance of the shift in meaning here is nicely (though inadvertently) illustrated by Ramsey's assertion that "We will never be anything more or anything other than the beings we always were in every cell and attribute" (1970: 67). It is clearly plausible to say that we will never be a being *other* than the being we were as a zygote, but it is clearly implausible to say that we will never be anything *more* than what we once were, at least if this means possessed of more rights than we possessed at some earlier point. As I noted in discussing the potentiality argument in Section 2.6, there are many rights that I possess now that I did not possess in earlier stages of my development. So why should we accept P2' so understood?

Those critics of abortion who make use of this claim seem to proceed as if it is simply obvious that the claim is true. Thus Liley, for example, ends his essay on the nature of the fetus with the words: "*Surely* if any of us count for anything now, we counted for something before we were born" (1972: 36, emphasis added). And in arguing from the ontological identity of the zygote and the adult who develops from it, Schwarz seems to treat as axiomatic the claim that "If the being at the later stages should be given the respect due to persons, then that same being should also be given this respect when he is at an earlier stage" (1990: 94).[21] But while this claim may turn out to be true, it simply is not plainly true. And in the context of the debate about abortion, in particular, it cannot reasonably be simply assumed to be true. After all, the debate over abortion is largely a debate over the moral status of the fetus, and the debate over the moral status of the fetus is largely a debate over whether or not it is the case that human beings have a right to life from

---

[21] Similarly Walker (undated a) treats the claim that "we are all essentially the same kind of entity as the preborn" as support for the claim that we all have the same "value" or "rights" as the preborn. See also Vieira (undated a).

the moment that they first come to exist. I am concerned in this book to examine those arguments with which a critic of abortion can attempt to convince those not already committed to the thesis that abortion is morally impermissible. Arguments that attempt to ground this thesis in such claims as that it is wrong to kill individuals like you and me or that it is wrong to kill newborn infants satisfy this requirement, since most people who do not accept the critic of abortion's thesis do nonetheless accept these claims. But in order for the essential property argument to establish that the fetus has a right to life, it must include as an assumption the very claim that is the subject of dispute between critics of abortion and their critics, the assumption that we have a right to life from the beginning of our biological existence. And this renders the argument circular in a way that the critic of abortion must acknowledge as unacceptable.

The proponent of the essential property argument therefore needs to provide an argument in defense of the claim that possession of a right to life is an essential property, an argument that does not beg the question in favor of the claim that the fetus has a right to life. And such an argument simply does not seem to be forthcoming. Why, then, would these writers treat the claim as self-evident? I suggest that the answer again lies in the distinction I noted in the context of the slippery slope argument in Section 2.5: that between what I referred to as existence value and integrity value. If to say that you are now a person is to say that you are now the sort of being whose existence is a good thing, then it may seem obvious that P2' is true. If what is morally wrong about killing you derives from the claim that the world is a better place when you exist in it than when you don't, then it seems natural to suppose that killing you at any point in your existence makes the world a worse place, and equally so. But, as we have already seen, this sense of value is inadequate for the critic of abortion's purposes. Killing an innocent person is supposed to be impermissible even if it makes the world contain more good (say, by preventing two other innocent people from dying). So the claim that you are a person must amount to the claim that you have integrity value: We need not think it makes things better that you exist, but given that you do, you have a kind of integrity that killing you would wrongfully violate. This is what P2' must mean in order for it to provide support for the claim that the critic of abortion seeks to defend. And on this meaning, it is far from obvious that P2' is true. I can easily believe that I have integrity now in virtue of properties that I now have accidentally rather than essentially. Indeed, as I have already had occasion to note, there are many rights that we believe we possess at some stages of our lives and not at others.

Finally, the claim that the right to life is an essential property of human beings has implications that many people on both sides of the abortion debate will find unacceptable. One implication concerns the case of the irreparably brain-damaged adult human being in a complete and irreversible coma. He is clearly the same individual living being as he was as a younger adult, so if his right to life is an essential property, it will follow that he has the same right to life while in a permanent coma. But this claim is far from being clearly true and to many will seem very clearly to be false. A second implication concerns the case of the convicted murderer. He, too, is clearly the same individual being as he was before he committed murder, so if his right to life is an essential property, it will follow that he retains his right to life after he has committed the murder. But this claim, too, is far from being clearly true. Many critics of abortion believe in the permissibility of capital punishment, and it would therefore be inconsistent for them also to maintain that the right to life is an essential property of human beings. And even if one denies that capital punishment is morally permissible, it seems difficult to maintain that it is impermissible merely in virtue of the fact that the murderer is a human being. The claim that irreversibly comatose adults and convicted murderers have the same right to life as you and I is not a claim that the critic of abortion can appeal to without further defense. As a result, a critic of abortion cannot rely on an argument for the conception criterion that proceeds as if it were. And this provides a further reason to reject the essential property argument.

One final response on behalf of the defender of the essential property argument merits notice. In invoking the claim that my personhood is an "essential" property of me, the writers I have cited are clear that they mean to be marking out a class of properties the loss of which is importantly different from the loss of purely accidental properties. And they are right to do so since, as we have seen, narrowing the scope of P3 is necessary in order for it to remain plausible. But as I have so far been understanding the distinction between essential and accidental properties, invoking the distinction salvages P3 only by undermining P2. In doing so, however, I have been using the term *essential* in a more specific manner than these writers typically do, and perhaps in doing so I have also used it in a more narrow manner than they intend. There is, in particular, a related but distinct idea that people often have in mind when referring to essential properties, and it might be thought that this is what is meant and that this could offer a way to rescue the argument. The idea is this: We often classify individuals into different kinds, and sometimes there are properties which it is necessary for an individual to possess in order for it to be an individual of that *kind*, even if it is not necessary in order for it simply to *exist*. On this use of the term, a property is an essential property of an individual of a given kind if the individual cannot lose the property without ceasing to be an individual of that kind even if he can lose the property without ceasing to exist. On this account, for example, being unmarried is an essential property of being a bachelor. If you are a bachelor and you get married, then you cease to be a bachelor even though you do not cease to exist. This broader notion of essential properties might at first seem to offer a successful compromise between the unacceptably broad claim made by P3 when it includes all properties, and the very narrow claim made by P3' that rendered it acceptable but unable to support the critic of abortion's conclusion. But this appearance is illusory. For what is the kind to which I belong only so long as I retain my personhood? The proponent of the argument will have to offer some sort of characterization. And whatever the answer is, it will remain the case that the argument simply assumes that a zygote is this kind of thing, and that there will be no reason for someone who is not already committed to the argument's conclusion to accept this assumption.

2.8. THE FUTURE-LIKE-OURS ARGUMENT

Perhaps the most powerful potentiality-based argument for the claim that the typical human fetus has the same right to life as the typical adult human being arises from the consideration that the kinds of future experiences that lie ahead of the typical human fetus are just the same as the kinds of experiences that lie ahead of the typical adult human being, and are thus of just the same kind of value. The argument is most widely associated with Donald Marquis's important article, "Why Abortion is Immoral" (1989), and I will focus my discussion in this section on Marquis's formulation of it, although the same sort of argument has also been defended by a number of other writers.[22]

---

[22] Marquis replies to some of his critics in Marquis (1994) and (1995), and I will incorporate some of his comments there into my discussion of the argument. For other defenses of the same sort of argument, see also Stone (1987, 1994, and 1995: 139n3), Schwarz (1990: esp. 9off.), and also Feezell (1987: esp. 44ff.). Although

2.8.1. The Argument

Marquis's argument can be understood as starting with the assumption that although defenders and critics of abortion differ sharply over the question of whether the fetus has the same right to life as you or I, they agree that in cases B, C, and D in the following list, the individuals in question have the same right to life as you and I do in E: (A) fetus, (B) infant, (C) suicidal teenager, (D) temporarily comatose adult, (E) you or me. Marquis can then be understood as suggesting that the following decision procedure be used to resolve the question about the status of the fetus: Identify the property that most plausibly accounts for the wrongness of killing in cases B–E, and then determine whether that property is possessed by the individual in case A. If it is, then the best account of the wrongness of killing in general provides a sufficient reason to conclude that the fetus has the same right to life as you or I. If it is not, then the best account of the wrongness of killing provides no such reason (though this will still leave open the possibility that killing the fetus is wrong for reasons other than the reasons that best explain why killing you or me is wrong). Marquis's thesis can then be put as follows: If the individuals in cases B–E have a right to life, then so does the typical human fetus.

Now as I noted in Section 1.3, some philosophers who have argued in defense of abortion would disagree with Marquis about case B, that of the human infant. If they are right in maintaining that the human infant has no right to life, then Marquis's conclusion will prove irrelevant. The claim that the fetus would have a right to life if the infant did will prove empty if the infant in fact doesn't. So one way to attempt to rebut Marquis's argument would be to attempt to establish that the infant does not have a right to life. I am not concerned in this work to argue against such an approach, but neither do I wish to rely upon it. For purposes of evaluating Marquis's argument, therefore, I will simply assume that Marquis is correct that the individuals in cases B–D have the same right to life that you and I have in case E. Marquis's claim is that on the best account of the wrongness of killing in these cases, the property that the individuals share and that is sufficient to make killing them seriously wrong is the property of having what he calls a "future-like-ours," a property that is also possessed by the typical human fetus.

there are some differences among these arguments, it seems clear to me that if Marquis's version is subject to the difficulties I identify here, then so are these other versions.

I will begin by briefly reconstructing Marquis's case for this claim and will then argue that although in one respect it is importantly correct, in another respect it is importantly mistaken. The result of its being importantly mistaken will be that the future-like-ours argument fails to provide satisfactory support for the conception criterion even if we accept the premises upon which the argument is based. But the result of its being importantly correct will be that a modified version of the argument will become available to provide support for an alternative position, one on which if Marquis is correct that the individuals in cases B–D have the same right to life that you and I have in case E, then the fetus only acquires this right at a much later stage in its development. That possibility will then be further developed near the end of Chapter 3.

Let us begin with case E. Suppose that Larry kills Moe, and we want to account for the truth of the claim that his doing so is seriously immoral. There would seem to be three sorts of considerations to which we might appeal in doing so: the effect of the action on others, the effect of the action on Larry, or the effect of the action on Moe. As Marquis convincingly argues, making the argument for the wrongness of the act rest on the effects of the act on others, say, the grief that Moe's death will cause to Curly and Shemp, will leave the argument subject to the charge that it cannot show why it is wrong to kill someone who is universally unloved (or, even more, who is universally hated). And making the argument rest on the effects of the action on Larry himself, say, by claiming that killing Moe will brutalize Larry, begs the question that is at issue, since the brutalizing effect on Larry's character of killing Moe will only properly be characterized as a negative one if there is some reason to believe that the acts that brutal people do are objectionable that is independent of considerations about the effects of such acts on their character. So if there is a reason that is sufficient for believing that it is wrong for Larry to kill Moe, it seems that the reason must be grounded in the effects of the killing on Moe himself. And there is one such effect, in particular, that seems to be a promising candidate: The killing of Moe deprives him of the entire set of experiences that constitutes his personal future. Marquis refers to the set of experiences that constitutes the personal future of a typical human being as a "future-like-ours," and so we can say that, on Marquis's account, the wrongness of killing Moe should be accounted for in terms of Moe's possession of a future-like-ours.

Why should it matter morally that Moe's death deprives him of a future-like-ours? There are several possible answers that might be given to this question, and thus several possible future-like-ours-based accounts of the wrongness of killing him. One suggestion might be this: Moe presumably places great value on the set of experiences that constitutes his personal future, and so what makes killing him wrong is that it deprives him of something he greatly values. On this version of the future-like-ours account, the property that Moe possesses that is sufficient to make him an individual with the same right to life as you or I is the property of "having a future-like-ours that one values." And this account can seem initially quite plausible, since it seems quite plausible to suppose that it is in general prima facie wrong to deprive people of what they value, and prima facie more seriously wrong to deprive people of what they more strongly value.

If we attempt to account for the wrongness of Larry's act by appealing to Moe's possession of a future-like-ours that he values, then we will be able to get case E right, and in an intuitively plausible manner. But, as Marquis argues, this will leave us unable to account for the wrongness of killing in the other uncontroversial cases, especially cases C and D.[23] The person in a temporary coma and the suicidal teenager do not currently value their personal futures, yet surely they nonetheless possess the same right to life that you or I have. So the account of the wrongness of killing Moe that turns on Moe's possession of the property of "having a future-like-ours that one values" must be rejected. What is needed is a way of modifying the account so that it retains its essential reference to Moe's possession of a future-like-ours, since this seems clearly to be relevant to the wrongness of killing him, but so that it also becomes able to account for the wrongness of killing in the cases of the temporarily comatose adult and the suicidal teenager.

There seem to be two distinct and promising ways in which this could be done. One turns on the claim that even if the individual in question does not currently *value* the set of experiences that constitutes his personal future, it is nonetheless true that that set of experiences is *of value* to him. The other turns on the claim that even if the individual in question does not *currently* value the set of experiences that constitutes his personal future, it is nonetheless true that he will come *to value* those experiences (if he is not killed). In his original presentation

---

[23] See, for example, Marquis (1989: 331, 1994: 359, 1995: 264). The case of the temporarily comatose adult, in particular, has seemed to many critics of abortion to present the strongest challenge to any attempt to tie the wrongness of killing people like you and me to our present (or actual) properties instead of our future (or potential) properties. See, for example, Schwarz (1990: 49, 90–4ff.), Rogers (1992), Schwarz and Tacelli (1989: 88–94), and Larmer (1995: 245, 247–8).

of the future-like-ours argument, Marquis distinguishes between these two possibilities and seems to express a clear endorsement of the first over the second. "It is, strictly speaking, the *value* of a human's future [rather than the human's future valuing of it] which makes killing wrong in this theory," he says of the theory he is endorsing (1989: 327, emphasis added). And he contrasts this position, which he at one point refers to as "the value-of-a-human-future" account, with one which would instead say that the morally relevant property possessed by the suicidal teenager and temporarily comatose adult is "the desire *at some future time* to live" (1989: 331, emphasis added).

But in the principal statement of what makes killing wrong in Marquis's original paper, the distinction between the "is of value" account and the "will come to value" account seems to collapse:

When I am killed, I am deprived both of what I now value which would have been part of my future personal life, but also [of] what I would come to value. Therefore, when I die, I am deprived of all of the value of my future. Inflicting this loss on me is ultimately what makes killing me wrong. This being the case, it would seem that what makes killing *any* adult human being prima facie seriously wrong is the loss of his or her future. (1989: 326)

Here "all of the value" of the experiences that lie in Marquis's future is cashed out in terms of whether he now values or would have come to value them. The "[t]herefore" indicates that we can determine that death deprives Marquis of "all of the value *of*" his future precisely because it deprives him of what he now values or would come *to value*. So the experiences that are contained in an individual's personal future are *of value* to that individual just to the extent that they are experiences of the sort that the individual either now values or will come *to value*. And this seems equally to be true in Marquis's most recent statement of the argument. In response to a challenge to produce an account of what it would mean to say that an individual's personal future is *of value* to him,[24] Marquis provides the following test: "Consider some class of human individuals at t_1. Consider the hypothesis that those human individuals have a future valuable to them at t_2. Verify this by asking those individuals at t_2 whether they believe that their lives at t_2 are worth living. Those who answer in the affirmative had a valuable future at t_1" (1995: 263–4). Assuming that those who believe at t_2 that their lives at t_2 are worth living do in fact value their lives at t_2 (and it is difficult to

---

[24] See Shirley (1995).

imagine that Marquis would mean to be denying this), it seems again to follow that the claim that an individual has a future *of value* to him and the claim that his future consists of experiences that he now values or will come *to value* amount to the same thing.[25] Since in both instances Marquis ultimately cashes out the claim that a future is of value to an individual in terms of the claim that the individual values or will come to value the experiences it contains, it is this latter consideration that seems to be the more fundamental on his account. As a result, we can say that the property that Marquis's account picks out as being sufficient in order to make one an individual with the same right to life as you or I is the property "having a future-like-ours that contains experiences of the sort that one now values or will later come to value (if one is not killed)." And, as Marquis notes, it seems straightforwardly to be true that a typical human fetus does, in fact, possess this property:

The future of a standard fetus includes a set of experiences, projects, activities, and such which are identical with the futures of adult human beings and are identical with the futures of young children. Since the reason that is sufficient to explain why it is wrong to kill human beings after the time of birth is a reason that also applies to fetuses, it follows that abortion is prima facie seriously morally wrong. (1989: 328)

Since this fact about the fetus's future will be true of it from the beginning of its existence, and since I am assuming that the fetus comes to exist at the moment of conception, it follows that the property that is sufficient to make one an individual with the same right to life as you or I is a property that the fetus acquires at conception. If the future-like-ours argument is successful, that is, then the conception criterion is true.[26]

---

[25] This is not to say that the first claim literally means the same thing as the second claim, but rather that the first claim is only true (or can only be said to be true) in cases where the second claim is true.

[26] I should point out that Marquis himself specifically avoids asserting that the future-like-ours argument entails that abortion is wrong from the moment of conception onward. This acknowledgment that the argument might not succeed all the way back to the moment of conception can be easily overlooked, since he mentions it only once, briefly and tentatively, in the middle of a sentence, "morally permissible abortions will be rare indeed unless, perhaps, they occur so early in pregnancy that a fetus is not yet definitely an individual" (1989: 210). In any event, Marquis clearly maintains that *if* a new individual human being comes to exist at conception, then the future-like-ours argument provides grounds for accepting the conception criterion. That is the claim I wish to challenge in this section.

2.8.2. The Challenge

Marquis's future-like-ours argument appeals to the fact that the human fetus has the potential to acquire properties that individuals like you and I already have. But it does so without fallaciously arguing from a potential property to an actual one. The future-like-ours argument, therefore, cannot be defeated by pointing to the objection that undermines the more common potentiality argument discussed in Section 3.6. The reason that this is so can be put in one of two ways. One is this: the future-like-ours argument appeals to an actual property that the fetus already has, the property of having a valuable personal future. This is an actual property it shares with us, not a potential it has to acquire a property which we already actually possess. Of course, one might object that saying that a fetus actually has a valuable future is really just shorthand for saying that it has the potential to enjoy many valuable experiences in the future. In this sense, Marquis's claim that the fetus already has the same right to life as you or I does rest on a claim about the fetus's potential. But in this sense, Marquis's claim that you and I have such a right also rests on a claim about our potential. So either Marquis's argument appeals to an actual property that we share with the fetus or it appeals to a potential property that we share with the fetus, but in neither case does it argue that the fetus has the same right to life that we have because it has the potential to have a property that we already actually have.

The potential of the human fetus to develop into an individual just like us seems to me to be the most promising property for a defender of the conception criterion to appeal to. And Marquis's argument seems to me to be the most promising way to make use of such an appeal. In addition, I believe that Marquis is correct that the future-like-ours principle that he defends can account for the wrongness of killing in cases B–E. I believe that he is also correct that the way in which this principle accounts for the wrongness of killing in these cases is intuitively plausible. And I believe that he is also correct in maintaining that an implication of this principle is that the typical human fetus has the same right to life as you or I. As a result, I believe that a successful rebuttal to Marquis's argument must do three things. First, it must identify another property that the individuals in cases B–E also have in common, and thus an alternative account of the wrongness of killing you or me which produces the same results in cases B–E. Second, it must show that, given that the alternative account and Marquis's account produce the same results in these cases, there is reason to prefer the alternative account to Marquis's. In particular, it must show that the property picked out by the alternative account does a better job of illuminating the wrongness of killing, that it more convincingly identifies a feature of killing that makes it prima facie seriously wrong.[27] Third, it must show that the alternative account of the wrongness of killing in cases B–E produces substantively different results in case A. The property picked out by the alternative account, that is, must either be one that is never possessed by the typical human fetus, or one that is only possessed by the typical human fetus after it has reached a relatively advanced stage of development.[28]

Since Marquis treats statements of the form "P values (or will come to value) X" as interchangeable with statements of the form "P desires (or will come to desire) that X continue,"[29] and since it will prove to be more natural to characterize the alternative property I wish to propose in terms of the language of desires, we can recast the principle underlying Marquis's account as follows:

If an individual P has a future-like-ours F *and* if either (a) P now desires that F be preserved, *or* (b) P will later desire to continue having the experiences contained in F (if P is not killed), then P is an individual with the same right to life as you or I.

Since on this account either a present or a future desire to enjoy one's personal future-like-ours is sufficient in order to be included in the scope of the principle, we can call this the "present or future desire" version of the future-like-ours principle.[30]

---

[27] In saying this, I am saying that I believe that Marquis is also correct about the appropriate criteria for evaluating his principle, which are essentially the same as the criteria I defend in Section 1.3 (see Marquis 1989: 326).

[28] When I say "relatively" advanced, I mean relative to the moral question that provides the context for Marquis's discussion. Approximately 90 percent of all abortions take place during the first trimester of pregnancy, so if the alternative account picks out a property that the fetus acquires significantly later than that point, then that will be late relative to when most abortions are performed, and most abortions will not, on that account, involve the death of an individual who has been shown to have the same right to life as you or I (for further details of the distribution of abortions by weeks of gestation, see Section 4.7.4).

[29] For example, Marquis writes that "comatose and suicidal people don't *desire* their futures," where this is clearly treated as saying that they do not currently value them (1995: 264–5, emphasis changed).

[30] For example, "[T]he value of my future to me is not simply based on my present beliefs or desires. It is based on the attitudes toward my life I will have (or would have) in the future" (Marquis 1995: 264). This is also another instance in which it is clear that "valuing" and "desiring" can be treated interchangeably in considering Marquis's argument.

Now suppose that the only uncontroversial case we had to account for was E, the case of killing individuals like you and me. In that case, there would be no reason to append the "or will later come to desire" clause (b) to the "now desires" clause (a). We would simply say that P has the same right to life as you or I if P has a future-like-ours that P now desires to preserve. In short, we would have no reason to prefer the "present or future desire" version of the future-like-ours principle to what could be called the "present desire" version. And since the present desire version is more parsimonious, we would have reason to prefer it instead. Marquis's argument for amending the "present desire" version of the future-like-ours principle by adding the extra clause turns, as I have said, on the claim that certain cases, especially C and D (the suicidal teenager and the temporarily comatose adult), force us to accept this revision. I want now to argue that he is mistaken about this. More precisely, I will claim that although it is true that on some ways of understanding what it means for P to currently desire X, the "present desire" version of the future-like-ours principle cannot account for the wrongness of killing in cases C and D, there is at least one way of understanding what it means for P to currently desire X on which the "present desire" version can and does account for the wrongness of killing in these cases. So in proposing an alternative account of the wrongness of killing in cases B–E, I will again be arguing with the critic of abortion on his own terms. I will, in effect, be accepting Marquis's future-like-ours *argument* but defending a different version of the future-like-ours *principle*. And I will defend the three claims about this alternative version of the principle that I said any successful rebuttal of Marquis's position must defend: that it produces the same results as does Marquis's in all of the uncontroversial cases, that it does so in a manner that more satisfactorily illuminates the wrongness of killing in those cases, and that it produces substantively different results in case A, that of the typical human fetus. I will begin by defending the first two claims in terms of cases C and D, and will then turn to the third claim before saying something in conclusion about case B (the infant).

2.8.3. Occurrent versus Dispositional Desires

So suppose that in response to case E, that of individuals like you and I, we have proposed the "present desire" version of the future-like-ours principle: If P has a future-like-ours that P now desires to preserve, then P has the same right to life as you or I. Suppose we have been convinced that, at least as far as this case is concerned, the "present desire" version is superior to the "present or future desire" version, since it produces the same result as that principle and more parsimoniously. And we are now considering how we should respond to case D, that of the temporarily comatose adult. Marquis's argument for the "present or future desire" version of the future-like-ours principle turns on the claim that the temporarily comatose adult does not currently desire that his future personal life be preserved. Nor, for that matter, does he currently desire anything else. After all, he is comatose. As a result, Marquis suggests that in order to account for the fact the temporarily comatose adult surely has the same right to life as you or I, we must modify the "present desire" version of the future-like-ours principle by adding "or would come to desire."

But while the claim that the temporarily comatose adult does not have any present desires is true in one sense, it is false in another. It is true that the temporarily comatose adult does not curently have any *conscious* desires. But even while he is unconscious, he still *has* desires. He is simply not aware that he has them. This is perhaps most clearly seen by comparing the case of desires with the case of beliefs. The chances are quite good that ten minutes ago you were not consciously thinking about the claim that a triangle has three sides. So in this sense, you were not at that time "believing" that a triangle has three sides. Still, that a triangle has three sides was surely one of your beliefs at that time. It was not what is standardly referred to as an *occurrent* belief, one that you were consciously entertaining at that time, but it was nonetheless something that you already actually believed, and not simply something that you had the potential to come to believe if at some point in the future someone asked you how many sides a triangle had. If I had asked you ten minutes ago how many sides a triangle has, you would surely have begun to consciously entertain the belief that a triangle has three sides. And this is not because the belief that a triangle has three sides would then suddenly have sprung into existence in you, as new beliefs do when you acquire them for the first time. Rather, it is because you were already disposed to respond to the question by forming the occurrent belief that a triangle has three sides and so already *had* the belief that a triangle has three sides in what is commonly referred to as the *dispositional* sense. And the same is true of you even while you are asleep or temporarily comatose. You do not lose all of your beliefs each time you go to bed and then acquire a new and identical set of beliefs each time you wake up. You retain your beliefs as dispositional beliefs and occasionally have some or others as occurrent beliefs.

All of this seems equally to be true in the case of desires. While you were eating breakfast this morning, the chances are that you were not consciously desiring that your future personal life be preserved. Still, surely this was one of your desires, and likely a very strong one. And it remains a desire that you have even while you are asleep or comatose, just as your belief that a triangle has three sides remains a belief that you have. So with respect to case D, at least, that of the temporarily comatose adult, we can conclude that Marquis's revision of the "present desire" version of the future-like-ours principle is necessary in one sense of "present desire" but not necessary in another. If by "present desire" we mean "present occurrent desire," then the revision is necessary. The temporarily comatose adult does not have a present occurrent desire that his future personal life be preserved, and Marquis is presumably correct that he will later have such a desire if we do not kill him. So one version of the future-like-ours principle that could successfully account for case D along with case E would be the "present or future occurrent desire" version. This is Marquis's version. But if by "present desire" we mean "present dispositional desire," then this revision is not necessary. The temporarily comatose adult does currently have a dispositional desire that his future personal life be preserved, just as he currently has a dispositional belief that a triangle has three sides. So a second version of the future-like-ours principle that could also successfully account for case D along with case E would be the "present dispositional desire" version. This is the version that I wish to defend.

I have argued so far that, at least with respect to case D, my version of the future-like-ours principle produces the same result as does Marquis's version. This was the first claim I said that any successful rebuttal to Marquis's position must be able to sustain. What about the second claim? Given that both versions of the principle produce the same result in the case of the temporarily comatose adult, is there is a reason to prefer my version of the principle to Marquis's? I believe that there are two distinct sorts of reasons. First, my version is more parsimonious than Marquis's. As I have already noted, we can plausibly account for the wrongness of killing individuals like you and me by appealing exclusively to our possession of present desires, in particular, the present desire we each have to enjoy the experiences contained in our personal futures. On Marquis's version of the principle, we then have to introduce an entirely new set of considerations about what an individual's desires will be or would have been in the future in order to account for the case of the temporarily comatose adult. But on my version of the principle, no such further complications are needed and all of the considerations that are sufficient to account for the wrongness of killing him are already available in the principle that is sufficient to account of the wrongness of killing you or me.

Second, and more importantly, the consideration that my version of the future-like-ours principle appeals to seems to be more salient than the consideration embodied in Marquis's version. The great merit of the future-like-ours approach in general is that it enables us to account for the prima facie wrongness of killing by understanding killing as one instance of a more general category of acts that are prima facie wrong: acts that frustrate the desires of others.[31] It is in general prima facie wrong to act in ways that frustrate the desires of others, and in general more seriously prima facie wrong to act in ways that frustrate their stronger desires. And surely the desire to enjoy one's personal future is one of the strongest desires that one expects others to have.[32] Yet surely throughout the entire range of cases in which our acts can be

---

[31] This is not to say that killing is only wrong for the same reason that these other acts are wrong. There may be further reasons that apply only to killing. But even if there are, it is surely still a merit of the future-like-ours approach that it shows that the grounds for the wrongness of killing are not entirely distinct from the grounds for the wrongness of other wrongful acts.

[32] The assimilation of the wrongness of killing with the wrongness of frustrating desires generally might be opposed by means of the following sort of example: Veronica wants Archie to marry her almost as strongly as Betty wants to go on living. If the reason that it would be wrong for Archie to kill Betty is primarily a function of the strength of her desire to go on living, then it would be almost as wrong for Archie to refuse to marry Veronica as it would be for him to kill Betty. But while it is prima facie seriously wrong for Archie to kill Betty, it is not even a little bit prima facie wrong for Archie to refuse to marry Veronica. So the wrongness of killing is not primarily a function of the fact that killing frustrates the desires of the victim.

This objection, however, neglects the distinction between acts and omissions. If Archie kills Betty, he does an act that deprives her of desirable experiences that she would otherwise have experienced. If he refuses to marry Veronica, he refrains from doing an act that would provide her with desirable experiences she would otherwise not have experienced. If acts and omissions are morally on a par when their consequences are comparable, then the future-like-ours account of the wrongness of killing will indeed imply that killing Betty and not marrying Veronica will be morally on a par. But one who holds that acts and omissions are morally on a par will likely accept this implication. And if one does not hold that acts and omissions are morally on a par, then the implication does not follow. We would instead have to compare Archie's refusal to marry Veronica to his refusal to provide needed life-saving assistance to Betty where providing such assistance

wrong at least in part because they frustrate the desires of others what matters is the desires that others have dispositionally, not merely those that they have occurrently. Imagine, for example, a man who justifies his adulterous affair by saying, "Oh, yes, sometimes my wife has the desire that I be faithful to her, and when she is having that desire I always act in accordance with it. But she isn't having that desire right now. Right now she is playing bridge with her friends, and so she is instead having the desire that she be dealt a good hand." It is true that we could try to account for the insufficiency of the husband's argument by claiming that his wife will later have the desire that he be faithful to her and that he is now acting in a way that will prevent that later desire from being satisfied when it arises. And we could also point out that there may be still further reasons for believing that adultery is wrong having nothing to do with the desires of either of them. But none of this seems to capture what is really wrong with the husband's argumentative ploy. What is wrong with it is simply that his wife *does* have a strong desire that he be faithful, that she has this desire even while she isn't consciously entertaining it as an occurrent thought, and that this fact shows that his desires are not the only ones that must be respected when he is deciding how to act.

This same sort of reasoning seems natural in a variety of other contexts, such as those in which you lie to someone on his death-bed or demean a colleague behind her back. Indeed, even in the case where it is beliefs rather than desires that are morally relevant, it seems clearly to be those that are dispositional and not merely those that are occurrent that matter. Consider, for example, the plausible claim that you should not be allowed access to sensitive military secrets if you believe that the government should be violently overthrown. Surely what should matter in such cases is not just whether you have the belief in question as an occurrent belief, but whether you have it as a belief at all. On my version of the future-like-ours principle, the best account of the wrongness of killing coheres easily and naturally with the best account of the wrongness of these other acts. On my version, you wrong the temporarily comatose adult by depriving him of something that he really does value right now. On Marquis's version, this is not so. You wrong the temporarily comatose adult only in virtue of the fact that you deprive

would impose costs on him comparable to the costs of being married to Veronica. The future-like-ours account of the wrongness of killing will imply that these are morally on a par, but this implication seems reasonable.

him of something that he would have come to value later if you hadn't killed him. And so if the two versions of the future-like-ours principle produce the same results in the uncontroversial cases, there is good reason to prefer my version to his.

Before moving on to case C, that of the suicidal teenager, let me note one objection that might be raised at this point. My version of the future-like-ours principle relies on the attribution of dispositional beliefs and desires to people. I have asserted, for example, that even while the temporarily comatose adult is unconscious he still has a strong desire that his personal future be preserved. But I have said very little about what this attribution involves or about how one could go about verifying it in particular instances. So it might be said that while my suggestion shows that there is the possibility that an alternative version of the future-like-ours principle might be developed, the possibility cannot be adequately characterized, let alone successfully defended, until one first provides a full-blown theory of dispositional beliefs and desires. Marquis's version, on the other hand, requires no such attribution and no such theory. And thus, it might be urged, in the absence of such a theory, his version must be preferred to mine.

I am not prepared to offer anything like a full-blown theory of dispositional beliefs and desires. But I do not believe that anything like this is necessary in order to justify preferring my version of the future-like-ours principle to Marquis's. It is true that in order to apply my version of the future-like-ours principle to the case of any particular individual, I must be able to justify the claim that the individual currently has a dispositional desire that his personal future be preserved. But it is equally true that in order to apply Marquis's version of the future-like-ours principle to the case of any particular individual, Marquis must be able to justify the claim that the individual will later have the desire to enjoy the experiences contained in his personal future. And I see no reason to believe that one task will be more or less difficult than the other in any particular case. If the temporarily comatose adult has what seems to us by all reasonable measures a valuable life ahead of him, then we should feel equally confident in attributing the dispositional desire to go on living to him and in predicting that when he wakes up he will be glad to be alive. Indeed, it is difficult to imagine what reason we could have for accepting the assumption that Marquis's version of the principle requires, the assumption that the temporarily comatose adult will experience an occurrent desire to enjoy the experiences contained in his personal future when he wakes up, if it is not simply a belief in the assumption that my version of the principle requires, the assumption that the temporarily comatose adult already has this desire as a dispositional one.

2.8.4. Actual versus Ideal Desires

I have argued so far that the "present dispositional desire" version of the future-like-ours principle is superior to Marquis's "present or future occurrent desire" version in terms of cases E and D. So let us now turn to case C, the suicidal teenager. Hans has been dumped by his girlfriend and has plunged into a deep depression. He can think about nothing else and has no desire to go on living. So not only does Hans not have an occurrent desire that his personal future be preserved, he has no dispositional desire that his personal future be preserved either. He just has no desire to go on living at all. If we kill Hans, then, we do not deprive him of anything that he currently values in either sense. But surely Hans nonetheless has the same right to life as you or I. So it would seem that even if the "present dispositional desire" version of the future-like-ours principle can account for cases E and D, it fails to account for case C. And since we presumably believe that Hans will later value his future life if we refrain from killing him, it seems that Marquis's "present or future occurrent desire" version has no difficulty accounting for this case. So case C seems to show that we should prefer Marquis's version of the future-like-ours principle to mine after all.

But the claim that Hans has no present desire that his personal future be preserved, like the claim that the temporarily comatose adult has no such desire, is true in one sense and false in another. It is true that the actual content of Hans's present desires, both occurrent and dispositional, does not include a desire that his personal future be preserved. But in many cases in which we believe that the present desires of others are morally significant, we distinguish between the actual content of the desire that a person has given her actual circumstances and the content the desire she actually has *would* have had if the actual desire had been formed under more ideal circumstances. This is especially true in cases involving individuals who are temporarily in conditions of great emotional distress. And when the distinction between actual and ideal desires is taken into account here, a further refinement in the "present desire" version of the future-like-ours principle emerges. As in the case of the apparent problem posed by the temporarily comatose adult, I want first to demonstrate that when the "present desire" version of the

70

future-like-ours principle is properly formulated it produces the same result as does Marquis's "present or future desire" version, and then to argue that it does so in a manner that does a better job than does Marquis's of illuminating *why* this is the proper result.

Let me begin with the distinction between actual and ideal desires itself. Suppose that Irving is nearing the end of a hike and comes to a fork in the trail. Although his primary desire is for his own personal safety, he also has desires to take trails that are easier rather than less easy and to take trails that are more scenic rather than less. He knows that the left-hand branch is both easier and more scenic than the right-hand branch, but he does not know that someone has planted a land mine on the left-hand branch, and that if he takes that route he will trigger it and suffer a serious and possibly fatal injury. As a result of his general desires about trails and his knowledge of his situation, Irving forms a particular desire about which fork to take, the content of which is a desire to turn left. Turning left is the content of both his present dispositional desire and his present occurrent desire. But even though the actual content of Irving's present desire about which way to turn is to turn left, it is clear that the content of this particular desire does not accurately reflect the true implications of his more basic desires. If he knew about the land mine, the actual content of his present desire would surely be to turn right. The actual content of people's desires arise under imperfect conditions, such as a lack of accurate information, and we can define their *ideal* desires as their actual desires idealized, where this involves "correcting" the actual content of their actual desires to account for the various distorting effects that such imperfect conditions may have caused. In this sense, Irving's present actual desire is to turn left, but his present ideal desire is to turn right. Strictly speaking, of course, it is misleading to describe this ideal desire as one that Irving "has." The content of what I am calling his ideal desire is not the content of any particular desire that he actually has. For purposes of brevity, however, I will nonetheless use locutions such as "Irving has a present ideal desire to turn right" as a shorthand for such more cumbersome expressions as "When the content of the present desire that Irving actually does have about which direction to turn is idealized to correct for the distorting effects of the imperfect circumstances under which that actual desire was formed, the result is a desire to turn right."

A lack of full and accurate information is one respect in which our desires are typically formed under imperfect conditions. But there are others. Sometimes our desires are formed while we are under duress, or while we are upset. For these reasons, and often for others, we may form desires without reflecting on our situation calmly and without giving a reasonable amount of weight to the implications our choices will have for our near and distant future. In short, our desires are often more shortsighted than they would be if they were formed under more ideal circumstances. This seems to be the case with Hans. As things stand, he is painfully aware of how unpleasant his immediate future is going to be, and barely aware, if aware at all, of how much pleasure and satisfaction lie in his future despite this temporary setback. It need not be that Hans lacks information about the many goods that his later future is likely to hold, it is simply that he is not able to put this information into proper perspective. If he were to look more objectively at what the rest of his life holds in store for him – some deep traumatic pain now but a much greater overall amount of satisfaction and happiness later on – then he would desire to persevere and get on with his life. The actual contents of Hans's present desires do not include a desire to go on living, then, but the idealized contents of his present desires do. And so, in the sense in which I am using these terms, Hans has no actual present desire to go on living, but does have an ideal present desire to go on living.

This analysis based on the distinction between present actual and present ideal desires is already sufficient to justify my first claim with respect to case C. In the case of killing Hans, that is, as in the case of killing the temporarily comatose adult, Marquis's addition of "or would later desire" to the "present desire" version of the future-like-ours principle is not necessary in order to account for the truth of the claim that the individual in question has the same right to life as you or I. If by "present desire" we mean "present actual desire," then the revision is necessary. Hans does not currently have an actual desire that his future personal life be preserved, and Marquis is presumably correct that he will later have such a desire as an occurrent desire if we do not kill him. So one version of the future-like-ours principle that could successfully account for case C along with cases D and E would be the "present or future actual occurrent desire" version. This, when all of the relevant distinctions are finally drawn, is the most accurate way to describe Marquis's version. But if by "present desire" we mean "present ideal desire," then this further revision is not necessary. Hans does currently have an ideal desire that his personal future be preserved, just as Irving currently has an ideal desire to turn right at the fork in the trail. So a second version of the future-like-ours principle that could also successfully account for case C along with cases D and E would be the "present ideal dispositional desire" version. This is the version that I wish to defend.[33]

What about the second claim? Given that both versions of the future-like-ours principle produce the same result in the case of the suicidal teenager, is there is a reason to prefer my version to Marquis's? I believe that there are three reasons. The first two reasons parallel considerations I identified in the case of the distinction between occurrent and dispositional desires. One is that my version of the principle is again more parsimonious than Marquis's. We are able to account for the wrongness of killing in cases E and D (you or me, and the temporarily comatose adult), by appealing solely to one kind of property possessed by the individuals in question: the property of currently having desires about their futures. It is because these individuals currently have desires about their futures that our desires about how to behave are not the only ones that are morally relevant. On Marquis's version, we then have to introduce a further kind of property in order to account for the wrongness of killing in case C (the suicidal teenager): the property of having the potential to have such desires in the future if one is not killed. But on my version, this multiplying of morally relevant properties is not necessary.

There is one sense, of course, in which present ideal desires are as structurally complex as actual future desires. Both must be spelled out counterfactually. To say that a person will have a given future desire is to say that he will later have that desire *if* he is not killed, and to say that a person has a present ideal desire is to say that he would now have that desire *if* his desires were formed under more perfect circumstances. But the account of the wrongness of killing that appeals to present ideal desires is nonetheless simpler than the account that appeals to future actual desires. To say that an individual's having a present ideal desire is morally relevant is to say that it matters morally that the individual actually has desires, that how things go matters to him and not just to us. To say that an individual's having present or future actual desires is morally relevant, on the other hand, is to say that it matters morally that the individual has either present desires or the potential to have such desires in the future. And so, on my version of the future-like-ours principle, but not on Marquis's, all of the kinds of properties that are needed in order to account for the wrongness of killing the suicidal

---

[33] Shirley briefly suggests, but does not explicitly defend, a proposal that is similar to this version of the future-like-ours principle at least in terms of the distinction between actual and ideal desires (1995: 87).

teenager are already available in the account that suffices to explain the wrongness of killing you or me or the temporarily comatose adult.

A second, and perhaps stronger, reason for preferring my version of the future-like-ours principle to Marquis's here is again the same as in the case of the distinction between occurrent and dispositional desires: It is superior in terms of moral salience. As I pointed out in that context, the great merit of the future-like-ours approach in general is that it enables us to account for the prima facie wrongness of killing by understanding killing as one instance of a more general category of acts that are prima facie wrong: acts that fail to respect the desires of others. And just as in such cases in general it is dispositional rather than merely occurrent desires that are morally relevant when desires matter morally, so is it ideal rather than actual desires that are morally relevant when desires matter morally, at least in those cases where the actual desires have arisen under importantly imperfect conditions.

Suppose, for example, that the adulterer's wife is not off playing bridge with her friends, but is instead visiting her therapist for help in dealing with the fact that her only child from a previous marriage has been diagnosed with a fatal disease. Trying to help her to focus on the sources of comfort that she has in her life, the therapist encourages her to think about the loving relation she now has with her current husband. But the woman is so distraught over the plight of her child that in her current state of mind this relationship seems utterly trivial in comparison. "The only thing I care about right now is my son's health. I could care less if my husband were sleeping with every woman in town," she says, and in her present state of mind she really means this. Suppose now that the husband appeals to this fact as a justification for his behavior: My wife doesn't currently have any actual desire that I be faithful to her, occurrent or dispositional. Again, we could try to account for the insufficiency of the husband's argument by claiming that his wife will later have this desire as an actual desire and that he is now acting in a way that will prevent that later actual desire from being satisfied. And we could again point out that there may be still further reasons to believe that adultery is wrong that have nothing to do with anyone's desires. But as in the case of the distinction between dispositional and occurrent desires, none of these replies seem to capture what is really wrong with the husband's ploy.

What is wrong with it is simply that his wife *already* has desires about the future, and that if she were able to reflect on these desires more clearly, they would already include the desire that he remain faithful to her. The fact that his wife has desires about her future means that the husband's desires are not the only ones that are relevant in his deciding how to act. Her desires matter, too. But her desires matter to the extent that they accurately reflect who she is and what matters most to her, and under such circumstances it is clearly her ideal desires rather than her actual desires that do this. In this sense, the wife in this variant of the story is just like Irving, who would have the actual desire to turn right at the fork in the trail, if his desires were formed under more perfect conditions. Suppose that there is a sign at the fork in the road warning of the land mine that has been planted on the left-hand branch, and that just before Irving reaches the fork, you remove the sign, ensuring that Irving will turn left rather than right when he reaches it. In that case, you could truthfully point out that Irving had no actual desire to turn right, of either an occurrent or dispositional sort, and that your act of removing the sign therefore did not prevent him from doing anything that he had an actual desire to do. Again, while other reasons could be given for saying that your act was wrong, none would directly identify the flaw in your justification unless they pointed to the simple fact that you acted in a way that Irving would not want you to act if the content of his desires were based on a more accurate understanding of his situation. The fact that Irving has strong desires about how his trip goes for him imposes constraints on how you may behave. Yours are not the only desires that matter: you have a prima facie reason to respect his desires that you would not have if he had no desires at all. And the fact that the content of his desire about how his trip goes has been importantly distorted by the imperfect conditions under which it has been formed gives you reason to consider the content of the desire that he would have, rather than the content of the one that he actually does have, in taking his desires into account.

On my version of the future-like-ours principle, the account of the wrongness of killing coheres easily and naturally with the best account of the wrongness of these other acts. On Marquis's version, this is not so. Suppose that someone kills Hans and tries to justify the act by saying that Hans had no actual desire to go on living, of either an occurrent or dispositional sort. On my account, it is sufficient to conclude that killing Hans is nonetheless wrong simply in virtue of the fact that he has desires about his life, which are such that, when corrected to take into account the imperfect circumstances under which they have been formed, tell strongly against our killing him. The killer's purported justification for his act depends on his taking advantage of the fact that imperfect circumstances are temporarily distorting the content of the desires that Hans actually has. And it seems very plausible to say that, in general, when someone's desires are such that they would very strongly desire that you not do something to them were they able to reflect more clearly on the question, then that counts as a very strong moral reason not to do it. But on Marquis's account, as in the case of the temporarily comatose adult, the wrongness of killing Hans does not cohere as strongly with these more general judgments. Killing Hans is wrong only because if you don't kill Hans he will later value the experiences he enjoys and so will later be glad that you did not kill him. On this account, the wrongness of killing is not explained by appealing to a feature that accounts for the wrongness of a more general class of wrongful actions. The wrongness of killing becomes an anomaly. Of course, if there were no alternative account available on which the wrongness of killing cohered more closely with the wrongness of a more general class of wrongful actions, then the fact that Marquis's account makes the wrongness of killing anomalous would not provide a decisive reason to reject his account. But, as I have argued, there is just such an alternative account available. And so if the two versions of the future-like-ours principle produce the same results in the uncontroversial cases, there is again good reason to prefer my version to his.

Finally, and perhaps most importantly, my version of the future-like-ours principle is superior to Marquis's because it is able to account for a counterexample that Marquis's version is unable to account for.[34] For consider the case of Hans's even more depressed brother, Franz. Like Hans, Franz does not currently value his personal future even though, as also in the case of Hans, his personal future contains many of the sorts of experiences that we take to be distinctively valuable. Due to a permanent and irreversible chemical imbalance in his brain, however, Franz is, and will always remain, completely unable to value the experiences that he has. Although he has a future-like-ours, he has no actual occurrent desire to preserve it and he will never have such a desire. On Marquis's "present or future actual occurrent desire" version of the future-like-ours principle, therefore, there can be no basis for saying that it would be immoral to kill Franz. If we kill Franz, we do not deprive him of anything that he does value or will come to value. But on the "present ideal dispositional desire" version of the future-like-ours principle, things look very different. For surely Franz's desires about his personal future

---

[34] I am grateful to Michael Tooley for bringing this to my attention.

would include the desire that it be preserved if his desires were formed in the absence of the chemical imbalance that prevents him from having this desire. Although he has no actual desire to go on living, that is, it does make sense to attribute this desire to him as an ideal desire. And given this, my version of the principle implies that Franz does have the same right to life as you or I. Since virtually every critic of abortion will agree that Franz has a right to life even if he will never care about it, this counts as a very strong reason to conclude that, on the critic's own terms, my version of the future-like-ours principle is superior to Marquis's.

Before moving on, let me again pause to consider some objections that might be raised at this point. Two objections turn on the claim that my version of the future-like-ours principle is subject to refutation by counterexample. First, a critic might point to the case of a fully developed adult human being whose brain has for some reason not yet developed to the point where he has been able to have any conscious experiences. Doesn't my position, the critic might ask, fail to account for the wrongness of killing him? Here the answer is that the critic is correct in claiming that my position does not entail that such an individual has the same right to life that you and I have, but mistaken in viewing this feature of the position as a failure. A human being whose body is fully developed but whose brain is still at the level of development of a preconscious fetus, after all, is morally on a par with a preconscious fetus. It is true, of course, that the fully developed adult would be much larger than a typical preconscious fetus, but surely mere differences in physical size are not morally relevant, a point that critics of abortion themselves are often quick to emphasize in other contexts. The assumption needed to treat this feature of my position as a problem, then, the assumption that such an individual has a right to life, simply amounts to the assumption that such fetuses have a right to life, and it would clearly beg the question for a critic of abortion to appeal to such an assumption when this is precisely the question that is at issue.

A second case that a critic might point to is that of the temporarily comatose amnesiac. Like the ordinary temporarily comatose adult, the temporarily comatose amnesiac has no occurrent desire to go on living. But unlike the ordinary temporarily comatose adult, the critic might argue, the temporarily comatose amnesiac has lost all of his previous beliefs and desires and so lacks even the dispositional desire to carry on with his life. And this would mean that, on my account (but not on Marquis's), there is no grounds for saying that it would be immoral to kill him. Here, I think, we have to be more careful in specifying what the case involves. On my (admittedly very limited) understanding of amnesia (see, e.g., Baddeley 1987), it is not true that an amnesiac retains no memories at all of his previous life. Although there are a variety of forms of amnesia, it seems always to be the case that amnesiacs remember some things unproblematically (how to speak, for example, or that putting your hand in a flame hurts) and retain many other memories dispositionally (such as names of relatives) even if they often have great difficulty in accessing them. So, on a fairly straightforward understanding of amnesia, it seems to be the case that a temporarily comatose amnesiac would still have a dispositional desire to go on living, and so would be as wrong to kill on my account as on Marquis's. Of course, the critic might instead appeal to an imaginary case in which a temporarily comatose adult has had the entire contents of his brain destroyed so that there is no more information contained in his brain than is contained in that of the preconscious fetus. In this case, it seems right that my position does not imply that such an individual has the same right to life as you or I. But, as in the case of the adult who has never had conscious experiences, a critic of abortion cannot appeal to such a case as a means of rejecting my position because we cannot assume ahead of time that killing such individuals is seriously immoral.

Finally, a critic of the position I have been defending here might argue as follows: My version of the future-like-ours principle relies on the attribution of ideal desires to people. But I have said extremely little about what this involves. So it might again be said that while my suggestion shows that there is the possibility that an alternative version of the future-like-ours principle might be developed, the possibility cannot be adequately characterized, let alone successfully defended, without a full-blown theory of ideal desires. Marquis's version, on the other hand, requires no such attribution and no such theory. And thus, in the absence of such a theory, his version must be preferred to mine.

I am no more prepared to offer a full-blown theory of ideal desires than I am to offer a full-blown theory of dispositional desires. But again I do not believe that anything like this is necessary. It is true that in order to apply my version of the future-like-ours principle to the case of any particular suicidal teenager, I must be able to justify the claim that he currently has an ideal desire to go on living. But it is equally true that in order to apply Marquis's version of the future-like-ours principle to the case of any particular suicidal teenager, Marquis must be able to justify the claim that he will in the future have a desire to enjoy the experiences that now lie ahead of him. And I again see no reason to believe that one task will be more or less difficult than the other. Indeed, with the exception of the case of Franz just noted, I again suspect that they will simply pick out the same range of cases, and when they do not, this will be to the advantage of my version of the principle rather than to the advantage of Marquis's.

2.8.5. Implications

I have so far defended two claims in terms of cases C, D, and E: that my "present ideal dispositional desire" version of the future-like-ours principle produces the same results as does Marquis's "present or future actual occurrent desire" version, and that my version of the principle is superior to Marquis's in terms of accounting for why killing is wrong in these cases. I will eventually have to say something about case B, that of the infant, but this will prove easier to do after I have attempted to defend my third and final claim: that my version of the future-like-ours principle produces a substantively different result from Marquis's in case A, that of the human fetus. On the face of it, at least, this claim might initially seem unlikely. With the exception of cases like Franz, who is permanently unable to value his personal future, I have already argued that the two principles would pick out essentially the same range of cases among temporarily comatose adults and suicidal teenagers, so it might seem that they ought to pick out precisely the same range of cases among fetuses as well. And it seems natural to suppose that if a fetus could reflect calmly on the future that lies ahead of it, it would desire to go on living as much as would anyone else.[35] Indeed, if anything, the typical human fetus has more to look forward to than we do, since we have already used up some portion of the valuable future that we had lying ahead of us when we were fetuses. But I want now to argue that this is not so. Case A should be broken down into two subcases: the human fetus prior to the point at which it begins to have conscious desires, and the human fetus from this point on. For simplicity's sake I will refer to these as the preconscious fetus and the conscious fetus, although this may in some respects be misleading. And I will argue that, unlike the cases of the temporarily comatose adult and the suicidal teenager, it is not reasonable to attribute to the preconscious fetus a

---

[35] Marquis makes this point in noting that a defender of the future-like-ours argument could respond to a counterfactual proposal by suggesting that "fetuses would desire to live if the thought had occurred to them" (1995: 265).

present ideal dispositional desire that its personal future be preserved. If this claim is correct, then my version of the future-like-ours principle does not imply that the conception criterion is correct, while Marquis's version does imply that it is correct.

The argument for the claim is this. In the case of the suicidal teenager, or the adulterer's wife, or the hiker at the fork of the trail, it is morally relevant that there is a particular desire that the individual *would* have under ideal conditions because there is a particular desire that the individual *does* have arising from other desires and less than ideal circumstances within which beliefs and desires have interacted to produce the particular desires that the individual does have. Given that Irving's actual desire to turn left was formed in the absence of complete information, and given that his actual desire to end the trip safely is stronger than his actual desire to end it quickly and scenically, for example, it is reasonable to say that his actual desire would be to turn right if he had more complete information and that this is morally relevant. Similarly, given that the desires of the suicidal teenager and the grieving mother were formed under conditions of severe emotional distress, it is reasonable to hold as morally relevant what they would instead desire if they were able to think more calmly and put things into proper perspective. As I emphasized in arguing that my version of the future-like-ours principle is more parsimonious than Marquis's, ideal desires in this sense are supervienient on actual desires. There is no desire that a rock would have under more ideal circumstances, for example, because a rock does not have any desires to begin with. But it follows from this that a particular ideal desire can meaningfully be attributed only to someone who has at least some other actual desires. And since the preconscious fetus has no actual desires, it follows that it has no ideal desires either.

Now the claim that the preconscious fetus has no actual desires, of course, requires some further explication. The term *desire*, after all, can mean many things. If by *desire* one simply means a disposition to behave in certain ways or to respond to certain stimuli in certain ways, then the preconscious fetus does, in fact, have desires. But if by desires one only means desires in this simple behavioral sense, then it is equally true that a thermostat has desires. The fact that the thermostat "desires" to raise the temperature in the room in this behavioral sense surely provides no moral reason for us to respect its desires, and so it is morally irrelevant that the preconscious fetus has desires in this sense. Another sense of desires, however, is clearly morally relevant. This is the sense in which to desire something is to be in a certain conscious state that involves caring about, valuing, wanting the object of desire. These are conscious and not merely behavioral desires. Some desires of this sort may essentially involve reference to certain propositions or sentences. But in order for a desire to be a conscious desire, at least as I am using the term here, such reference is not necessary. All that matters is that the individual have an attraction to a given subject that is associated with certain conscious states and is not merely behavioral in nature in the way that the thermostat's desires are. This is all that matters because it is enough to matter morally that something has desires in the sense of having conscious desires. This matters morally because the fact that it has desires in this sense means that things matter to it in a way that things do not matter to thermostats. In typical cases, what matters to a being with conscious desires is best reflected in its actual conscious desires, but in those cases in which its actual desires are formed under importantly imperfect conditions, this is not so. In these cases, I have argued, it is ideal desires rather than actual desires that best reflect what matters to it and thus ideal desires rather than actual desires that matter morally. But since this is so only to the extent that desires reflect what matters to it, and since only a being with conscious desires is a being that has things matter to it, the sense of desires that the present ideal desire version of the future-like-ours principle appeals to must be conscious desires. Since the preconscious fetus is not conscious, it does not have ideal desires in this sense. And so, on this account, the best account of why you and I and temporarily comatose adults and suicidal teenagers have a right to life does not imply that the preconscous fetus does.

Marquis responds to a somewhat similar argument suggested briefly by Shirley (see Shirley 1995: 86–7), and it is important to see how his response to that argument fails to undermine the argument I am making here. Marquis argues that if we insist that an individual satisfy a counterfactual conditional in order to have the same right to life as you or I, and if we argue that fetuses fail to satisfy the requirement by appealing to the claim that "a fetus is not capable of having a desire. The thought corresponding to the desire cannot occur to it," then this will also rule out the case of the temporarily comatose adult, since *"there is a sense* in which someone who is temporarily unconscious is incapable of having thoughts also" (1995: 265, emphasis added). But there are two reasons that this problem does not arise in the case of the counterfactual conditional identified by the present ideal dispositional desire version of the future-like-ours principle that I have been defending. The first is that, on my account, it makes all the difference *which sense* of having a thought we are talking about. The temporarily comatose adult is as incapable as the preconscious fetus of having occurrent beliefs and desires. But the temporarily comatose adult, unlike the preconscious fetus, can have, and does have, dispositional beliefs and desires. And on my account, these are what are morally relevant when beliefs and desires matter morally. The temporarily comatose adult, unlike the preconscious fetus, has actual dispositional beliefs and desires and these are sufficient to warrant the attribution to him of present ideal desires. If Irving fell asleep during his hike, for example, it would remain the case that he had an actual desire to turn left based on his actual beliefs and desires, and it would remain the case that it would be reasonable to say that if his actual desire had been based on more complete information, he would now (while asleep) have an actual (dispositional) desire to turn right. So the counterfactual consideration that excludes the preconcious fetus from the scope of my version of the future-like-ours principle does not exclude the temporarily comatose adult.

The second reason that Marquis's response to Shirley cannot be used against the principle I am defending here is that, strictly speaking, the position that I am defending need not deny that the preconcious fetus has the *capacity* for beliefs and desires. In some sense, it might be said, even the preconcious fetus has the *capacity* for both. A preconscious human fetus, I have been following the critic of abortion in assuming, is simply a human being at a very early stage of development. And since the human being that the fetus is will eventually have beliefs and desires, it might be said that there is therefore at least some sense in which the human being that the fetus is already has the capacity for having such beliefs and desires. In this sense, the preconscious fetus and the temporarily comatose adult would, indeed, be on a par so far as their capacities are concerned: Neither of them currently has the ability to entertain an occurrent belief or desire, and both of them, if they are not killed, will later have such abilities.

But, again, what matters morally on the account that I have been defending is the possession of *actual* dispositional desires, not the capacity for having such desires in the future, and in this respect the two cases are fundamentally different. The temporarily comatose adult currently has actual dispositional desires that he has developed under actual conditions. To the extent that the content of these desires has been distorted by the fact that they were formed under imperfect conditions, we are entitled to consider as his ideal desires those he would have formed had these conditions been more ideal. And to the extent that it is his ideal desires rather than his actual ones that more accurately reflect what actually matters most to him, it is these desires that are capable of underwriting moral constraints on our treatment of him. The preconcious fetus, on the other hand, currently has no dispositional desires about conscious states it would like to enjoy in the future. Since it has no such desires, it has no such desires whose content may have been distorted by various sorts of imperfect conditions. And since it has no such desires whose content may have been distorted by such imperfections, there is no other such desire that it would now have instead under more ideal circumstances. The fact that it has the *capacity* for such desires (in the sense that it has the potential to develop the neural equipment requisite for having them) does not suffice to warrant the attribution to it of ideal desires. It suffices only to warrant the attribution to it of the *capacity* for having such desires, and the mere capacity for having such desires is not what makes killing wrong on the version of the future-like-ours principle that I have been defending. To say that someone has a strong ideal desire that a certain act not occur is to say that there is someone to whom it strongly matters that the act not occur. To say only that someone has a capacity for having such a desire is to say only that there is someone who is capable of having it strongly matter to them that the act not occur. And, at least on the account of the wrongness of killing that I have been defending, this is not enough.

I have argued that the "present ideal dispositional desire" version of the future-like-ours principle does a better job than does Marquis's version of accounting for the wrongness of killing in those cases, such as C, D, and E, about which defenders and critics of abortion alike are almost entirely in agreement. And I have argued that this version of the future-like-ours principle, unlike Marquis's, does not entail that the preconscious fetus has the same right to life as you or I. I have not yet said anything, however, about the other case that Marquis appeals to in defending the future-like-ours argument, that of the human infant (case B). And surely it is the case of the newborn infant that critics of abortion in general are most likely to appeal to, in arguing that the denial of rights to the fetus is inconsistent with other moral judgments that most people are likely to accept. But if what I have said to this point is correct, the case of the human infant should pose no difficulty for my account. A newborn infant does have actual conscious desires. He has a desire to enjoy the sensation of warmth, for example, and the experience of satisfying his hunger. It is true, of course, that the infant cannot put the content of his desires into words, and so there is one sort of conscious desire that he does not have. But this does not mean that he does not have any conscious desires at all. It is also true that the newborn infant does not yet possess the concept of himself as a continuing subject of experience, and it is true that he does not understand that death involves the annihilation of such a subject. Indeed, it seems unlikely that he has any concepts at all and so in this sense unlikely that he understands anything. But if he did understand these things, he would surely desire that his future personal life be preserved since he would understand that this is necessary in order for him to enjoy the experiences that he does already consciously desire to enjoy. And in this sense, at least, he is no different from the hiker who would desire to turn right if he understood that this was necessary in order for him to satisfy the strongest desires that he does in fact have. On the account that I have been defending, then, all that is required for the newborn infant to satisfy the conditions sufficient for having the same right to life as you or I is that he have a future-like-ours and that he have actual conscious desires that can be satisfied only if his personal future is preserved (even if he does not understand that his personal future must be preserved in order for him to satisfy these desires). I do not believe that it is controversial to maintain that the newborn infant has conscious desires in this fairly minimal sense, and so the account that I have been defending as superior to Marquis's can easily accommodate the claim that the newborn infant has a right to life.[36]

Indeed, I believe it is uncontroversial to maintain that conscious desires of this limited sort arise in the fetus at some point prior to birth. Studies have consistently demonstrated, for example, that newborn infants recognize and express a preference for the sound of their mother's

---

[36] It might be objected that my proposal also implies that this is so of many non-human animals, since many nonhuman animals presumably also have conscious desires in the fairly minimal sense in which I am using that term. And surely most critics of abortion would deny that nonhuman animals have the same right to life as you or I. But my proposal will only imply this if we agree that such animals also have a future that is sufficiently like ours. If they do have a future-like-ours, then my proposal will imply that they have a right to life, and so will Marquis's. If they do not, then neither proposal will imply this. Determining whether or not a dog, say, has a future that is sufficiently like ours to merit inclusion within the scope of the principle would require further considerations about what makes our lives distinctively valuable, and the future-like-ours position, on either Marquis's version or the alternative I have been suggesting, can remain neutral on this question. Either version of the position, therefore, is compatible with either view about the rights of nonhuman animals, and this strikes me as a further merit of the position.

voice. And it is difficult to imagine how this could plausibly be accounted for other than by saying that at some point in the pregnancy, the infant began to enjoy the conscious experience of hearing the sound of his mother's voice and had formed a desire for hearing that voice rather than other voices. So it is an implication of the account that I have been defending as superior to Marquis's that there is some point in fetal development after which the fetus is an individual with the same right to life as you or I. This implication, however, does not pose a problem for the argument that I have been concerned to advance in this section. I have been concerned here only to argue that Marquis is mistaken in claiming that typical human fetuses have this right from the moment of conception, not to argue that there is no point in fetal development at which they do. And this implication will also provide the basis for the positive suggestion I will make in chapter 3 about when the fetus is best understood as acquiring this right, given the assumption that you and I and human infants have this right. Before turning to that topic, however, I will address one final argument for the conception criterion, an argument that is importantly different from all of those considered thus far.

2.9. THE PROBABILITY ARGUMENT

A final argument for the conception criterion does not turn directly on any claims about the fetus's species membership, or about its continuity relation to us, or about its potentiality. Instead, it turns on the claim that the chances that a sperm or ovum will eventually become a child increase dramatically at conception. This argument is most frequently associated with Noonan, and I will follow others in focusing my discussion on his defense of it here. But it should be noted both that others have defended this argument as well (e.g., Pluhar 1977: 167–8) and that while Noonan's critics typically treat the argument as his primary defense of the conception criterion, Noonan himself is careful to defend it not as a positive argument for the criterion, but rather as "a 'buttressing' consideration, showing the plausibility of the standard," which he thinks should be adopted primarily for other reasons (1970: 59).[37] To stick with

---

[37] Strasser, for example, begins his paper by writing that "Noonan argues that abortions are morally impermissible because of the great likelihood that foetuses will become moral agents who can feel and reason," and treats Noonan's dependence on an argument based on genetic identity as merely another one which he "also"

Noonan's numbers[38] (and to follow his emphasis on the sperm as the future child rather than the ovum), we can put the argument like this: The odds that a sperm will become a zygote are 1 in 200,000,000, and since the odds that a zygote will become an infant are 4 in 5, the odds that a sperm will become an infant are 1 in 250,000,000. The difference between 1 in 250,000,000 and 4 in 5 represents an immense difference in probabilities, and since moral distinctions can and should reflect such differences, there should be a moral distinction between the rights of the sperm and the rights of the zygote. In particular, the difference is significant enough to justify the conclusion that a zygote has a right not to be killed while a sperm does not have such a right. So we have:

P1: The difference between the chances that a sperm will develop into an infant and the chances that a zygote will develop into an infant is immense.

P2: If the chances that P will develop into an infant are immensely greater than the chances that Q will, then P has importantly greater rights than Q does.[39]

C: A zygote has importantly greater rights than a sperm does.

I will refer to this as the probability argument.

There are several problems with the probability argument. Let me begin with P1. P1 is ambiguous. It could mean one of two things:

P1a: For any sperm and any zygote, the chances are immensely better that the zygote will become an infant than that the sperm will.

P1b: If you randomly select a sperm and a zygote, the chances are immensely greater that the zygote will become an infant than that the sperm will become an infant.

Noonan supports P1 by appealing to the facts that only 1 in 200,000,000 sperm will get the chance to become a zygote, and that 4 in 5 zygotes

makes (1987: 199, 199n1). But this is misleading; Noonan does not argue that abortions are morally impermissible *because* of the change in liklihood. He argues only that the change in liklihood counts as confirmation of the view provided that the view receives independent support. And he is clear that "The positive argument for conception as the decisive moment of humanization is that at conception the new being receives the gentic code" (1970: 59; see also Noonan (1979: 155)).

[38] Although it is worth noting that more recent research suggests that only about 1 in 5 zygotes naturally survive to term (Seller 1993: 137).

[39] Strictly speaking, Noonan need not assume this; he might add a proviso that the chances of P developing into a child must themselves be nonnegligible. Nothing said here turns on the inclusion of this proviso, so it is omitted from the discussion.

become infants. These facts show that P1b is true. If only 1 in 200,000,000 sperm becomes a zygote, then if you randomly select one, the chances that it will become a zygote are 1 in 200,000,000, and similarly for the chances of a zygote becoming an infant. But if P1 is true only in the sense of P1b, then even if P2 is true this will justify only the conclusion that if you randomly select a sperm and a zygote, the expected outcome will be that the zygote has greater rights than the sperm.[40] And this conclusion is far too weak for Noonan's purposes. Noonan wishes to conclude that the difference in probabilities supports the conclusion that every zygote has a right to life and that every sperm lacks such a right, and that conclusion does not follow from P1b and P2.

In order for P1 to lend support to C in the sense in which C provides at least supplemental support for the conception criterion, then, it must be construed as P1a. And it is clear that, to the extent that Noonan is aware of the distinction, this is how he intends P1 to be understood: "If a spermatozoan is destroyed, one destroys a being which had a chance of far less than 1 in 200 million of developing into a reasoning being" (1970: 59). This is clearly meant to be a claim about every sperm, not just about the typical sperm. But P1a is plainly false. For consider a particular sperm S that is swimming ahead of the other 199,999,999 sperm in its group, and is just about to merge with a healthy ovum in a healthy woman. Its chances of becoming a zygote are excellent, and its chances of becoming an infant are very good. Now consider a particular zygote Z that has just been conceived in a woman whose uterine walls suffer from a condition that makes successful implantation all but impossible. Its chances of becoming an infant are practically zero. Indeed, not only do the facts about conception therefore fail to support Noonan's conclusion even if we assume that P2 is true, they turn out to support precisely the opposite conclusion: that this particular sperm has much greater rights than does this particular zygote. But surely the critic of abortion must reject the claim that killing this particular sperm would be morally worse than killing this particular zygote. Noonan's argument, then, is impaled on the horns of a dilemma: Either P1 is true but fails to support the conception criterion, or P1 supports the conception criterion but is false.

This problem seems to me sufficiently fatal to warrant rejecting the argument, and it arises even if we accept the comparison as Noonan has formulated it. But there is in fact something very misleading about the way in which Noonan frames his comparisons, and this reveals yet

---

[40] Galvin makes essentially this point also (1988: 81–3).

further difficulties. One problem is that Noonan focuses his comparison on the sperm rather than on the egg; but since an act of intercourse involves millions of sperm but only one egg, this gives a highly misleading picture of the difference in probabilities involved. If one looks at the chances that a given egg will develop into a child rather than that a particular sperm will, things look much more as they do in the case of the zygote. There is no immense shift in probabilities between the pre- and postfertilized ova, and this would suggest that even if Noonan's argument could justify the distinction between killing sperm and killing zygotes, it would fail to justify a comparable distinction between killing eggs and killing zygotes, and that failure is just as unacceptable on the abortion critic's own terms.

A second problem is that Noonan compares killing one sperm to killing one zygote. But a spermicide does not randomly kill one sperm out of an ejaculate containing 200 million. It kills all of them. Killing one individual with a 1 in 200 million chance of becoming a child may be much less significant than killing an individual with a four in five chance, but it is not at all obvious that this is so of killing 200 million such individuals.[41]

But let us suppose that I am mistaken about all of this, and examine P2 nonetheless. P2 amounts to the claim that the greater the chances that an individual will develop into an infant, the greater the individual's rights. One reason to reject this claim has already been given: It implies that the sperm at the head of the pack has a much greater right to life than the zygote having difficulty implanting in the uterine wall, and this seems extremely implausible. In addition, Noonan's defense of P2 is unconvincing. Noonan argues that "most moral reasoning is an estimate of probabilities" and cites as an example of this the fact that whether or not one is morally negligent often turns on whether or not one has taken into account probabilities (1970: 58–9):

If the chance is 200,000,000 to 1 that the movement in the bushes into which you shoot is a man's I doubt if many persons would hold you careless in shooting; but if the chances are 4 out of 5 that the movement is a human being few would acquit you of blame.

Now, this argument can itself be understood in one of two ways. Noonan's critics typically take the claim to be that the risk you take

---

[41] Strasser notes this difficulty with Noonan's analogy (1987: 202–3); see also Dore (1989: 280).

in the first case is morally on a par with the risk involved in killing a sperm while the risk in the second is morally on a par with the risk involved in killing a zygote or fetus. On this account, if you believe that it would be wrong to take the second risk but permissible to take the first, then you should also think it wrong to kill a zygote or fetus but permissible to kill a sperm. If this is what Noonan means, then the argument does seem to be easily defeated. It overlooks the distinction between running the risk of harming someone knowing that if you do harm someone, the someone will be a human being, and harming someone running the risk that the someone you harm would have become a human being had you not harmed him.[42] This does seem to be at least part of Noonan's intent, and to that extent, at least, his failure to attend to this distinction does undermine his defense of P2. But Noonan need not be understood as resting the case for P2 solely on the analogy itself. At least part of his argument seems to be that the example demonstrates that there are at least some instances in which probabilities constitute an important part of moral reasoning. We might take this as some evidence for his more general claim that "most" moral reasoning involves such considerations, and that claim in turn as support for the conclusion that such considerations are relevant in the case of P2. This way of understanding Noonan's point does not render it subject to the refutation just noted, but it leaves the argument unconvincing nonetheless. For an isolated example hardly supports the claim that this is true of most of moral reasoning, the claim itself seems implausible, and even if it is true we need some reason to think that it is true in the case of P2.

Finally, it is worth noting a problem for Noonan's position that has arisen with the development of *in vitro* fertilization (IVF). As Singer and Dawson note, the typical success rates for IVF and for subsequent implantation are such that there is a relatively small difference between the probabilities of a child resulting from an IVF-produced zygote on the one hand, and the pre-IVF-treated sperm and egg on the other. A laboratory's success rate for fertilization may be around 80 percent, but the percentage of zygotes that successfully implant often rises no higher than 10 percent. Using these figures, the probability of a typical IVF zygote becoming a child is 10 percent, while the probability of a typical

---

[42] This objection is noted by Galvin (1988: 86–7) and Strasser (1987: 199, 200). As Brody points out (1974: 236), the example also blurs the morally relevant distinction between asking whether an act is morally permissible and asking whether an agent is blameworthy for performing it.

sperm or egg in a petri dish prior to IVF becoming a child is 8 percent (1988: 89–90). Even if Noonan's argument were not subject to the various objections I have already raised against it, then, it would entail that while killing a non-IVF-produced zygote is much worse than killing a sperm or an egg, killing an IVF-produced zygote is not. And this is an implication that a critic of abortion cannot accept. I conclude, then, that the various arguments that have been offered in defense of the conception criterion should be rejected on the abortion critic's own terms, and that the probability argument fails to provide any further support for it.

Chapter 3

Postconception Criteria

3.0. OVERVIEW

In Chapter 2, I considered a number of arguments in defense of the claim that the typical human fetus acquires a right to life at the moment of its conception, and argued that none of them are successful on the abortion critic's own terms. Critics of abortion have failed to provide a good reason to believe that a zygote has a right to life. But I am assuming, at least for the sake of the argument, that you and I do have such a right, and that we developed gradually from such zygotes. So if we did not acquire this right at the moment of our conception, there must be some point after conception at which we did. The question that remains, then, is: When is that? This question is crucial to assessing the rights-based argument against abortion, understood as an argument for the thesis that abortion, at least in typical cases, is morally impermissible. Approximately one half of all abortions take place within the first nine weeks of gestation, approximately 90 percent within the first trimester, and virtually all by the twentieth week of gestation. If the fetus acquires a right to life after conception but within the first several weeks of gestation, then abortion in typical cases does involve the death of an individual with the same right to life as you or I even if the conception criterion is mistaken. But if the fetus acquires this right at some later stage, then abortion in typical cases does not involve the death of an individual with a right to life, even if a number of abortions in unusual circumstances do prove to involve such a death. A variety of distinct stages after conception have traditionally been held out as alternatives to the conception criterion. Some of these postconception criteria lie relatively early in fetal gestation and others lie relatively late. Rejecting the conception criterion, therefore, is not sufficient for rejecting the rights-based argument against abortion.

In addition, one must also justify rejecting the other relatively early criteria and justify accepting one of the relatively later ones. This chapter attempts to do both.

As in Chapter 2, I will attempt to present a fair account of the arguments that have been offered in defense of the criteria that I reject and will attempt to show that these arguments are inadequate on terms that the critic of abortion accepts. In addition, I will attempt to provide a positive defense of one of these positions, the claim that the fetus acquires a right to life when its brain reaches a certain level of maturity. Even here I will argue that some of the arguments that have been offered in defense of this view should be rejected. But I will also argue that there is at least one argument for this view that succeeds on the abortion critic's own terms – indeed, on the very terms that are established by the argument widely viewed as the most powerful argument against abortion, the future-like-ours argument. Since it turns out that the level of brain development picked out by this criterion is reached well after the vast majority of abortions are performed, the defense of this criterion will suffice to undermine the first of the two claims made by the rights-based argument against abortion. And since both claims made by that argument must be sustained in order for it to successfully establish its conclusion, this result will be sufficient to warrant rejecting the rights-based argument against abortion itself.

3.1. IMPLANTATION

Implantation marks the stage at which the developing conceptus, which has to this point been freely floating down the fallopian tube, becomes firmly embedded in the uterine wall. This generally occurs six to eight days after fertilization. If the conceptus acquires a right to life at this stage and not before, then some forms of birth control result in the death of the conceptus before it acquires this right, while virtually all abortions in the standard sense of the term result in its death after it has done so. The implantation criterion is significantly different from the conception criterion, then, because, unlike the conception criterion, it would provide grounds for considering such abortifacients to be morally like contraception rather than like abortions. Is there good reason to believe that this is the stage at which the right to life begins?

Let me begin by pointing out that there is one fact about implantation that sometimes obscures discussion of this question. When the conceptus implants in the uterine wall, the impact triggers certain hormonal changes in the pregnant woman, a reaction that is sometimes characterized as the woman's "accepting" the nascent embryo. This fact is sometimes used as support for the claim that pregnancy begins at implantation, rather than at fertilization. Indeed, the claim that implantation is "the point at which pregnancy begins" is sometimes offered and accepted with no justification at all, particularly in the medical literature (e.g., Kaplan and Tong 1994: 51). And the claim that pregnancy begins at implantation has the implication, which is then sometimes made explicit, that methods of birth control that prevent implantation should be understood as methods that prevent pregnancy, rather than as methods that terminate pregnancy. And so it might be thought that this consideration shows that such methods are morally on a par with contraception rather than with abortion.

This line of reasoning may be tempting, but it is flawed. If we agree that pregnancy begins at implantation rather than at fertilization, this is only because we are distinguishing pregnancy as a state of the woman's body from pregnancy as the condition in which a new individual member of our species has come into existence. To say that a given method of birth control prevents pregnancy from occurring rather than terminating pregnancy in this sense, then, does not entail that it prevents a new member of our species from coming into existence. The use of such methods will still result in the death of such an individual, while the use of contraception does not. And so such considerations provide no support for the implantation criterion.

A second argument for the moral significance of implantation might run as follows: Prior to implantation, a woman can prevent herself from bringing a child to term simply by preventing the conceptus from implanting. After implantation, she can do so only by destroying it. She can prevent implantation by rendering the uterine wall inhospitable to the conceptus, and this might be characterized as an instance of declining to aid the conceptus or letting the conceptus die. But, it might be argued, she can prevent the implanted conceptus from continuing to develop only by killing it. The claim that there is a morally relevant difference between killing and letting die seems plausible to many people, and is accepted by many critics of abortion, and if this claim is true, then it would seem to support the claim that there is a morally relevant line to be drawn at implantation.

There are several ways in which one could respond to this argument. One could, of course, deny that there is a morally relevant difference between killing and letting die, or one could argue that methods of birth control that prevent implantation are better understood as involving killing than as involving letting die. But even if we accept both the general moral claim and the particular factual characterization, this argument still fails to locate the line we are looking for. If accepted, the argument would not show that the conceptus prior to implantation lacks the same right to life that you or I have, but only that even if it has such a right, there is a means of preventing it from developing further that does not violate that right. So this argument, too, fails to support the implantation criterion.

Nathanson defends the implantation criterion by appealing to a still further consideration. He characterizes implantation by saying that "this is when [the conceptus] announces its presence as part of the human community by means of its hormonal messages." Prior to implantation, on this account, the conceptus "is incomplete, lacking the essential element that produces life: an interface with the human community and communication of the fact that it is there" (1979: 216). But this is implausible. Communication is not necessary to "produce" life, though it may be needed to sustain it, and the fact that the conceptus "announces" its humanity here implies, if anything, that its humanity is something that it already possessed.

A final argument for the implantation criterion might run as follows:[1] the chances that a given conceptus will successfully develop into an infant rise sharply at the point of implantation. So, following Noonan's suggestion that the line between having a right to life and not having one should reflect some significant change in probabilities, one could conclude that the line should be drawn here. But the fact that there are different points at which the probabilities shift dramatically should itself cast doubt on the moral relevance of this criterion. And, in any event, we saw in Section 2.9 that there are several compelling reasons to reject the probability argument itself, regardless of where the probability shift is said to occur. So considerations about probability, too, fail to support the implantation criterion.

---

[1] Wennberg notes and then rejects this argument (1985: 70). It is also sometimes argued that implantation is morally relevant because it corresponds closely to the point after which twinning can no longer take place. But twinning can take place after implantation, and this should in any event be treated as a distinct criterion.

3.2. EXTERNAL HUMAN FORM

During the first few weeks after fertilization, the human fetus does not look noticeably different from the fetuses of many other species. But by the time a human infant is born, he is indisputably one of us. This prompts two questions: at what point does the fetus acquire its distinctively human appearance, and is the acquisition of its distinctively human appearance morally relevant in a way that could justify the claim that this is when the fetus acquires a right to life? In short, we want to know what the external human form criterion would commit us to, and whether there is good reason to accept it.

The answer to the first question surely depends in part on the degree of biological knowledge of the viewer. A specialist might be able to discern the differences between relatively undeveloped fetuses that would elude the rest of us. If there is going to be an argument for the fetus's appearance being morally relevant, however, it seems likely that it will have to turn on claims about differences that would be apparent to ordinary people. And here there seems to be a general consensus that the fetus is recognizably human after six weeks, and certainly after eight. So if the external human form criterion is accepted, then it will turn out that a great number of abortions involve the death of the fetus after it has acquired a right to life.

I am not aware of any even prima facie credible arguments that have been offered in favor of the external human form criterion. Why should whether or not an individual has the same right to life as you and I depend on what the individual looks like? There is, however, a related argument that is sometimes offered in the abortion literature that could be construed as or modified to become such a defense, and the resulting argument is worth briefly considering, partly in the interests of completeness, but partly because even though virtually every critic of abortion will surely reject it, its rejection raises a difficulty for one tactic commonly exploited by critics of abortion. The argument turns on the claim that morality requires us to inculcate in ourselves and others attitudes and dispositions that enable us to carry out our moral duties, and that psychologically, we would be unable to carry out our duties toward each other without our accepting at least some restrictions on our treatment of fetuses that give rise to similar sorts of sympathetic emotions. Jane English is one philosopher who has defended this sort of argument, using the terminology of personhood: "If our moral rules allowed people to treat some person-like non-persons in ways we do not want people to be treated, this would undermine the system of sympathies and attitudes that makes the ethical system work." And as a result, she argues, morality "must prohibit certain treatment of non-persons which are significantly person-like" (1975: 302). Strictly speaking, English does not defend the claim that the human-looking fetus has the same right to life as you or I, or even that we should treat it as if it does, but rather the significantly weaker claim that morality does not permit us to treat such a fetus in just any way we choose. This claim is clearly inadequate for purposes of the critic of abortion. Still, we can use English's argument as a model from which to construct what may be the only defense of the external human form criterion worth considering. So construed, the argument would have to run roughly as follows:

P1: It is morally impermissible to kill individuals like you or me.
P2: Morality requires us to maintain those moral sentiments that are necessary in order for us to fulfill our moral duties to individuals like you or me.
P3: The moral sentiment that enables us to accept and act on the belief that killing individuals like you or me is morally impermissible is incompatible with accepting and acting on the belief that killing human-looking fetuses is morally permissible.
C: Morality requires us to accept and act on the belief that killing human-looking fetuses is morally impermissible.

When the argument is put in this way, the problem with it becomes quite clear: P3 is simply implausible. There is simply no reason to believe that people who accept the permissibility of aborting human-looking fetuses find it any more psychologically difficult to fulfill their duties not to kill individuals like you or I than do people who reject the permissibility of killing such fetuses. There is, then, so far as I can see, no good reason to accept the external human form criterion.

I suspect, in fact, that virtually every critic of abortion will, at least upon reflection, agree that the external human form criterion should be rejected. After all, virtually every critic of abortion believes that aborting the fetus is morally impermissible even before it takes on its distinctively human appearance. What the fetus looks like in the first few weeks of its gestation, such critics would say, is irrelevant to how it should be treated. And if it turned out that the human fetus looked like a grotesque cockroach until very late into its gestation, such critics would surely, and justly, complain that this fact would do nothing to support the moral permissibility of killing it. But given the irrelevance of the fact that the early fetus does not look distinctively human, it is difficult for such critics consistently to appeal to the fact that the later fetus does look distinctively human. Yet this is one of the most common appeals made by those who are opposed to abortion, both in print and in public forums. Schwarz's book, for example, to which I have referred at a number of points, contains photographs of fetuses at 10, 19, and 27–9 weeks of gestation (1990: 126–7).[2] What the human fetus looks like is not relevant to whether it has the same right to life as you or I. For that reason, the external human form criterion should be rejected. But so, too, should the use of visual representations of fetuses that do look like human infants, and for precisely the same reason.

3.3. ACTUAL FETAL MOVEMENT

Before turning to the more promising candidates based on some kind of fetal brain activity, I will briefly mention, for the sake of completeness, two further possibilities for which there may possibly have been some plausible support in the past, but which can easily be dismissed for our purposes. The first criterion proposes that the fetus acquires a right to life when it first begins to move on its own. Ultrasound imaging indicates that this begins at between five and six weeks after fertilization (Burgess and Tawia 1996: 10). If the fetus acquires such a right at this time, most abortions do involve the death of an individual with a right to life. It might perhaps at one time have plausibly been held that the fetus does not begin to be a living being until it begins such movement, and that might in turn have plausibly been used to ground a defense of the actual fetal movement criterion. But since we no longer have any reason

---

[2] Examples of such appeals among activists opposed to abortion are ubiquitous. An advertisement for a scale model of a human fetus called "Young One," for example, includes testimony from an activist opposed to abortion who says he has protested in front of his local abortion clinic weekly for the last ten years and found Young One to be "the most effective tool we have" ("Young One" 1995). And a catalog published by Heritage House '76 advertises a product called "Precious Feet," which "represent the exact size of an unborn baby's feet at 10 weeks after conception" and can be purchased as pins, necklaces, tie bars, and earrings. The copy includes testimonials from opponents of abortion who have successfully used the Precious Feet to persuade women not to have abortions (The Precious Foot People (1995: 3–4)). For an analysis of the use of such images, see Condit (1990: chap. 5, esp. 88–9).

to believe this, there is no reason to believe that the point at which the fetus first begins moving is morally significant.

3.4. PERCEIVED FETAL MOVEMENT (QUICKENING)

A second and related candidate is quickening, which refers to the point at which the fetus's movement is first perceived by the woman who is carrying it. Typically, this occurs approximately sixteen to seventeen weeks after fertilization. If the fetus acquires a right to life at the moment of quickening, then the vast majority of abortions occur before the fetus acquires this right, and so do not involve the death of an individual with the same right to life as you or I. While quickening has historically been a popular candidate for the criterion we are interested in, however, this too seems to have been so for reasons that have since become obsolete.

One reason that can be seen to be intelligible in its historical context is that prior to quickening, a woman could not determine with certainty whether her swollen abdomen was the result of a developing pregnancy or of a dangerous intestinal obstruction requiring medical treatment. Prior to quickening, then, a doctor could claim in good conscience to attempt to cure her, but after this point he could not think he was doing anything other than destroying a fetus. The cogency of this position is debatable even on its own terms, but since a woman can now determine whether she is pregnant well before this point, the issue is moot.

The same sort of response also applies to a second historically understandable justification that was sometimes offered for the quickening criterion. At one point, quickening may have been the best available evidence of fetal viability, and this may have been taken to be morally relevant. But we no longer identify the point of quickening with the point of viability, and even if we did, we would still require an argument for the relevance of viability itself (see Section 3.7). So we have no good reason to accept the claim that the fetus acquires a right to life at the moment of quickening.

3.5. INITIAL BRAIN ACTIVITY

A zygote does not have a brain. You and I do. On the face of it, this seems to be morally significant. If you discovered an alien from Mars with a brain exactly like ours, you might well think that the alien was entitled to the same respect that we demand of each other. And if you discovered that someone you thought had a brain like ours was in fact an automaton with no brain at all, you would likely think that destroying that individual was not morally on a par with destroying you or me. A newborn infant, moreover, has a brain as well, and so is in this sense like you and me and unlike the zygote. All of this suggests that there is some stage of development between zygote and newborn at which the fetus acquires a property, namely, the possession of a brain like ours, that might account for its having the same right to life as you and I. One might, in short, propose the brain criterion: The fetus acquires a right to life when it acquires a brain.

3.5.1. The Brain

This initial suggestion is unacceptably imprecise for a least three distinct reasons. First, you and I and the newborn do not merely possess a brain. We possess a functioning brain. The zygote, on the other hand, possesses no brain at all. Since possession of a brain and possession of a functioning brain are two distinct properties, we would first have to specify which of the two we claimed to be morally relevant before specifying which of the two we meant to propose as a criterion for acquiring a right to life. Second, the brain is not an organ with a single function. It is composed of a number of distinct areas or regions which perform largely (though not entirely) distinct tasks. So we would have to specify which part or parts of the brain we were taking to be morally relevant, as well as whether these parts merely had to exist or had to be functioning before we could more precisely formulate our proposal for a brain-based criterion. Finally, the brain taken as a whole, and the parts considered individually, are not simply acquired all at once. They develop gradually and they begin to function gradually. Nor do the parts develop sequentially. Although some mature more rapidly than others, for the most part the various regions of the brain develop simultaneously. So we would have to specify how much development or functioning, as well as in what part or parts of the brain, we were taking to be morally relevant before we could make our proposal satisfactorily determinate and begin to subject it to critical scrutiny. In short, there is not one brain criterion to consider; there are many brain criteria.

In principle, there are innumerable such criteria. But in practice there seem only to be a few that are likely to generate even prima facie support. Before considering the arguments that can be given for and against them, then, we need to render the proposals themselves more clear, and before we can do that, we need to say something more about the brain itself. What follows is a brief synopsis of what seems to represent the standard and uncontroversial picture of the human brain.[3] It is important to note, however, both that I am not myself competent to assess the accuracy of this picture, and that if the facts should prove to be relevantly different from the way they are set out here, then the arguments based on them will to that extent have to be revised or rejected.

So briefly: The brain is standardly divided for purposes of analysis into the *brain stem* and the *forebrain*. The brain stem, as the name implies, serves as the foundation upon which the forebrain is placed. The brain stem, in turn, consists of two regions, the *midbrain* and the *hindbrain*. The hindbrain is located at the base of the brain, where the brain meets the spinal cord. It consists of three primary organs: the *medulla*, the *pons*, and the *cerebellum*. Each of these organs serve to assist in the control of basic body functions. The medulla helps to regulate such functions as blood pressure and respiration, the cerebellum assists in helping the body maintain balance and posture, and the pons serves as a conduit which allows information to pass between the cerebrum (discussed below) and the cerebellum. The functioning of all three organs is nonconscious and automatic. The medulla is regulating your blood pressure even as you read this book, but you are not aware of this activity, nor are you aware of the information that is being passed through your pons. The cerebellum contributes to movements of your body that you are aware of and that you sometimes deliberately initiate, but the contributions made by the cerebellum itself remain undisclosed to you. If you consciously decide to throw this book against the wall, for example, the cerebellum will play no role in your deliberately moving your arm, but it will automatically oversee subtle adjustments in other parts of your body that are needed for you to maintain your balance, and you will not be aware of these adjustments taking place. The other part of the brain stem, the midbrain, is located above the pons at the end of the spinal column. It regulates eye movement and processes information from the ears. Again, this part of the brain fulfills its functions without your being aware of it. The midbrain helps your body respond to auditory stimuli, but if you

---

[3] The facts are taken primarily from Morowitz and Trefil (1992: esp. 93–101), and checked against a number of other sources, especially Diagram Group (1987), Restak, M.D. (1979), Ornstein and Thompson (1984), and Smith (1984).

had no forebrain, this would happen without your being aware of any sound.

This brings us to the forebrain. The forebrain, which rests on top of the brain stem and is substantially larger than it, can also be understood in terms of two parts, the *diencephalon*, which rests immediately above the brain stem, and the *cerebrum*, which constitutes the remainder of the forebrain. The diencephalon can itself be divided into two regions, the *thalamus*, which like the pons serves as a conduit through which information can pass from one part of the brain to another, and the *hypothalamus*, which regulates metabolic functions, such as hormonal balance and, in the case of women, the menstrual cycle. As is the case with the organs of the brain stem, the functioning of the regions of the diencephalon is automatic and nonconscious. You are not aware of information passing through your thalamus or of the influence that your hypothalamus is exerting over your metabolism.

The rest of the forebrain is the cerebrum. The cerebrum is divided into two lobes, and it is this part of the brain that people typically have in mind when they think of what a human brain looks like. The cerebrum is in turn divided into two parts, the *lower cortex*, which lies near the diencephalon, and the *cerebral cortex*, the twisted, wrinkled outer layer of the cerebrum that is the most familiar part of the brain in its appearance. The lower cortex regulates such functions as those associated with the sense of smell. It also contains part of the *limbic system*, a network of tissue that extends down into the diencephalon and that governs such primal emotions as fear, anger, and sexual arousal. The cerebral cortex can itself in turn be divided into numerous specific areas which are involved in such diverse activities as language use, conscious movement, processing of sensory information, and so forth. Knowledge of this division arises primarily from cases in which damage has occurred in localized areas of the brain. Extensive damage to certain regions of the left temporal lobe, for example, can result in the loss of linguistic ability, while damage to the right temporal lobe impairs spatial activities such as the ability to draw. The cortex could thus be subdivided in a number of ways, but a further analytical division is unnecessary for our purposes, since the feature of the cerebral cortex that is most likely to be thought of as morally relevant cannot be definitively assigned to any particular region within it and so must be thought of as a feature associated with possession of the cerebral cortex as a whole.

3.5.2. The Cerebral Cortex

The feature I have in mind concerns the relationship between the cerebral cortex and consciousness. The relationship itself resists a simple, clear explication for two distinct reasons: It is extremely difficult to say what, exactly, we mean by consciousness, and it is extremely difficult to understand what, precisely, the relationship between consciousness and the cerebral cortex is. While either problem could occupy a book on its own, however, I believe I can say enough about the relationship here to justify the claim that if consciousness is morally relevant, then possession of a cerebral cortex is relevant to answering the question of what stage of fetal development marks the point at which the fetus acquires a right to life. We will have to wait until later to consider whether, and if so how, this relevance can provide a satisfactory answer to the question.

The first problem we confront in trying to set the stage for a consciousness-based defense of a cortical brain activity criterion is that the term *consciousness* seems to elude clear definition. The entry under "Consciousness" in *The International Dictionary of Psychology*, for example, reads in part as follows: "The term is impossible to define except in terms that are unintelligible without a grasp of what consciousness means. . . . Consciousness is a fascinating but elusive phenomenon: It is impossible to specify what it is, what it does, or why it evolved. Nothing worth reading has been written about it" (cited in Chalmers 1996: 3).

It seems to be correct that any attempted definition of consciousness will in the end prove circular. It is tempting to say that to be conscious is to be aware of something, for example, but then *awareness* will surely have to be defined in terms of being in a conscious state. But it does not follow from this that nothing worthwhile can be said about it. This would follow if our inability to define the term meant that we had no idea what was being referred to when the term *consciousness* was being used. If I were to advance a number of claims about the moral significance of "gockiness," for example, while conceding that I could offer no definition of the term, you would be justified in expecting that you would learn nothing from what I said. But consciousness is different in this respect. You do know what I am talking about when I talk about consciousness, despite my inability to define it for you. As Nagel famously put it, using an expression that has since become ubiquitous in discussions of the subject, "an organism has conscious mental states if and only if there is something that it is like to *be* that organism – something it is like *for* the organism" (1974: 166). Even if this does not constitute a definition of consciousness, you do know what I am talking about when I refer to the fact that there is something that it is like to be you when you see a clear blue sky, hear a shrill scream, feel a sharp prick, or a cold wind, or a burning itch. And this is enough to make clear what is meant by the claim that there is a morally relevant difference between an organism that is conscious in this sense and an organism that is not.

The second problem with setting the stage for a consciousness-based defense of a cortical brain activity criterion is that even if we are sufficiently clear about what we mean by the term *consciousness*, we are deeply puzzled about its relation to the brain. In one sense, this is certainly true, and the puzzle of consciousness constitutes one of the central topics in the philosophy of mind. How could a purely physical organ, an interconnected set of individual cells, give rise to conscious experiences? How can it be the case that an organism's having a certain set of physical properties makes it the case that there is something that it is like to *be* that organism? But in another sense, the relation between consciousness and the brain, and, more specifically, between consciousness and a functioning cerebral cortex, is less controversial. The relation is simply that without the latter, we do not have the former. This is well established by considering cases involving brain damage. As one textbook on physiological psychology reports, "Severe brain damage can reduce a person to a reflex machine that shows no sign of consciousness or mind. Damage limited only to the cerebral cortex, the highest region of the brain, appears to abolish completely all human characteristics, abilities, and *awareness*" (cited in Morowitz and Terfil 1992: 99, emphasis added). And as Burgess and Tawia note, "All the relevant empirical evidence suggests that the destruction of the cortex will suffice for the cessation of consciousness" (1996: 2n). Even though it remains utterly mysterious *how* this could be the case, it is generally accepted *that* this is the case.[4] And for our purposes, this is all that is needed to get a

---

[4] It might be objected that the claim I am appealing to here, the claim that possession of an active cerebral cortex is necessary for consciousness, is more controversial than I am acknowledging. In particular, it might seem that this claim entails that it is impossible for people to survive the deaths of their bodies. But many people believe that there is an afterlife in this sense, and many more believe that it is at least possible that there is. Critics of abortion, in particular, may be likely to believe this, and so if the claim that my argument is resting on here is inconsistent with this belief, then the argument itself will fail to engage critics of abortion on terms that they can accept.

But the claim that I am appealing to here is entirely neutral with respect to the existence of an afterlife. If a particular human organism permanently loses its

consciousness-based defense of a cortical brain activity criterion off the ground.

The claim that possession of an active cerebral cortex is *necessary* for consciousness should not be confused with the claim that cortical brain activity is *sufficient* for consciousness or that consciousness occurs within, or is a property of, the cortex itself. Although some neurologists once expected to "locate" consciousness within the cortex, much as Descartes had once claimed that it resided in the pineal gland at the top of the brain stem, more recent research indicates that an essential role is played by a network of cells in the brain stem itself, known as the *reticular formation*. This point is worth emphasizing in order to avoid a possible misundertanding of the claim being made here. One popular presentation of information about the human brain, for example, characterizes the current state of knowledge about consciousness as follows: "It now seems likely that consciousness is a function of the reticular formation" (Diagram Group 1987: 92n). And since the reticular formation lies within the brain stem, this can give rise to the impression that consciousness itself arises from the brain stem, and that it can thus occur prior to or independent of activity in the cerebral cortex.

But this is to misconstrue the role of the reticular formation. The point is simply that its functioning, too, is necessary for consciousness; a tumor or blood clot near the reticular formation as small as the head of a match can cause an irreversible coma, but this is consistent with the claim that the cortex is also necessary for consciousness. A patient with cortical damage in the state known as coma vigil, for example, may have a functioning brain stem, and this may allow the patient's eyes to follow visual stimuli across a room, but such patients are not conscious (Restak 1979: 265).

3.5.3. *The Initial Brain Activity Criterion*

I will return to the cortical brain activity criterion in Section 3.6 and focus for the remainder of this section on other possible brain-based

---

cerebral cortex, for example, then the claim will entail that that particular organism is no longer conscious. But it says nothing at all about whether there might be an immaterial soul that contains the consciousness that previously inhabited that organism. A defender of a cortical brain activity criterion is committed to the claim that in such a case the organism no longer has a right to life, but can certainly agree that if there is a soul that contains the consciousness that was formerly associated with the organism, then destroying the soul would be morally impermissible.

criteria. Given the complex nature of the brain, one could in principle propose any number of brain-based criteria in addition to the cortical brain activity criterion. But for most of the distinctions that might be drawn it is difficult to imagine an even remotely plausible case that could be made for accepting them. Let us begin by asking whether a credible brain criterion could appeal to mere possession of a brain as opposed to possession of a functioning brain. It is difficult to see how this could be done. At approximately 22 days after conception, the embryo has formed what is known as the *neural tube*, the product of waves of tissue that fuse together along what will become the back of the embryo and that serves as the basic structure of the spinal cord and brain. Within another 24 hours or so (around day 23), a pair of bulging structures emerges from the front end of the neural tube. These are the beginnings of the brain. By day 25, this developing structure already exhibits division into three areas that foreshadow the development of brain stem, midbrain, and forebrain. So we could say that at some point during this period the brain comes into existence, and that what happens afterward is that it develops further and becomes functional. Estimating conservatively, we could say that the embryo has a brain once the bulging structure emerges from the neural tube, or we might wait until the point at which it seems to possess the rudimentary division into regions, but either way we would probably place the point at which the embryo obtains a brain somewhere between 22 and 25 days after fertilization.

But what argument could be made for the claim that this marks a morally important development? The collection of cells is not yet doing any of the sorts of things that brains do when we think of brains as morally important. The cells are merely constructing the structures that will later do those things. We might appeal to the potential which exists at this point. Once there is a nascent brain, the basic cells have become sufficiently differentiated so that now there are brain cells and not just the uniform, undifferentiated cells with which we began. So we might say that now we have the sorts of cells that can do the morally important work of completing and activating the brain. But this is misleading. These cells will have to continue to differentiate and develop in order to do those things. If no further differentiation occurred, we would never get a functioning brain. And if one then tried to appeal to the claim that we already have the cells that will produce those more specialized cells, then we could point out that when we had the conceptus without a brain, we already had the cells that produced these cells. Indeed, when we had the zygote, we had the cell that produced all of them. The only credible-looking argument that initially points toward the moral relevance of mere brain possession, then, would seem in the end to push us either backward or forward. And since I have already rejected the arguments for going backward, the only alternative seems to be to move forward. If there is a credible brain-based criterion, then, it must turn on claims about a functioning brain.

This restriction still leaves us with innumerable possibilities, but most of the distinctions we could draw again seem to be plainly irrelevant. What reason could be given for thinking that there is a morally relevant difference between having a functioning thalamus but not a functioning hypothalamus and having a functioning hypothalamus but not a functioning thalamus? In practice, then, there seem to be two only alternatives. Either one takes the onset of activity in any part of the brain to be morally significant or one focuses in particular on the functioning of the cerebral cortex. I will focus here on the claim that the fetus acquires a right to life as soon as it has brain activity of any sort and will defer until Section 3.6 the claim that it acquires this right as soon as it has a particular kind of activity in the cerebral cortex. I will refer to the claim that the fetus acquires a right to life at the onset of brain activity as the initial brain activity criterion. Before asking what arguments might be offered for it, we should ask when this onset of activity first occurs, what sort of activity it is, and where in the brain it occurs.

When we talk about activity in the brain, we are talking about electrical activity. It is difficult to determine precisely when this begins to occur. Such activity has consistently been detected in fetuses at as early as 10 weeks of gestation, but there is at least one report of such activity being detected in a fetus of 6 weeks gestation (Burgess and Tawia 1996: 20). Let us assume conservatively that electrical activity in the brain begins at six weeks. In that case, if initial brain activity is taken to justify attributing a right to life to the fetus, then the vast majority of abortions involve the death of an individual with a right to life. Indeed, if this account is correct, then some women may never have the option of aborting the fetus before it acquires this right since they may not discover that they are pregnant until after this period has passed.

The next question is: What kind of electrical activity are we talking about? There are two possibilities. Either the activity is organized or it is unorganized. If the electrical activity in the brain is random and unorganized, then we can infer very little about what is going on in the brain from it. Every cell in the human body exhibits some degree of electrical activity, and the fact that an electrical signal can be detected from the brain cells in this sense shows merely that they are alive. If the electrical activity is organized, however, then we may be able to conclude more than this, at least if it is located in the cerebral cortex. Organized electrical activity in the brain can be measured with an electroencephalograph (EEG). Two electrodes are attached to different locations on the subject's skull, and the voltage between them is measured. The voltage level changes over time, and when the levels are plotted on paper or depicted on a monitor the result is the oscillating pattern we think of as brain waves. The procedure itself is not especially complex and has been in practice in roughly the same form for over 50 years.

Now, in one sense, EEG patterns are unilluminating. Although it is presumed that the organized electrical activity they represent is in some way related to the actions of individual neurons in the brain, just what precisely this relationship is remains obscure. We don't really know, that is, just what an EEG reading is a reading *of*. But in another sense, EEG patterns are extremely useful. Although we don't know exactly why, different patterns arising from electrical activity in the cerebral cortex turn out to correspond to different mental states, and experience has made it possible to identify uncontroversially certain patterns with certain states. In particular, neurologists standardly distinguish between four kinds of EEG pattern based on their frequency: *beta* (greater than 13 cycles per second), associated with alertness and attentiveness; *alpha* (8–13 cycles per second), associated with a restful state; *theta* (four–seven cycles per second), associated with a drowsy state; and *delta* (less than four cycles per second), associated with deep sleep. As Burgess and Tawia put it, "In neuropsychology, it is regarded as uncontentious that there is a link, close enough to amount to supervenience, between genuine behavioural evidence of consciousness and electrical activity in the cortex which can be measured by an EEG" (1996: 8). So if the electrical activity characteristic of the brain in its early state of development is organized cortical activity, then we may be able to draw certain conclusions about the mental state of the fetus at that point. The sorts of considerations that may legitimately be advanced in favor of the initial brain activity criterion, then, depend largely on the location and kind of electrical activity that occurs in the period from 6 to 10 weeks after fertilization during which the brain first becomes active.

A claim often made in writings opposed to abortion (and not infrequently conceded in works defending it) is that during this early stage of fetal development the human brain begins to produce recognizable, organized electroencephalographic waves. Baruch Brody, for example, who defends what I am calling the initial brain activity criterion, refers to the claim that "electroencephalographic waves are noticeable" at "about six weeks after conception" as a "fact," although he cites no evidence for this (1975: 83), and this claim is also forwarded uncritically by Schaeffer and Koop (1979: 40) and Schwarz (1990: 50–1) among others. If this claim is true, then while the distinction between organized and unorganized brain activity will remain important in theory, it will prove to be irrelevant in practice: When the brain acquires the one, it acquires the other. And if this activity occurs in the cortex as well as in the lower parts of the brain, then the important distinction in principle between cortical and noncortical brain activity will also prove practically irrelevant. Any argument for the moral relevance of organized cortical brain activity will, in effect, be an argument for attributing a right to life to the fetus as soon as its brain first becomes active, some time between 6 and 10 weeks after fertilization.

But as Morowitz and Trefil have more recently demonstrated (1992: 122–5), the claim that what is present when brain activity first begins in the human fetus is the kind of organized electrical activity that produces EEG waves is unfounded. Morowitz and Trefil traced the origins of this often repeated but rarely documented claim to a 1968 conference at the Charles University in Prague, whose proceedings in turn referred back to a 1963 study published by Bergstrom and Bergstrom in the Finnish Annals of Surgery and Gynecology. Bergstrom and Bergstrom had performed a series of Cesarean abortions on fetuses ranging in development from 59 days ($8\frac{1}{2}$ weeks) to 158 days ($22\frac{1}{2}$ weeks), and after surgically removing live fetuses from the uterus had measured the voltage from electrodes inserted into three different regions of the brain: the brain stem, the hypothalamus, and the top of the cortex. They measured some activity in the brain stem even in the early fetuses, and detected a few signals from the hypothalamus in the oldest fetuses, and no activity whatsoever in the cortex of any of the fetuses, even those of $22\frac{1}{2}$ weeks gestation. None of the readings taken in the study, then, "showed any trace of the kind of organized activity we associate with the EEG" (1992: 125).

Rather than revealing organized brain activity in the cortex of fetuses between 6 and 10 weeks gestation, then, the Bergstroms' study uncovered only unorganized brain activity and only in the brain stem.

This finding, moreover, is precisely what one would expect, given two further facts about human brain development.

One concerns the brain activity of prematurely born infants. As Donald Scott reports in his book, *Understanding the EEG: An Introduction to Electroencephalography*, "Attempts have been made to record cerebral activity of premature infants and they have succeeded (only) if the gestational age was 25 weeks or more" (quoted by Morowitz and Trefil 1992: 122). If electrical activity were detectable in the cortex of fetuses between 6 and 10 weeks of gestation, then it would certainly be detectable in the much more fully developed brains of premature infants from 20 to 24 weeks. The fact that such activity has not been detected in such infants provides strong evidence that it has not been detected in such fetuses.

The second set of facts that confirms this picture of nascent fetal brain activity concerns the development of synaptic connections between individual brain cells. As Morowitz and Trefil put it, "Before synapses are formed, the fetal brain is just a collection of nerve cells. The fetus is incapable of awareness or volition. After the synapses have formed, the brain is functional" (1992: 116). The question of what sort of brain activity occurs during the period from 6 to 10 weeks after fertilization when brain activity first occurs, then, turns largely on the further question of whether a sufficiently large number of synaptic connections are formed during this time. Two sources of information help to answer this further question: studies of brain tissue from the autopsies of stillborn or prematurely delivered infants, and studies of fetal brain tissue taken from monkeys and other primates. The results of both sorts of studies converge around the following picture: "As a general rule, embryologists reckon that cells grow and migrate from Months 2 to 5, differentiate and form the cortex structure . . . in Month 6, and form large numbers of synapses starting in Month 7." In particular, on this account, "there is a period between twenty-five and thirty-two weeks when the cortex is coming into existence as a functional entity" (Morowitz and Trefil 1992: 118, 119). This picture, moreover, seems to be common in standard reference works on the subject. According to the entry on "Brain Development," in *The Oxford Companion to the Mind*, for example, the increase in the brain's bulk in the last two months of gestation "is due, not to multiplication of cortical neurones, but to their branching and to the formation of the first connections that integrate the powerful cortical integrating tissues with the rest of the brain to make *conscious* perception, voluntary action, and intelligent learning possible" (Trevarthen 1987:

107, emphasis added).[5] Given that there is so little synaptical connectivity prior to 25 weeks of development, and given that cerebral activity has not been recorded on premature infants born before this stage, we would expect that there would be no indication of such activity in fetuses prior to this point. And that, despite the assertions to the contrary that have mistakenly arisen from erroneous characterizations of the Bergstroms' report, is perfectly consistent with what the Bergstroms actually observed.

There is one further piece of evidence that critics of abortion often offer in defense of the claim that the fetus becomes conscious well before this point. This is the fact that the fetus is capable of responding to physical stimuli well before this point. Graphic depictions of such behavior, such as that presented in the video *Silent Scream*, are often dismissed by defenders of abortion as a mere appeal to emotion, but this response is unfair. It is simply a fact that a human fetus at 9 or 10 weeks of gestation responds to stimulation of the palm of its hand by partly closing its fingers and to stimulation of the sole of its foot by flexing its toes. The fact that the fetus can respond to such physical stimuli in this manner does count as some prima facie evidence that it is conscious, and it is sheer dogmatism to refuse to take such evidence into account. Indeed, if we did not know what we do know about the development of synaptical connections, and the brain activity of fetuses and prematurely born infants, the inference might well be warranted. But given what we do know, it is not. The fetus's behavior is better explained nonconsciously, as is the similar behavior of an unconscious patient during surgery: "In surgery, for example, unless sufficient local or systemic anaesthesia is administered, an unconscious subject will still respond appropriately to stimuli by jumping, withdrawing, and so on, even though the subject is not conscious and hence cannot interpret the physical impulses as pain" (Knight and Callahan 1989: 216).

Attending to the distinction between simple brain activity and organized cortical brain activity of the sort that is associated with EEG waves helps to make sense of much of the confusion within the literature critical of abortion.[6] Brody, for example, writes that Glanville Williams

---

[5] Similarly, Derbyshire refers to the "broadly accepted conclusion that recorded responses to noxious stimulation prior to 26 weeks gestation are *reflex* responses, not dependent on conscious appreciation" (1999: 29).

[6] Burgess and Tawia make essentially the same suggestion (1996: 6–7, 18).

endorsed the relevance of fetal brain activity "but only because he mistakenly thought that foetal brain *activity* is first detectable in the seventh month," rather than after the sixth week (1974: 240n., emphasis added; see also 1975: 154n.). Yet what Williams in fact claimed in the work that Brody refers to is that "brain *waves*" are first discernible at that time (1957: 231, emphasis added). Similarly, Goldenring cites Hellegers as support for the claim that "*EEG* activity has been demonstrated at eight weeks," (1985: 200, emphasis added), but in the source that Goldenring cites, Hellegers says only that "*readable* brain electric activity" is present (1970: 197, emphasis added). Both Brody and Goldenring, then, seem to have conflated simple brain activity in general with the specific sort of organized cortical brain activity that produces the familiar patterns found in EEG waves. If the fetus acquires a right to life in virtue of its initial brain activity sometime between 6 and 10 weeks after fertilization, then, the claim will have to be that it does so in virtue of its possessing simple electrical activity in its brain stem. If the fetus acquires a right to life in virtue of its acquiring organized electrical activity in its cerebral cortex, then the claim will have to be that it acquires this right at a substantially later stage. Morowitz and Trefil locate this stage at the period between 25 and 32 weeks of gestation. Burgess and Tawia locate it at 30 to 35 weeks. But whatever difficulties we may have in pinning down the precise point in time at which this occurs, it will clearly be a distinct and later stage from the first onset of initial brain activity. I will focus for the remainder of this section on the argument for the initial brain activity criterion and will turn to the organized cortical brain activity criterion in the section that follows.

Given the significant limits on the kind of brain activity that can justifiably be appealed to in attempting to defend the initial brain activity criterion, it may seem difficult to imagine what kind of argument might be offered in its defense. The brain stem, it is important to remember, governs only the most fundamental, automatic bodily functions such as heartbeat and respiration. And, as has also been noted, some degree of electrical activity occurs in every cell in the human body. Indeed, as Morowitz and Trefil discovered when they went back to the original Bergstroms' report, "the Finnish surgeons saw similar electrical activity when they stimulated the fetus's leg muscles" (1992: 124). As Morowitz and Trefil put it, the electrical activity identified here means at most that "the circuits that carry signals to the cerebellum have been completed" (1992: 124).

3.5.4. The Symmetry Argument

There is, however, one sort of argument that is likely to be offered in defense of the initial brain activity criterion so understood, and that merits our attention. The argument begins with what seems to be an extremly plausible assumption: that there must be a kind of symmetry between when the right to life begins and when it ends. More specifically, we might say that the property whose permanent loss makes an individual no longer possess a right to life is the same as the property whose initial acquisition makes an individual possess a right to life in the first place. I will call this the symmetry assumption. The symmetry assumption seems reasonable to many people.[7] Indeed, we might even think that it follows necessarily from the conceptual symmetry between adding and taking away. If removing a side from a square makes it a triangle and no longer a square, after all, then surely what needs to be added to the triangle to make it a square must also be a side. From here, the argument takes it that although there is a great deal of debate about when the right to life of an individual human being begins, there is substantially less debate about when the right to life of an individual human being ends. If this is so, and if the symmetry assumption is true, then we can answer the difficult question of when the right to life begins by appealing to the answer to the less difficult question of when it ends.

The less difficult question, of course, is still difficult. Even if we do agree that an individual loses his right to life when brain death occurs, the question of when exactly that is seems open to multiple interpretations. Indeed, the question of just when a person with a right to life ceases to exist may itself seem so insoluble (leading at least one writer to propose in exasperation that "Death is the time at which the brain-death forms are completed" [quoted in Smith 1984: 297]), that the strategy behind the symmetery argument may seem to amount to little more than clarifying the obscure by the equally obscure. In order for the question to yield a justification for the initial brain activity criterion, in any event, we will have to answer it by saying that as long as an individual still has at least some electrical brain activity in his brain stem, then even if his cerebral cortex has been permanently destroyed, he remains an individual with the same right to life as you or I. Once he permanently loses all electrical brain activity, then he no longer possesses this right, even

---

[7] The main proponent of the symmetry argument is Brody (1975). See also Brody (1974), Veatch (1983), Goldenring (1982, 1985), Engelhardt (1974: 220–3), and Matthews (1979: 155–6).

if he remains biologically alive. When this claim is conjoined with the symmetry assumption, the result is what I will refer to as the symmetry argument for the initial brain activity criterion:

P1: The property whose permanent loss makes one lose a right to life is the same as the property whose initial acquisition makes one gain a right to life.

P2: The property whose permanent loss makes one lose a right to life is the property of having electrical brain activity.

C: The property whose initial acquisition makes one gain a right to life is the property of having electrical brain activity.

If P1 and P2 are true, then C is true. And if C is true, then the initial brain activity criterion is true.

But there is good reason to doubt both P1 and P2. Let me begin with P1, the symmetry assumption. If we deny this assumption, then we can agree that loss of brain activity is what makes you stop having a right to life without being committed to the view that gaining brain activity is what makes you begin to have one. There are two sorts of objection that can be raised here. One is indirect. We might argue that if there are good reasons for accepting one criterion for death and another criterion for life, then these reasons will themselves count as reasons to deny the symmetry assumption. Granted, the assumption has a certain surface appeal, we might say, but we shouldn't let it force us into accepting a criterion for rights possession that can't be rendered plausible on independent grounds.[8] This objection has a certain degree of force, and it is true that many who rely on the symmetry assumption treat it as if it stands in need of no defense. But I suspect that in the end it is insufficient to warrant rejecting the argument in the absence of a compelling alternative.

The second objection to P1 is direct and, it seems to me, decisive. P1 rests on the assumption that birth and death are symmetric, but there is an important respect in which this is not so. The asymmetry arises from a feature of the two that is easy to overlook not because it is so subtle, but because it is so obvious: birth comes before death, but death comes after birth. Time, that is, runs in one direction, and birth and death are not symmetric to each other with respect to it. This asymmetry in turn undermines the symmetry assumption embodied in P1 for the following

---

[8] I take it that something like this motivates the criticism of the symmetry assumption in Moussa and Shannon (1985).

reason: When a person lacks a certain quality because he has lost it to death, then he lacks not just the quality itself, but also the prospect of having that quality in the future. But when a person lacks a certain quality because he has not yet acquired it, then he does not lack the prospect of having that quality in the future. It follows from this that the parallel between birth and death does nothing to favor P1 over what I will call

P1': The property the permanent loss of future prospects for which makes one lose a right to life is the same as the property the initial acquisition of future prospects for which makes one gain a right to life.

And P1' is insufficient to generate the argument's conclusion. If we accept P2, we will agree that the property whose permanent loss makes an individual lose a right to life is the property of having electrical brain activity. But we will insist that this is so not because the permanent loss of this property entails the absence of this right, but because the permanent loss of this property entails the permanent loss of prospects for acquiring (or reacquiring) it in the future, which in turn entails the absence of this right. And since the absence of a given property prior to acquiring it does not entail the absence of prospects for acquiring it in the future, it will not follow that the individual prior to acquiring the property does not have a right to life.[9] Considerations about the parallel between birth and death do nothing to rule out appeal to this principle rather than to P1, and so there seems not to be a sufficient reason to accept P1 of the symmetry argument.

But let us suppose that we nonetheless accept P1. There remains the even greater problem of P2. P2 simply sets the standard for losing one's right to life too low. It would deem an irreversibly comatose patient whose cerebral cortex had been permanently destroyed but who nonetheless retained some minimal electrical activity in the brain stem to have the same right to life as you and I. This is surely implausible.[10] A

---

[9] This sort of objection to the symmetry argument is offered by Crum (1992: 41) and Ford (1988: 16, 81–2).

[10] Crum complains that P2 sets the standard for death too *high*. While brain death might be a "socially popular definition" he urges, the argument must rest on "a scientific one." And from a biological point of view, he notes, a brain-dead individual can still be a living organism (Crum 1992: 44). But defining death in this way clearly deprives it of its moral significance. After all, as Crum himself notes (1992: 43), the hair on a body placed in a coffin continues to grow so that the

defender of the claim that the human fetus acquires a right to life when it first comes to have some minimal brain activity in its brain stem cannot appeal to an argument that entails that people in irreversible comas do as well. A defender of the initial brain activity criterion, therefore, cannot depend on the symmetry argument. And since there seems to be no other even prima facie plausible argument for the initial brain activity criterion, I conclude that there is no good reason to accept it.

3.6. ORGANIZED CORTICAL BRAIN ACTIVITY

3.6.1. The Proposal

For purposes of this discussion, organized cortical brain activity refers to electrical activity in the cerebral cortex of the sort that produces recognizable EEG readings. As I noted in Section 3.5.3, there is no evidence to suggest that this occurs prior to approximately the 25th week of gestation, and ample evidence to suggest that it does begin to occur sometime between the 25th and 32nd week. If the onset of such activity marks the point at which the fetus acquires a right to life, then the vast majority of abortions do not involve the death of an individual with a right to life. So if the organized cortical brain activity criterion (cortical criterion for short) is accepted, then the rights-based argument against abortion, understood as an argument for the claim that abortion in typical circumstances is morally impermissible, will be defeated. I propose to argue in this section that the organized cortical brain activity criterion should, in fact, be accepted, and on terms that the critic of abortion already accepts.

I am hardly the first person to defend the cortical criterion. Indeed, both Morowitz and Trefil, explicitly, and Burgess and Tawia, implicitly, draw this moral conclusion from the empirical evidence that they present and that I have, in part, made use of in distinguishing simple brain activity from organized cortical brain activity. But the argument I wish to propose in defense of the cortical criterion differs significantly from that of both pairs of writers. And although I agree with both that the moral conclusion can be grounded in the empirical premises, I believe that the route from the one to the other employed in each of their arguments may be seriously flawed. Since I

individual is in this sense still alive, but surely destroying the individual at that point is not morally on a par with destroying you or me.

believe that my defense of the cortical criterion is capable of avoiding the problems that may ultimately undermine theirs, I will begin by briefly discussing each of these other arguments before turning to my own. The central claim of this section will therefore be that the cortical criterion should be accepted even if these other arguments in its defense are unsuccessful. It is worth emphasizing, however, that if I am mistaken in believing that these other arguments are unsuccessful, then the cortical criterion will still prove to be justified, though for their reasons rather than for mine. I will then conclude the section with a response to the concern that we must acknowledge a sizeable gray area within which we cannot confidently judge whether or not the fetus is conscious.

3.6.2. Rival Arguments

One argument that can be offered for the organized cortical brain activity criterion has already been discussed in Section 3.5.4: the symmetry argument. The symmetry assumption that underlies that argument maintains that the property whose permanent loss makes an individual no longer possess a right to life is the same as the property whose initial acquisition makes an individual possess such a right. When this claim is conjoined with the claim that the property whose permanent loss makes an individual no longer possess a right to life is the property of having organized cortical brain activity, the result is a defense of the cortical criterion. As I noted in that section, the symmetry argument is often advanced as a defense of the claim that the fetus acquires a right to life at a much earlier point in its development. Indeed, the symmetry argument is advanced in the popular *Handbook on Abortion*, written by one of the nation's most active opponents of abortion, as if it is obvious that it supports a strong anti-abortion conclusion: "The scientist measures the definitive end of human life by the end of human brain function as measured by the E.E.G. Why not also then use the onset of that same function as measured on that same instrument as the latest time when a scientist would say that human life begins!" (Wilke and Wilke 1975: 18). But surely it is much more plausible to maintain that one ceases to have a right to life when one no longer has any organized cortical activity even if one still has some simple electrical activity in the brain stem. The presence of such simple electrical activity, it is important to remember, means only that such automatic functions as the regulation of blood pressure and respiration are taking place nonconsciously. And on this view, the symmetry argument, if it succeeds at all, provides a defense not of the initial brain activity criterion, but rather of the organized cortical brain activity criterion. Although Burgess and Tawia do not explicitly discuss abortion in their account of fetal consciousness that I in part appealed to in Section 3.5.3, for example, they do seem to endorse precisely this argument: "If conscious experiences – or, rather, *some* conscious experiences – are the aspect of our lives we value when we *look forward*, considerations of symmetry *dictate* that we first acquire a capacity for what we most value in our lives when we first become conscious" (1996: 2).

I am not prepared to rest my acceptance of the cortical criterion on this revised version of the symmetry argument. As I suggested in Section 3.5.4, the symmetry assumption underlying the argument seems to be importantly flawed. The symmetry between looking forward and looking backward is imperfect: Existing after one permanently loses consciousness is the same as existing after one permanently loses the capacity for consciousness, but existing before one has first gained consciousness is not the same as existing before one has gained the capacity for consciousness. Symmetry considerations, therefore, need not dictate that we first acquire a capacity for what we most value when we first *become* conscious. Rather, they can equally well be understood as dictating that we acquire such a capacity when we acquire the *capacity* to become conscious. And since we presumably acquire that capacity at some point before we become conscious, the symmetry argument will fail to provide satisfactory support for the cortical activity criterion. I do not want to insist that this objection to the symmetry argument is decisive, nor need I do so. If this objection to the symmetry argument can be overcome, then this defense of the cortical criterion should be accepted. A defense of the cortical criterion that avoids the need to overcome this objection will be even stronger, however, and I will attempt to provide such a defense in Section 3.6.3.

A second argument in defense of the organized cortical brain activity criterion is offered by Morowitz and Trefil.[11] Morowitz and Trefil propose to replace the well-worn question, "When does human life begin?" with the question "When does the fetus acquire those properties that make humans uniquely different from other living things?" which they

---

[11] The argument discussed here is also essentially the same as that offered by, among others, Blumenfeld (1977: 262ff.), Seller (1993: 137), and Kuhse and Singer (1990: 69–70).

also express as the question "When does a fetus (or embryo or zygote) acquire humanness?" This question, they propose, "can be answered totally within the framework of science. We first look at human beings and determine what property or properties distinguish them from other living things. Then, we examine the development of a human being from a single fertilized egg to birth and determine when those properties are acquired" (1992: 9). The answer they defend is that possession of a functioning cerebral cortex distinguishes human beings from other species, and that the human fetus thus acquires "humanness" when its cerebral cortex begins to function.

Now, Morowitz and Trefil may well be correct that the question as they formulate it can be construed as a purely scientific one. But so construed, it sheds no light on the moral status of the fetus. Merely identifying the point at which a human being acquires that property or set of properties that distinguish it from other species says nothing about when it acquires that property or set of properties in virtue of which it merits the same respect due to individuals like you and me. And indeed at times Morowitz and Trefil seem to recognize this. A biologist, they recognize, "cannot provide a definition of *individual life* (at least as that term is used in the abortion debate) solely from the biological sciences" (1992: 7). Yet despite this fact, they insist that their formulation of the question is "the relevant question" (1992: 9), and despite their avowal that they are not asking a moral question, they insist that answering their question provides an answer to moral questions. In explaining how their question relates to the abortion controversy, for example, they write as follows:

There would be no abortion debate if abortion did not involve a conflict of rights [between the pregnant woman and the fetus]. ... The crucial point is what or who is exercising the respective rights. The woman, of course, is an adult human being, a person. The fetus, on the other hand, changes daily, rapidly acquiring new characteristics and properties all the time. Before it has acquired humanness, however, it does not possess those properties that distinguish humans from other animals. Therefore, the conflict of rights is between someone who has acquired the property of humanness and an entity that has not. In such a situation, it seems obvious to us that the presumption must be on the side of the woman – that the rights of a person who has acquired humanness must prevail over those of a fetus or embryo that has not (1992: 18).

Now, if "humanness" is taken to be a value-neutral category, as Morowitz and Trefil insist that it be taken, this passage is one long non sequitor. If the claim that a given individual has acquired "human-ness" is not a claim that the individual has acquired some sort of special moral standing, then how can the truth of the claim make it obvious (or even provide partial support for the claim) that the individual's rights should prevail over those of another who has not yet attained it? This would be like arguing that since a parrot's ability to mimic words is what most clearly distinguishes it from other species of bird, it follows that the rights of a parrot who has already developed this ability must trump those of a parrot who has not yet developed it. And whatever moral status one thinks that parrots are entitled to, this claim is hardly obviously true and almost certainly false.

This problem threatens to render Morowitz and Trefil's entire book ir-relevant to the abortion debate. Determining the point at which the fetus attains "humanness" will tell us nothing about the morality of abortion if humanness itself is not a morally relevant property. The problem can be remedied, however, if we take their argument to contain the follow-ing tacit premise: Human beings are morally special *because of* those nonmoral properties that distinguish them from the rest of the animal kingdom. Moreover, there is at least one place where Morowitz and Trefil come very close to acknowledging that they are, and must be, making this assumption. In criticizing the approach that instead asks when human life begins, they rightly note that "the answer [to that question] would say nothing about what it is that makes human beings different *and special*" (1992: 9, emphasis added). Now, what makes hu-man beings different from tigers is something that a scientist can tell us, but a scientist cannot tell us what makes human beings morally special unless we already agree that we are morally special just in virtue of these properties. Another way of putting the point is this: One could find many differences between humans and other species. The aver-age length of gestation and birthweight of offspring, for example, is probably not literally identical to that of any other species. So we could consider that to be what makes us distinctively human. But we surely believe that other differences are more important, and to say that is it-self to make a moral judgment. When Morowitz and Trefil justify their claim that "acquisition of the enlarged cerebral cortex sets humankind off from the rest of the living world" they point to its ability to allow us to "reason and make tools" (1992: 62). Again, to say that we merit special respect because we can do these things is to make a moral judgment, not a scientific one. So provided that they are willing to rescind their claim to pure scientific objectivity, we can attribute to Morowitz and

Trefil the following argument for the organized cortical brain activity criterion:

P1: You and I have a right to life in virtue of those qualities that distinguish us from the rest of the animal kingdom.

P2: Those qualities that distinguish us from the rest of the animal kingdom arise from our having organized electrical activity in our cerebral cortexes.

C1: You and I have a right to life in virtue of our having organized electrical activity in our cerebral cortexes.

C2: Fetuses acquire a right to life when they acquire organized electrical activity in their cerebral cortexes.

Following Morowitz and Trefil, we can call this the humanness argument.

The problem with the humanness argument it that is invalid. Let us agree that you and I have substantially greater moral standing than do members of other species because of the things that we can do that they cannot. And let us also agree that it is in virtue of our having organized electrical activity in our cerebral cortexes that we are able to do these morally important things. These assumptions do suffice to establish that having organized electrical activity in the cerebral cortex is *necessary* for having the special moral standing that we have. If having such activity is necessary in order to be able to do certain sorts of things, and if the capacity for doing these sorts of things is in turn necessary for having this special moral standing, then having such activity is necessary in order to have such moral standing. But it does not follow from this that having such activity is *sufficient*. I need to have organized electrical activity in my cerebral cortex in order to balance my checkbook, for example, but it does not follow that every human being that has such activity can do this. A fetus, even after it has acquired organized electrical activity in its cerebral cortex, cannot do this. Nor, for that matter, can an infant or even a toddler. So if we acquire a right to life only when we reach the point at which we can actually do such things as reason and make tools, it will turn out that infants and toddlers lack this right.

It is possible, of course, that a defender of abortion could simply accept this implication, and agree that human infants and toddlers lack a right to life. And, as I noted in Chapter 1, a number of philosophers have maintained that, at least in the case of infants, this is, in fact, the case. But, as I also suggested in Chapter 1, it would be a serious mistake for a defender of abortion to depend on this being the case. A defense of abortion that attempts to argue on the abortion critic's own terms will be much stronger if it can show that abortion is permissible even while assuming it is true that the newborn human infant has the same right to life as you or I. From this point of view, the fact that Morowitz and Trefil's argument seems to imply that the infant and even toddler does not have a right to life is a serious problem for that argument.

There are two ways in which a defender of Morowitz and Trefil's argument could attempt to show that the argument does not have this implication. One would be to maintain that my example of balancing a checkbook sets the intellectual bar too high. Perhaps one could establish lower standards of reasoning that even a newborn infant could uncontroversially satisfy. The problem with this approach is that any such test will also be passed, and much more easily, by any mature, adult member of any number of nonhuman species. One need not have an unduly sentimental or anthropomorphic view of such animals in order to recognize that, by any plausible measure, dogs and cats, cows and pigs, chickens and ducks are more intellectually developed than a newborn human infant. It would then follow that killing such animals is morally worse than killing a newborn infant. Again, some defenders of abortion might be willing to accept this implication, but it is difficult to imagine how such a position could succeed in engaging critics of abortion on their own terms, since surely virtually every critic of abortion would find this implication unacceptable.

The other response that a defender of Morowitz and Trefil could make to the objection I have raised would be to acknowledge that a newborn infant cannot balance a checkbook, but to point out that the infant's brain will eventually develop to the point where it can do so, while this is not true of the brains of animals of any other species. The problem with this response is clear: It is equally true of a fetus at just a few weeks of gestation that it has a brain that will eventually develop to the point where it can balance a checkbook. So the considerations about what is morally significant about our brains seem in the end either to push the line for acquiring a right to life too far forward, so that even newborn babies fail the test, or to push it too far backward, at least so far as the defender of the cortical criterion is concerned.

Indeed, the failure of Morowitz and Trefil's argument here is instructive in that it highlights what would seem to be an insurmountable problem for any defense of the organized cortical brain activity criterion: Either one insists that all that matters is what the brain can currently do, in which case infants and toddlers will be excluded from the class of individuals with a right to life, or one allows that what the brain will later be able to do also matters, in which case embryos and fetuses will be included in that class from a much earlier stage of development. The challenge is to identify a reason for holding that the potential of the human brain is morally relevant once it has organized electrical activity in its cerebral cortex but is not morally relevant before that point, a reason that is not itself merely an ad hoc device for reaching the conclusion the defender of the cortical criterion wishes to reach. I will now present an argument that attempts to meet this challenge.

3.6.3. The Modified Future-Like-Ours Argument

To say that I will now present such an argument is in an important sense misleading. I have, in effect, already presented the argument, in my response to Marquis's future-like-ours argument in Section 2.7. What remains is only to make explicit its implications.

According Marquis's version of the future-like-ours argument, it must be remembered, the best account of the wrongness of killing an individual like you or me or a temporarily comatose adult or a suicidal teenager rests on the wrongness of depriving an individual of a future-like-ours. A future-like-ours contains a variety of valuable experiences of the sort that the individual either currently desires to enjoy or will later come to enjoy, and so killing him is wrong because it deprives him of all that he now values or will later come to value. And since a typical human fetus has a future-like-ours from the beginning of its existence that it will later come to enjoy, it follows on this account that a typical human fetus has the same right to life as you or I from the beginning of its existence.

I argued in Section 2.8 that Marquis's position is ultimately undermined by a failure to account for two important distinctions, that between occurrent and dispositional desires, and that between ideal and actual desires. A desire of yours is an occurrent desire if it is one that you are consciously entertaining. If this discussion is striking you as tedious, for example, then you may right now be experiencing an occurrent desire to put this book down. A desire of yours is dispositional if it is a desire that you do have right now even if you are not thinking about it at just this moment. I suspect, for example, that when you began to read this sentence you really did want to live beyond tomorrow evening, even though it is unlikely that you were entertaining just that desire consciously as you began to read this sentence. If we limit the sorts of desires that matter morally to occurrent desires, then Marquis's example of the temporarily comatose adult will successfully demonstrate that a present desire to preserve one's personal future is an unsatisfactory basis upon which to construct an account of the wrongness of killing. The temporarily comatose adult has no present occurrent desire that his personal future be preserved, yet surely killing him is as wrong as killing you or me. And since the temporarily comatose adult will presumably have such a desire when he regains consciousness, the most natural response to this problem will be to follow Marquis's suggestion that we appeal to the wrongness of frustrating a desire that he either has now or will later come to have if he is not killed. But as I argued in Section 2.8.3, it is dispositional desires, rather than occurrent desires, that matter most when desires matter morally. The desires of others make legitimate demands on you because they show that yours are not the only desires there are to be satisfied. The fact that a woman desires that her husband be faithful to her thus constitutes a legitimate moral reason against his having an affair regardless of whether she is currently entertaining that desire as a conscious desire or entertaining some other conscious desire, or no conscious desires at all. And when we formulate a future-like-ours account of the wrongness of killing in terms of dispositional desires, we find that we can account for the wrongness of killing the temporarily comatose adult without complicating the initial scheme on which killing is wrong in terms of an individual's present desires. I thus argued that a present dispositional desire version of the future-like-ours account of the wrongness of killing was superior to the present or future occurrent desire version that Marquis endorses on grounds of both parsimony and salience.

The actual content of a desire of yours is the content of a desire that you in fact have (either occurrently or dispositionally). If you are thirsty right now and there is a glass of water in front of you, for example, then you may well have an actual desire to drink from that glass. Actual desires are often formed under less than perfect conditions, and in such cases we can often reasonably refer to the desire that you would have had under more perfect conditions by idealizing your actual desire to take the circumstances into account. If we know that the water in the glass in front of you contains a deadly toxin, for example, while you do not know this, then while your actual desire will be to drink from the glass, we may confidently consider your ideal desire to be to avoid drinking from the glass, given that your actual (though likely dispositional rather than occurrent) desire not to be killed strongly outweighs your actual (even if occurrent) desire to quench your thirst. And we can say the same sort of thing about those desires that overtake us when we are under conditions of great stress or grief. If we limit the sorts of desires that matter morally to actual desires, then Marquis's example of the suicidal teenager will successfully demonstrate that a present desire to preserve one's personal future, even when desires are construed to include dispositional and not merely occurrent desires, is an unsatisfactory basis upon which to construct an account of the wrongness of killing. The suicidal teenager has no present desire that his personal future be preserved of either an occurrent or dispositional sort, yet surely killing him is as wrong as killing you or me. And since the suicidal teenager will presumably have such a desire when he overcomes his present difficulties, the most natural response to this problem will again be to follow Marquis's suggestion that we appeal to the wrongness of frustrating a desire that he either has now or will later come to have if he is not killed.

But, as I argued in Section 2.8.4, it is ideal desires, rather than actual desires, that matter most when desires matter morally, at least in those cases where actual desires arise under importantly imperfect conditions, such as crucially mistaken information or severe degrees of emotional trauma. The fact that you have desires about how your future goes imposes legitimate moral demands on me, and the fact that your ideal dispositional desire not to be killed more deeply and accurately reflects what matters to you than does your actual occurrent desire to drink the glass of water in front of you makes your ideal rather than your actual desire the morally relevant one. And when we formulate a future-like-ours account of the wrongness of killing in terms of ideal desires, we again find that we can account for the wrongness of killing the individual in question, in this case the suicidal teenager, without complicating the initial scheme on which killing is wrong in terms of an individual's present desires. I thus concluded that a present ideal dispositional desire version of the future-like-ours account of the wrongness of killing was superior to the present or future actual occurrent desire version that Marquis endorses on grounds of both parsimony and salience.

Chapter 2 was concerned with what I have been calling the conception criterion, the claim that the fetus acquires a right to life at the moment of its conception. Since ideal desires, as I defined them, are simply the content of actual desires corrected to account for the distorting influences of imperfect circumstances, and since a zygote has no actual desires to suffer such distortion, I concluded that the best version of the future-like-ours account of the wrongness of killing failed to establish that the conception criterion should be accepted. But I ended Section 2.8.5 by conceding that it did not follow from this that there was no point in fetal development at which the argument would justify attributing to the fetus such moral standing. Since I was only concerned in that section to argue against Marquis's claim that the typical human fetus *always* has this moral standing, this concession did nothing to undermine the position I was taking. But since we are now concerned to establish at what point after conception the fetus does acquire this standing, this concession might seem crucial.

And, in fact, it is crucial. But it is not a concession. Rather, it is the missing piece needed to complete a satisfactory defense of the organized cortical activity criterion that does not fall prey to the objection that ultimately renders arguments such as that of Morowitz and Trefil unacceptable. The problem, remember, was that any appeal to what the brain can do at various stages of development would seem to have to appeal either to what the brain can already do or to what the brain has the potential to do in the future. If it limits appeals to what the brain can already do, then it will be unable to account for the presumed wrongness of killing infants and toddlers. If it allows appeals to what the brain has the potential to do in the future, then it will have to include fetuses as soon as their brains begin to emerge, during the first few weeks of gestation. The challenge was to identify a reason for holding that the potential of the brain is morally relevant once it has organized electrical activity in its cerebral cortex but is not morally relevant before that point, a reason that is not itself merely an ad hoc device for reaching the conclusion the defender of the cortical criterion wishes to reach. And what remains of Marquis's future-like-ours argument, if both my objection to his argument and my concession about the limits of that objection are accepted, provides just such a reason.

For on the account of the wrongness of killing that results from this modification of the original future-like-ours argument, the existence of other individuals makes a legitimate moral demand on us in virtue of their having at least some actual desires about how their lives go. As a result, an individual cannot begin to acquire this special moral standing until it begins to have at least some actual desires. The fact that an individual will later have such desires is not, on this account, morally relevant. A human fetus has no such desires prior to the point at which it has conscious experiences, and it has no conscious experiences prior to the point at which it has organized electrical activity in its cerebral cortex. It therefore has no such desires prior to the point at which it has organized electrical activity in its cerebral cortex. One implication of this account of the wrongness of killing, then, is that the fetus does not acquire the moral standing that you and I have prior to the point at which it has such activity. The fact that the human fetus prior to this point has the potential to develop such activity is not in itself morally relevant.

But it is also a feature of this account of the wrongness of killing that merely having some actual desires is not enough to ensure that one has the same right to life as you or I. Killing people like us is the severe wrong that it is not only because it thwarts a desire that we have, but because it thwarts a particularly important desire that we have: the desire to preserve our future-like-ours. We have this particular desire, at least as an ideal desire even if it is not always one of our actual desires, because we do, in fact, have a future-like-ours. And we have a future-like-ours only because we have a brain which will enable us to enjoy, in the future, the kinds of conscious experiences that make our lives distinctively valuable to us. Thus, on this account of the wrongness of killing, the potential of our brains is morally relevant within a limited scope. Prior to developing actual conscious desires, an individual cannot have the same moral standing as you or I. Once an individual does develop such desires, the potential that his brain has for developing further becomes morally relevant: It is because a human infant's brain has a potential that the brain of a mature cow or pig does not have that the human infant uncontroversially has a future-like-ours, whereas the cow or pig does not. And it is because of this that the conscious desire that an infant has provides a solid foundation for attributing to it an ideal dispositional desire that its future-like-ours be preserved, whereas this cannot be said of the conscious desires of the cow or the pig.[12] That the potential of the individual's brain is morally relevant once the individual first becomes conscious but not prior to that point, therefore, is not an

---

[12] To say that a cow does not uncontroversially have a future-like-ours is not to insist that it does not have such a future. It is to say only that one would need an argument to establish that the kinds of experiences contained in a cow's future are sufficiently like the kinds of experiences contained in our futures to merit including cows within the scope of the principle. As I noted in a footnote to my discussion of Marquis's argument in Section 2.8, the proponent of the future-like-ours approach can remain neutral about whether nonhuman animals's futures are sufficiently like ours to warrant inclusion within the scope of the principle, and this seems to me a merit rather than a defect of this approach.

ad hoc stipulation tossed in simply to achieve a desired result with respect to the human fetus. Rather, it is the natural result of improving the "past or future actual occurrent desire" version of the future-like-ours account of the wrongness of killing in general by making it more salient and parsimonious. And, intended or not, the result is still the same: The fetus acquires the moral standing that you and I have when it first begins to have conscious desires. The fetus comes to have conscious desires during the period when it begins to have organized electrical activity in its cerebral cortex, and so to say this is to say that the fetus acquires this status when it begins to have such activity. And to say this is to endorse the organized cortical activity criterion.

3.6.4. The Gray Area

I have argued that, on the account that does best by the critic of abortion's own standards, the fetus acquires the right to life that you and I have when it begins to have conscious desires, that this occurs when it begins to have a certain kind of electrical activity in its cerebral cortex, and that this occurs at some point from 25 to 32 weeks after fertilization. If all of this is correct, then the vast majority of abortions take place well before the point at which the fetus acquires a right to life. This does not in itself demonstrate that such abortions are morally permissible, but it does show that the rights-based argument against abortion fails to show that they are impermissible. And since very few abortions take place between the 25th and 32nd weeks of pregnancy, it makes very little difference that we cannot be more specific in locating the precise point at which the fetus's aquisition of this right occurs on this account. While the gray area between 25 and 32 weeks thus produces few practical difficulties for the position defended here, however, it must be conceded that there is also a gray area extending further back. Even if we recognize that the often-repeated claim that the fetus becomes conscious as early as six weeks after fertilization arises from a confusion between simple electrical activity in the brain stem and organized electrical activity in the cerebral cortex, that is, we must still allow that there is substantial room for doubt about precisely when the fetus does become conscious. And this threatens to weaken the extent to which the organized cortical brain activity criterion can serve to undermine the rights-based argument against abortion in typical circumstances.

At this point, however, it is important to emphasize that the vast majority of abortions take place substantially before even the 25th week of gestation. According to figures from the Alan Guttmacher Institute from February 2000, for example, only 1 percent of all abortions performed in the United States in 1996 took place after the 20th week of pregnancy.[13] So even if we push the gray area back from 25 weeks to 20 weeks, it will still turn out that 99 percent of abortions take place before the fetus acquires a right to life. Burgess and Tawia identify 20 weeks of gestation as "the most conservative location we could plausibly advocate" as the beginning of what they call "cortical birth," because it is at this point that "the first 'puddle' of cortical electrical activity" of an "extremely rudimentary nature" begins to appear in brief spurts (1996: 23). Adopting this very conservative estimate seems advisable given our lack of more definitive knowledge, but doing so has no effect on the conclusion that abortion in typical cases, indeed the vast majority of actual cases, does not involve the death of someone with a right to life. Indeed, even if we decide to push the gray area back to just 15 weeks of gestation, it will turn out that approximately 94 percent of abortions take place before the fetus acquires this right. If the gray area is pushed back to 12 weeks, it will turn out that approximately 88 percent of abortions will still take place before the fetus acquires a right to life, and even if we were to push it back as far as 10 weeks, it will turn out that a substantial majority of abortions, approximately 77 percent, take place before the fetus acquires this right.[14] Moreover, if it were widely accepted that abortion

---

[13] The statistics can be found at http://www.agi-usa.org/pubs/fb_induced_abortion.html. The particular figures are taken from 1996, the most recent year for which such information is currently available in the United States, but there is relatively little variation in these figures for all of the years since 1973 for which such statistics are available.

[14] It is worth noting in this context that even critics of abortion who have been concerned to emphasize this gray area have not tried to push it back as far as this. A *London Times* article posted on a web site sponsored by one organization opposed to abortion, for example, cites Vivette Glover, identified as one of Great Britain's "foremost researchers on foetal pain," as questioning the results of a national report on fetal pain. That report, "Foetal Pain – An Update of Current Scientific Knowledge," sponsored by the Health Department and published in May 1995, had concluded that "there was no evidence that the foetus could feel pain earlier than 26 weeks because its brain and neurological system were not sufficiently developed." Dr. Glover is then quoted as agreeing that consciousness depends on electrical activity in the cortex of the brain, but then adding the proviso that: "Below 13 weeks' gestation, the foetus has no such cortical activity. After 26 weeks the full anatomical system is present and the foetus is quite likely to feel pain. The area of uncertainty is between 13 and 26 weeks" (Laurance 1997). But, in the United States at least, the vast majority of abortions take place even before this area of uncertainty begins. So even allowing room for the generous gray area

was permissible up to a certain point and not after that point, a greater percentage of women who have abortions would presumably ensure that they had them prior to that point. And it may, ironically, be in part due to strategies supported by some critcs of abortion, such as the impositions of waiting periods and the picketing of abortion facilities, that some women who would abort relatively early in their pregancies wait until relatively later. I do not want to trivialize the importance of the difference between drawing the line at 25 weeks and drawing it at, say, 12 or 10. Nor do I have anything further to say about how one should go about assessing the size of the gray area within this range. But the thesis of this book is not meant to be more specific than the claim that abortion in typical circumstances is morally permissible, and the rights-based argument against this claim is undermined by the organized cortical brain activity criterion regardless of where between 10 and 32 weeks we draw the line. I conclude that the organized cortical brain activity criterion should be accepted, and that, as a result, the rights-based argument against abortion in typical cases should be rejected. I will go on, in the next chapter, to assume for the sake of the argument that I am mistaken about this and that the fetus acquires the right to life at the moment of its conception. And I will argue that even if this is so, the rights-based argument against abortion should still be rejected. But before doing so, I will conclude this chapter with a brief discussion of one other rival criterion.

3.7. VIABILITY

Viability refers to the point at which it becomes possible for a fetus to survive outside of the womb. The exact moment at which this occurs cannot be determined precisely, but it is generally acknowledged to occur at some point toward the end of the second trimester, between 20 and 23 weeks after fertilization. Since the vast majority of abortions occur well before even the most conservative estimates for viability, greater specificity is unnecessary for our purposes. If the fetus acquires a right to life when it becomes viable, then on any plausible account of when viability occurs it will turn out that the vast majority of abortions do not involve the death of an individual with a right to life.

that such critics of abortion demand, the organized cortical brain activity criterion would still entail that abortion in typical cases occurs before the fetus acquires a right to life.

The claim that viability is morally relevant is often dismissed out of hand as a claim associated only with an extremely permissive attitude toward abortion and as one that is easily rebutted by one or two quick observations. But both of these responses are unwarranted. The first is misleading because even one who opposes abortion in general might think that viability is morally relevant. He might say, for example, that a woman who is raped or whose life is endangered by her pregnancy may have an abortion, but only if this is done before the fetus is viable. Or he might say that even though all abortions are bad, abortions on viable fetuses are even worse, a sentiment that may underlie much of the opposition to what critics of abortion have referred to as "partial birth" abortion. And the second claim is misleading because the usual rebuttals to the viability criterion, although superficially appealing, are ultimately unsatisfactory.

One common objection to the viability criterion is that it excludes from the class of individuals with a right to life people who clearly have such a right, such as, according to one such critic, people with pacemakers or on heart-lung machines (Werner 1976: 204).[15] But this is a puzzling objection. A fetus that could survive on a heart-lung machine is a paradigmatic example of a fetus that *is* viable, not one that is unviable. Why should the claim that a fetus that can survive on such a machine *does* have a right to life be taken to imply that an adult who can survive on such a machine does not? Presumably, what the critic of the viability criterion has in mind here is the idea that being viable means being independent and self-sustaining, and that people who require heart-lung machines are neither of these. But viability means merely the ability to survive outside of the womb of the woman in whom the fetus is conceived. We can distinguish between being dependent on a particular person and being dependent on some person or other. The viability criterion maintains that the former property is morally relevant, while the purported counterexamples establish only that the latter is morally irrelevant. But the moral irrelevance of the former is not entailed by the moral irrelevance of the latter, and so such examples, although quite common, are ultimately ineffective.

A second common objection to the viability criterion is that it would make one's moral status dependent on, and relative to, the existing state of technology. At some point in the past, for example, a seven-month-old fetus could not survive outside of the womb; because of

---

[15] The same objection is also raised by, for example, Carrier (1975: 393).

medical advances, a seven-month-old fetus now can survive outside of the womb. At present, a five-month-old fetus cannot survive outside the womb, but perhaps at some point in the future a five-month-old fetus could. But tying the fetus's right to life to the question of its viability can then seem to have absurd consequences. As one of the many writers who have pressed this objection has put it, "Does a 5-month-old fetus then *become* a person when that stage of technology exists? Can personhood be a condition relative to and dependent on technology?" (Cooney 1991: 161).

I would suggest that the best response to this objection, when the term *person* is being used in a morally relevant sense, is simply to answer yes. If personhood were instead meant to denote a purely descriptive biological claim about the fetus's species membership, of course, this answer would be absurd. Whether or not an individual is a member of one species rather than another cannot depend on contingent facts about currently available technology. But there is nothing comparably objectionable with the claim when it is understood as a claim about the fetus's having the same right to life as you and I. Indeed, rather than being absurd, it seems to fit naturally with other moral judgments that most of us would be inclined to make. Consider, for example, an adult human being with a particular form of brain injury that has caused him to lapse into an irreversible coma. Most people would agree that he does not have the same right to life as you and I. But it is of course possible that technological advances might some day make it possible to bring people with precisely the same form of brain injury out of their comas. Were that to happen, we would surely say that the individual did have the same right to life as you or I, since this is what we say of people who are only temporarily unconscious. This would be to make his moral standing relative to the existing state of technology, and in a way that seems perfectly appropriate.[16] So the fact that the viability criterion makes the fetus's moral standing relative to technological development also provides no reason for rejecting it.

A related objection complains that the viability criterion would make the fetus's moral standing relative to its location, or to the income of the woman carrying it. So two fetuses of identical condition, one in a poor area and one in a rich one, would differ in their moral standing. But this objection presupposes a needlessly narrow understanding of viability. The proponent of the viability criterion is best understood as

---

[16] This point is also noted by Zaitchik (1981: 24–5).

claiming that a fetus is viable if the technological means of keeping it alive outside of the womb are in principle available somewhere, even if not to this particular fetus. And so this objection, too, must ultimately be rejected.

The viability criterion, then, cannot be dismissed as quickly as many people have seemed to suppose. But this does not mean that it should be accepted. And, indeed, I believe that it should not be accepted. I believe this not because I believe that the claim itself has plainly objectionable implications, but because I do not believe that there are any good reasons to accept it. Justifying this belief would require consideration of those arguments that have been offered in defense of the viability criterion, but justifying this belief is unnecessary for the purposes of this work. The central claim of this chapter and the chapter that preceded it has been that the first premise of the rights-based argument against abortion – the claim that the fetus has the same right to life as you and I – is false in typical cases of abortion, and can be shown to be false on terms that critics of abortion already accept. I have argued that this is so on the grounds that the falsity of this premise is entailed by the organized cortical brain activity criterion and by arguing that the organized cortical brain activity criterion should be accepted. But if it turns out that I have been mistaken about the organized cortical brain activity criterion, and that the viability criterion should be accepted instead, it will still turn out that the first premise of the rights-based argument against abortion should be rejected, since its falsity is also entailed by the viability criterion. Whether I am correct or mistaken in rejecting the viability criterion, therefore, the cumulative result of this and the previous chapter remains the same: The first premise of the rights-based argument against abortion should be rejected.

Chapter 4

The Good Samaritan Argument

4.0. OVERVIEW

The rights-based argument against abortion turns on two claims: that the fetus (at least in typical cases of abortion) has the same right to life as you and I, and that if this is so, then abortion (at least in typical circumstances) is morally impermissible. In Chapters 2 and 3, I considered the first of these claims in some detail and argued that it should be rejected on the critic of abortion's own terms. The fetus should instead be understood as acquiring a right to life only after its brain reaches a certain level of maturity, a development that occurs well after the vast majority of abortions are performed. If this analysis is correct, then the rights-based argument fails for most, but not all, cases of abortion. But let us now suppose that I have been mistaken about this, and that the fetus acquires a right to life at the moment of its conception. This concession will vindicate the rights-based argument against abortion only if we also accept the argument's second claim, the claim that if the fetus has this right, then abortion (at least in typical circumstances) is morally impermissible. I will argue in this chapter that this second claim should also be rejected on the abortion critic's own terms.

The argument I will defend against this claim turns on the thesis that cases of a woman's carrying a pregnancy to term should be subsumed under the broader category of good samaritanism. From the moral point of view, that is, a woman who carries a pregnancy to term is like a person who generously offers at some considerable cost to herself to provide what another needs but does not have the right to, while a woman who declines to carry a pregnancy to term is like a person who declines to offer such assistance. It is not the case that abortion violates the requirements of morality, on this account, but rather that continuing to incur the burdens involved in a typical pregnancy goes beyond them, even if the fetus does have the same right to life that you or I have. I will refer to the argument that attempts to reconcile the moral permissibility of abortion with the claim that the fetus has a right to life in this manner as the good samaritan argument.

The good samaritan argument is not original. It was first proposed by Judith Jarvis Thomson in her 1971 article, "A Defense of Abortion," and has been defended, or at least endorsed, by a variety of writers since then.[1] But while Thomson's paper has become "the most widely reprinted essay in all of contemporary philosophy" (Parent 1986: vii) as well as one of the most widely discussed, it has hardly become one of the most widely accepted. One writer has compared Thomson's argument to Anselm's ontological proof of the existence of God (Davis 1983: 260), while another has compared it to Zeno's paradoxes of motion (Wilcox 1989: 212), and the comparisons represent what seems to be a widespread feeling: that while the good samaritan argument is surely "ingenious" (a word that recurs like a mantra in nearly every attack on Thomson's article), it is just as surely flawed. I will not argue in this chapter that Thomson herself has provided a satisfactory defense of the good samaritan argument. Indeed, with respect to two of the most influential objections to it, I will argue that the good samaritan argument is not only stronger than it is typically taken to be but is stronger than Thomson herself claims it to be. But while I will not attempt to defend Thomson's defense of the good samaritan argument, I will attempt to defend the argument itself.

---

[1] See, for example, Bolton (1979: esp. 42, 44), Rothbard (1973: 121; 1983: 97–99), McDonagh (1996: 10–11), Harrison (1983: 39–40), and, most importantly, Kamm (1992). A variant of the good samaritan argument as an argument against legal restrictions on abortion has also been defended by such writers as Tribe (1992: 130–5), Swensen (1991), Neff (1991: 351), and Walen (1997). The only genuine historical antecedents to Thomson's 1971 article of which I am aware seem to come from theological arguments about abortion in the case of life-threatening pregnancies made within the Catholic Church. The Spanish Augustinian Basilio Ponce (1569–1629), for example, argued that bloodletting was permissible to save the life of a pregnant woman even if this resulted in the death of the fetus, since this amounted to depriving the child of nourishment which more rightfully belongs to the mother. And the 1867 edition of *Casus conscientiae* by the French Jesuit Jean Pierre Gury (1801–66) contains an argument (which may have been inserted by his editor after his death) from an analogy with withholding nutrition from a child after birth: just as a woman would not be bound to feed her child after birth if doing so endangered her life, so she is not bound to continue supporting the fetus with her body during pregnancy if doing so threatens her life (Connery 1977: 158, 216–18).

4.1. THE ARGUMENT

The target of the good samaritan argument is the rights-based argument against abortion, which Thomson puts as follows: "Every person has a right to life. So [assuming for the sake of the argument that the fetus is a person] the fetus has a right to life. No doubt the mother has a right to decide what shall happen in and to her body; everyone would grant that. But surely a person's right to life is stronger and more stringent than the mother's right to decide what happens in and to her body, and outweighs it. So the fetus may not be killed; an abortion may not be performed" (Thomson 1971: 132). The argument to which Thomson offers the good samaritan argument as a response can be represented as follows:

P1: The fetus is a person.
P2: Every person has a right to life.
C1: The fetus has a right to life.
P3: The woman has a right to control her body.
P4: The right to life outweighs the right to control one's body.
P5: Abortion kills the fetus.
C2: Abortion is morally impermissible.

Thomson then attempts to demonstrate that "something really is wrong" with this argument by placing the reader in a now (in)famous set of circumstances:

You wake up in the morning and find yourself back to back in bed with an unconscious violinist. A famous unconscious violinist. He has been found to have a fatal kidney ailment, and the Society of Music Lovers has canvassed all the available medical records and found that you alone have the right blood type to help. They have therefore kidnapped you, and last night the violinist's circulatory system was plugged into yours, so that your kidneys can be used to extract poisons from his blood as well as your own. The director of the hospital now tells you, "Look, we're sorry the Society of Music Lovers did this to you – we would never have permitted it if we had known. But still, they did it, and the violinist is now plugged into you. To unplug you would be to kill him. But never mind, it's only for nine months. By then he will have recovered from his ailment, and can safely be unplugged from you." (1971: 132)

Thomson takes it that you will think it morally permissible for you to refuse to remain plugged into the violinist for nine months. That is certainly my response to the story, and I will assume for now that it is yours as well. But, as Thomson points out, the director of the hospital could say to you: "All persons have a right to life, and violinists are persons. Granted you have a right to decide what happens in and to your body, but a person's right to life outweighs your right to decide what happens in and to your body. So you cannot ... be unplugged from him" (1971: 114).² If unplugging yourself from the violinist is morally permissible, then clearly there is something seriously wrong with the argument the hospital director is making. And if the argument the hospital director is making is relevantly analogous to the rights-based argument against abortion, then there is something seriously wrong with that argument as well, even if it is true that the fetus has the same right to life as you or I or a famous violinist.

It is tempting to suppose that it is clear what the problem with the director's argument is supposed to be, and to turn immediately to the question of whether that argument really is relevantly like the rights-based argument against abortion. To many readers, it seems obvious that the lesson of the story is supposed to be that in this case your right to control your body really does outweigh the violinist's right to life. And if that is the point of the story, then the good samaritan argument in defense of abortion will have to rest on the parallel claim that a pregnant woman's right to control her body outweighs a fetus's right to life. Thomson's objection to the argument as sketched above, on this account, will be that even if you assume that P1 is true, P4 is false and shown to be false by the case of you and the violinist. This, for example, is how the editors of the anthology from which I have been citing Thomson's article characterize her position in the introductory note they provide for the reader: "She rejects the idea that the fetus has a right to life which overrides the mother's right to her own body" (Pojman and Beckwith 1994: 131).

But this is a mistake. Thomson's example is not meant to deny that the violinist's right to life outweighs your right to control your body. If there were a genuine conflict between your right to control your body and the violinist's right to life, Thomson would surely agree that his right to life would trump your right to control your body. If you met the violinist at one of his concerts and wanted to exercise your right to control your body by swinging your fists in a manner that would cause him to be pummelled to death, for example, she would plainly acknowledge that his right to life would outweigh your right to control

---

² Strictly speaking, this quote comes in response to a variation that Thomson presents in which you must remain plugged in for the rest of your life.

your body. But Thomson's claim is precisely that there is no such conflict between these two rights in the case she has presented, that unplugging yourself from the violinist does not violate his right to life in the first place. Even though he has a right to life, that is, he has no right to the use of your kidneys. So in unplugging yourself from him, you do nothing that conflicts with his right to life, even though you do something that brings about his death. The lesson of the story, therefore, is not that it is sometimes permissible for you to violate the violinist's right to life, but rather that the violinist's right to life does not include or entail the right to be provided with the use or the continued use of whatever is needed in order for him to go on living. And if, as Thomson suggests, the rights-based argument against abortion proceeds in a relevantly similar manner, then this will be the objection to that argument as well: not that the fetus's right to life does not outweigh a woman's right to control her body. Surely if the fetus has the same right to life as you and I, then that right does outweigh a woman's right to control her body, and if the two come into conflict, then it is the fetus's right to life that must prevail. Rather, the objection will turn on the claim that the fetus's right to life does not include or entail the right to be provided with the use or the continued use of whatever is needed in order for it to go on living. In terms of the argument represented above, then, Thomson's objection is not that P4 is false, but rather that C2 does not follow even if it and all of the other premises of the argument are true. C2 would follow only given a further premise, which the rights-based argument against abortion tacitly assumes to be true, namely:

P6: If abortion kills the fetus, then abortion violates the fetus's right to life.

This is the premise that the good samaritan argument is designed to attack. As Thomson puts the point later in her article, the rights-based argument against abortion "treats the right to life as if it were unproblematic. It is not, and this seems to me to be precisely the source of the mistake." Once it becomes clear that the right to life does not include or entail the right to life support, that is, it becomes clear that it is not enough for the critic of abortion to establish that the fetus has a right to life: "We need to be shown also that killing the foetus violates its right to life, i.e., that abortion is unjust killing. And is it?" (1971: 136, 138). It is important to be clear at the outset that this is the question that Thomson's violinist example is meant to raise in order to ensure that the argument based on the example receives a fair hearing. The claim that your right to control your body could outweigh someone's right to life is implausible on the face of it, but the claim that someone else's right to life does not include or entail the right to be provided by you with the use or continued use of whatever they need in order to go on living is not at all implausible. And if the right to life does not include or entail this further right, then it is not at all clear that P6 is true.

Of course, it is not at all clear that P6 is false either. It does seem clearly to be false that unplugging yourself from the violinist violates his right to life. When you unplug yourself from him, you bring about his death by depriving him of something to which he has no just claim. But whether this provides support for the conclusion that P6 is false depends on whether the two cases are sufficiently alike in all morally relevant respects. We can thus picture Thomson's example, and the argument that is based upon it, as having two distinct goals. The first is to show that the rights-based argument against abortion as she presents it is unsuccessful. In this sense, Thomson's claim seems to me to be plainly correct. The rights-based argument against abortion as formulated here is invalid and can be remedied only by adding a further premise, one which is not obviously true. The second, and more ambitous, goal is to show that the rights-based argument is not only unsuccessful as it stands, but is incapable of being successfully revised. This amounts to showing that P6 is false, or at least is false in many cases. It is at this point that a defender of the good samaritan argument must maintain that unplugging yourself from the violinist is morally on a par with aborting a fetus. If this claim can be successfully defended, then the argument will have established that abortion is morally permissible even if the fetus does have the same right to life as you or I.

Since the argument at this point turns crucially on the analogy between a woman's being pregnant and your being plugged into the famous violinist, the argument's critics are left with essentially three lines of response: They can attempt to identify a morally relevant disanalogy between the two cases, they can embrace the conclusion that it would be impermissible for you to unplug yourself from the violinist, or they can reject the authority of such arguments from analogy. The most popular strategy by far has been to attempt to uncover a morally relevant disanalogy between the case of you and the violinist and that of the pregnant woman and the fetus. If such a disanalogy is successfully identified, then the critic of abortion can accommodate our intuition that it is morally permissible for you to unplug yourself from the violinist without having to concede that it is morally permissible for a pregnant woman to have an abortion. Since a great number of objections of this form have been defended in the literature prompted by Thomson's article, and since a good number of these objections are potentially quite powerful, the vast majority of this long chapter will be devoted to examining them in some detail and to arguing that all of them fail on the abortion critic's own terms. Before turning to a detailed examination of these objections, however, I want first to consider an objection that maintains that the good samaritan argument is without force even if no such disanalogy can successfully be uncovered. This objection is hardly the most prominent of the many that have been aimed at the good samaritan argument, and many readers may find it of little force. But those readers who are attracted to the objection at all may well find it compelling. Such readers will believe that it makes very little difference whether or not Thomson's analogy can be vindicated, and so will think that the vast majority of the arguments made in this chapter are simply beside the point. I will therefore begin my defense of the good samaritan argument by attempting to show that they are mistaken.

4.2. THE WEIRDNESS OBJECTION

So let me assume for a moment that you agree that there is no morally relevant difference between the violinist case and the case of a typical unwanted pregnancy, and that you also agree that it would be morally permissible for you to unplug yourself from the violinist. If you accept both of these claims, then it might seem obvious that I would be entitled to conclude that you will also, even if grudgingly, accept the conclusion that abortion in the case of a typical unwanted pregnancy is morally permissible. But this would be premature. For you might simply reject the authority of such arguments from analogy to begin with. Moreover, there is one feature of the good samaritan argument that you might plausibly appeal to as a way of justifying your refusal to assent to the argument's conclusion while at the same time accepting its premises. As one of the argument's critics has put it, "the violinist example is *weird*" while "pregnancy is the opposite of weird" (Wilcox 1989: 214–15). Indeed, many people who first encounter the good samaritan argument, whether they are inclined to accept its conclusion or not, find it difficult to take the argument seriously precisely because of its weirdness. This sort of resistance to the good samaritan argument can take one of two forms.[3] On the one hand, one can argue that the weirdness of the violinist example undermines the argument's validity, that there is something about the nature of moral argument that makes such inferences illicit. On the other hand, one can concede that the argument seems to be formally sound, but find that its weirdness renders it utterly unpersuasive nonetheless. The first sort of response challenges the argument's objective validity, while the second challenges its subjective force. I will consider each in turn.

The case for maintaining that the weirdness of the violinist example undermines the soundness of the argument itself is put well by Wilcox: "The moralities we have represent some ways of dealing with the realities and regularities of human life; and they may not fit well the irregularities or impossibilities. . . . So what is appropriate for kidnapped kidney bearers and their violinist parasites might not be appropriate for mothers and the babes in their wombs" (Wilcox 1989: 215).[4] This is a common response to the increasing tendency in recent philosophical writings to attempt to illuminate real moral issues by appealing to surreal examples: If morality is to be a practical science, we need not worry if our principles yield counterintuitive results in impractical if not impossible cases.

Hypothetical examples can indeed become so artificial that their practical significance vanishes. So it is difficult not to have some sympathy with the weirdness objection so understood. Still, it is even more difficult to accept it. The fact that hypothetical examples are sometimes misused, after all, cannot count against their use in general. And to remove them from the philosopher's bag of tools entirely would be to eliminate a valuable method for testing the relative significance of the many different features that constitute real life cases of moral choice.

To see that this is so, it is important to begin by distinguishing the complaint that an example is extremely unusual from the complaint that it is literally impossible. In each kind of case there can be grounds for legitimate objections to the way that an example is used, but in neither case do they successfully apply to the way that the violinist

---

[3] I am grateful to Andrew Tardiff for bringing this distinction to my attention and for convincing me that a defender of abortion should try to say something about both.

[4] Wilcox does not explicitly defend this view, maintaining only that it is "arguable," but he does say that the difference between the two cases is significant, and it is difficult to see why he thinks this if not for this reason. For a similar defense of this objection, see also Levi (1987).

example is used in the good samaritan argument. Consider first the claim that an example appealed to in a given discussion is extremely unusual. In some contexts, this fact about an example does render its use objectionable. Suppose, for example, that you have endorsed the claim that theft of legitimately acquired private property is seriously immoral. And suppose that, in response, someone presents a case in which you must steal a small amount of some drug from a billionaire who will never notice that it is missing (indeed, if you don't steal it, it will simply sit in his medicine cabinet until its expiration date passes and it is thrown away) in order to prevent your husband or wife from dying a horribly painful death. Assuming that you agree that your stealing the drug would be morally permissible in this case, your interlocutor then urges that this shows that there is nothing wrong with stealing after all.

There is something objectionable about the use of this example, and the objection does arise from the fact that the case appealed to is so unusual. But the problem is not the unusualness of the example per se, but rather that it is unusual in specific respects that make it different from typical cases of theft in ways that are uncontroversially morally relevant. It is clearly morally relevant, for example, that this act of theft causes no discernible harm to anyone while typical acts of theft do cause discernible harm to someone. And it is clearly morally relevant that this act of theft is needed in order to prevent someone from dying while typical acts of theft are not. This is why one cannot infer from the fact that stealing in this case is permissible that stealing in general is. So understood, the fact that this particular use of an unusual example is objectionable does nothing to support the claim that the good samaritan argument's use of the violinist example is objectionable. The violinist scenario is very strange, but I am assuming in this section that the particular qualities that make it different from cases of unwanted pregnancy are not, in themselves, morally relevant. If one or more of the differences between the cases does prove to be morally relevant, after all, then *that* will be the reason for concluding that the argument is unsound. If the differences do not themselves prove to be morally relevant, then the mere strangeness of the example in and of itself will provide no further reason for rejecting the argument's soundness.

A second reason that might be given for rejecting appeals to very unusual cases is that they might be thought to generate uncertain or unreliable responses. This objection, too, is sometimes correct. Suppose, for example, that you are asked for your intuitive response to the following case: As a result of exposure to radiation, there is a mutant strain of cockroach that, if immersed in salt water, develops the potential to metamorphize into a being with abilities just like yours or mine. One such cockroach is about to crawl into a puddle of such water in front of you. If left to do so, and then left alone for nine more months, it will turn into something just like a human infant with all the potential that any other human infant has. Would it be permissible for you to kill the mutant roach before it becomes immersed in the water? Such an example might be posed as a way of discerning the moral significance of the fetus's potential to develop into an infant and later adult relevantly like you or me. It might be said that you should use your response to the question of whether it would be morally permissible for you to kill the cockroach at this stage as a guide to thinking about the permissibility of killing a fetus when it is no more developed than a cockroach. But here it seems very likely that your response to the case will be uncertain. Without knowing more about the imagined process of metamorphosis, it is extremely difficult to know if killing the cockroach prevents *it* from later having all sorts of wonderful experiences, or whether it simply prevents some not yet existing being from coming into existence. Indeed, to the extent that you have any clear reaction at all, it is likely that you will let your views about killing the fetus inform your reaction to the cockroach case rather than vice versa, so that appealing to such a case in the first place would amount to little more than attempting to illuminate the difficult by the obscure.

But the violinist example is nothing like this. Finding yourself plugged into a famous unconscious violinist might be every bit as bizarre as coming across a mutant cockroach. But while your response to the cockroach case may well be confused at best, it is difficult to imagine that this is so of the violinist case. If you are like most people, your response is quite clear and unequivocal: Morality simply does not require us to make such sacrifices on behalf of others, even others who have the same right to life that we have. The mere fact that the violinist case is so unusual, then, cannot count against its use in the good samaritan argument.

What about the complaint that a given example is impossible? Here, too, we must distinguish between two sorts of complaint: the complaint that a given example is physically or technically impossible, and the complaint that a given example is logically or conceptually impossible. Suppose that an example involves no logical contradiction, but is such that, at least at present, there is no way for it to occur. This certainly seems to describe the violinist example. But why should this be a problem?

Suppose, for example, that you had been asked your response to the following scenario: You are driving a car when the brakes suddenly fail, and you can either steer left and run over five people or right and run over one. There is nothing difficult to understand about this example and your response to it is presumably quite clear. But now suppose that I add that this car you are driving is powered by a tiny nuclear reactor in the glove compartment. This makes the case fantastic, but there is no reason to suppose that this feature of the example could alter the clarity or significance of your reaction to it. And the same goes for the violinist example. The fact that the technology involved in making the violinist dependent on you is exotic rather than mundane is morally irrelevant.

If an example comes closer to being logically impossible, on the other hand, then serious problems will indeed arise. Suppose, for example, that you are asked whether it would be permissible for you to travel back in time and assassinate Hitler before he was guilty of committing any crimes. To the extent that one views time travel as conceptually incoherent, one may well be unable to formulate any clear response to the question. But, of course, the violinist case is nothing like this, either. I conclude that the cogency of the good samaritan argument is not threatened by the oddness of the violinist example.

Let us now consider the case of a critic of abortion who concedes, at least for the sake of the argument, that the premises of the good samaritan argument seem to be true and that the argument itself seems to be formally sound, but who complains that he nonetheless finds the argument as a whole entirely unpersuasive. It may be tempting for the defender of abortion simply to label such a critic irrational and to leave the argument at that. But such complacency is irresponsible. Sometimes it is not unreasonable to remain unmoved by an argument even when one can find no reason to reject any of its premises and can detect no flaw in its reasoning. Many people, for example, can see that all of the premises of Zeno's paradoxes of motion are true, yet if they are unable to follow mathematical arguments making use of calculus, they may prove to be unable to understand how the paradoxes can successfully be dissolved. But surely this does not mean that they should therefore stop believing that things move, or even that they should seriously doubt that they do. A critic of abortion may find that he responds to the good samaritan argument in the same way, and responding in this way need not be unreasonable, let alone irrational.

It may be that there is nothing that can be said in response to this kind of concern. If you find such arguments to be entirely without force, then it may be that you would also find any possible argument in defense of such arguments also to be entirely without force, and for precisely the same reason: that they ultimately issue in conclusions that you find you simply cannot accept (in this case, the conclusion that it is unreasonable not be persuaded by sound arguments that make use of fantastic examples). If this is so in your case, then I believe that I can do no more than to acknowledge that it need not be unreasonable for you to remain unmoved by the good samaritan argument and ask that in return you acknowledge that those who do find themselves moved by it are reasonable in believing that they have provided a sound defense of their position. I suspect, however, that there is at least something more that can be done to try to open your mind to the subjective force of such arguments, and so I will briefly try to do so.

The first thing to do is to note that in the case of Zeno's argument, it is the conclusion itself that is fantastic, while in the case of the good samaritan argument, it is the example used in order to reach the conclusion that some find objectionably bizarre. Some people, of course, may find that, subjectively, wild examples are as impotent as wild conclusions. But I suspect that many others will not. I believe that many people who are unmoved by arguments that seem to establish wildly counterintuitive conclusions will find that they can be moved by arguments that use wildly unrealistic examples to establish conclusions that are themselves neither obviously true nor obviously false. So attending to this distinction may have some effect on whether you are open to being persuaded by the good samaritan argument.

In addition, while the claim that abortion is morally on a par with unplugging yourself from the violinist may strike you as outrageous, I suspect that the conclusion that motion does not exist will seem even more obviously false to you. If you are inclined to insist that you find the two claims equally unacceptable, there is probably little more that I can say other than to suggest that you consider that many intelligent, reasonable people find the former claim to be at least plausible, and some of them believe it is actually true, while no one seriously doubts that the latter claim is simply false. Again, some people may find that the claim made within the good samaritan argument is as absurd as the conclusion resulting from Zeno's, but I suspect that many others will not.

A further consideration is this: I have asked you to assume at least for the sake of the argument that you agree with the good samaritan argument's premises and that, in particular, you agree that there is no morally relevant difference between the violinist case and the pregnancy case. But if you find the argument to be completely lacking in persuasive force, I strongly suspect that you do not, in fact, believe that the two cases are morally on a par. If I am right about this, of course, this does not show that you will find the argument persuasive if you are later convinced that it is objectively sound. But I suggest, to the extent that this is possible, that you ask yourself whether you really believe that you would be entirely unmoved by the argument if you were really convinced that every substantive objection you had to the analogy could be decisively answered. This is not an easy question to answer, but I suspect that in many cases it will turn out that it is belief in the argument's objective flaws that largely underwrites confidence in its subjective emptiness.

Finally, I will add a few observations based on discussions I have had about the violinist example over the past few years with students and colleagues.[5] This sampling base is still relatively small, but I suspect that my comments may have force for at least some readers. The first thing I would note is this: I have had a number of students tell me that they were opposed to abortion before they read Thomson's article and that they were still opposed to abortion after they studied it, but that Thomson's argument had convinced them that abortion is morally permissible in cases of pregnancy arising from rape. They were convinced that this was so because they were convinced (as are many people) that the violinist analogy is successful in rape cases, but only in rape cases. It is true that in some obvious respects this is a relatively small change in their view. But the point remains: They changed their view about abortion precisely to the extent that they believed that the violinist analogy was accurate. They thought it was accurate only in a very narrow range of cases, and so they changed their view in only a very narrow range of cases. But in the narrow range of cases about which they were convinced that the analogy held, it had subjective force to them despite the fact that it is so artificial.

A related phenomenon worth noting is this: When I teach Thomson's article, I begin by presenting her argument in the strongest possible way before moving on to present objections to the argument. Virtually every time I have presented the argument, there have been at least one or two students who have expressed the sort of attitude that I have been

---

[5] What I say in what follows is consistent with my experience teaching other articles that make use of similarly artificial examples, but I will limit myself here to my impressions based on teaching Thomson's paper in particular.

considering here: that the weirdness of the example makes them feel that their opposition to abortion is not in the least challenged by the argument. Yet every time this has happened, I have also found that when I go on to identify potentially serious disanalogies, these students become much more confident in their rejection of the argument. Indeed, I have found that it is often the students who claim to find the argument simply absurd who do the best job of identifying such disanalogies. The lesson again seems to be that the argument did have some initial force for them despite its weirdness and despite their own initial belief that it didn't. People do not become more confident that motion exists after they learn how to dissolve Zeno's paradoxes because they are not in the least persuaded that motion doesn't exist in the first place. But my experience has been that virtually everyone who rejects the argument based upon the weirdness of the violinist example feels significantly more confident in rejecting the argument after they have identified important disanalogies between the violinist and pregnancy cases. This again suggests that the argument had some subjective force to them to begin with, despite their claims to the contrary. None of this, of course, counts as proof that you should be persuaded by the good samaritan argument if you accept its premises. Arguing about whether an argument should be persuasive is in a sense like arguing about whether a joke is funny. But I do suspect nonetheless that at least some readers will find that these considerations make them feel less certain that they can simply dismiss the good samaritan argument without considering whether there are sound objections to the argument itself.

I have argued that the weirdness of the violinist example does not threaten the objective validity of the good samaritan argument, and I have tried to respond to the concerns of the person who finds such arguments utterly unpersuasive even when they are formally sound. In all of this, my attitude toward the weirdness of the violinist example has been defensive. But it is also worth noting that in one important respect the weirdness of the violinist example is a virtue, and not merely not a flaw. This is so because focusing our attention on bizarre cases can help us to avoid succumbing to an unwarranted form of moral conservatism. Although I have been treating abortion as a discrete moral problem, virtually no one who has an opinion about abortion thinks of it entirely in this way. Many critics of abortion, for example, see the relatively widespread acceptance of abortion as part of a larger decline in traditional family values. Similarly, many defenders of abortion see the protection of access to abortion as part of a larger defense of equality for women. When we engage in discussions about abortion with those with whom we disagree, it may often be that we end up retaining our initial views about abortion in particular, at least in part, because even though the explicit focus of the debate has been on abortion in particular, we have been subtly and tacitly influenced by our associating abortion with these broader concerns. In addition, it may be that we retain our views about abortion at least in part because we have or perceive ourselves to have a personal interest in abortion's being available (or in its being unavailable). We can come to see that this is what we are doing (if it is what we are doing) only by considering our response to a case that we take to be relevantly similar to abortion in all respects except for its being so unusual that it allows us temporarily to set aside these larger issues and personal interests. That is precisely what the violinist example attempts to provide. So if our responses to the two cases differ, and if we can identify no further relevant disanalogies, we should take this as reason to revise our assessment of the abortion case, and not as reason to doubt the relevance of the violinist case. And all of this, it is important to stress, is perfectly consistent with the belief that our moral views should be developed with an aim toward making them appropriate to the realities and regularities of everyday life. It is because we are concerned with abortion as it typically is that we begin with its distinguishing features; it is because we wish to attain a more clear and impartial view of it that we then attempt to consider these distinguishing features more clearly by abstracting away from the familiar context that may lull us into moral complacency or prejudice.

It might be objected to all of this that our intuitions about such peculiar cases are not to be trusted, that claiming to discern our deepest moral values by focusing on such artifical cases is akin to claiming to get in touch with some deeper reality by taking LSD. But this analogy seems to me to get things backwards. In the case of LSD, we understand how use of the drug interferes with the normal functioning of the brain and thus leads to distorted perceptions, and as a result we are likely to view the perceptions of reality that we have while we are under the influence of the drug as less reliable than those we have when we are free of its influences. But in the case of abortion, what we understand is that in the real world abortion is connected to many other issues and interests that can distort our judgments about it as a moral issue on its own. As a result, it is the artificial cases that permit us to avoid distortion, rather than the realistic ones. In any event, I will assume for the remainder of this chapter that we accept the legitimacy of arguing from such examples.

The question now is: Is there a morally relevant difference between the violinist case and the pregnancy case?

4.3. THE TACIT CONSENT OBJECTION

There is at least one obvious difference between the two cases that seems plainly to be of moral significance. In the case of you and the violinist, the situation in which you find that there is a violinist whose life is dependent on you does not arise from any voluntary action of yours. But when a woman becomes pregnant, except in cases where the pregnancy arises from rape, the situation in which she finds that there is a fetus whose life is dependent on her does arise, at least in part, from a voluntary action of hers. If she had not voluntarily engaged in sexual intercourse, she would not have become pregnant. Moreover, the distinction between situations that arise from voluntary actions and those that do not seems plainly to be a morally relevant one. And so, according to this objection, even if the violinist analogy is successful in every other respect, it still establishes only that abortion is permissible in cases involving rape.[6] Your being plugged into the violinist against your will is like a woman being impregnated against her will, that is, but it is not like a woman becoming pregnant as a result of consensual intercourse.

4.3.1. Consent versus Responsibility

The objection that the good samaritan argument is undermined by the moral significance of the difference between situations that arise from voluntary actions and those that do not can be developed in two importantly distinct ways. The distinction corresponds to the two components of Thomson's initial reply to this objection in the following passage:

I suppose we may take it as a datum that in a case of pregnancy due to rape the mother has not given the unborn person a right to the use of her body for food and shelter. Indeed, in what pregnancy could it be supposed that the mother has given the unborn person such a right? It is not as if there were unborn persons drifting about the world, to whom a woman who wants a child says "I invite you in." (1971: 138)

---

[6] This objection to Thomson's argument is ubiquitous in the literature. In addition to the proponents of the objection discussed in this and the following section, see also, for example, Wennberg (1985: 160–2), Wilcox (1989: 216ff.), Warren (1973: 232), Feinberg (1978: 143), Boss (1993: 102), Donagan (1977: 169–70).

Thomson's response to the objection that the good samaritan argument fails in cases where pregnancy arises from voluntary intercourse can be understood as resting on the conjunction of the following two claims: that the fetus cannot acquire the right to the use of the woman's body unless we can suppose that the woman has *given* the fetus this right, and that we cannot suppose that the woman has given the fetus this right unless she has *explicitly* agreed to do so. Even in cases of voluntary intercourse, a woman does not explicitly agree to give the fetus the right to the use of her body. And so, if these two claims are correct, then if the good samaritan argument is successful in rape cases, it is successful in nonrape cases as well.

But each of these claims can be challenged. The second claim can be challenged by appealing to the plausible notion that sometimes a person consents to a state of affairs not by explicitly agreeing to accept it, but by doing some voluntary action that amounts to *tacitly* agreeing to accept it. The objection to the good samaritan argument that arises from the denial of the second claim therefore maintains that because the woman's pregnancy in nonrape cases is the (foreseeable) result of a voluntary action of hers, she should be understood as having tacitly waived her right to expel the fetus or (what amounts to the same thing) as having tacitly granted the fetus a right to stay. I will call this the tacit consent objection. The first claim can be challenged by appealing to the plausible notion that a person can acquire the right to your assistance when his need for your assistance (foreseeably) arises from a voluntary action of yours on the grounds that you are responsible for his state of need, even if in doing the action that led to his being in a state of need you did not "give" him the right to your assistance either explicitly or tacitly. It is plausible, for example, to maintain that an innocent bystander who is accidentally shot by a hunter and who as a result now needs the hunter's aid in order to survive has acquired a right to the hunter's assistance even if by voluntarily choosing to go hunting the hunter cannot reasonably be understood as having agreed, even tacitly, to grant this right to those whose need for assistance arises from his voluntary actions. The objection to the good samaritan argument that arises from the denial of Thomson's first claim therefore maintains that because the woman in nonrape cases is responsible for the fact that there is a fetus whose life now depends on the use of her body in order to survive, the fetus has acquired a right to the use of her body even if the woman has not "given" this right to the fetus, explicitly or otherwise. I will call this the responsibility objection. Both objections are prima facie quite plausible, and if either or both can be sustained, then the good samaritan argument will fail in cases in which the woman's pregnancy arises, at least in part, from a voluntary action of hers.

4.3.2. *The Significance of the Objection*

The claim that when pregnancy arises from the woman's voluntary action the fetus has acquired the right to the use of her body for as long as it needs it to survive seems to many people to be a devastating objection to the good samaritan argument, and Thomson herself does not provide a satisfactory reply to it. She responds by suggesting that a woman who becomes pregnant because of contraceptive failure cannot reasonably be thought of as having agreed to or as being responsible for the pregnancy,[7] and by downplaying the significance of the claim even if it is sustained:

It seems to me that the argument we are looking at can establish at most that there are some cases in which the unborn person has a right to the use of its mother's body, and therefore some cases in which abortion is unjust killing. There is room for much discussion and argument as to precisely which, if any. But I think we should sidestep this issue and leave it open, for at any rate the argument certainly does not establish that all abortion is unjust killing (1971: 121).

This reply is unsatisfactory for several reasons. First, and perhaps most obviously, even if one concedes to Thomson the case of contraceptive failure, the response itself seems to concede that the fetus does acquire the right to the use of the pregnant woman's body in cases where the woman and her partner neglected to use contraception in the first place. A significant number of pregnancies arise in just this way, and the result would then be that, so far as Thomson's defense of the good samaritan argument is concerned, it is morally impermissible for women to have abortions under such circumstances.

Second, and more importantly, it can plausibly be argued that since contraceptive devices are known to be imperfect, a woman who has intercourse while using one consents to or is responsible for the results since she knowingly and voluntarily runs the risk of becoming

---

7 She is not completely explicit about this, but this is plainly the point of her examples of bars or screens failing to prevent unwanted burglars or people-seeds from getting into a house through a window.

pregnant.[8] A hunter, for example, can plausibly be held responsible for taking care of an innocent bystander she accidentally shoots, even if she takes every reasonable precaution to avoid such an accident short of not going hunting in the first place. So if the good samaritan argument cannot provide a defense of abortion in the case where contraception is not used, then it may well prove unable to provide a defense of abortion even in the case where contraception is used. And if that is so, then the good samaritan argument will provide, at most, a defense of abortion in cases of rape.

This leads to a third problem. Many proponents of the rights-based argument against abortion, though far from all of them, wish to (or are at least willing to) make an exception to their opposition to abortion in cases where the pregnancy arises from rape. But they are confronted with a problem. Since their opposition to abortion in typical cases arises from the conviction that abortion violates the fetus's right to life, it is difficult to see how they could consistently treat rape cases differently from nonrape cases. A fetus conceived as a result of rape, after all, surely has the same right to life as any other fetus. But if the good samaritan argument is accepted and the tacit consent or responsibility objection is then sustained, then this problem with the abortion critic's position will be solved: Abortion will prove to be impermissible in nonrape cases not because the fetus has a right to life, but because it has acquired a right to the use of the woman's body. And since the fetus will not have acquired this right in rape cases, on this account, the exception for rape cases will then prove well grounded. And this in turn renders Thomson's response to these objections unacceptable. Since only a very small fraction of abortions involve pregnancies arising from rape, and since a significant portion of those who generally oppose abortion are willing to make an exception in such cases anyhow, it will turn out that if the tacit consent or responsibility objection can be sustained, then Thomson's defense of the good samaritan argument will prove a greater contribution to the position held by critics of abortion than to the position held by its defenders. While Thomson is surely right that these objections would not defeat her general claim that abortion can sometimes be morally permissible even if the fetus has a right to life, therefore, she is just as surely wrong to sidestep the issue. It is crucial to consider whether the

---

[8] This point has been pressed recently by Lee (1996: 118–19) among others.

good samaritan argument can be extended to cover cases in which the woman voluntarily engages in intercourse without using contraception. And although Thomson herself not only refrains from insisting that the argument can be extended in this way but seems tacitly to concede that it may prove incapable of being so extended, I will argue here that it can.

The tacit consent objection and the responsibility objection must be considered separately, and I will focus on the former in the remainder of this section and on the latter in the whole of the next. But before doing so, it is important to make explicit one assumption that I will be making in my treatment of both. I will be assuming that in cases that do not involve rape, a woman who engages in sexual intercourse with a man can properly be characterized as acting voluntarily. This assumption is worth noting for two reasons. One is that it has been denied by some people, including some prominent feminists (e.g., MacKinnon 1984). On their account, intercourse in nonrape cases is often (or perhaps always) involuntary, or at least is not voluntary in any meaningful sense. Although the justification for this claim varies somewhat from one proponent to another, the typical argument maintains that women often have, or at least are often made to feel that they have, no genuine alternative to submitting to the pressures exerted on them by their partners. And if this is so, the argument runs, then their choices cannot justly be treated as free. I will not argue against such a view here, but I will not make use of it either. I am concerned in this book to argue that the case against abortion can be defeated on terms that critics of abortion generally accept, and surely critics of abortion will not generally accept the claim that nonrape instances of intercourse should be construed as involuntary. If one does accept the view that nonrape instances of intercourse should be construed as involuntary, then this will count as one way to rescue the good samaritan argument from the charge that it succeeds, if at all, only in cases involving rape. But for purposes of this book, what is important is to see that the good samaritan argument can be vindicated even if it is deprived of such support.

The other reason this assumption is worth noting is that although this analysis of what would typically be described as voluntary intercourse is one that most critics of abortion will surely reject, it in fact closely parallels a claim that many critics of abortion persist in advancing. This is the claim that women who have abortions should themselves be understood as victims of the practice. As one such critic has put it, "in many cases women are the second victims of abortion. In one sense they choose, but in a deeper and more significant sense, they succumb, because they see no realistic alternative. They feel coerced, their situation presents itself to them as leaving no other choice, they experience an absence of choice" (Schwarz 1990: 128).[9] If this claim is meant to highlight the hardships an unwanted pregnancy can impose on women, then it is well taken. But it often seems to be invoked as a way for the critic of abortion to allow himself to claim that abortion is an evil act without having to accuse women who have abortions of voluntarily committing evil acts. And in this sense, the claim is difficult for such critics to sustain. For if a woman who has an abortion because her boyfriend threatens to leave her if she doesn't is not held to be responsible for her choice, then it is difficult to see why a woman who has intercourse with her boyfriend because he threatens to leave her if she doesn't should be held responsible for hers. And if she is not responsible for her having engaged in sexual intercourse in the first place, then the pregnancy that results from her action should be treated as on a par with one that results from rape, a result that few critics of abortion would be willing to accept. In any event, I will be assuming here that women who engage in intercourse in nonrape cases should be understood as acting freely and voluntarily. The question, then, is whether granting this assumption, the good samaritan argument can still overcome the problems raised by the tacit consent and responsibility objections.

4.3.3. The Objection's Two Claims

I will begin with the tacit consent objection, which seems to be the more common version of the objection grounded in the distinction between voluntary and involuntary acts, and which, indeed, is often pressed even by those of Thomson's readers who are generally sympathetic with her conclusions. As one such writer has put it, "the fetus *does* have a right to use the pregnant woman's body [in nonrape cases] because she is (partly) responsible for its existence. By engaging in intercourse, knowing that this may result in the creation of a person inside her body, she *implicitly gives* the resulting person a right to remain" (Steinbock 1992: 78, second emphases added). The tacit consent objection turns on two claims: that because the woman's act of intercourse is voluntary, she should be understood as having tacitly consented to something with

---

[9] Similarly, Reardon writes that "data suggest that rather than 'choosing' abortion, many women, perhaps even most, are just 'submitting' to abortion" and characterizes this as "the illusion of choice" (1996: 140–1).

respect to the state of affairs in which there is now a fetus developing inside of her body, and that what she should be understood as having tacitly consented to with respect to this state of affairs is, in particular, the fetus's having a right to have the state of affairs continue for as long as this is necessary for it to remain alive. I will argue that both claims should be rejected.

4.3.4. Rejecting the First Claim

Let me begin with the first claim, the claim that the fact that the woman's act of intercourse is voluntary counts as evidence of her having tacitly consented to something with respect to the resulting state of affairs. There is surely something plausible sounding about this, since if the notion of tacit consent is to make sense at all it must arise from voluntary rather than involuntary actions. But I want to argue that this appearance arises from a confusion between a person's (a) voluntarily bringing about a certain state of affairs, and (b) voluntarily doing an action foreseeing that this may lead to a certain state of affairs. My claim is that only (a) is a plausible candidate for grounding tacit consent in the relation between an agent and a state of affairs she is (or is partly) responsible for having brought about, and that any plausible attempt to apply tacit consent to nonrape cases of pregnancy must appeal to (b).[10] If this analysis is correct, then we have no grounds for concluding that the woman who has intercourse without contraception has tacitly consented to anything with respect to the state of affairs in which a fetus is now developing inside her body.

To see this, let us first consider what one would have to believe about tacit consent in general in order to affirm the particular claim that when a woman has voluntary intercourse without contraception and becomes pregnant as a result she has tacitly consented to give the fetus a right to stay. Assuming that the fetus is a person with the same right to life as you or I, the general structure of the woman's situation is this: A person has done a voluntary act that has caused a certain state of affairs to exist, where this state of affairs is one in which a second person is now infringing on some right that the first person has to something.[11] Our question

---

[10] For two possible exceptions to this claim, see footnote 16.

[11] This formulation might seem to beg the question, since if we conclude that the voluntariness of the first person's doing the act counts as evidence of his having consented to the resulting state of affairs, then it won't be the case that the state

is: What conditions would be sufficient to make it be the case that the first person has tacitly consented to give the second person the right to continue doing this? We could say that it is sufficient that the person's act be voluntary and that it cause the resulting state of affairs. But this would imply that by voluntarily acting, a person consents to the continuation of a state of affairs he produces even if he had no knowledge that his action could lead to such a state of affairs. And this would amount to saying that if a woman has intercourse without contraception and does not understand that intercourse can lead to conception, then she has tacitly consented to carry the fetus to term. Since this is plainly implausible, we must at least add the requirement that the act cause the state of affairs in a manner that is foreseeable to the person performing the act.

Let us then assume that these three conditions – voluntariness, causality, and foreseeability – must be accepted as necessary conditions for tacit consent in order to avoid producing implications that are plainly unacceptable.[12] It seems correct that all three conditions are satisfied in the case where a woman's pregnancy arises from voluntary intercourse: Her action was voluntary, was the proximate cause of the pregnancy that now infringes on her right to control her body, and was the cause of this state of affairs in a manner that was foreseeable to her (assuming that she understood that intercourse without contraception can lead to pregnancy). But all of this will show that a woman who engages in intercourse without contraception has tacitly consented to something with respect to the resulting state of affairs only if these general conditions are not merely necessary for tacit consent, but sufficient. And I want now to argue that the claim that these conditions are sufficient for having consented to something with respect to the resulting state of affairs is implausible.

One could, of course, argue against the claim that these conditions are sufficient for consent by arguing that no conditions short of explicit consent are sufficient. But I want to identify an implication of the claim that these conditions are sufficient that should be unacceptable to all critics of abortion, including those who embrace the general notion of

---

of affairs involves the second person's infringing on some right of his. Strictly speaking, we should say that the state of affairs in question is one in which the second person is doing something that counts as infringing on the first person's right to something *unless* the first person does or has done something to grant the other person the right to do this.

[12] These requirements are typically acknowledged and defended by those who defend the tacit consent objection. See, for example, Langer (1992).

tacit consent. I want to assume, therefore, that tacit consent in and of itself is a perfectly reasonable doctrine and to argue by means of an example that puts this assumption in a favorable light. So let us focus on a relatively uncontroversial instance of tacit consent: If you voluntarily leave some money on the table in a restaurant as you are leaving after your meal is over, then you have tacitly waived your right to it and have consented to allow the waiter to have it. You have made no explicit announcement that you intend to relinquish control of the money, of course, and have said nothing explicit that would indicate that you wish the money to go to the waiter rather than the chef or the busboy or the owner, but it nonetheless seems reasonable to maintain that your action amounts to a tacit declaration of just this sort. And surely it is the voluntariness of your act that makes this assessment reasonable. If you had instead left the money on the table because you had been forced to do so by a knife-wielding assailant, we would not be inclined to say that you had tacitly consented to anything about it.

But now consider the cases of Bill and Ted, each of whom has voluntarily exited a restaurant having voluntarily placed some money on the table at which he was dining alone. In Bill's case, the state of affairs in which he is no longer in the restaurant and some of the money that was originally in his pocket is now on the table is a state of affairs he brought about voluntarily: After he finished eating, he stood up, took some money out of his wallet, placed it on the table, and walked out the door. In Ted's case, the same state of affairs is not one which he brought about voluntarily, but rather one which foreseeably arose from a voluntary action of his. As he sat down to eat, Ted discovered that the crumpled wad of dollar bills in his pants pocket made him uncomfortable, so he put them down on the table while he was eating, intending to put most of them back in his pocket when it was time to leave. A friend who was leaving the restaurant when Ted sat down saw this and warned Ted not to put the money there on the grounds that he might forget about it, but Ted foolishly refused, and when the friend urged that he at least tie a piece of string around his finger to remind himself to put most of the money back in his pocket before leaving, Ted declined, saying that he didn't like the way having a piece of string tied around his finger "made him feel" while he was trying to enjoy a meal. Unfortunately, Ted was so lost in the rapture of his meal that he did indeed forget to put most of the money back in his pocket, and about ten minutes after he left the restaurant, he suddenly realized his mistake and headed back to clear things up.

Now clearly Ted has no one to blame but himself. It is not as if someone else forcibly removed the money from his pocket and put it on the table. Still, it is surely unreasonable to insist that by putting the money on the table when he sat down Ted tacitly agreed to let the waiter keep all of it if, as a foreseeable consequence of this act, the money was still on the table when he left.[13] Yet if the three conditions identified as necessary conditions for tacit consent are also taken to be sufficient conditions, there can be no way to account for the distinction between the cases of Bill and Ted. In Ted's case, just as in Bill's, all three conditions for waiving one's rights are satisfied: Ted's putting his money on the table without tying a piece of string on his finger was voluntary, was the proximate cause of his leaving the money in the restaurant, which in turn was a foreseeable (though unintended) consequence of his act. Maintaining that these three conditions are sufficient for tacit consent, then, renders one unable to distinguish betwen the case of Bill and Ted precisely because the conditions overlook the distinction between (a) and (b) noted above. The cases are relevantly different because Bill voluntarily brings about the state of affairs in which he has left the restaurant with his money still on the table, while Ted does not. Ted voluntarily puts the money on the table, foreseeing that this may result in the state of affairs in which he has left it in the restaurant. And the lesson of this is that even if voluntarily bringing about a certain state of affairs constitutes consent to bear the burdens it imposes on you (as in the case of Bill), it does not follow that voluntarily doing an action foreseeing that this may lead to a certain state of affairs constitutes such consent (as in the case of Ted).[14]

---

[13] In response to this example, Michael Davis has suggested that even though it is clear that Ted has not waived his right to the use of his money, it may still be that he has become liable in virtue of something like a "quasi-contract": One could argue that Ted's act of putting the money on the table is negligent because it foreseeably risks causing the confusion, harm, and so on, that may result from the money being left there, and that negligence of this sort warrants treating Ted *as if* he has agreed to bear the resulting costs even if, strictly speaking, he has not so agreed. On this account, however, the tacit consent objection slides into the responsibility objection, and if my response to that objection in the following section is successful, then Davis's suggestion must be rejected as well.

[14] For those who find plausible the common claim that voluntarily crossing a national border constitutes tacit consent to be governed by that nation's laws, a similar lesson arises from the real-life case of William Barloon and David Daliberti, who accidentally strayed across the border from Kuwait into Iraq while trying to visit a friend with the United Nations force monitoring the area. Their eight-year jail sentence was universally condemned as an outrageous case of injustice (they were

This analysis has the following implications for the application of tacit consent theory to cases of voluntary intercourse.[15] A woman whose pregnancy arises from voluntary sexual intercourse has not voluntarily brought about the state of affairs in which the fetus is making demands

released shortly thereafter), yet on the account of consent I am arguing against here, there would be no legitimate cause for complaint. The maximum sentence for illegally entering Iraq is 20 years in prison, and the two men went on their trip voluntarily, which was the proximate cause of their crossing the border, which was in turn a foreseeable (but unintended) consequence of their actions (Powell (1995: A-3)).

[15] It might be objected that very little, if anything, about cases of voluntary intercourse follows from my analysis of the sufficient conditions for consent on the grounds that the analysis itself arises from a relatively trivial example. Relatively little is at stake in the question of who has the right to the use of (what was at least initially) Ted's money, but a great deal is at stake in the question of who has the right to the use of the pregnant woman's body. So one might well think that even if Ted has the right to take the money back from the waiter, it does not follow that the woman has the right to take the use of her body back from the fetus, and that attending to the example of tipping can thus do little to illuminate the moral problem of abortion.

I certainly agree that the woman's right to abort the fetus does not follow from Ted's right to reclaim his money. There may be any number of important differences between the two cases. But viewing this as a problem for my analysis misconstrues the purpose of the example. I am not arguing that the woman has a right to abort the fetus because she has not consented to refrain from doing so. Rather, I am responding to an argument that claims to show that she lacks the right to abort the fetus because she has consented to refrain from doing so. That argument turns on the claim that the voluntariness of the action which produced the state of affairs justifies the attribution of consent, not on the claim that she is obligated to sustain the fetus because its very life is at stake. And the example of Bill and Ted demonstrates that this foundational claim about consent is untenable.

It may be worth noting, however, that the importance of the distinction between (a) and (b) for which I have been arguing would be revealed even if we focused on less straightforward and more controversial examples of consent. Suppose one believed, for example, that if you take off your coat and put it in the arms of a homeless person who needs the coat in order to survive the winter, then you have tacitly consented to let him keep the coat for as long as he needs it. It might be thought that in some respects this is more representative of what is at stake in cases of abortion. Still, this would not support the conclusion that if you take your coat off on a windy day because you want to experience the pleasure of a chilling breeze against your bare skin, then you must let the homeless person keep it if, as a foreseeable (but unintended) consequence of your action, the coat is blown into his arms. Again, there may be good reason to believe that you would be obligated to let the homeless person keep the coat, but the reason cannot plausibly be grounded in the claim that you have consented to let him keep it, and that is the claim I am concerned to address in this section. I have avoided appealing to such cases (you let someone into your house because it is cold outside, etc.) in

on her body. Rather, she has voluntarily brought about the state of affairs in which a man is having sexual intercourse with her, foreseeing that this might bring about the further state of affairs. In this respect, she is like Ted rather than like Bill. And since Ted's relation to the unwanted state of affairs he has foreseeably produced is not sufficient to warrant the claim that he has consented to bear the burdens it imposes on him, the same is true of her. We cannot justifiably insist that she has tacitly consented to waive the right to the control of her body. Suppose that once she discovers that she is pregnant she endeavors to have the pregnancy terminated. Then she is like Ted when he returns to the restaurant to retrieve most of his money after he discovers that he has (foreseeably, but not intentionally) left all of it on the table. It is clear that in Ted's case, we must take this to mean that he has not agreed to waive his right to the control over the money. Similarly, we must take this to mean that she did not give and has not given the fetus a right to the use of her body. The mere fact that her pregnancy resulted from voluntary intercourse for which she is (partly) responsible, then, cannot reasonably be understood as evidence that she has consented to anything with respect to the state of affairs in which there is now a fetus making unwanted demands on her body.[16]

developing my argument for the importance of the distinction between (a) and (b) because it is less clear that people who believe in tacit consent will agree that you have consented to let the person keep the coat (or stay in your house) for as long as he needs to even in the case where you deliberately hand it to him (or let him in; perhaps you mean only to let him use the coat until you are ready to go home or to remain in your home until you are ready to go to bed), and I want to work from a case that puts the tacit consent position itself in the most favorable possible light.

[16] Two exceptions might be urged here. One is the case of a woman who freely chooses to have an embryo implanted in her. This does seem to be a case in which she voluntarily brings about the state of affairs in which there is a fetus making demands on her body, rather than one in which she merely foresees that her action may lead to such a state of affairs. It thus seems plausible to think of it as a genuine case in which, if one belives in tacit consent, one will have good grounds for thinking that consent has been given. The other is what might be called the case of intentional conception, one in which the woman deliberately refrained from using contraception because she wanted to become pregnant. She does seem to do more than merely foresee that the subsequent state of affairs may arise, and so it can again seem plausible to suppose that in this case she has consented to it.

These cases, of course, would represent at most a tiny fraction of abortions, so even if accepted they pose no real threat to the position taken in this chapter. Still, it is worth noting that while each seems plausible, each also raises certain difficulties. In the case of the embryo implant, for example, we would need to be

Let me make one further point about the distinction between voluntarily bringing about a state of affairs and voluntarily acting with the foresight that a state of affairs may result: its importance is revealed by seeing what happens when it is ignored, and it is ignored in an analogy that is commonly offered by critics of the good samaritan argument. Langer, for example, motivates his defense of the tacit consent objection with the following example:

Imagine a person who freely chooses to join the Society of Music Lovers, knowing that there was a 1 in 100 chance of being plugged into the violinist if she joins the society. She certainly does not desire to be plugged into the violinist, but at the same time she desires to join the society, and feels the one in one hundred odds are an acceptable risk. She goes ahead and joins, and much to her chagrin, her name is selected as the person to be plugged into the violinist. Is it unreasonable to say that she has waived her right to control over her own body? I think not.[17]

On this account, the woman who risks an unwanted pregnancy by voluntarily engaging in intercourse is like the woman who risks being plugged into the violinist by voluntarily joining the Society of Music Lovers. And since the second woman clearly waives the right to the control of her body, so does the first.

The problem with the analogy is this. Langer says that the second woman "freely chooses to *join*" the society, and this sounds as if it means that her voluntary action is the act of agreeing to abide by the society's

careful about specifying the content of the rights waiver that was being imagined; as Sara Worley has pointed out to me, it may seem implausible to suppose that a woman who consents to have multiple embryos implanted in her as a part of her infertility treatment should be understood as waiving the right later to remove one in order to improve the prospects of survival for the others. And as Marcia Baron has noted, such a woman might also be understood as tacitly agreeing only to bear at least one child by virtue of the procedure without having agreed to bear all of them. In the case of the intentional conception, on the other hand, there is a sense in which it does not seem quite right to say that, strictly speaking, the woman intentionally becomes pregnant. She does what she hopes will lead to pregnancy, but there are many factors beyond her control that may lead one to conclude that the pregnancy should not be understood as a state of affairs that she voluntarily creates. I will leave the question about how to treat both cases open, and thus accept the possiblity that my argument against the tacit consent objection does not apply in either or both of these cases. Since abortions arising from such cases are presumably very rare, however, this is at most a very small concession.

17 Although Langer does not note this, the same example is also used to make the same point by Warren (1973: 232–3).

rules. And since the society's rules include entering every member in a lottery to decide who will be plugged into the violinist, it follows that her act is the act of agreeing to be entered into the lottery, from which it of course follows that if her name is selected she must be understood as having waived her right to the control of her body. This is because her voluntary action *is* the act of entering the lottery, rather than an action with the foreseeable consequence that others will treat her as if she had. In order for the two cases to be parallel, then, we must assume that the first woman has similarly agreed to enter her name in a comparable pregnancy lottery by virtue of her having engaged in voluntary intercourse. But we cannot assume that she has so agreed because whether or not she has is precisely the question we are attempting to answer.[18]

The problem with the analogy becomes more apparent if we set it straight by simply having the second woman freely choose to do some action foreseeing that the action may lead to her finding herself plugged into the violinist. It is tempting to suppose that this can be accomplished simply by picturing a case such as one in which the society was known to have hired kidnappers who were lurking in the park at night and you nonetheless voluntarily engaged in the act of walking through the park without carrying any protection.[19] Surely in that case, no one will say that by walking in the park you have tacitly consented to remain plugged into the violinist if you are kidnapped. And, indeed, it is common for defenders of abortion to compare a woman who has voluntary intercourse knowing that this may lead to her becoming pregnant to a woman who voluntarily goes for a walk in a dangerous neighborhood knowing that this may lead to her being assaulted (e.g., McDonagh 1996: 43–4, 49–50). Again, surely no one will say that by walking in the dangerous neighborhood, the woman has tacitly consented to being assaulted or that she has tacitly waived her right to resist such assaults, and with deadly force if necessary. But while these sorts of analogy represent an

---

[18] It might be argued that in a society which legally prohibits abortion, a woman who engages in voluntary intercourse enters precisely such a lottery. But even if we agree that a woman in such circumstances does tacitly consent to carry the resulting fetus to term, this will only be because she has tacitly agreed to obey a law, not because she has tacitly waived her right to the control of her body. And the good samaritan argument is designed to show that abortion is morally permissible even if the fetus has the same right to life that you and I have, not to show that it is morally permissible even if it requires violating a legal prohibition.

[19] I myself succumbed to this temptation in an earlier discussion of this objection (Boonin 1997: 296–7).

improvement over the lottery story in terms of the distinction between voluntarily creating a state of affairs and voluntarily acting with the foresight that a state of affairs may result, they are flawed for a different reason. The kidnapper or attacker does something to you that he has no right to do, and it is plausible to suppose that this is the reason that your act cannot count as consenting to allow him to do it. But there is no such culpable agent in the case of the woman whose pregnancy arises from voluntary intercourse, and so one can agree that you do not consent in the kidnapping case while still maintaining that the woman does consent in the voluntary intercourse case.

But this problem with the analogy can be avoided by eliminating the causal role of the culpable agent. So suppose instead that your having become plugged into the violinist was merely the result of a benign computer malfunction. You had voluntarily checked into the hospital on the night of December 31, 1999, for some optional cosmetic surgery, knowing that there was a possibility that a Y2K-related computer error might lead to your having the wrong procedure done, a kind of mistake that you knew occurs from time to time even in the absence of computer errors. Your friends urged you not to take such chances with your body, but you ignored their warnings. And after falling asleep for the evening, you woke up discovering that even though no one had deliberately done anything to you that they weren't supposed to do, you were nonetheless mistakenly plugged into the ailing violinist as a result of a random computer glitch. In this version of the story, there is no culpable human agent who plugs you into the violinist. As in the case of the conception of the fetus resulting from voluntary intercourse, your becoming plugged into the violinist is merely the result of a random occurrence, though one that could only occur because a prior act of yours had made it possible for it to occur. But surely no one will say that because you knew that this random event might occur after you checked yourself into the hospital, your checking yourself in counts as consent to remain plugged into the violinist. And so, by parity of reasoning, we cannot say that because the woman who engaged in voluntary intercourse knew that conception might occur, her engaging in intercourse counts as consent to carry her pregnancy to term.

A proponent of the tacit consent objection, of course, might complain that there is an important difference in the probabilities in the two cases: Such computer errors are relatively rare while pregnancies resulting from voluntary intercourse are not. But this consideration can provide the critic with little comfort. For the analogy can simply be revised so that the chances of a computer error occuring are stipulated to be precisely the same as the chances of conception occurring from a single act of intercourse without contraception. In that case, the proponent of the objection will have to maintain that you truly have consented to remain plugged into the violinist if the computer error occurs, a concession that it is extremely difficult to imagine a critic of abortion making. And even worse, from the point of view of the critic of abortion, the analogy can be revised so that the woman who has intercourse has serious fertility problems, such that conception occurring from an act of intercourse in her case is extraordinarily unlikely, as unlikely as having a doctor mistakenly initiate the wrong procedure on you when you check into a hospital. In that case, the proponent of the tacit consent objection will have to concede that the woman has not given the fetus the right to make use of her body. But surely no critic of abortion will maintain that whether or not abortion violates the fetus's right to life varies with the fertility of the pregnant woman. And so the critic of abortion cannot attempt to rescue the tacit consent objection by appealing to such differences in probabilities.

I have been arguing against the first claim made by the tacit consent objection, the claim that because the woman's act of intercourse is voluntary, she should be understood as having tacitly consented to something with respect to the state of affairs in which there is now a fetus developing inside of her body. My argument to this point has focused on the distinction between deliberately bringing about a state of affairs and deliberately doing an action foreseeing that a given state of affairs may arise as a result. But before turning to the second claim made by the objection, I want to note a further difficulty with the first claim that remains even if we picture the woman as deliberately becoming pregnant rather than merely foreseeably causing her pregnancy. So return for a moment to the case of Bill, who deliberately left some of his money on the restaurant table after his meal and proceeded to walk out the door. Why are we so confident that this counts as evidence that he has consented to transfer his right to control the money to the waiter, rather than to the owner, or the busboy, or the customers at the next table? Or why don't we take it simply as a waiver of his right to the money with the result that whoever sees it first is entitled to take it? Presumably, this is because there is a well-established convention that constitutes the background against which Bill's act is performed. If the act of leaving money on the table took place in a culture where there was no such convention about tipping, then it would be unreasonable to take the act as consenting to transfer the right to the money to the waiter. And this suggests that there is at least one further necessary condition for an act to count as evidence of consent: It must take place in a culture where there is a convention by which it is so understood. Indeed, this is presumably true of explicit consent as well, insofar as a handshake or a signature will be evidence of explicit consent only if it takes place in a context where it is so understood.

But this creates a further problem with the attempt to use tacit consent theory as grounds for raising an objection to the good samaritan argument. It is unclear, to say the least, that in our culture there is such a convention, and it is certainly clear that in cultures that do not treat abortion as immoral there is no such convention. Indeed, in some cultures, there may even be a convention by which some acts of intercourse would best be understood as evidence of consent *not* to carry a resulting pregnancy to term, such as cultures in which there is a conventional limit on the number of children that a woman may have, or that disapprove of children conceived outside of marraige or between members of different races or classes. It seems patently false to insist that a woman in such circumstances tacitly agrees to allow the fetus to remain in her body if she becomes pregnant as a result of her voluntarily engaging in intercourse. If anything, she should be understood as having tacitly agreed *not* to allow the fetus to make use of her body, though I do not mean to press this suggestion here. The point is simply that a person's act cannot reasonably be taken as evidence of tacitly consenting to something unless it takes place in a context in which it is generally understood as constituting such consent.[20]

4.3.5. Rejecting the Second Claim

I have been concerned to this point to argue against the first claim made by the tacit consent objection, the claim that because the woman's act

---

[20] In addition, it is worth noting that not every act is a suitable candidate for counting as evidence of consent to something. If the act is such that refraining from performing it is itself a substantial burden to the agent, then viewing the act as consenting to something amounts to coercing people into consenting to it, and expressions of consent which are coerced are generally recognized to be nonbinding. And, as Smith points out, a strong case can be made for saying that refraining from voluntary intercourse is a substantial enough burden to undermine the suitability of voluntary intercourse as a sign of consenting to anything (1983: 237–8) (though see also Tooley (1983: 48) for a rejoinder).

of intercourse is voluntary, she should be understood as having tacitly consented to something with respect to the state of affairs in which there is now a fetus making demands on her body. If my argument has been successful, then the woman who has intercourse without contraception is not like you if you voluntarily plug yourself into the violinist. Rather, she is like you if you voluntarily engage in some pleasurable activity with the foresight that this might end up causing you to become plugged into the violinist. And in that case, if my analysis of tacit consent has been correct, you have not agreed to give the violinist the right to the use of your body. But let us now suppose that I have been mistaken about this. Let us suppose that the woman whose pregnancy arises from voluntary intercourse is instead like you if you freely walk into the violinist's room, sit down next to him, and deliberately plug yourself in. I will take it that this implies that you have consented to the act of becoming plugged into the violinist. But what follows from this?

At least one thing seems reasonably enough to follow: Suppose that the procedure involved in unplugging you from the violinist is itself somewhat painful and costly. If you were plugged into the violinist involuntarily, then whoever forced you to be plugged in should have to bear the costs of, and compensate you for the suffering involved in, the unplugging. But if you freely plugged yourself in, then you should have to bear these costs on your own. So we might say that freely plugging yourself into the violinist constitutes consent to bear the costs of unplugging yourself. But does it constitute consent to more, and in particular, does it, as the second claim made by the objection maintains, constitute consent to remain plugged in for the nine-month period that the violinist requires? This strikes me as extremely implausible. Suppose that because of your unique compatibility, the violinist will die unless you undergo a series of nine painful bone marrow extractions over the next nine months, and with a clear understanding of the nature of the procedure and its potential risks, you freely volunteer to undergo the first extraction. After the second round of extraction, however, you find that the burden is considerably more than you are willing to bear on his behalf. Do you really believe that it would now be morally impermissible for you to discontinue providing aid to the violinist merely because you began providing aid voluntarily? To say that doing so would be impermissible would be to say that the violinist's right to life does not entitle him to seven more extractions of bone marrow from you if the first two were done involuntarily, but that it does entitle him to seven more extractions from you if the first two were done voluntarily. It is extremely difficult to believe that critics of abortion will be willing to endorse such a view.[21] But unless they are willing to accept it, they must conclude that even if the first claim made by the tacit consent objection is true, and a woman's voluntarily engaging in sexual intercourse really is taken to be evidence of consent to something (and I have already argued that it should not be), the second claim is nonetheless false: Her act cannot reasonably be taken as evidence of consent to keep the fetus in her care for as long as is necessary for the fetus to survive.[22]

One final point merits notice. The tacit consent objection claims that in virtue of her action's being voluntary, the woman whose pregnancy arises from voluntary intercourse should be understood as having tacitly agreed to give up the right to the exclusive control of her body. I have been assuming to this point that the right to control one's body is an alienable one, a right that is at least in principle possible to give away by consent. My claim has simply been that the fact that her engaging in intercourse was voluntary provides no good reason to suppose that she has in fact done this. But the assumption that the right to control one's body is alienable is itself open to doubt. Suppose, after all, that a woman made the following explicit agreement: Give me some money today, and tomorrow you can use my body in any way that you want even if by that time I have changed my mind and no longer want you to. Most of us would think this sort of contract to be simply invalid. As at least one writer sympathetic to the good samaritan argument has urged, "one cannot legitimately enslave oneself by waiving in advance one's right

---

[21] Among other things, as Kamm has pointed out, accepting the view that voluntarily beginning to aid someone makes discontinuing aid impermissible would deter many people from offering aid in the first place. Many people might be genuinely uncertain about whether they would be willing to provide all of the aid needed, and would be willing to start as long as they remained free to stop if they so desired (1992: 108).

[22] There may, of course, be other important differences between the bone marrow case and the pregnancy case. The cost in terms of suffering may be different, for example, and refraining from giving more bone marrow might seem to be a case of letting die while refraining from continuing the pregnancy might seem more a case of killing. One might, then, consistently believe that you don't have to keep giving bone marrow while the pregnant woman does have to keep supporting the fetus. My point here is simply that this will have to be for reasons other than the fact that the support was begun voluntarily, so that the mere fact of voluntary initiation of support does not imply a duty to continue it. But the tacit consent objection depends on its being the case that the fact of voluntary initiation itself does imply such a duty. The objections that Thomson's analogy is undermined by the distinction between killing and letting die and by the difference in burdens in the two cases are addressed in Sections 4.5 and 4.9.

to control one's own body" (Long 1993: 189).[23] And if this is so, then even if we thought that by her actions the woman could legitimately be understood as *attempting* to consent to waive this right, we would still have to conclude that she had not in fact done so.

I conclude that both claims needed to sustain the tacit consent objection must be rejected on grounds that the critic of abortion can and does accept, and that the objection thus fails to undermine the violinist analogy for typical nonrape cases, including those in which a woman voluntarily has intercourse without contraception. If the good samaritan argument is successful in rape cases, then the tacit consent objection fails to show that it is not also successful in nonrape cases as well.

4.4. THE RESPONSIBILITY OBJECTION

Let us now consider what I am calling the responsibility objection. In deriving the fetus's right to the use of the pregnant woman's body in nonrape cases from the fact that the pregnancy arose from a voluntary act of the woman's, this objection dispenses with the claim that the woman has tacitly consented to assist the fetus. It maintains instead that, morally speaking, the woman is like someone whose voluntary actions foreseeably lead to an accident that causes an innocent bystander to be in need of her assistnace. Tooley, for example, argues that the good samaritan argument is undermined by considering a case in which you engage in a pleasurable activity knowing that it may have the unfortunate side effect of destroying someone's food supply. You did not intend to cause the loss of food, let us assume, but it nonetheless resulted from your voluntary actions, and in a manner that was foreseeable in the sense that you knew your actions risked causing a loss of this sort (1983: 45). Surely most of us will agree that you do owe it to the bystander or victim to save his life even at some considerable cost to yourself, even though you need not be understood as having tacitly consented to do so in virtue of your having undertaken the risky action voluntarily. But if this is so, then the woman whose pregnancy is the accidental but foreseeable result of her voluntary action owes the fetus the use of her body even if she did not tacitly consent to grant it this right.[24]

---

[23] A similar point is made by Paul and Paul (1979: 135) and Rothbard (1982: 98), and hinted at though not clearly endorsed by Kamm (1992: 24).

[24] The same objection is made by means of similar examples by, for example, Beckwith (1992: 111–12; 1994: 164), Carrier (1975: 398–9). Similar examples are

Let me begin by noting one reason to be suspicious of analogies of the sort that proponents of the responsibility objection generally employ. Beckwith, for example, argues that the claim that voluntarily engaging in intercourse with the foresight that this might result in pregnancy imposes a duty to care for the offspring "is not an unusual way to frame moral obligations, for we hold drunk people whose driving results in manslaughter responsible for their actions, even if they did not *intend* to kill someone prior to becoming intoxicated" (1992: 111–12; 1994: 164).[25] But in the case of drunk or negligent driving, we already agree that people have a right not to be run over by cars, and then determine that a person who risks running over someone with a car can be held culpable if he has an accident that results in a violation of this right.[26] And the same is true in the other sorts of cases that proponents of the objection typically appeal to: It is uncontroversial that you have a right not to be deliberately shot by a hunter's bullet, or to have your food supply intentionally destroyed, and from this we derive a right that people not negligently act in ways that risk unintentionally causing these things to occur. In the case of an unintended pregnancy, on the other hand, the question of whether the fetus has a right not to be deliberately deprived of the needed support the pregnant woman is providing for it is precisely the question at issue. So it is difficult to see how an argument from an analogy with such cases can avoid begging the question.

4.4.1. Two Senses of Responsibility

But there is an even more fundamental problem with the responsibility objection. The problem can most clearly be identified by first asking precisely why we are so confident that the one who stands in need of your assistance has acquired the right to it in the sorts of cases that critics such as Tooley, Beckwith and Carrier employ. Presumably, as a first approximation, a proponent of the responsibility objection would say something like this: "It is because if you *hadn't* done the voluntary action that foreseeably led him to be in need of your assistance, he wouldn't

also used in a series of position papers published by an organization called Libertarians for Life (e.g., Gordon 1993: 1–2; 1994a: 6; 1994b: 7; 1995: 134; Walker undated b); Walker and Gordon 1993: 7; Vieira 1978: 3).
[25] Beckwith makes this claim in the context of defending the father's responsibility to care for the offspring, but it is presumably meant to apply equally to the case of the mother.
[26] Although even this claim is by no means unproblematic, as the literature on moral luck demonstrates.

be in need of your assistance in the first place. Since your voluntary act foreseeably brought about the state of affairs in which he is in need of your assistance, you are responsible for the fact that he is in need of your assistance. And since you are responsible for the fact that he is in need of your assistance, you have acquired an obligation to provide him with such assistance." And this seems reasonable enough.

But now consider that there are two distinct ways in which the counterfactual proposition, "If you had not done the voluntary action, then he would not now need your assistance in order to survive," can be true:

(1) If you had not done the act, then he would not now exist (and so would not now need your assistance in order to survive).

(2) If you had not done the act, then he would now exist, and would not need your assistance in order to survive.

Assuming that your voluntarily doing the action makes you responsible for the resulting state of affairs, we can recast this distinction as one between two different senses in which you might be responsible for bringing about the state of affairs in which another person now stands in need of your assistance in order to survive:

Responsibility (1): You are responsible for the fact that the other person now exists.

Responsibility (2): You are responsible for the fact that, given that the other person now exists, he stands in need of your assistance.

And this means that the claim, "If you are responsible for the fact that he now stands in need of your assistance, then you have acquired an obligation to provide him with such assistance," can mean two different things. The seemingly simple claim underlying the responsibility objection turns out not to be so simple.

I want now to argue that the claim, "If you are responsible for the fact that the person now stands in need of your assistance, then you have acquired an obligation to provide the person with such assistance," is true in one of the two senses of responsibility I have identified and false in the other. And I will argue that in the sense in which the claim is true, the pregnant woman is not responsible for the fact that the fetus now stands in need of her assistance in order to survive, and that in the sense in which it is true that the pregnant woman is responsible for the fact that the fetus now stands in need of her assistance in order to survive, the claim that such responsibility generates an obligation to provide assistance is false. Silverstein has offered a similar defense of the good samaritan argument on this point, and I will make use of some examples based on his in developing my case for it. And although I will argue in the end that the sort of example that Silverstein exploits is subject to a fatal objection, I will also argue that the central insight the examples are meant to reveal is nonetheless sound.

Since the argument will become difficult to follow if the reader must continually pause to remember which sense of responsibility is sense (1) and which is sense (2), let me first introduce the following convention. When I mean to say that "You are responsible in sense (1) for the fact that the person now stands in need of your assistance," I will sometimes say that you are responsible for the needy person's *existence*, or responsible for the fact that he now exists. When I mean to say that "You are responsible in sense (2) for the fact that the person now stands in need of your assistance," I will sometimes say that you are responsible for the needy person's *neediness*, or responsible for the fact that he is needy, given that he now exists. Having said this, we can begin by noting that in Thomson's story about you and the violinist, you are not responsible for the fact that the violinist stands in need of your assistance in either of the two senses of responsibility that I have identified. You are responsible, that is, neither for the violinist's existence nor for his neediness, given that he does exist. You did not create the violinist, so there is no voluntary action that you did such that had you not done it the violinist would not now exist. And you did not give the violinist the rare kidney ailment, so there is no voluntary action that you did such that had you not done it the violinist would now exist and would not need your assistance in order to survive. The proponent of the responsibility objection agrees that the violinist has not acquired the right to the use of your body and concedes that unless there is another morally relevant asymmetry, this case is relevantly similar to that of a woman whose pregnancy results from rape. He then argues that the case of a woman whose pregnancy results from voluntary intercourse is different. In that case, the critic urges, the woman is responsible for the fact that the fetus now stands in need of her assistance. So that case is relevantly different from Thomson's violinist case. Furthermore, the critic maintains, the voluntary intercourse case is relevantly similar to the sorts of cases cited by Beckwith, Carrier, and Tooley, in which a voluntary act of yours foreseeably (but not intentionally) causes an accident that leads an innocent bystander to be in need of your assistance in order to survive. For in those cases, too, you are responsible for the fact that another person now stands in need of your assistance.

In those cases, we are surely inclined to agree that the bystander has acquired a right to your assistance. And so, it is argued, we should also agree that, in the case of pregnancy resulting from voluntary intercourse, the fetus has acquired a right to the use of the woman's body.

In one important respect, the responsibility objection is correct. Cases of voluntary intercourse are relevantly different from Thomson's example. But in another important respect, the objection is mistaken. Cases of voluntary intercourse are also relevantly different from cases such as those cited by Beckwith, Carrier, and Tooley. In those cases, when you are responsible for the fact that another stands in need of your assistance, you are responsible in sense (2) and not in sense (1). You are responsible for their neediness given that they exist, that is, but you are not responsible for the fact that they exist in the first place. It is not the case that the hunter, for example, did some voluntary action such that had he not done it the innocent bystander would not now exist. Rather, it is that the hunter did some voluntary action such that had he not done it the innocent bystander would now exist and would not need the hunter's assistance in order to survive. But in the case of a pregnancy that results from voluntary intercourse, the correct attributions of responsibility are precisely the opposite: When the woman is responsible for the fact that the fetus now stands in need of her assistance, she is responsible in sense (1) and not in sense (2). It is the case that the woman did some voluntary action such that had she not done it the fetus would not now exist. If she had not voluntarily had intercourse, the fetus would not now exist. But it is not the case that she did some voluntary action such that had she not done it the fetus would now exist and would not need her assistance in order to survive. There was no option available to her on which the fetus would now exist and not be in need of her assistance. So there is no voluntary action that she did such that had she not done it the fetus would now exist and not be in need of her assistance. And so, in the sense in which I defined these terms above, a woman whose pregnancy arises from voluntary intercourse is responsible for the fetus's existence, but she is not responsible for its neediness, given that it exists.

Because of the distinction between these two senses of responsibility, we cannot yet conclude that the difference between the rape case and the nonrape case is morally relevant. We can say only that the rape case is like the nonrape case in terms of responsibility in sense (2) (in both cases, the woman is not responsible for the fact that the fetus is in need of her support, given that the fetus exists), and that the rape case is unlike the nonrape case in terms of responsibility in sense (1) (in the rape case, the woman is not responsible for the fact that the fetus exists, while in the nonrape case, the woman is responsible for the fact that the fetus exists). And this means that the responsibility objection can be sustained only if we agree that responsibility in sense (1) alone is sufficient to generate an obligation to provide the needed assistance. The question, then, is what we should say about cases in which one individual is responsible for the fact that another now stands in need of her assistance in sense (1) but not in sense (2) – is responsible for the needy person's existence, that is, but not for his neediness given that he exists.

4.4.2. The Significance of the Distinction

It is perhaps not immediately apparent how to go about answering this question. One wants to consider cases in which someone now stands in need of your assistance in order to survive and in which you have done some action such that, had you not done it, this dependent person would not now exist, and given that you did do it, this person exists and needs your assistance in order to survive. And it may seem that there really are no such cases other than those in which the act is simply the act of conceiving the person. If that is so, then we cannot usefully illuminate the case of voluntary intercourse by appealing to other cases, and may have to conclude that what we have here is simply an anomalous case that cannot be resolved one way or the other by appealing to those more general beliefs about responsibility that critics and defenders of abortion alike generally share. But this pessimism is premature. For there is another kind of action such that had you not done the action the person would not now exist: not the act of *creating* his life, but the act of *extending* it. Suitably constructed, such cases offer a means of testing the relative significance of the two different senses of responsibility that are at issue here. And when they are consulted, the claim needed to sustain the responsibility objection, the claim that responsibility in sense (1) alone is sufficient to generate an obligation to provide the needed assistance, is undermined.

To see this, consider first the following variation on Thomson's story:[27]

Imperfect Drug I: You are the violinist's doctor. Seven years ago, you discovered that the violinist had contracted a rare disease that was on the verge of killing

---

[27] This is a condensed and slightly modified version of an example given by Silverstein (1987: 106–7).

him. The only way to save his life that was available to you was to give him a drug that cures the disease but has one unfortunate side effect: Five to ten years after ingestion, it often causes the kidney ailment described in Thomson's story. Knowing that you alone would have the appropriate blood type to save the violinist were his kidneys to fail, you prescribed the drug and cured the disease. The violinist has now been struck by the kidney ailment. If you do not allow him the use of your kidneys for nine months, he will die.

In Imperfect Drug I, you are responsible in sense (1) for the fact that the violinist now stands in need of your assistance. You are responsible, that is, for his existence. You did a voluntary action such that had you not done it, the violinist would not now exist. If you had not given him the drug, he would not now exist. But you are not responsible in sense (2) for the fact that the violinist now stands in need of your assistance. You are not, that is, responsible for his neediness, given that he exists. It is not the case that you did a voluntary action such that, had you not done it, the violinist would now exist and not need your assistance in order to survive. For there was no course of action available to you seven years ago that would have caused it to be the case both that the violinist would now be alive and that he would not be in need of the use of your kidneys.[28] So you are responsible for the needy violinist's existence, but you are not responsible for his neediness, given that he exists. This is what makes Imperfect Drug I importantly different from what I will call

Imperfect Drug II: This is the same as Imperfect Drug I, except that you could also have given the violinist a perfect drug that would have cured him with no side effects. But out of indifference or laziness you chose to give him the imperfect drug. The violinist has now been struck by the kidney ailment. If you do not allow him the use of your kidneys for nine months, he will die.

In Imperfect Drug II, you are responsible for the fact that the violinist now stands in need of your assistance in both senses. If you had not voluntarily given the violinist one or the other of the drugs, he would not now exist. And if you had not voluntarily given him the imperfect drug rather than the perfect drug, he would now exist and would not be in need of your assistance in order to survive. So in Imperfect Drug

---

[28] In his response to an objection raised by Langer, Silverstein is more clear that this is the central point of his example. See Langer (1993: 348–9), Silverstein (1993: 361ff.).

II, you are responsible both for the needy violinist's existence and for his neediness, given that he exists.

It is extremely difficult to avoid the conclusion that you do owe the violinist the use of your kidneys in Imperfect Drug II, but that you do not in Imperfect Drug I. We might put the reason for this in a few ways. We might say that in Imperfect Drug II, there is a clear sense in which you harmed the violinist by choosing to give him the imperfect drug, while in Imperfect Drug I there is no sense in which you harmed him by giving him the imperfect drug. Or we might put it like this: Suppose that in Imperfect Drug I, you had told the violinist that you could either give him the imperfect drug or no drug at all, and that if you gave him the imperfect drug you would refuse to lend him the use of your kidneys for nine months should he later develop the kidney ailment. Presumably, the violinist would have chosen to take the imperfect drug rather than the alternative. But suppose that in Imperfect Drug II, you had told the violinist that you could either give him the imperfect drug or the perfect drug or no drug at all, and that if you gave him the imperfect drug and he later developed the kidney ailment, you would refuse to lend him the use of your kidneys for nine months. Presumably, in that case, the violinist would have chosen to take the perfect drug. So we can account for our different responses to the two cases by saying that you do not incur a further duty to assist the violinist when you make the choice that leaves him best off, or the choice that is the one that he would have selected, but that you do incur such a duty when you fail to do so. And either way, if this is our response to the two cases, then we must conclude that in cases where you are responsible in sense (1) and not in sense (2) for the fact that another now stands in need of your assistance – in cases, that is, where you are responsible for the needy person's existence but not for his neediness, given that he exists – the individual in need has not acquired the right to your assistance. And if this is so, then the responsibility objection fails: Pregnancies that arise from voluntary intercourse are relevantly similar to Imperfect Drug I rather than to Imperfect Drug II.[29] A woman whose pregnancy is the result

[29] Of course, one might maintain that even in Imperfect Drug II, the doctor does not owe the violinist the use of his kidneys (and one could hold this even while believing that the violinist was nonetheless entitled to something as compensation or punitive damages). And it would then follow that the good samaritan argument would be secure even if it turned out that the case of a pregnancy arising from voluntary intercourse was more like Imperfect Drug II than like Imperfect Drug I. Since this assessment seems controversial at best, and since I claim that the good

of voluntary intercourse, that is, is responsible for the existence of the fetus, but is not responsible for the neediness of the fetus, given that it exists. If the good samaritan argument succeeds in rape cases, therefore, the responsibility objection fails to show that it does not also succeed in nonrape cases as well.[30]

4.4.3. Three Objections

Three objections that might be raised against this argument merit notice. The argument rests on the claim that when you are responsible in sense (1) but not in sense (2) for the fact that another now stands in need of your assistance, then the individual in need has not acquired the right to your assistance. But this claim can be challenged in two ways. The first arises from the possibility that there could be cases in which, even though you are responsible in sense (1) and not in sense (2), your action still harmed the individual who now needs your assistance in order to survive, or your action was other than he would have chosen to have you do. If this is so, then it will seem that even though you are only responsible for the fact that the individual exists, and not for the fact that he is needy given that he exists, he will still have acquired the right to your assistance. And if this is so, then the claim upon which my argument against the responsibility objection rests will have to be revised or rejected. Consider, for example, the case of

Imperfect Drug III: This is the same as Imperfect Drug I, except that the situation arose a few weeks ago, and the only way to save the violinist's life that was available to you was to give him a drug that in every case causes continuous excruciating pain for a few weeks, which then ceases with the onset of the sort of kidney failure described in Thomson's story. Knowing that the drug would

---

samaritan argument can be defended without it, I will not rely on it here though I do not mean to be insisting that it is mistaken.

[30] One might well be inclined to object at this point that the woman has acquired an obligation to provide aid to the fetus precisely *because* there was no way for her to make it the case that the fetus exist without making it the case that the fetus exist in a state of dependence on her, while there was a way for her to avoid making it the case that the fetus exist in the first place: She could simply have abstained from having intercourse. But this would imply that you have acquired an obligation to provide aid to the violinist in Imperfect Drug I. There was no way for you to make it the case that the violinist (still) exists without making it the case that he exists in a state of dependence on you, but there was a way for you to avoid making it be the case that he still exists in the first place: You could simply have abstained from giving him the drug.

certainly cause both the pain and the kidney failure, and knowing that you alone would have the appropriate blood type to save the violinist once his kidneys failed and to enable him to then go on and live a healthy, happy, indpendent life, you gave him the drug that cured the disease and caused the pain to begin. The violinist has now been struck by the kidney ailment.

In this case, as in Imperfect Drug I, you are responsible for the fact that the violinist now exists, but not for the fact that he is needy, given that he exists. Now let us assume, what some might deny, that the violinist in this case would be better off dying right away of the rare disease rather than taking the drug, if taking the drug would only provide him with a few weeks of agony and then death from the kidney failure. And let us also assume that he would be better off still if he took the drug and endured the pain and was then saved from the kidney failure so that he could go on to enjoy the rest of his life. In that case, even though you are only responsible in sense (1) and not in sense (2) for the fact that he stands in need of your assistance, it is nonetheless true that if you refrain from assisting him now, he will have been made worse off by your having given him the drug than he would have been had you let him die at that time (or that he would have chosen no drug at all over the drug with no subsequent kidney assistance). And this makes it plausible to suppose that you now have an obligation to save him from the kidney failure, even at some substantial cost to yourself. If we accept this analysis, then we must modify the claim I presented against the responsibility objection to read as follows: If a voluntary action of yours makes you responsible in sense (1) and not in sense (2) for the fact that another now stands in need of your assistance in order to survive, then the individual has not acquired the right to your assistance *unless your assistance is needed to make him as least as well off as he would have been had you not done the voluntary action in the first place.*[31]

I am inclined to accept this emendation. Accepting this modification of the argument, however, will affect its ability to undermine the responsibility objection only if we believe that a fetus is made worse off by being conceived and then aborted than it would have been had it

---

[31] Silverstein himself accepts this emendation (1987: 111), and it also runs parallel to the notion of a "baseline" employed by Kamm, who argues that you are (or may be) obligated only to ensure that the violinist not be made worse off than he would have been had you not been hooked up to him in the first place (1992: e.g., 26, 43, 89–90).

never been conceived in the first place.[32] This claim is implausible at best, unintelligible at worst (since the fetus would not "have been" anything had it not been conceived) and the sorts of arguments that have typically been advanced in its defense are unsatisfactory. Moreover, one of the few considerations that might be appealed to in its support in other contexts cannot be appealed to in this context without begging the question that is at issue. This is the thought that may well arise when one compares the case of a man who is murdered in his sleep with one who dies of natural causes in his sleep. Although it may be difficult to provide a satisfactory account of the thought, many people find that they are inclined to believe that the murder victim has been more seriously harmed than has the other. And if this is so, then the fact that the fetus that is conceived and then aborted is *killed*, while if it had not been conceived then it would not have been killed, might seem to lend support to the claim that conceiving and then aborting it leaves it worse off than it would otherwise have been.

The problem with this line of argument is that if the original example shows anything, it shows only that it is worse to die an unjust death than to die an ordinary death. And even if that claim is accepted, it clearly cannot be used here because the question of whether or not abortion causes an unjust death is precisely the question at issue. So what the defender of the responsibility objection really has to maintain in order to exploit the revision I have accepted to the principle I have been defending is not merely the claim that a fetus is worse off being conceived and then *aborted* than it would have been had it never been conceived in the first place, but that it is worse off being conceived and

---

[32] It is worth noting that there is an important difference between the following two claims: (1) By being conceived and then aborted, the fetus is put in a condition that is *not worse* than the condition of having never been conceived, and (2) by being conceived and then aborted the fetus is put in a condition that is *identical* to the condition of having never been conceived. Lee has challenged the sort of argument I am defending here by maintaining that the argument depends on claim (2) being true and by arguing that claim (2) is false (1996: 125–6). But the argument depends only on claim (1) being true. We can agree that we have put the fetus in a condition or position that is different from what would otherwise have been the case, but if doing so is not worse for it, then, on the account developed here, we have not yet been given a reason for thinking that we owe it further assistance (on p. 127, Lee actually slips into claiming that we cannot say of the unborn child that he "has not been placed in a condition worse than what he would have been in" had he not been conceived, but this is preciesly what we *can* say, and saying so is sufficient for the purposes of the argument I am defending here).

then simply dying than it would have been had it never been conceived. And this makes the claim even more difficult to believe. Consider, for example, what it would imply about women who are highly prone to miscarriage. If the claim is true, then if such a woman chooses to try to become pregnant, she seriously harms each fetus that she fails to carry to term.[33] It would take a very strong argument to establish that the claim is true, given that the claim itself is implausible and has consequences that are implausible, and the arguments that have been offered in its defense cannot bear this weight.

Michael Davis offers one such argument for the claim that the fetus is made worse off by being made to live a short time and then being killed than it would have been had it never existed at all by appealing to the following example (1983: 277):

[T]o be killed is bad, so bad that merely being brought into existence for a time is not necessarily enough to make up for it. We would not, I take it, allow a scientist to kill a ten-year-old child just because the scientist had ten years ago "constructed" the child out of a dollar's worth of chemicals, had reared it for ten years in such a way as to make it impossible for the child's care to be given to anyone else for another eight years, and now found the care of the child a far greater burden than he had expected.

But this example does not support the conclusion for two reasons. The first arises from the fact that in Davis's story, the scientist deliberately makes the child exclusively dependent on him. Since the scientist could have avoided doing this, with the result that the child could now be cared for by someone else, what he does in making the child dependent on him is like what you do in making the violinist dependent on you in Imperfect Drug II, when you could instead have rendered him independent of you, rather than what you do in making the violinist dependent on you in Imperfect Drug I, when there was no alternative available to you that would have rendered him independent of you. When we agree that in Imperfect Drug II you now owe the violinist the use of your kidneys, it is because you made him dependent on your support when you could have avoided doing so, not because we believe that if he dies now he will be made worse off than if you had not saved him seven years ago. And in just the same way, when we agree that in Davis's story the scientist now owes the child another eight years of support, it is because the scientist made him dependent on such support when he could have

---

[33] This point is noted by Kamm (1992: 85–6).

avoided doing so, not because we believe that if the child dies now he will be made worse off than if the scientist had not created him in the first place.

There is a second problem with Davis's argument that arises independently of this first problem. For suppose we agree that we would not allow such a scientist to kill his or her child. Davis simply assumes that this must be so because the killing is so bad *for the child* that the high quality of the child's (short) life does not make up for it. Only on this assumption would our saying that the scientist does something immoral commit us to the claim that one is made worse off by being made to live a short time and then being killed than if one had never existed. But this assumption is unwarranted. It is much more likely that our response to Davis's example (assuming that we share his response) reveals instead that we believe that some acts are wrong even though they leave no one worse off than they would otherwise have been. Suppose, for example, that a woman knows that if she conceives a child now it will live a just barely worthwhile life and die at the age of fifteen but that if she waits a month she will conceive a child who will live an extremely happy life to a ripe old age. We might well criticize her if she chooses to conceive the first child rather than the second, but that is no evidence that we think that this child is made worse off than if he had never lived. It is instead evidence that we think (if we do criticize her) that there are wrongs that harm no one. Similarly, if we share Davis's response to his example, this is not because we think the child would have been better off never having been conceived.

A second defense of the claim that a fetus is made worse off by being conceived and then aborted than it would have been had it never been conceived arises from the following set of considerations: Death, especially premature death, is a great harm to the one who suffers it, while the provision of a very short amount of life, especially life of the sort one enjoys during the first few months after conception, is a relatively small benefit to the one who receives it. So one who is conceived and then aborted is granted a relatively small benefit and then a relatively great harm, which seems to add up, on the whole, to a worse state than that of one who is not conceived in the first place and who thus receives neither the small benefit nor the great harm.

This argument is unacceptable for two reasons. In the first place, as Nagel has pointed out, "If death is an evil at all, it cannot be because of its positive features, but only because of what it deprives us of" 1970: 1). But if saying that death is a great harm to the fetus amounts to saying that death deprives the fetus of great goods it would enjoy if it were to go on living, then this provides no support for the claim that the fetus would have been better off still had it enjoyed no such goods in the first place.[34] In addition, the argument would seem equally to imply that a six-year-old child who leads a happy life and then dies in her sleep would have been better off never having been conceived. After all, the totality of the goods she is deprived of by death is much greater than the totality of goods she has so far enjoyed, so if the harm of death consists in the greatness of the good it deprives one of, then this would mean that the harms in her life greatly outweigh the benefits. But as tragic as her death is, the critic of abortion will surely be unwilling to insist that she would have been better off never having been conceived. Of course, it is open to the proponent of the responsibility objection to attempt to articulate and defend a conception of the nature of death on which it turns out both that the fetus is worse off being conceived and then dying in the womb than not being conceived and that this is not so of the six-year-old who dies in her sleep. But in the absence of such a defense, the attempt to undermine my argument against the responsibility objection by apealing to such cases as Imperfect Drug III is unsuccessful on the abortion critic's own terms.

A second objection to the argument I have developed to this point would be to insist that there can be cases in which you do a voluntary act such that you are responsible in sense (1) but not in sense (2) for the fact that another person now stands in need of your assistance, keeping the person alive is *not* needed in order to make him at least as well off as he would have been had you not done the voluntary act in the first place, and yet it is nonetheless still the case that the person in question has acquired the right to your assistance. Langer offers what seems to be a plausible example of just this sort of case: his relationship with his one-year-old son (1993: 351–2):

I am responsible for his existence, but I am not responsible for the condition in which he finds himself.... He is in a condition which requires constant physical attention, long-term financial aid, and significant psychological nurture...I have caused his existence, but I certainly have not caused him to be in this terrible, needy condition. Do I not have an obligation to care for his needs?

This is plainly a case in which an individual is responsible for the fact that another now exists (since if Langer had not had intercourse, his son

---

[34] This point is also pressed persuasively by Kamm (1992: 84–7).

would not now exist) and is not responsible for the fact that the other is needy, given that he exists (since there was no option available to Langer when his son was conceived on which his son would both exist now as a one-year-old and not be in this needy condition). And (I am assuming) it is also a case where it is not true that if the child were to die today this would leave him worse off than if he had never been conceived. So if the claim I have to this point been using against the responsibility objection is true, then Langer has acquired no obligation to care for his child. But Langer takes it that we will think that he does have such an obligation since "the laws and moral intuitions of our society strongly oppose child abandonment" (1993: 352). And if that is so, then an individual can acquire the right to your assistance even in cases where a voluntary action of yours makes you responsible for his existence but not for his neediness given that he exists, and in which your assistance, although needed to keep him alive, is not needed in order to make him at least as well off as he would have been had you not done the voluntary action in the first place. And this seems precisely to describe the case of the woman whose pregnancy results from voluntary intercourse.

Let us assume that we agree that you have a duty to care for your one-year-old son in such circumstances.[35] It does not follow from this that the individual in need *always* acquires the right to your assistance when you are responsible for his existence and not responsible for his neediness given that he exists. It follows only that he *sometimes* acquires this right in such cases. This concession would indeed force a further revision in the claim I have been defending as an argument against the responsibility objection. I would now be unable to insist that an individual's being worse off than he would have been had you not done the voluntary action is necessary in order for the individual to acquire the right to your assistance in those cases where your voluntary action makes you responsible for the fact that he exists but not for the fact that he is needy given that he exists. However, even this revision, strong

---

[35] Although it is worth noting that even this part of Langer's argument is subject to doubt. After all, it does not follow from the claim that "child abandonment" is immoral that a parent has a duty to provide for his child's needs. That would follow only if one also believed that a parent had a duty not to put his child up for adoption; but most people (especially, perhaps, opponents of abortion) believe that it is perfectly permissible for a parent to have someone else incur the costs of raising his child. So one might reply to Langer's question simply by saying that no, he does not have an obligation to care for his son's needs. If he no longer wishes to be a parent, it is morally permissible for him to place his son up for adoption.

as it is, does not suffice to rescue the responsibility objection from the problem I have identified. The objection, remember, claims that nonrape cases are relevantly different from rape cases *because* they differ in terms of responsibility in sense (1) only. The objection is forceful, then, only if being responsible in sense (1) is, in and of itself, enough to make the difference between an individual's acquiring the right to your assistance and his not acquiring it. Your being responsible for the needy person's existence, that is, must be a sufficient condition for the individual's acquiring the right to your assistance. But the fact (assuming that it is a fact) that the needy individual can *sometimes* acquire the right to your assistance in cases where you are responsible for his existence but not for his neediness, given that he exists, does not show that your being responsible for his existence is, in and of itself, sufficient for him to acquire that right. The argument presented above still shows that your being responsible in this sense is not sufficient to generate this right since it does not generate this right in the case of Imperfect Drug I. If the right to assistance is only *sometimes* acquired in cases in which you are responsible for the fact that the other exists and not responsible for the fact that he is needy given that he exists, then your being responsible for his existence in itself is sufficient for the acquisition of the right only in conjunction with (and perhaps only because of) some additional considerations. And the burden would then be on the proponent of the responsibility objection to show that these other considerations obtain in the case of pregnancy arising from voluntary intercourse and not just in the case of the father who is raising a one-year-old. Unless it is shown that these further considerations do obtain in both cases, the claim that the individual sometimes has a right to your support in cases where you are responsible for his existence but not for his neediness given that he exists (as in the case of the one-year-old) is too weak to undermine my argument. For that claim is perfectly consistent with the claim that the mere fact that the woman in nonrape cases is responsible for the fetus's existence but not for its neediness given that it exists is not sufficient to provide the fetus in such cases with a right to the use of the woman's body if the fetus in rape cases does not have such a right.

And there is good reason to doubt that such a case could be made. For, somewhat ironically, what seems plausible about the tacit consent objection seems to come back to haunt the responsibility objection. After all, it is surely plausible to suppose that a mother (to switch back to the woman's perspective and keep the analogy tighter) who brings a baby to term and takes it home with her has tacitly agreed to care for it.

Nothing that was said against the tacit consent objection would count against this claim, since voluntarily bringing a baby into one's home is voluntarily bringing about the state of affairs in which the baby is under one's care, while voluntarily having intercourse is only acting in a way that foreseeably may lead to the further state of affairs in which there is a developing fetus in the womb. And if this is so, then we can account for Langer's duty to his one-year-old son while showing that the conditions sufficient for his son to acquire the right to his assistance do not obtain in the case of the woman whose pregnancy results from voluntary intercourse. We can say that the mother (and father) of the one-year-old owe care to their child either because (a) such a duty follows from tacit consent alone, which is reasonably inferred from bringing the child home after it is born but not merely from engaging in voluntary intercourse (in which case the fact that the parent is responsible for the fact that the child exists is entirely superfluous to accounting for the child's right to assistance from his parent), or because (b) such a duty follows from tacit consent only when it is conjoined with responsibility in sense (1) (in which case the fact that the parent is responsible for the fact that the child now exists is necessary but not sufficient for the child's having such a right). The first of these two accounts seems far more plausible, since (b) is difficult to square with the assumption that the duty adoptive parents have to the children they adopt is the same as the duty biological parents have to the children they conceive.[36] But choosing between the two accounts is not necessary: On either one, the morally relevant distinction that explains why the parent of a one-year-old son has a duty to care for him while the victim of rape does not have a duty to care for her fetus would fail to distinguish the woman whose pregnancy arises from rape from the woman whose pregnancy arises from voluntary intercourse.[37]

---

[36] Even if the "adoption" is really a kidnapping, as in the case where a woman steals a baby from the hospital and takes it home to raise as her own, we still presumably believe that her duty to care for the infant is as strong as the duty of any parent to care for her child, and this would again favor (a) over (b).

[37] None of what is said in this paragraph, it should be noted, implies or presupposes that a woman who declines to bring her newborn home has no duty to care for it at all. Suppose that she gives birth to a child in an abandoned field. One might hold the view that there are no positive duties to assist others, in which case one will hold that if she does not wish to raise the child herself she is morally free to walk away and leave the infant to die. But a proponent of the good samaritan argument need not hold this view. One could believe that there are positive duties to assist others, at least in cases where the burden is relatively small and the

183

A third objection to my argument against the responsibility objection focuses on the sorts of examples I have used in trying to show that there is a morally relevant difference between the two senses of responsibility I have identified.[38] In trying to show that there is an important difference between these two kinds of responsibility, I have to this point followed the sort of example exploited by Silverstein, in which you are the violinist's doctor and the violinist has not acquired the right to your assistance in cases, such as Imperfect Drug I, in which you are responsible for the fact that he now exists, but are not responsible for the fact that he needs your assistance given that he exists. My argument, in short, has turned on the claim that although cases of voluntary intercourse which result in pregnancy are relevantly different from Thomson's violinist case, they are relevantly like Imperfect Drug I rather than Imperfect Drug II or Imperfect Drug III. But it is open to a proponent of the responsibility objection to agree that voluntary intercourse is like Imperfect Drug I in this particular respect, but to insist that there is a much more important sense in which the cases differ and which undermines the analogy.

In particular, there is the following difference between a woman who voluntarily conceives and then aborts a fetus, and you when you voluntarily cure and then later refuse to save an ailing violinist: In curing

benefit relatively great, and so hold that the woman would at least be obligated to incur the cost of carrying the child to town and providing for it until it could be taken to a hospital or shelter. But one who holds this view will also hold that she would have this obligation equally even if she were to come across a newborn that someone else had abandoned in the field, so this will again fail to support the claim that the good samaritan argument is undermined by the difference between the voluntariness of intercourse in nonrape cases and the involuntariness of the kidnapping in the violinist case. And, in addition, it would hardly follow that a woman would therefore be obligated to sustain her pregnancy since the burdens of a typical pregnancy are far more intimate and extensive than the burden of dropping a baby off at a hospital or police station.

Of course, one might endorse the existence of a positive duty to assist another who will otherwise die even where the burden to you in doing so is quite substanial, provided that (a) the benefit to the other still significantly outweighs the burden to you and (b) you are the only one who can save the individual. This would justify a duty to continue the pregnancy even granting that the burden is substantially greater than what we are typically required to undergo for the benefit of others. But then it will equally follow that you are obligated to remain plugged into Thomson's violinist for nine months, since the benefit to him significantly outweighs the burden to you and you are the only one who can save him. So even this view of positive rights would fail to undermine Thomson's analogy.

[38] I am grateful to Alec Walen for bringing this objection to my attention, and to Jeff McMahan for identifying some difficulties with an earlier version of my response to it.

the violinist, you greatly benefit him, providing him with several more years of valuable experiences that he would otherwise not have had. When the woman conceives the short-lived fetus, she does not benefit it at all, since it will not go on to have any valuable experiences that it would otherwise not have had. This fact can be used to undermine the sort of example I have been borrowing from Silverstein in a few distinct ways. One could argue that since you have already greatly benefitted the violinist, you have no duty to benefit him further, while since the woman has not yet benefitted the fetus, she does have a duty to so benefit it. One could argue that your motives in saving the violinst were benevolent, whereas the woman's motives in engaging in intercourse were not. And, most forcefully, one could argue that you were morally obligated to cure the violinist, whereas the woman was not morally obligated to engage in voluntary intercourse. The voluntary act that rendered you responsible for the fact that the violinist now exists was the act of giving the violinist the only drug available that could save his life, and it would have been morally impermissible for you to have failed to give the violinist the drug. But the voluntary act that rendered the woman responsible for the fact that the fetus now exists was the act of engaging in sexual intercourse. And the woman surely had no moral obligation to do that. So one could argue that the reason the violinist does not acquire the right to the use of your body in Imperfect Drug I is not because you are only responsible in sense (1), but because of the *way in which* it came to be the case that you are only responsible in sense (1). Because you were morally required to give the violinist the drug, your giving him the drug cannot confer on him a further right to your assistance that he would not otherwise have had. But because the woman whose pregnancy results from voluntary intercourse was not morally required to engage in voluntary intercourse, her engaging in voluntary intercourse can confer on the fetus a right to her further assistance that it would not otherwise have had. Thus, one could agree that the violinist has the right to your assistance in Imperfect Drug II but not in Imperfect Drug I, and also agree that it is Imperfect Drug I rather than Imperfect Drug II that resembles the case of voluntary intercourse in terms of both senses of responsibility, and still conclude that the woman's voluntarily acting in a way that makes her responsible for the fetus's existence is itself sufficient for the fetus to acquire a right to her assistance, while your voluntarily acting in a way that makes you responsible for the violinist's existence is not sufficient for the violinist to acquire a right to your assistance in Imperfect Drug I.

I believe that this objection to the examples I have appealed to is successful, and that the argument against the responsibility objection as I have thus far developed it cannot be sustained for that reason. I have nonetheless presented the argument to this point in terms of examples adapted from Silverstein's discussion for two reasons. First, they provide a natural way to bring out the distinction between the two senses of responsibility at issue, since the strategy involves appealing to cases where one's act extends a person's life and performing such acts is typical of what doctors do. Second, it is important to see the flaw in Silverstein's examples before asking whether the examples can successfully be modified. The reason for this is that the examples can, in fact, be successfully modified. And seeing how this can be done reveals how easily even defenders of the good samaritan argument such as Silverstein can be mistakenly led to attribute a greater degree of responsibility to the pregnant woman than the circumstances warrant.

In particular, when your voluntary act causes you to be responsible for the fact that the violinist exists in Imperfect Drug I, your act deliberately brings about the state of affairs in which the violinist is still alive. You give him the drug, after all, in order to save him. But when the woman's voluntary act causes her to be responsible for the fact that the fetus exists, this is not so. She does not deliberately bring about the state of affairs in which the fetus is now alive. Rather, she deliberately brings about the state of affairs in which she is now enjoying sexual intercourse, while foreseeing that the state of affairs in which there is a fetus alive and dependent on her may later result. The kind of example that Silverstein uses to develop his case against the responsibility objection, then, fails because it neglects the distinction that I appealed to in arguing against the tacit consent objection. Because it does so, it mistakenly compares the pregnant woman to one who has voluntarily brought about the state of affairs in which there is now an individual who needs her assistance in order to survive. And if we reconstruct the argument against the responsibility objection with this distinction in mind, we can produce an analogy that vindicates the argument against the objection while avoiding the problem that ultimately undermines Silverstein's argument against it. For now consider

Hedonist: You are a hedonist who wishes to engage in a very pleasurable activity. The activity is such that if you engage in it, there is a chance that it will cause some gas to be released that will result in adding a few extra months of unconscious existence to the life of some already-comatose violinist in the world. As things now stand, this violinist has no more conscious life ahead of him. But if the gas is released, and if he does have a few extra months of unconscious life added as a result, it will then become possible for you to bring him out of his coma by giving him the use of your kidneys for nine months. There are certain devices that you can use during the pleasurable activity which reduce the chances of gas emission but do not eliminate them entirely, but you do not like the way the use of such devices "makes you feel" when you engage in the pleasurable activity. So you engage in the pleasurable activity, and without such devices. As a (foreseeable but not intended) result, some gas escapes, causing some extra unconscious time to be added to the life of an already comatose violinist, and making it possible for him to then be brought out of his coma if you remain plugged into him for nine months.

In this case, as in Imperfect Drug I, you are responsible for the fact that the violinist now exists, but you are not responsible for his neediness, given that he exists. There was no action available to you on which the violinist would still exist at this point and not be in need of the use of your kidneys. In this respect, you are like the woman whose pregnancy is the result of voluntary intercourse. And in this case, unlike Imperfect Drug I, you did the voluntary act that caused you to be responsible for the violinist's existence not because it would greatly benefit the violinist, or because you were benevolent, or because you were morally required to do it, but merely because doing the act would be pleasurable.[39] The case of the Hedonist, then, eliminates all of the differences that ultimately undermine the sort of examples I have to this point taken from Silverstein. But surely the critic of abortion will be unwilling to insist that in the Hedonist case you are morally required to provide the violinist with the use of your body. Such insistence here seems no less implausible than in Thomson's original story. Why should the fact that you have already provided the violinist with a few months of unconscious existence that he would not otherwise have had mean that you are now morally required to add even more months to his life, even given that your motive in performing the action that foreseeably added those months to his life was purely selfish? I conclude that my argument against the

---

[39] In setting the example up in this way, I do not mean to be insisting that a woman's motivation in having sexual intercourse must always be as trivial as the mere pursuit of pleasure. As in the stipulation that her motivation for not using contraception is solely because she does not like the way that it makes her feel, this surely oversimplifies and trivializes things. But again, as with that case, I want to assume for the sake of the argument that her motives are as trivial as possible and argue that the objection to the good samaritan argument still fails.

responsibility objection can overcome this third objection, even though the related argument developed by Silverstein cannot, and that the responsibility objection, like the tacit consent objection, must ultimately be rejected on grounds that the critic of abortion already accepts. If the good samaritan argument is successful in rape cases, then it is successful in nonrape cases as well, including cases of voluntary intercourse in which contraception is not used. The question that remains, then, is whether the argument is successful in rape cases in the first place. I will argue in the remainder of this chapter that it is.

4.5. THE KILLING VERSUS LETTING DIE OBJECTION

The responsibility objection and the tacit consent objection to the good samaritan argument both turn on the claim that there is a morally relevant difference between the way in which the relationship between you and the violinist begins in Thomson's example and the way in which the relationship between the pregnant woman and the fetus begins in cases where the pregnancy results from voluntary intercourse. I have argued that although Thomson herself fails to satisfactorily address these objections, the objections themselves should nonetheless be rejected. Two of the most powerful further objections to the good samaritan argument turn on the claim that there is a morally relevant difference between the way in which the relationship beween you and the violinist ends when you unplug yourself in Thomson's example and the way in which the relationship between the pregnant woman and the fetus ends when a woman has an abortion. The first objection maintains that there is a morally relevant difference between killing a person and letting a person die, and that abortion kills the fetus while unplugging yourself merely allows the violinist to die. The second objection maintains that there is a morally relevant difference between intentionally causing a person's death and foreseeably causing a person's death, and that abortion intentionally causes the fetus's death while unplugging yourself merely foreseeably causes the violinist's death. I will consider the first of these objections in this section and the second in the following section.

4.5.1. The Objection

So consider the claim that the good samaritan argument is undermined by the moral significance of the difference between killing a person and letting a person die. Assuming that you share my response to Thomson's example, you agree that it would be morally permissible for you to unplug yourself from the violinist with the result that the violinist is allowed to die of his kidney ailment. But in the case of abortion, one does not merely allow the fetus to die. A person who performs an abortion must either first kill the fetus and then remove it or kill it in the process of removing it. And once the analogy is set right in this way, the objection maintains, the good samaritan argument is undermined: Do you really think that you are permitted to unplug yourself from the violinist if in order to do so you must first dismember or burn him to death? Two of the most influential rebuttals to Thomson's original paper cite this as the single greatest problem with the good samaritan argument. Baruch Brody urges that "Thomson has not established the truth of her claims about abortion, *primarily* because she has not sufficiently attended to the distinction between our duty to save X's life and our duty not to take it" (1975: 30, emphasis added). And John Finnis points to the distinction between killing and letting die as "perhaps the decisive reason why abortion cannot be assimilated to the range of Samaritan problems and why Thomson's location of it within that range is a mere (ingenious) novelty" (1973: 141).[40] How should the defender of the good samaritan argument respond?[41]

One way of responding to this objection would simply be to deny the general claim upon which it rests: that there is a sufficiently significant

---

[40] Or at least, like Thomson (1973: 156), I take it that this is what Finnis is referring to here; as Thomson points out, his discussion is somewhat ambiguous. The claim that the distinction between killing and letting die undermines Thomson's argument is also pressed by Schwarz and Tacelli (1989: 84–7), Schwarz (1990: 115–16), Kamm (1992: 74–6), Feinberg (1978: 143), Benson (1990: 43–4), Ajzenstat (1990: 50–1), Beckwith (1992: 116–7; 1994: 167–8), Brody (1971b: 338–9), and Gordon (1993: 1; 1995: 132).

[41] In addition to the responses developed below, it is difficult to resist adding an *ad hominem* response. For it seems extremely unlikely that those who believe that abortion is morally impermissible would be inclined to revise their views if they were assured that from now on all aborted fetuses would die a lingering death from exposure or neglect shortly after being safely removed from the uterus rather than a more directly caused death by some other means shortly before (or while) being removed. Indeed, in works opposing abortion that describe the various procedures involved, there is rarely a suggestion that it makes a moral difference whether the fetus is killed or left to die, and typically an emphatic declaration that it makes no such difference. As one such writer puts it, "The effect on the baby is the same: the baby is dead" (Powell 1981: 147). But if Thomson's critics would themselves deny the claim that the permissibility of abortion turns on whether the fetus is killed or left to die, then why should her defenders have to accept it?

general moral difference between killing a person and refraining from saving a person. This is the response that Thomson herself offers in her reply to Finnis:

Now it had not actually escaped my notice that the mother who aborts herself kills the child, whereas a man who refuses to be a Good Samaritan – on the traditional understanding of Good Samaritanism – merely does not save. My suggestion was that from a moral point of view these cases should be assimilated: The woman who allows the pregnancy to continue, at great cost to herself, is entitled to praise in the same amount, and, more important, of the same kind, as is the man who sets forth, at great cost to himself, to give aid. That is why I proposed we attend to the case of you and the violinist (1973: 156).

Thomson takes it, that is, that the proposition needed to maintain the objection to her argument, the proposition that "the difference between killing and not saving makes a sufficiently profound difference as to make the assimilation [of the violinist and abortion cases] improper," is false and *"shown to be false* by the story of you and the violinist" (1973: 157, emphasis added).

This response may satisfy a fair number of people, particularly those who are already predisposed to view the distinction between killing and letting die with some suspicion. If we do not already have a strong commitment to the moral significance of the distinction, Thomson's analogy may well feed the intuition that the distinction is relatively unimportant. But for the rest of us, this seems only to leave the discussion in a stalemate. Other possible disanalogies aside, that is, Thomson seems to agree with Finnis that the permissibility of abortion follows from the permissibility of unplugging yourself from the violinist if and only if killing is not substantially worse than letting die. Thomson seems to take this to show that since the cases are sufficiently analogous, killing is not substantially worse than letting die. Finnis takes it to show that since killing is substantially worse than letting die, the cases are not sufficiently analogous. But the claim that the analogy stands or falls with the distinction itself provides support for neither conclusion. As a result, Thomson's response to the killing versus letting die objection leaves her position vulnerable to those who think that there are sound independent reasons to place great moral weight on the distinction between killing and letting die. Since I am attempting in this book to argue from premises that critics of abortion generally accept, and since many critics of abortion surely accept the claim that killing is worse than letting die, a stronger response to this objection is needed than the one Thomson has provided, a response that begins by taking seriously the claim that killing is substantially worse than letting die and then shows why the good samaritan argument should be accepted nonetheless. I will now attempt to develop such a response.

Since I want here to take seriously the claim that there is a morally relevant distinction between killing and letting die, it will be useful to have available a pair of cases that puts this claim in a favorable light. So consider what I will call, following Foot (1984: 282–3, details modified), Rescue I and Rescue II. In both cases, you are on a trolley heading north and about to come to a fork where you can either turn left or right. You have driven the trolley over this section of track many times before, and so you know that the two branches of the fork reunite a few miles later, shortly before the line ends at a local hospital. You also know that if you turn right you get to the end of the line substantially sooner than if you turn left, both because the route to the right is more direct and because the route to the left goes up and down a number of steep hills, whereas the route on the right is flat. But there is the following difference between the two cases. In Rescue I, you learn that there are five dying people lying by the side of the track near the middle of the left-hand branch, and one dying person lying by the side of the track near the middle of the right-hand branch. In Rescue II, you learn that there are five dying people lying by the side of the track near the middle of the left-hand branch, and one healthy (but temporarily unconscious) person stuck to the track near the beginning of the left-hand branch. Refer to Figure 4.1 for a diagram of the two situations.

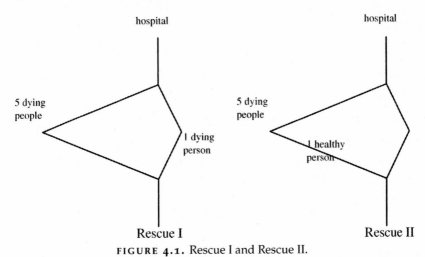

FIGURE 4.1. Rescue I and Rescue II.

In each case you have two options: Turn left or turn right. In Rescue I, if you turn left, you can get the five dying people to the hospital in time to save them. If you do this, however, there will not be enough time to go back and rescue the sixth dying person. Similarly, if you turn right, you can get the one dying person to the hospital in time, but then there will not be enough time to go back and rescue the other five. In Rescue II, if you turn left, you can get the five dying people to the hospital in time to save them. If you do this, however, you will run over and kill the healthy person who is stuck on the track. If you turn right, on the other hand, then (you know that) the healthy person will have time to work himself free from the track before another trolley comes along, but by the time you get to the point where the two forks converge and start to double back to save the five, it will be too late to save them. So in both cases, if you turn left, the final result will be that five people are alive and one is dead, and in both cases, if you turn right, the final result will be that one person is alive and five are dead. And so if the consequences of your decision are all that matter, then choosing to go left in Rescue I is morally on a par with choosing to go left in Rescue II.

Many people will find it plain that it is morally permissible to turn left in Rescue I but morally impermissible to turn left in Rescue II. You can fail to save one innocent person in order to save five others, they will say, but you cannot kill one innocent person in order to save five others. Of these, some will think it true that it would be morally impermissible for you to drive over the unconscious healthy person in Rescue II even if doing so were necessary in order to save a million dying people, while others will think that in such an extreme case killing the one would be morally permissible. But whether killing an innocent person is taken to be absolutely prohibited or merely substantially more difficult to justify than letting an innocent person die makes no difference to the objection to the good samaritan argument. Either way, the difference between the two cases demonstrates that you cannot conclude from the fact that it would be permissible for you to let someone die in a given situation that it would also be permissible for you to kill someone in relevantly similar circumstances. But drawing such an inference seems to be precisely what the good samaritan argument requires us to do. Assuming that it really is permissible to turn left in Rescue I but impermissible to turn left in Rescue II, then, what can be said in defense of the good samaritan argument?

4.5.2. Letting the Fetus Die

The first thing that can be said is that even if one acepts the moral relevance of the distinction between killing and letting die, there is at least one method of abortion, hysterotomy, that is more plausibly described as a case of letting die rather than a case of killing. Hysterotomy involves removing the living fetus through an abdominal incision of the uterus and then allowing it to die.[42] This procedure is more invasive and more dangerous to the woman than are other procedures, and for this reason it is typically reserved for later stages of pregnancy when other techniques are no longer feasible.[43] But there is no reason in principle why it could not be performed much earlier, if other methods were thought for some reason to be morally impermissible.[44] In addition, a woman with an unwanted pregnancy could always have a hysterectomy, removing both the uterus and the fetus within it. This would again permit her to be detached from the fetus without having to kill the fetus before or in the process of removing it. It would, again, be more invasive and dangerous, and would leave her unable to have children in the future, but the point remains that it is an available method of terminating a pregnancy that is more plausibly characterized as a case of letting die rather than a case of killing. In both of these cases, abortion seems simply to be a means by which a woman who has been providing needed life support to the fetus she is carrying can effectively discontinue her provision of such support; and when an agent discontinues providing another with needed life support, this seems clearly to be a case of letting die rather than of killing.[45] So if underestimating the significance of the

---

[42] Of course, it is possible that in some cases the fetus is in fact killed after its removal rather than left to die soon after, but presumably neither the woman seeking the abortion nor the person providing it would object to letting the fetus die instead if this were thought to render an otherwise impermissible procedure permissible.

[43] According to one anti-abortion tract, at least, the mortality rate for women who have an abortion by hysterotomy is 15 times greater than for those who have a saline abortion (Schaeffer and Koop 1979: 42). See also Knight and Callahan: "Because of its invasiveness and the attendant risks to the woman, [hysterotomy] should be utilized only late in gestation and only in special situations in which the life of the woman may be in peril (1989: 195; see also Kaplan and Tong (1994: 144)).

[44] Morowitz and Trefil, for example, refer to abortions that were performed using such methods on fetuses as early as $8\frac{1}{2}$ weeks into pregnancy (1992: 123), and this is about as early as abortions are typically performed using any other procedures.

[45] Or at least this is so in those cases in which the provision of life support is terminated by the provider or by someone authorized to do so by the provider. As

distinction between killing and letting die were taken to be the primary or decisive objection to the good samaritan argument, then its critics could at most establish that some but not all methods of abortion are morally permissible. And this would not impugn the good samaritan argument in defense of abortion any more than the claim that some forms of execution are immoral would undermine an argument in defense of the permissibility of capital punishment.[46] This is, admittedly,

McMahan (1993) has convincingly argued, whether an act of discontinuing life support counts as an act of killing or of letting die can depend on who is performing the act. If you unplug yourself from the violinist, this seems plainly to be a case of letting the violinist die. But suppose you decide to remain plugged into him for nine months and I break into the room in the middle of the night and disconnect you from him against your will. Here it seems plausible to say that I have killed the violinist. When you unplug yourself from the violinist, you simply stop keeping him alive, and to stop keeping someone alive is to let them die. But when I disconnect the violinist from you, it is not as if I am merely declining to keep him alive. I was not keeping him alive in the first place, and so when I deprive him of the life support that you are trying to give to him, I am doing more than simply refraining from keeping him alive. I am assuming here that the abortions in question are performed at the request of the women involved, and thus allow that if a doctor were to perform a hysterotomy against the woman's will this would count as his killing the fetus and not merely as his letting it die. Since the good samaritan argument is not meant to defend the claim that abortion is permissible when it is done against a woman's wishes, however, this restriction does not affect the substance of the argument, so I will continue to speak in the text simply of abortion per se.

[46] It might be objected that even though it is true that the good samaritan argument would remain sound as a defense of the permissibility of abortion in principle, its practical significance would be greatly reduced if it could only justify abortion by hysterotomy. Practically speaking, after all, the argument is important only to the degree that it corresponds to actual cases of abortion. And very few abortions are performed using this method. In this sense, the concession that the good samaritan argument succeeds, but only in cases of abortion by hysterotomy, might be compared to the concession that the argument succeeds, but only in cases of pregnancies arising from rape. That position, too, is consistent with the claim that abortion in principle can be permissible, but surely its significance as a defense of abortion as it is actually practiced is severely limited.

In one respect, this objection is correct. An argument in defense of abortion is of practical interest only to the extent that it provides a defense of actual abortions. But there is an important difference between limiting abortions to those performed by hysterotomy and limiting abortions to those that end pregnancies caused by rape: Any woman who wants an abortion can choose to have a hysterotomy performed on her, but a woman whose pregnancy arose from voluntary intercourse cannot choose that it be the case that her pregnancy arose from rape. If the good samaritan argument justified abortion only in rape cases, that would greatly reduce its practical significance, but if it justifies only a particular method of abortion, then, provided that the method could be made generally available, it will not.

a contingent fact about abortion, but it is a fact about abortion nonetheless.

Now, of course, one could object to the characterization of a procedure such as hysterotomy as an instance of letting die rather than killing. One might argue that since removing the fetus from the uterus (or the fetus and the uterus from the woman) actively deprives the fetus of the support it needs in order to survive, the remover causes the death and does not merely allow it to happen. Indeed, at least one critic of abortion has characterized hysterotomy as just this kind of killing, describing an example of such a procedure by saying that the doctor "made the incision, then reached in *to suffocate the baby* by disconnecting the baby's placenta from the womb" (Powell 1981: 50, emphasis added).[47] On this understanding, the very act of doing the disconnecting is itself a killing. But if we are to characterize hysterotomy as killing on these grounds, then by parity of reasoning we will also have to say that unplugging yourself from the violinst kills him and does not merely let him die, since it is equally true that unplugging yourself from him actively disconnects the violinist from the support that he needs in order to survive.

At this point, however, it is open to the critic of the good samaritan argument to concede that hysterotomy and unplugging yourself from the violinist are both killings but to insist that there is a morally relevant difference in the way in which they are killings. Foot herself argues that in the end the morally important difference we are inclined to insist upon in distinguishing between Rescue I and Rescue II is not between killing and letting die per se, but between initiating a fatal sequence of events and allowing a fatal sequence of events to run its course. And she suggests that this distinction does undermine the violinist analogy.

---

[47] Or as the Italian seminarian Daniel Viscosi argued in 1879, if you take a fish out of the water, you kill it and, similarly, taking a nonviable fetus from the womb amounts to the same thing (Connery 1977: 248). Similarly, Noonan compares abortion by hysterotomy to causing the death of an infant by exposure: "The death of the unborn child is caused by exposure to an environment he or she is not developed enough to function in" (1979: 167–8). And Walsh and McQueen argue as follows: "Intrauterine maternal sustenance is as necessary to the fetus's survival as air, food and fluids are for life outside the womb. To remove a person from these natural means of life support is direct killing" (1993: 361; see also Walker 1993).

Other critics of abortion, however, do not characterize hysterotomy in this way. A pamphlet prepared for the American Life League, for example, describes it as follows: "A surgical incision is made, the womb cut open and the infant removed, very much alive. Most babies are laid aside to perish. Some 'compassionate' doctors kill them to end their struggle for life" (Colliton undated).

When you unplug yourself from the violinist, that is, "The fatal sequence resulting in death is not initiated but is rather allowed to take its course." But the case of abortion, she argues, is "completely different. The fetus is not in jeopardy because it is in its mother's womb; it is merely dependent on her in the way children are dependent on their parents for food. An abortion, therefore, [even by hysterotomy] originates the sequence which ends in the death of the fetus" (1984: 288–9).

The problem with this argument is that Foot fails to establish that the act of removing the fetus from the womb is the act that originates the fatal sequence of events in the case of procedures such as hysterotomy. To point out that the fetus while in the womb is not in jeopardy does not suffice to establish that the act of removing it from the womb is the act that originates the fatal sequence. After all, the violinist while plugged into you is not in jeopardy either, and the act of unplugging yourself is not the act that originates the fatal sequence in that case: It merely allows a preexisting sequence to continue. Unplugging yourself results in the violinist's death only because his condition is such that he cannot survive on his own, and thus the act that originates the fatal sequence that you allow to continue is whatever act led to its being the case that the violinist had this condition. Similarly, then, since removing the fetus from the womb results in the fetus's death only if his condition is such that he cannot survive on his own, the act that would count as initiating the fatal sequence should be the act that led to its being the case that the fetus had this condition. Let us suppose that the fetus dies after it has been removed because its lungs are insufficiently developed to breathe on its own. Then whatever caused the fetus to have such poorly developed lungs at this point in time is what initiated the fatal sequence. And since it is presumably part of the normal course of things that a fetus at an early stage of gestation has lungs of this level of development, the act which causally led to this state of affairs was simply the act of conceiving it in the first place. This means that removing the fetus from the womb does not initiate the fatal sequence of events but merely allows the death to occur, which would have occurred in any event once conception had occurred if the woman had not been sheltering the fetus.

Two objections might be raised at this point. One arises from the fact that the fetus has been in the womb from the beginning of its existence, while the violinist was sick before he was plugged into you. So one might argue that there never was an already existing fatal sequence in the case of the fetus but that there was an already existing fatal sequence in the case of the violinist. And this would imply that removing the fetus does initiate the fatal sequence of events in the case of hysterotomy while unplugging yourself from the violinist does not. But this difficulty can be avoided merely by revising Thomson's story in the following way: You wake up in the morning and discover that last night some practical jokers kidnapped you and plugged you into a perfectly healthy violinist. In the middle of the night, though, his kidneys unexpectedly failed as a result of a predisposition to such failure that he inherited genetically. As a result, you must remain plugged into him for nine months or he will die. Surely if you think it is permissible to unplug yourself from the violinist in Thomson's version, you will think it permissible to unplug yourself in this version. What difference could it make whether the violinist got sick before or after he was plugged into you? But this version renders the violinist case just like the fetus case in terms of the chronology of the fatal sequence. There was never a time when the violinist was in danger of dying before he was plugged into you, just as there was never a time when the fetus was in danger of dying before it was in the womb. If you unplug yourself in this case, are you initiating a fatal sequence or allowing one to continue? I am inclined to say that you are allowing to continue a fatal sequence of events that began when the violinist was conceived with this genetic disposition, and if this is what we say, then we should similarly say that removing the fetus allows to continue a fatal sequence of events that began when the fetus was conceived with the genetic disposition to have insufficient lung development for independent survival at an early stage in its development. Granted, this is a genetic disposition that all human beings have, while the violinist's is a genetic disposition that only some human beings have. But it is difficult to see how this could be relevant to the question of whether in those cases in which an individual does receive the given disposition at conception this does or does not count as the initiation of the fatal sequence of events.

On the other hand, one might insist that in this variation on Thomson's story you are instead initiating a new fatal sequence of events. Perhaps we could say that by the act of unplugging yourself you are making it be the case that the failed kidney is fatal when it otherwise would not have been. I will not argue against this characterization, and if it is accepted, then, by parity of reasoning, it will follow that hysterotomy initiates a fatal sequence and does not merely allow one to continue, whereas unplugging yourself from the violinist in Thomson's original story does merely allow a fatal sequence to continue. But in that case, unless the critic of abortion is now willing to agree that unplugging yourself from the violinist is impermissible in my practical joker variation, he must concede that the distinction between initiating a fatal sequence and allowing one to continue is not the one we are looking for when we accept the distinction between Rescue I and Rescue II. So whether we characterize hysterotomy as killing or as letting die or as a peculiar kind of variation of one or the other, the essential point needed to sustain the good samaritan argument will remain: The case of the woman and the fetus and the case of you and the violinist (in my practical joker version of the story if not in Thomson's) are morally on a par in the case of abortion by hysterotomy even if killing is substantially worse than letting die.

My characterization of hysterotomy as allowing a preexisting fatal sequence of events to continue rather than as initiating a new fatal sequence of events may also be denied for a second reason: It seems tantamount to saying that all of life is a process of dying, and this can seem to stretch the notion of dying beyond its normal meaning. I am not myself convinced that this counts as a problem for the analysis I am proposing. A person whose death does not arise from some external cause does eventually die, and it seems to me that the beginning of his dying cannot non-arbitrarily be located at any point other than the point when he began to exist. And I suspect that what resistance there might be to my characterization arises from an ambiguity in such terms as *fatal, lethal,* and *threatening.* In one sense, these terms suggest a force that is external to the victim and not a natural part of his existence. In this sense, there is no such preexisting sequence in the case of the healthy fetus while there is in the case of the unhealthy violinist. But in another sense, such terms refer to whatever ultimately causes it to be the case that a death is going to occur which would otherwise not have occurred. This is the sense in which there seems to be a morally relevant difference between initiating such a sequence and allowing one to continue, and in this sense the fetus in the woman's womb is just as threatened as is the violinist plugged into you. In both cases, an act has already initiated a sequence of events in which an individual now stands in need of life support and will die if that support is discontinued.

But even if we reject this characterization and insist that there is no meaningful sense in which the fetus in the womb is threatened, the attempt to exploit Foot's analysis as a means of defending the killing versus letting die objection to the good samaritan argument must still be rejected. For if we agree that there is no preexisting threat to the fetus whose death comes about because it is prematurely removed from the womb, then we must equally agree that there is no preexisting threat to the young infant whose death comes about because nobody feeds it. Surely a person who fails to feed a hungry infant allows it to die and does not kill it, and so the result will then be that there need not be a preexisting threat to someone in order for it to be the case that by declining to provide support for him we do not kill him but rather let him die.[48] If this is the case, then, again, the distinction between initiating a fatal sequence of events and allowing one to continue is not the one we are looking for when we agree that there is a morally relevant difference between Rescue I and Rescue II, and so it will not matter if that distinction picks out a difference between hysterotomy and the case of you and the violinist. The distinction itself will be morally irrelevant. So whether we characterize hysterotomy as killing or as letting die or as a peculiar kind of variation of one or the other, the central claim made by the good samaritan argument will again remain intact: The cases of the woman and the fetus and of you and the violinist remain morally on a par even if killing is substantially worse than letting die.

4.5.3. Killing the Fetus

I have argued so far that even if you accept the claim that there is a morally relevant difference between Rescue I and Rescue II, this does not support the claim that there is a morally relevant difference between unplugging yourself from the violinist and abortion by hysterotomy. If this is so, then the good samaritan argument can succeed at least as a defense of hysterotomy even if killing is much worse than letting die. But let us now consider what we should have to say about those methods of abortion that do involve killing the fetus either prior to or in the process of removing it. On the face of it, accepting the distinction between the Rescue cases would seem to undermine any attempt to use the good samaritan argument as a defense of such methods. The way in which these methods bring it about that the fetus is dead, after all, is clearly like the way in which your running over the person stuck to the track in Rescue II brings it about that he is dead rather than the way in which your declining to save the person by the side of the track in Rescue I brings it about that he is dead. But I want now to argue that this impression is misleading. If we accept my argument to this point, that the distinction between killing and letting die does not undermine the analogy between unplugging yourself from the violinist and abortion by hysterotomy, and if we also recognize that hysterotomy poses greater

---

[48] This is the analysis that McMahan defends (1993: 404–6).

risks to the pregnant woman than do those methods of abortion that involve killing the fetus prior to or in the process of removing it, then we must conclude that a woman's choice to abort a fetus by means of a method that involves killing it rather than to have the fetus removed by hysterotomy or to carry it to term takes place in a context that is importantly unlike that involved in either of the Rescue cases. It instead takes place in the context of a set of choices that is relevantly like what I will call Rescue III.

In Rescue III, as in the other cases, there are again five dying people lying by the side of the track near the middle of the left-hand branch. But in this case, there is one unconscious dying person stuck to the track ahead of you before the track branches in two. You have the ability to stop the trolley, get out of it, free the unconscious dying person and put him in the trolley with you, before continuing on your way. However, in order to do so, you will have to expose yourself to some noxious fumes that will cause your trip to be more hazardous and potentially fatal to you than it would be if you were to remain in the trolley and simply drive over him. And in order to prevent the trapped person from dying, if you do stop to free him, you will then have to turn right at the fork and take the shorter route to the hospital, leaving the five by the side of the left-hand branch to die. If you free the trapped man and then turn left, he will die, but you will still be able to get to the five in time to save them. Refer to Figure 4.2 for a diagram of the three cases.

In Rescue III, there are three salient options:[49] (a) stop and free the trapped person, exposing yourself to the noxious fumes, then turn left at the fork, thus saving the five and allowing the (formerly) trapped person to die; (b) run over the trapped person, avoiding exposure to the noxious fumes, then turn left at the fork, thus saving the five and killing the trapped person; (c) stop and free the trapped person, exposing yourself to the noxious fumes, then turn right at the fork, thus saving the (formerly) trapped person and allowing the five to die.

I want now to make a number of claims about Rescue III. The first is that it is the choice you face in Rescue III, not the choice you face in

---

[49] In addition to the three possibilities I discuss here, there is, of course, a fourth option: You could run over the trapped person and then turn *right*, with the result that all six people end up dead. But I am assuming that no one would seriously propose this course of action, and that no woman would choose the course of action that would seem most closely to correspond to it: to abort the fetus and then nonetheless to choose (assuming this were possible) to suffer all of the burdens of an unwanted pregnancy.

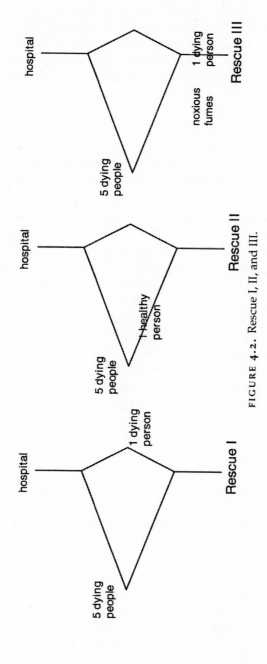

FIGURE 4.2. Rescue I, II, and III.

Rescue II, that parallels the structure of the choice a woman faces when she considers ending an unwanted pregnancy. Such a woman can (a) have the fetus removed by hysterotomy while exposing herself to higher costs and risks than if she had an abortion by some other method, thus avoiding the burdens of an unwanted pregnancy and allowing the fetus to die; (b) have an abortion by some other method, thus sparing herself the higher costs and risks of hysterotomy, killing the fetus and avoiding the burdens of an unwanted pregnancy; (c) carry the pregnancy to term, thus sparing the fetus and incurring the burdens of an unwanted pregnancy. Thus, in order to demonstrate that the good samaritan argument justifies all methods of abortion even if killing is substantially worse than letting die, I need not defend the claim that it would be morally permissible for you to run over the healthy person in Rescue II even if killing is substantially worse than letting die. I need only defend the claim that it would be morally permissible for you to run over the dying person in Rescue III even if killing is substantially worse than letting die. And this is a very different claim.

My second claim about Rescue III is a claim about the response that most people are likely to have to the case: I suspect that most people who agree that it would be impermissible for you to run over the trapped healthy person in Rescue II will nonetheless allow that it would be permissible for you to run over the trapped dying person in Rescue III. If it is morally permissible for you to allow one person to die in order to save five people in Rescue I, after all, then surely it will also be permissible for you to allow one to die in order to save five in Rescue III. So it would, at the least, be morally permissible for you to expose yourself to the noxious fumes and free the trapped man, and then turn left with the result that he dies anyhow and you save the five other people. But given that it would be permissible for you to let the currently trapped person die if you were to free him first, it is difficult to believe that it would be morally *required* for you to first expose yourself to the fumes in order to free him, given that in doing so you would then turn left and allow him to die anyway. And if you are not morally required to free him, then you are morally permitted to run over him, since stopping to free him and running over him are your only two options.

What I have said about the permissibility of running over the trapped person in Rescue III to this point amounts essentially to an appeal to intuition. Of course, it may be that the claim that killing is worse than letting die itself must ultimately rest on an appeal to intuition. And if this is so, then my claim that it would be morally permissible for you to run over the trapped dying person in Rescue III is every bit as firmly established as is the claim that it would be morally impermissible for you to run over the trapped healthy person in Rescue II. Still, those who hold that killing is worse than letting die often attempt to ground this claim in more general considerations, and it is worth asking whether, in this sense, more can be said in support of the claim that it would be morally permissible for you to run over the trapped dying person in Rescue III even if killing is worse than letting die. And I believe that something more can be said.

The something more stems from two thoughts. The first is the thought that any plausible defense of the claim that killing is worse than letting die must be part of a more general defense of the claim that causing harm is worse than allowing harm to happen, that it is worse to cut off a man's arm than to refrain from preventing it from being cut off, worse to give him a drug that will make him ill than to refrain from giving him an antidote when he has accidentally swallowed such a drug, and so on. The second is the thought that a plausible defense of the claim that causing harm is worse than allowing harm will at some point depend on the claim that when you cause harm to someone, you make him worse off than he would have been had you not happened on the scene, while if you merely allow harm to come to him as a result of an action that someone else has already initiated, you leave him no worse off (though also no better off) than if you had never come along.[50] In Rescue II, when you run over the trapped healthy person, you leave him worse off than he would have been had you not come along in the first place. Had you not come along in the first place, he would have freed himself from the track before another trolley came along. But in Rescue III, as in Rescue I, you do not leave the person who ends up dead worse off than he would have been had you not come along in the first place. In both cases, the person who ends up dead needed your assistance to go on living, and and so in both cases, they would have ended up dead even if you had

---

[50] I set aside complications arising from cases in which you prevent others from providing aid. In these cases, you do make the person worse off than they would have been had you not come along, since had you not come along, the person would have been rescued by others. And this raises some difficulties in terms of whether such cases should count as cases of causing harm. Such complications, however, do not affect the general point appealed to here, that merely allowing harm is less wrong than causing harm in virtue of the fact that merely allowing harm does not make the person worse off than they would otherwise have been. This is the sense in which killing the trapped person in Rescue III is morally on a par with not saving the dying person in Rescue I.

not come along in the first place. In this sense, you do not cause harm to the dying man by running over him in Rescue III, while you clearly do cause harm to the healthy man by running over him in Rescue II. And so the reason that is most likely to be invoked in support of the moral relevance of the difference between merely allowing harm by letting someone die in Rescue I and causing harm by killing someone in Rescue II fails to establish that killing is impermissible in Rescue III and cases relevantly similar to it. Cases of abortion that involve killing the fetus prior to or in the act of removing it rather than the substantially more invasive method of hysterotomy are relevantly like the killing in Rescue III. And so the claim that there is a morally relevant difference between Rescue I and Rescue II, the claim at the heart of the killing versus letting die objection, fails to undermine the good samaritan argument as a defense of these methods of abortion.

4.5.4. Two Objections

I have argued that it would be morally permissible for you to run over the trapped person in Rescue III even if killing is worse than letting die. And I have argued that if this is so, then the distinction between killing and letting die fails to undermine the good samaritan argument not only for methods of abortion such as hysterotomy, but also for methods of abortion that uncontroversially involve killing the fetus prior to or in the process of removing it. I want now to consider two objections that might be raised against my argument.

The first is an objection to my claim that those who maintain that killing is worse than letting die will generally agree that it would be morally permissible for you to run over the trapped dying person in Rescue III. For it might seem that the claim that it would be morally permissible for you to run over this person in Rescue III is inconsistent with other claims that virtually any proponent of the distinction between killing and letting die will defend. And if this is so, then the scope of my reply here is severely limited.[51] Consider, for example, the doctor who makes the following argument following the outline of my analysis of Rescue III: "We have a number of cases here at the hospital in which we determine that it would be permissible for us to discontinue treatment and allow a patient to die. Right now, for example, I am planning to

---

[51] I am grateful to an anonymous referee from *Social Theory and Practice* for identifying this objection in response to an earlier version of my Rescue III.

discontinue treatment of a cancer patient because the treatment itself causes her to suffer and she is going to die soon anyway. But once we discontinue treatment, she is still going to linger on for a few days, taking up a valuable bed space in our already strained hospital, and using up resources that could better be spent helping others. If it is permissible for you to run over the trapped person in Rescue III on the grounds that you are not going to save him anyway and are not morally required to, then once we have decided that it would be permissible for us to let her die and that we are, in fact, going to let her die, then we have no duty to incur the additional burdens of keeping her here, and so are entitled to kill her." And surely if there is anything that proponents of the distinction between killing and letting die will agree on it is that it is morally impermissible for the doctor to kill this patient even if it is permissible for the doctor to let her die.

There are a number of reasons to reject this objection. One is this: Although the discussion of the morality of killing versus letting die often takes place within the context of the debate over active versus passive euthanasia, it is not at all clear that those who think that killing is worse than letting die need think that active euthanasia is worse than passive euthanasia. After all, if we have a genuine case of passive euthanasia, we have decided that it is in the patient's own interest to die now rather than later, and so in killing her we would not be harming her. And if killing is worse than letting die because causing harm is worse than allowing harm, then the doctrine will simply fail to apply in cases where death is not a harm. Even if there are no further replies to this objection to my argument, then, I can conclude that the critic of the good samaritan argument is entitled only to the claim that the argument fails if one agrees that killing is worse than letting die even in cases where causing death does not harm the victim, and this seems to me a substantially weaker claim to be making.

But let us go ahead and assume that it would be a problem for my analysis of Rescue III if it entailed that it would be permissible for the doctor to kill the dying cancer patient. There are several reasons why my analysis does not entail this. One is that there is a difference between the duties that doctors have toward patients they care for in their hospitals and the duties that you have toward strangers you encounter on trolley tracks. Since the former are clearly stronger than the latter, it does not follow that if it would be permissible for you to treat a stranger in a certain way it would also be permissible for a doctor to treat a patient in a relevantly similar way. And, indeed, opposition to active euthanasia often turns crucially on the claim that it is incompatible with the duties that a doctor has to her patients in particular simply in virtue of being a doctor. A second reason that my analysis does not have this implication is that there is a difference in the kinds of burdens involved in the two cases. The cost of removing the trapped person from the track in Rescue III rather than running over him is an increased risk to your own health, while the cost to the doctor of withholding treatment rather than killing his patient is that it uses up additional resources which might more efficiently be used elsewhere. And it does not follow from the fact that it would be permissible to do something to avoid a risk to your health that it would also be permissible to do the same thing to avoid using some valuable resources that could more efficiently be used in other ways. In addition, the person trapped on the track is unconscious, while the dying patient in this example is not. And it does not follow from the fact that it would be impermissible to kill a conscious person under certain circumstances that it would also be impermissible under relevantly similar circumstances to kill an unconscious person who will never regain consciousness if you refrain from killing her and instead allow her to die. Finally, and in some respects most importantly, if the doctor wanted to avoid expending any further resources on the patient, he could simply discharge her from the hospital, letting her die rather than killing her. But that option is not available to you in Rescue III. In order to ensure that you allow the trapped person to die rather than kill him, it is necessary that you incur the unwanted burden. Accepting my claim that it is permissible for you to run over the trapped dying person in Rescue III, therefore, does not commit you to agreeing that active euthanasia is permissible whenever passive euthanasia is. So even those proponents of the distinction between killing and letting die who believe that killing is worse in those cases where death is not a harm to the one who is killed have no reason to reject my claim that it is permissible to run over the dying person in Rescue III.

A second objection to my response to the killing versus letting die objection agrees that it is morally permissible for you to run over the dying person in Rescue III, but denies that this shows that it is permissible for a woman to have an abortion by a method that involves killing the fetus rather than by a method that involves removing it and allowing it to die. One could agree that *sometimes* it is permissible to kill one whom you will otherwise permissibly let die in order to avoid some risk of harm to yourself, but maintain that whether or not this is so depends on how strong one's justification for letting the person die is in the first place.[52] In Rescue III, the justification for letting the person die is very strong: It is necessary in order to save five others. But in cases of hysterotomy, the justification for allowing the fetus to die is less strong: It is necessary in order for the woman to avoid the burdens of an unwanted pregnancy. So one could agree that in Rescue III it is permissible for you to kill the trapped person because you will otherwise permissibly let him die while maintaining that in the case of unwanted pregnancies killing the fetus is impermissible even if it will otherwise permissibly be allowed to die.

There is something right about this objection. If we believe that killing is worse than letting die when all else is equal, then we should at the very least be wary of the claim that it is *always* permissible to kill one whom you will otherwise permissibly let die in order to avoid some risk of harm to yourself. But there is also something wrong about this objection. If there are cases where it would be impermissible to kill one whom you will otherwise permissibly let die in order to avoid some risk of harm to yourself, then what makes the difference between the permissibility of killing and of letting die is not how strong the justification for letting die is in the first place, but rather how serious the cost to you of letting die rather than killing is. That this is so can be established by attending to two variations on Rescue III. In both cases, the configuration is the same as in Rescue III: There is one unconscious dying person trapped on the track ahead of you before the fork in the line, you will have to expose yourself to some unhealthy fumes in order to free him before continuing on your way, and there are some dying innocents lying by the side of the left-hand branch of the track whom you can save if and only if you either kill the trapped person and then turn left or allow him to die by freeing him and then turning left. But the two cases differ in terms of the two variables whose moral relevance is at issue in assessing this objection to my argument: how strong your justification for letting the trapped person die is, and how great the cost to you would be of letting him die rather than killing him.

Rescue IIIa: Lying by the side of the track on the left-hand branch is one dying person and one dying dog. So you can either save the life of the trapped person or save the life of the nontrapped person and the dog. If you can either save one person or save one person and one dog, it is a bit better to save one person and one dog, but not tremendously better. So while you are certainly justified

---

[52] I am grateful to Jeff McMahan for raising this objection in the context of an earlier version of my Rescue III.

in allowing the trapped person to die, your justification for letting the trapped person die is relatively very weak. The noxious fumes that you will have to expose yourself to in order to remove the trapped person from the track are very strong. They will cause a tremendously painful burn over the entire surface of your body, which will persist for a year and that resists all known forms of treatment. So the cost to you of letting the trapped person die rather than killing him is relatively very great.

Rescue IIIb: Lying by the side of the track on the left-hand branch are 500 dying people. So you can either save the life of the trapped person or save the life of the 500 other people. If you can either save one person or save 500 people, it is tremendously better to save 500 people. So your justification for letting the trapped person die is relatively very strong. The noxious fumes that you will have to expose yourself to in order to remove the trapped person from the track are very weak. They will cause you a very minor itch on the surface of your nose, which will persist for five minutes. So the cost to you of letting the trapped person die rather than killing him is relatively very small.

I assume that anyone who agrees that you may run over the trapped person in the original Rescue III will agree that you may run over him in Rescue IIIa. If it is implausible to suppose that you are morally required to subject yourself to the relatively milder fumes in the original Rescue III case, it is difficult to see how the fact that there are fewer innocents by the side of the left-hand branch in Rescue IIIa could make it be the case that you are morally required to subject yourself to the relatively stronger fumes which threaten you in that case. And while some who agree that you may run over the trapped person in the original Rescue III may also believe that you may do so in Rescue IIIb, I suspect that many will not. Moreover, refusing to allow that one may run over the trapped person in Rescue IIIb while agreeing that one may do so in Rescue IIIa seems quite reasonable. Suppose, after all, that there were no cost to you at all involved in letting the trapped person die rather than in killing him. Suppose that there were actually two points ahead of you where the tracks diverged and then reunited, that the trapped person was stuck to the left-hand track on the first fork, and that some number of dying people were lying by the side of the left-hand branch of the second. This case, which I will refer to as Rescue IV, is illustrated in Figure 4.3.

In Rescue IV, you must surely need some sort of justification for turning left at the first fork rather than right, and this seems to be so no matter how many dying innocents there are lying by the side of the track on the second left-hand branch. And if all of this is so, then it is

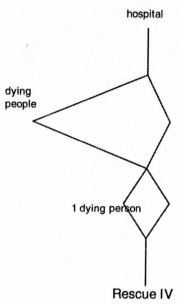

Rescue IV

FIGURE 4.3. Rescue IV.

the increased level of cost to the agent of letting die instead of killing, and not the strength of the agent's justification for letting die in the first place, that determines whether or not it is permissible for the agent to kill the person whom he will otherwise permissibly let die.

This response to the objection I am considering does not immediately vindicate the claim that the permissibility of abortion procedures in general follows from the permissibility of abortion by hysterotomy if it is permissible to run over the trapped person in the original version of Rescue III. The response does show that it does not matter how strong the woman's justification for having an abortion is so long as it is strong enough to justify having an abortion by hysterotomy. But it must still be asked how much greater the cost to her is of having the fetus removed in this way than it would be to have an abortion by some other method. If the extra costs and risks to her are more like the cost to you of getting out of the trolley in Rescue III or Rescue IIIa, then it will be permissible for her to have the fetus killed if it is permissible for her to have it removed and allowed to die. But if the extra costs and risks are more like the cost to you of getting out of the trolley in Rescue IIIb or of turning right at the first fork in Rescue IV, then it may be impermissible for her to have the fetus killed even if it is permissible for her to have it removed and allowed to die.

I am not at all confident that I can satisfactorily characterize the extra degree of risk and harm that a woman exposes herself to in having an abortion by hysterotomy as opposed to having one by some other method. But I am confident that in either case the good samaritan argument can be sustained. My sense from reading the literature as a non-expert is that the level of cost to the woman is such that if the noxious fumes imposed a comparable degree of cost on you, we would think it permissible for you to run over the trapped person in Rescue III. And if this is so, then the good samaritan argument succeeds in justifying all methods of abortion, even if killing is worse than letting die. But perhaps this is not so, and the extra cost to the woman in having a hysterotomy is relatively trivial. If this is the case, then the argument most likely fails to justify abortion by other means.[53] But now this becomes a very trivial concern. If it hardly matters to a pregnant woman what method of abortion she uses, then it hardly matters what methods of abortion turn out to be morally permissible so long as at least some of them do.

My argument here has turned on the claim that those who accept the moral relevance of the distinction between Rescue I and Rescue II will accept that it is permissible for you to run over the dying trapped person in Rescue III rather than expose yourself to the noxious fumes. But while I suspect that this is true for most such people, I do not want to insist that it is so for all. I suspect that most justifications that can be given for distinguishing between Rescue I and Rescue II produce the result that you are permitted to drive over the trapped man in Rescue III rather than incur the burden of exposing yourself to the noxious fumes and then allowing him to die instead. But there are surely some justifications which might be offered for distinguishing between Rescue I and Rescue II, and thus some proponents of the distinction between killing and letting die, whose accounts would not produce this result. And while I believe that most accounts of the distinction between killing and letting die do turn on the assumption that in killing a person you are making him worse off than he would have been had you not come

---

[53] I say "most likely" but not certainly because one could still argue that it would be permissible to run over the trapped person in Rescue IIIb, in which case even the tiniest increase in risk would suffice to justify having an abortion by some other method.

along, this too need not be so of all accounts. Indeed, on some accounts, killing a person is wrong even if you benefit him by doing so, say, by putting him out of excruciating, incurable suffering. Proponents of these positions will insist that the distinction between killing and letting die is of such great importance that you are truly required to incur the burden of releasing the trapped man before continuing on your way in Rescue III even though this does him no good and causes you substantial harm (and some of these would insist that you must do so even if doing so harms the man himself as well as you, say, by waking him up and forcing him to spend his last few hours of life in great pain rather than asleep). Indeed, a number of writers have clearly maintained that even in cases where the fetus and woman will both die if an abortion is not performed, abortion is still morally impermissible. As one such writer has put it, "it is preferable by far that a million mothers and fetuses perish than that a physician stain his soul with murder" (Healy 1956: 196).

To such people, I can say only that they must still grant the permissibility of abortion by hysterotomy while they deny its permissibility by other methods, unless they are willing to maintain that it would be morally impermissible for you to unplug yourself from the violinist. Still, I suspect that the fact that their account of the distinction between Rescue I and Rescue II would commit them to forcing you to incur such costs just so that you can ensure that the trapped dying man die from one set of causes rather than another (and possibly from a more painful set of causes) in Rescue III will be taken as a serious problem for their position even by most people who are in general sympathetic to the distinction between killing and letting die and who admit the distinction between Rescue I and Rescue II. For most people who accept the distinction between Rescue I and Rescue II, then, (as well, of course, as for all of those who reject it) the good samaritan argument should be taken as sound for all methods of abortion, including those that involve killing rather than merely letting die. Those who would resist this conclusion cannot rest their case, as they have to this point, merely on the claim that there is a morally relevant difference between cases like Rescue I and Rescue II. Instead, they must rely on the further and much more controversial claim that it is morally impermissible to run over the trapped dying person in Rescue III. Until they provide a satisfactory defense of this claim, they cannot expect their objection to the good samaritan argument to be accepted by those who agree that killing is worse than letting die.

4.6. THE INTENDING VERSUS FORESEEING OBJECTION

There is a separate objection closely related to and easily confused with the claim that the violinist analogy fails to respect the distinction between killing and letting die. This is the objection that it fails to respect the distinction between acting with the intention of causing a person's death and acting with the foresight that a person's death will result. This objection is not as frequently raised against the good samaritan argument in particular, but it has recently and forcefully been pressed in this context by Lee (1996: 111ff.),[54] and the distinction it rests on is commonly invoked in discussions of whether people who oppose abortion in general should make an exception for cases where the woman's life is threatened if the abortion is not performed.

4.6.1. The Objection

The claim underlying the objection here is that in at least some sorts of cases, such as those in which a woman's cancerous uterus must be removed in order to save her life, it can be permissible to do an action that foreseeably brings about the death of the fetus (since the fetus will surely die if the uterus is removed), even though it would not be permissible intentionally to kill the fetus, say, by crushing its skull in order to prevent it from killing the woman during the process of delivery (e.g., Reardon 1987: 164). This argument is commonly raised in the philosophical and theological literature on abortion, but it also appears in pamphlets and other documents produced by organizations opposed to abortion (e.g., Brown and Young 1994: 22–3, Rice 1986: 13–14, American Life League 1995 [pamphlet]). The distinction the argument rests on can apparently be applied to the violinist example as well. The result is what I will refer to as the intending versus foreseeing objection, which can be put as follows: When you unplug yourself from the violinist, you do an act foreseeing that the violinist will die as a result, but the death of the violinist is not what you intend. When an abortion is performed, on the other hand, the act itself is intended to kill the fetus. Since there is a morally relevant difference between intending death and foreseeing

---

54 The objection is also explicitly raised by Hurka (1994: 121), and, perhaps, also by Finnis in the argument interpreted in Section 4.5 as more likely referring to the distinction between killing and letting die.

it, it does not follow from the fact that unplugging yourself from the violinist is permissible that abortion is also permissible, even if there are no further disanalogies between the two cases.

As in the case of the killing versus letting die objection, one could defend the good samaritan argument from the intending versus foreseeing objection by denying that the distinction appealed to is a morally relevant one. But since I want to attempt to defend the good samaritan argument while relying on claims that critics of abortion will generally accept, I want again to consider what a defender of the argument can say even if we grant the assumption that the distinction itself is perfectly appropriate. So I will again begin by appealing to the sort of case that proponents of the distinction will likely favor as presenting the distinction itself in a favorable light, and then argue that even if one accepts it, the distinction fails to undermine the good samaritan argument.

So consider the following scenario: Nation A is fighting a just war against Nation B. Nation B is starting to run low on ammunition and on morale, but is continuing to inflict severe casualties nonetheless, resulting in retaliation and heavy losses on both sides. In Nation B, there is a large ammunitions plant closely surrounded by buildings that house athletes training to compete for Nation B in the Olympics. Two bombers fighting for Nation A each decide to drop a bomb on the center of the ammunitions plant and each do so because this will hasten the end of the war saving many lives on both sides. But the values that underlie their reasoning differ in the following manner:

Bomber I: I want to force the enemy to surrender by reducing its already low ammunition supply. The best way to do this is to destroy as many of its weapons as possible and the most efficient way to do that is to drop a single bomb on the ammunitions plant. I recognize that when I drop the bomb the explosion will also kill some innocent civilians, and this is a very bad thing, but their deaths are not a part of my plan or intention; I merely foresee that they will occur. And the good of ending the war suffices to outweigh the evil of their deaths.

Bomber II: I want to force the enemy to surrender by reducing its already low morale. The best way to do this is to kill as many of its most popular civilians as possible, and the most efficient way to do that is to kill all the Olympic athletes living around the ammunitions plant, since that can be done by blowing the plant up with a single bomb. This plan has the added bonus of reducing the enemy's weapons supply as well, but that is just the icing on the cake; the point is to use the death of the athletes to cripple support for the war among the enemy's population, thus ending the war and saving countless lives on both sides. I recognize, of course, that killing innocent civilians is in itself a very bad thing, but I intend to kill them nonetheless, since the good of ending the war suffices to outweigh the evil of killing them.

This example is constructed so that if we view the two bombings from the outside, as it were, they are identical. Each bomber drops a bomb in exactly the same spot with exactly the same results in exactly the same order. So we might well be inclined to insist that there can be no morally relevant difference between the two *actions*, though we may well agree that Bomber II is a morally worse *person* than Bomber I. If this is our response to the cases, then the good samaritan argument will be immune to the intending versus foreseeing objection. A proponent of the argument can agree that a woman who has an abortion is a worse person than you are if you unplug yourself from the violinist. The claim made by the argument is merely that if your act of unplugging yourself is morally permissible, then so is the pregnant woman's act of aborting her pregnancy.

But I am assuming at least for the sake of the argument that this is not our response to the two cases. We reject the notion that an act can be fully understood independently of the intentions that bring it about (or, we might say, that at least in part constitute it). In this sense, we insist that what Bomber I and Bomber II *do* are different and, in particular, that what Bomber I does is permissible, whereas what Bomber II does is impermissible. The claim that there is a morally relevant difference between the intentions of the two bombers can be rendered more precise by asking the following counterfactual question of each: If the athletes were living elsewhere, so that dropping the bomb here would destroy the ammunitions plant but not kill the athletes, while dropping the bomb elsewhere would kill the athletes but not destroy the ammunitions plant, would you still have dropped the bomb here? To this question, Bomber I would answer yes. This demonstrates that his true intention is simply to destroy the plant. But Bomber II would answer no. If the athletes were living somewhere else, then he would drop the bomb there instead. This demonstrates that his true intention is to cause their deaths. So we can say that in accepting that there is a morally relevant difference between Bomber I and Bomber II, we are insisting that there is a morally relevant difference between those who would answer the counterfactual question yes and those who would answer it no. In saying this, we accept some version of the Doctrine of Double Effect. Assuming that we do accept this, what, if anything, follows about the analogy underlying the good samaritan argument?

4.6.2. Intentionally Letting the Fetus Die

Let me again proceed by distinguishing abortion by hysterotomy from abortion by methods that involve killing the fetus before or in the process of removing it, and by beginning with the case of hysterotomy. When put in terms of the two Bomber cases, the intending versus foreseeing objection rests on the conjunction of two distinct claims: that in terms of intentions, unplugging yourself from the violinst is analogous to what Bomber I does and that in terms of intentions, a woman aborting a pregnancy is analogous to what Bomber II does. The first claim maintains that when you unplug yourself from the violinist, you foresee that the violinist will die as a result of your action, but that this is not a part of what you intend to accomplish. The second claim maintains that when the woman has an abortion by hysterotomy, she intends that the fetus end up dead and not merely that it end up removed. I will assume that the first claim is true in your case. What about the second?

A defender of the good samaritan argument could, I suppose, maintain that in typical cases of abortion, the woman merely wants to be relieved of the unwanted burden of carrying the developing fetus and would have no objection to the removed fetus then being safely transferred to an artifical incubator or another woman's womb, if that were possible. Since such transfers are not currently possible, this response would argue, she foresees that the fetus will die as a result of its removal, but this is no part of her intention. On this account, her intention would run parallel to that of you when you unplug yourself from the violinist, and so the violinist analogy would not be undermined by the moral relevance of the distinction between intending death and foreseeing it. Whatever the merits of this empirical claim might prove to be, however, it is difficult to believe that a typical critic of abortion will be willing to accept it. If part of what divides critics and defenders of abortion is their sense of what motivates women to have abortions in typical cases, then a response to the intending versus foreseeing objection that rests on such a claim will be viewed by critics of abortion as begging the question, and with at least some justification. I believe, therefore, that a defense of abortion that attempts to engage critics of abortion on their own terms should concede, at least for the sake of the argument, that in typical cases of abortion, the pregnant woman wants more than merely to be relieved of the burden of the pregnancy itself. She wants to be relieved not only of the burden of pregnancy, but also of the burden of knowing that she has produced an offspring being raised by someone else somewhere in the world. For her, the death of the fetus developing inside her is a part of her intention in seeking an abortion.

If this is, in fact, the case, then the intending versus foreseeing objection is in one important respect correct: The pregnant woman's intention is not parallel to that of the intention of Bomber I, while your intention in unplugging yourself from the violinist is parallel to that of the intention of Bomber I. But in another important respect, the objection is mistaken: Even though it is true that the intention of the woman in such cases does not run parallel to the intention of Bomber I, it is also true that the intention of the woman in such cases does not run parallel to the intention of Bomber II. I want now to argue that her intention instead is more like that of a still further bomber, and that accepting the distinction between Bomber I and Bomber II does not commit us to concluding that what this further bomber does is impermissible. If this analysis is correct, then accepting that there is a morally relevant difference between intending death and foreseeing it does not undermine the good samaritan argument at least as a defense of abortion by hysterotomy.

The possibility of a still further kind of bomber arises from the fact whenever an act produces two distinct effects, there is always a third alternative to intending one effect and merely foreseeing the other. One can simply intend both. An overweight person who goes on a diet, for example, may do so intending to improve his health while merely foreseeing that this will make him more attractive. He may also do so intending to make himself more attractive while merely foreseeing that doing so will also improve his health. But he may also go on a diet with the intention of producing both results. In such a case, it would be misleading to speak of either of the effects of his diet as merely a foreseeable consequence. Two versions of this third case must be distinguished. In one version, at least one of the dieter's intentions is such that it would be strong enough to motivate him to go on the diet even if it turned out that it was his only reason for dieting. Even if the diet improved his health and not his appearance, for example, a dieter in this sort of case would still stick to his diet. I will refer to an intention of this sort as a sufficient intention. The fact that an intention is sufficient means that it would be enough in itself to motivate an agent to action even in the absence of further intentions. But the fact that an intention is sufficient does not mean that there are not, in fact, any other intentions. The dieter may have a sufficient intention to improve his health, but he may still intend to improve his appearance nonetheless. In a second version of this sort of case, the presence of both intentions is necessary in order to motivate the dieter to stick to his diet. Neither the improvement in health alone nor the improvement in attractiveness alone strike him as sufficient to justify the sacrifices involved. But given that he can accomplish both goals simultaneously, he concludes that the diet is justified. So in both cases the dieter has both intentions, even though the second of the two would quit if he learned that the diet would only improve his appearance, whereas the first would not.

With the distinction between sufficient and insufficient intentions in mind, we can identify two further versions of the bomber case, which I will call Bomber III and Bomber IV. Both do precisely the same act as Bomber I and Bomber II, and both do so intending both to cause the destruction of the ammunitions plant and to cause the death of the innocent civilians. But they differ in the way that the two dieters with both intentions differ.

Bomber III: I want to force the enemy to surrender by reducing its already low ammunition supply *and* by reducing its already low morale. The best way to satisfy this combination of desires is to drop a single bomb on the ammunitions plant, destroying some of their weapons and killing some of their Olympic athletes. If dropping the bomb only destroyed the ammunitions plant and didn't kill any innocent civilians, then dropping the bomb would still be justified. Destroying the plant would be a sufficient reason to drop the bomb. But since the bomb will also kill the Olympic athletes, and since I view that as another legitimate goal, I drop the bomb with the intention of causing both effects.

Bomber IV: I want to force the enemy to surrender by reducing its already low ammunition supply *and* by reducing its already low morale. The best way to satisfy this combination of desires is to drop a single bomb on the ammunitions plant, destroying some of their weapons and killing some of their Olympic athletes. If dropping the bomb only accomplished one of these two objectives, then the decision to drop the bomb would not be justified. If it only killed the civilians and didn't destroy the ammunitions plant, then the bomb would be better used elsewhere where it could do more damage. And if it only destroyed the ammunitions plant and didn't kill any innocent civilians, then it would again be better used elsewhere where it could do more damage. But as things stand, dropping the bomb will have both effects, and for that reason I view the decision to drop the bomb as justified.

I want now to make two claims about these further cases. The first is that accepting the distinction between Bomber I and Bomber II is consistent with maintaining that what Bomber III does is permissible even though what Bomber IV does is impermissible. The second is that the intention of a woman who has an abortion is relevantly like the intention of Bomber III rather than that of Bomber IV. If both of these claims are correct, then accepting the distinction between Bomber I and Bomber II does not undermine the good samaritan argument, at least in the case of abortion by hysterotomy.

The main reason for accepting the first claim is simple. What most clearly distinguishes Bomber I from Bomber II is their different answers to the counterfactual question: If the athletes were living elsewhere, so that dropping the bomb here would destroy the ammunitions plant but not kill the athletes, while dropping the bomb elsewhere would kill the athletes but not destroy the ammunitions plant, would you still have dropped the bomb here? To this question, Bomber I answers yes and Bomber II answers no. This is what makes it the case that causing the deaths of the innocent civilians is essential to the act that Bomber II does but not essential to the act that Bomber I does. And it seems plausible to many people to suppose that this difference is a morally relevant one. But in this respect, Bomber III is like Bomber I and Bomber IV is like Bomber II. When asked the same question, that is, Bomber III would answer yes and Bomber IV would answer no. And so if the difference in intentions accounts for the judgment that what Bomber I does is permissible while Bomber II does is not, then this judgment does not imply that what Bomber III does is impermissible even if it does imply that what Bomber IV does is impermissible.

This is not to say that there is no morally relevant difference between Bomber I and Bomber III. Surely there is. Bomber III is walking around with a wholly unacceptable intention, whereas Bomber I is not. But Bomber III has this intention even when he is not acting on it, say, when he is just watering his flowers, and the mere presence of this intention is not enough to render such acts impermissible. And when Bomber III drops the bomb, unlike when Bomber IV does, the presence of this intention is not essential to the act he is performing. So we are entitled to criticize the kind of person Bomber III is even though we are not entitled to criticize the kind of person Bomber I is. But this does not mean that we are entitled to criticize what Bomber III does.

Further support for this assessment of the permissibility of what Bomber III does can be found by applying the distinction between sufficient and insufficient intentions directly to Thomson's violinist story. In unplugging yourself from Thomson's violinist, I am assuming that you intend only to relieve yourself of the burden of remaining plugged into him, and that his death is purely a foreseeable but unintended consequence. In this sense, you are like Bomber I. We can imagine a variation on this case in which you would be just as happy to stay in the hospital for nine months – perhaps you have nothing better to do with your time and the food is to your liking – but you decide to unplug yourself solely in order to bring about the death of the violinist. In that case, your intention would run parallel to the intention of Bomber II, and if we agree that what Bomber II does is impermissible, we must also agree that what you do in this version of the story is impermissible as well.

But now consider what would, in effect, amount to Violinist III and Violinist IV. In both cases, you would like to be free to leave the hospital, since staying there is a substantial infringement on your liberty, and in both cases you would also like to see the violinist end up dead, say, because you are also a violinist in the local symphony and he is your chief rival. In Violinist III, the harm to you of having to stay in the hospital for nine months is itself sufficient to motivate you to unplug yourself. You would unplug yourself even if doing so would not cause the violinist to die, but given that it will cause the violinist to die, the bringing about of his death is also one of your intentions, since you do have a desire that he die. In this respect, you are like the dieter whose intention to improve his health would suffice to motivate him to stick to his diet, but who nonetheless also intends to improve his physical appearance and does not view that as a merely foreseeable side effect. In Violinist IV, on the other hand, you do not view the harm of being stuck in the hospital for nine months as a sufficient motivation to unplug yourself. You view being in the hospital as a bit undesirable, but if the violinist were not someone you wanted to see end up dead, you would choose to remain plugged in for nine months. In this resepct, you are like the dieter who is motivated to diet only by the conjunction of improving his health and his physical appearance.

It is not difficult to see how the belief that what Bomber II does is impermissible would entail the belief that unplugging yourself in Violinist IV is also impermissible. In both cases, the agent would not do the act he does were it not for the fact that the act will bring about a bad outcome. And so, in both cases, the agent's immoral intention plays an essential role in his acting as he does. But it is extremely difficult to see how this could lead us to say that it would be morally impermissible for you to unplug yourself in Violinist III. In Violinist III, after all, you have a permissible intention that suffices to motivate you to be unplugged – the intention to free yourself from being stuck in the hospital for nine months. And this would seem to suffice to make it morally permissible for you to unplug yourself. After all, imagine that you are the doctor in Violinist III. The person plugged into the violinist has called you over to his bed demanding that you unplug him from the violinist. You are about to unplug him, since you agree that the violinist has no right to use this person's kidneys to stay alive, but then at the last moment you discover that not only does the person intend to liberate himself from the hospital by being unplugged from the violinist, but he also intends to improve his chances of becoming first chair in the local symphony by bringing about the death of his main rival. Could you really maintain that you must now leave the person plugged into the violinist because one of his intentions is unacceptable? This seems an extremely implausible position to take. But unless the critic of abortion is willing to take it, he must concede that the acts done in cases like Bomber III and Violinist III are morally permissible.

Finally, let us consider the case of a woman whose reason for seeking an abortion is not merely that it will relieve her of the burdens of an unwanted pregnancy but that it will cause the death of the fetus. I suppose we can imagine cases in which a woman's intention is *only* to cause the death of the fetus and has nothing at all to do with the effects of the pregnancy on her body. We might, for example, picture a woman who has always wanted to experience the physical transformations involved in pregnancy and who would enjoy carrying a pregnancy all the way to birth, but who is deterred from doing so only by the fact that she does not want to raise children and does not want to have offspring of hers being raised by others. But presumably this is not what critics of the good samaritan argument have in mind. The case they very plausibly point to is the one in which a woman wants to avoid the burdens of pregnancy *and* wants to avoid the fate of having offspring of hers being raised by others. The intention of such a woman is thus clearly different from the intention of Bomber I and of Bomber II. The question is whether it is relevantly like the intention of Bomber III or of Bomber IV.

The way to answer this question is again to ask a suitably constructed counterfactual question. Critics of abortion themselves often exploit this sort of strategy effectively in establishing that for many women who seek abortions the death of the fetus is not merely a foreseeable side effect. How, they ask, would a woman who seeks an abortion respond if after the procedure was over she were told that the fetus had successfully been removed, but that it had been kept alive and would be brought to term and then raised by someone else? Presumably, many women would feel that they had not gotten all that they had asked for. And this counts as good reason to conclude that, in such cases, the woman's intention in seeking an abortion does include the death of the fetus and not merely its removal. But in order to determine whether this intention is essential to her act in such cases, whether, that is, she is relevantly like Bomber III or like Bomber IV, we must ask whether she would still choose to have such a procedure done if that were the only alternative to carrying the pregnancy to term. Suppose, in short, that she were told that no matter what happens, the fetus she was carrying was going to survive. The only question was whether she wanted it removed now or not. Perhaps there are some women who in such circumstances would choose to continue the pregnancy. But presumably for most women who seek abortions, being relieved of the burdens of an unwanted pregnancy is itself a sufficient reason to have an abortion, even if it is not the only reason they act on. In this respect, they are like the dieter for whom an improvement in appearance is a sufficient reason to stick with his diet even if it is not the only reason he acts on. And, more importantly, they are thus like Bomber III, who, like Bomber I, would still drop the bomb on the ammunitions plant even if it would not cause the death of any innocent civilians. If this analysis is correct, and if I have been correct that the distinction between Bomber I and Bomber II does not commit us to saying that what Bomber III does is impermissible, then we can accept the claim that there is a morally relevant difference between intending death and foreseeing it without abandoning the good samaritan argument, at least as it applies to abortion by hysterotomy.

4.6.3. *Intentionally Killing the Fetus*

I have argued thus far that if you agree that it is permissible for you to unplug yourself from the violinist, then accepting the importance of the difference between intending harm and foreseeing it fails to undermine the violinist analogy at least as it applies to hysterotomy. And as I noted in my discussion of the killing versus letting die objection in Section 4.5, the conclusion that some methods of abortion are impermissible does not suffice to undermine the good samaritan defense of abortion itself. But let us now ask what implications the distinction would have for those methods of abortion that involve killing the fetus before or in the process of removing it. As in the case of the distinction between killing and letting die, it might at first seem clear that accepting the distinction between intending harm and foreseeing it will suffice to undermine the analogy. In cutting the fetus into pieces in order to remove it, the doctor clearly acts with the intention of killing the fetus and not merely the foresight that the fetus will die. It is true, of course, that he intends this not as an end in itself but as a means to a further end, but that is equally true of Bomber II, and we are assuming here that we agree that what Bomber II does is impermissible, whereas what Bomber I does is not. But I want now to suggest that whether or not accepting the distinction between Bomber I and Bomber II undermines the violinist analogy for such methods of abortion depends on *why* we think the distinction is justified.

Here is one plausible suggestion:[55] Bomber I is aware that innocent civilians will die as a result of his action, but he does not propose to use their deaths as a means to his end. If he could destroy the ammunitions plant without causing their deaths, he would. Bomber II, on the other hand, seeks to secure the death of the civilians precisely as a means to his end. If destroying the ammunitions plant would not cause their deaths, he would use some other means to kill them. There is thus an important sense in which the two bombers take a different attitude toward the civilians. In particular, Bomber II (but not Bomber I) views the civilians as if they exist for his purposes, and this is essential to his act. But, we may well insist, people have value as ends in themselves, not merely as means to the ends of others (no matter how worthy those ends may be). So Bomber II acts with an unjustified attitude toward his victims, whereas Bomber I does not, and this attitude is essential to the act that Bomber II does. This, it can plausibly be argued, accounts for and justifies the distinction between our response to the two cases.

Let us suppose that something like this is our reason for concluding that what Bomber I does is permissible, whereas what Bomber II does is not, and now consider the case of a further bomber who finds himself in a different set of circumstances. In this case, the innocent civilians are all sleeping on top of the ammunitions plant, and there are two different ways in which he can destroy the plant. He reasons as follows:

Bomber V: I want to force the enemy to surrender by reducing its already low ammunition supply. The best way to do this is to destroy as many weapons as

---

[55] The suggestion is a simplified version of Quinn (1989: 190–3).

possible and the most efficient way to do that is to destroy the ammunitions plant. There are two ways I can do this. One is to drop Bomb A on the plant. For reasons peculiar to its design, however, Bomb A cannot be successfully detonated if there are living human beings on the roof of the building. So in order to use Bomb A, I will first have to fly over the plant and kill all of the sleeping civilians with a lethal gas. Then, after they are all dead, I can return and drop Bomb A. The alternative is to drop Bomb B. It has a special guidance system that will allow it to enter from the side of the plant, allowing the civilians to continue their sleep without disturbance until the bomb detonates. They will then die as a result of the plant being blown up. But Bomb B also releases a dangerous form of radiation that will reach as far as my cockpit, making this method more dangerous and potentially fatal to me.

I suspect that most of us will say that it is permissible for Bomber V to drop Bomb B. If it is permissible for Bomber I to drop his bomb, after all, it is extremely difficult to see why it would not be permissible for Bomber V to drop this one. But let us now ask whether it would be permissible for Bomber V instead to gas the sleeping civilians and then drop Bomb A. If our justification for the distinction between intending harm and foreseeing harm in general is of the sort I have described, it seems plausible to conclude that this, too, is permissible. In killing the civilians in this case, Bomber V does not view the civilians as if they exist for his own purposes. If there were a way for him to safely remove them from the roof before destroying the plant, he would do so. In this respect, gassing the sleeping civilians and then dropping Bomb A would make Bomber V relevantly like Bomber I rather than like Bomber II. And in choosing Bomb A over Bomb B, Bomber V is not using the death of the civilians as a means to his end. The civilians will be killed by his actions in either case, and so it is not their dying rather than not dying (or even their being killed by him rather than their being allowed to die by him) that enables Bomber V to avoid the risks associated with Bomb B, but simply their being killed by Bomber V's releasing of some lethal gas rather than by Bomber V's dropping of one of his bombs. It is easy to see that making a person die rather than live so that you can achieve some goal, however worthy, is using him as a means to your end. But it is extremely difficult to see how causing a person to die by one means rather than causing him to die by another, in cases where it is permissible to cause the death by the first means and the cause of death makes no difference to him, is using him as a means, or failing to respect him as an end. And so the claim that there is a morally relevant difference between Bomber I and Bomber II does not support the conclusion that it is morally impermissible for Bomber V to gas the innocent civilians and then drop Bomb A.

Now, this conclusion may at first seem little short of sophism. The claim that there is a morally relevant difference between Bomber I and Bomber II, after all, just *is* the claim that there is a morally relevant difference between intending death and foreseeing death. And the difference between Bomber V's gassing the innocent civilians and then using Bomb A, on the one hand, and his instead using Bomb B, on the other, just *is* the difference between his intentionally causing their deaths, on the one hand, and his foreseeably causing them on the other. So how could it be the case that judging Bomber II's act to be impermissible fails to entail that it is impermissible for Bomber V to gas the innocent civilians and then drop Bomb A?

But the argument I have been making here points to a crucial difference between the two pairs of cases. When we compare intentionally causing death and foreseeably causing death in the cases of Bomber I and Bomber II, we compare a case where a person chooses intentionally causing death over not causing death to one who chooses foreseeably causing death over not causing death. And, if we accept the moral relevance of the distinction, we affirm that the permissibility of the latter does not imply the permissibility of the former. But if Bomber V chooses to gas the sleeping civilians and then drop Bomb A, he does not choose intentionally causing death over not causing death. Rather, he chooses intentionally causing death over foreseeably causing death, in a context where the choice between the two makes no difference to the ones who will die but does make a difference to him in terms of the degree of risk of harm he will face. This is a fundamentally different kind of choice. And so the conclusion that the choice made by Bomber II is impermissible does not carry over to the choice made by Bomber V.

If this analysis is correct, then if the intending versus foreseeing objection fails to undermine the good samaritan argument in the case of abortion by hysterotomy, as I argued in Section 4.6.2, then it also fails to undermine the argument in the case of abortion by other methods. Thomson's violinist scenario is like Bomber I: Unplugging yourself from the violinist with the foresight that the violinist will die is relevantly like destroying the ammunitions plant with the foresight that the surrounding athletes will die. The proponent of the objection agrees with this characterization, but claims that the woman who has an abortion is instead like Bomber II, who kills the innocent civilians intentionally and not just foreseeably. And since what Bomber II does is impermissible even though what Bomber I does is permissible, the critic argues that what the woman who has an abortion does is impermissible even though what you do in unplugging yourself from the violinist is not. But because of the existence of procedures such as hysterotomy, the case of a pregnant woman who chooses to have an abortion in which the fetus is killed before or during its removal rather than to have a hysterotomy or to carry the fetus to term takes place in a context that is importantly unlike that of Bomber II. It is instead relevantly like the case of Bomber V choosing to gas the sleeping civilians and then drop Bomb A rather than to drop bomb B and suffer exposure to the radiation or to allow the ammunitions plant to remain standing. One can agree that there is a morally important difference between Bomber I and Bomber II and still maintain that if it is permissible for Bomber I to drop his bomb, then it is permissible for Bomber V to gas the sleeping civilians and then drop Bomb A. And so one can agree that there is a morally important difference between Bomber I and Bomber II and still maintain that if it is permissible for a woman to have an abortion by hysterotomy, then it is also permissible for her to instead have an abortion by a less risky and invasive method that involves killing the fetus before or in the process of removing it.

That this is so can again perhaps best be seen by considering a further variation on Thomson's story. Suppose you agree that you are permitted to unplug yourself from the violinist in a way that foreseeably leads him to die. But you then discover that you can save yourself a fair amount of harm and reduce your risk of death by intentionally killing him first and then unplugging yourself. As in the case of Bomber V, it seems to me that if you are permitted to foreseeably cause his death in the first place, then accepting the moral significance of the difference between Bomber I and Bomber II does nothing to show that you are required to take the more dangerous and harmful route when the results are the same for him (remember, he is unconscious). The two seem equally to respect him as an end, since you are only intentionally killing him because it is permissible for you to foreseeably cause his death anyway and because foreseeably causing his death would impose a greater cost on you. Again, it is not his death that you are using as a means to your end in this case, but rather your causing his death by one means rather than your causing his death by another means. And nothing about accepting the claim that there is a morally relevant difference between Bomber I and Bomber II commits you to believing that this is impermissible. If this analysis is correct, then the pregnant woman who has an abortion that involves killing the fetus before or while removing it can say precisely the same thing: Since it would be permissible for her to undergo a more dangerous and invasive procedure that would foreseeably cause the fetus's death, she does no disrespect to its value as an end by choosing to have it aborted in this way instead.

I do not want to insist that the considerations I have advanced in favor of the permissibility of Bomber V killing the innocent civilians and then using Bomb A are decisive on every account of the justification for the distinction between intending death and foreseeably bringing death about. I suspect that the autonomy-based justification I have briefly sketched for distinguishing between Bomber I and Bomber II is not the only justification which would produce the result that Bomber V is permitted to kill the civilians and then drop Bomb A rather than suffer the risk of exposure to the radiation from dropping Bomb B. But there are surely some justifications that might be offered for distinguishing between Bomber I and Bomber II, and thus some proponents of the distinction between intending death and foreseeably bringing it about, whose accounts would not produce this result. Proponents of these positions will insist that the distinction is of such great importance that you truly are required to run the risk of exposure to the radiation from Bomb B even though this does no good for the civilians who will be killed by your actions either way, and causes you substantial harm. To such people, I can again say only that they must still grant the permissibility of abortion by hysterotomy while they deny its permissibility by other methods, or admit the impermissibility of unplugging yourself from the violinist. Still, I suspect that the fact that their account of the distinction between Bomber I and Bomber II would commit them to forcing you to incur such costs just so that you kill the civilians by one means rather than by another in the case of Bomber V will be taken as a serious problem for their position even by most people who are in general sympathetic to the distinction between intending and foreseeing and who admit the distinction between Bomber I and Bomber II. For most people who accept the distinction between Bomber I and Bomber II, then, (as well, of course, as for all of those who reject it) the violinist analogy underwriting the good samaritan argument should be taken as sound for all methods of abortion, including those that involve killing the fetus before or in the process of removing it. And those who would argue that the good samaritan argument still fails to justify those methods of abortion that involve killing the fetus rather than foreseeably causing its death cannot rest their case, as thay have to this point, simply on the claim that there is a morally relevant difference between cases such as Bomber I and Bomber II. They must instead rely on the claim that it is impermissible for Bomber V to gas the sleeping civilians and then drop Bomb A given that if he doesn't he will cause their deaths by dropping Bomb B. This is a much stronger claim than the claim that there is a morally relevant difference between Bomber I and Bomber II, and it is not supported by the claim that there is a difference between those two cases. And until they provide a satisfactory defense of this claim about such cases as Bomber V, they cannot reasonably expect their objection to the good samaritan argument to be accepted by those who agree that there is a morally relevant difference between intending harm and foreseeing it.

4.7. THE STRANGER VERSUS OFFSPRING OBJECTION

Consider the case of Laverne and Shirley, each of whom declines to make a substantial sacrifice on behalf of a three-year-old child who is in need of her assistance. In Shirley's case, the child is a stranger, but in Laverne's case the child is her daughter. Surely this will make a difference in our moral assessments of the two cases. But this suggests a further difficulty with the good samaritan argument: the violinist in Thomson's analogy is a stranger, unrelated to you, but the fetus is a blood relative, the son or daughter of the pregnant woman. And this again suggests that we cannot move from the claim that it is permissible for you to unplug yourself from the violinist to the conclusion that it is permissible for the woman to abort her fetus. Schwarz puts the objection as follows: "The person hooked up to the violinist (we are assuming) has no duty to sustain him, for he is a total stranger, standing in a relation to the person that is most unnatural. This is exactly the opposite of the mother-child relation, which is most natural and proper. We do not have the obligation to sustain strangers artificially hooked up to us, but we do have the obligation to sustain our own children" (Schwarz 1990: 118).[56] What can a defender of the good samaritan argument say in response to this objection?

---

[56] This objection is also raised by a number of other writers, including Schwarz and Tacelli (1989: 82–4), Wennberg (1985: 159), Wilcox (1989: 215–16), Whitbeck (1983: 254), Gensler (1986: 239).

The first thing to say is that it does not follow from the fact that there is a morally relevant difference between what Laverne does and what Shirley does that there is a difference in terms of the moral permissibility of what they do. For consider the case of Thelma and Louise, each of whom murders a three-year-old child in order to collect payment from someone who wants the child dead. The child Louise kills is a stranger, but the child Thelma kills is her own daughter. Surely this will make a difference in our moral assessments of the two cases here, too, just as it did in the case of Laverne and Shirley. Our moral intuitions almost invariably judge that as horrible as both acts are, Thelma's is worse. But it is clear in this case that we do not really believe that Louise's victim had any less of a right not to be killed than Thelma's. There is no difference here in terms of moral permissibility. This does not mean, however, that our differential intuitions in this case should be abandoned. They should merely be recharacterized. We should be willing to concede that their actions are equally impermissible, but to insist that it takes an even more base and reprehensible character to be able to bring yourself to kill your own child.[57] And this suggests that at least a good deal of our intuitive response to the case of Laverne and Shirley can be accounted for by saying that Laverne is a worse person than Shirley, rather than by saying that Laverne does something she has no right to do while Shirley does something she has a right to do. And if that is how we account for such cases, then the good samaritan argument will be immune to the objection based on the difference between strangers and relatives: The claim made by the argument is not that a woman who has an abortion is no worse a person than you are if you unplug yourself from the violinist, but simply that if what you do is morally permissible then so is what she does.

But let us assume that we are not fully satisfied with this response. It remains to ask why it should be the case that Laverne's daughter has a stronger right to assistance from her than the stranger has to assistance from Shirley. One possibility is that she has this right simply in virtue of the fact that she is the biological offspring of Laverne, whereas the

---

[57] The same, presumably, would be said about the difference between killing innocent adults and killing innocent children. We typically think worse of child murderers than of typical murderers, but this cannot plausibly be taken as evidence that we think that adults have less of a right not to be murdered than children have.

stranger is not biologically related to Shirley. This is the explanation that Schwarz defends:

> The parents of a particular child have this obligation to him, and not someone else, because they are his biological parents; because they, and not someone else, begot and conceived the child. It is the biological bond that creates the obligation of parents to take care of their children, and also the rights that accompany this obligation (1990: 118).

If it is this difference in terms of biological relatedness that grounds the differential judgment in the case of Laverne and Shirley, then the analogy underlying the good samaritan argument will be defeated, since you are not biologically related to the violinist while the pregnant woman is a biological parent of the fetus she is carrying.

But there are several difficulties with this account of the difference between the cases of Laverne and Shirley. The first is simply that it seems to be utterly mysterious how the mere fact of biological relatedness could, in and of itself, generate such a difference in moral obligations. It would not be mysterious if the claim turned on the fact that the woman did some voluntary action that led to the conception of the child, since the moral salience of the distinction between voluntary and involuntary actions is relatively straightforward. And at least part of Schwarz's argument might be taken to support this interpretation: It seems right to say that the woman "begot" the child in cases of voluntary intercourse, but not so in the case of pregnancies arising from rape. To beget a child is to *cause* it to exist, and in rape cases the woman does not do anything to cause the child to exist. But if this were the explanation of the moral relevance of the biological relation between parent and child, then the stranger versus offspring objection would simply reduce to the tacit consent or responsibility objection all over again. And while it would certainly have a high degree of prima facie plausibility, it would also remain subject to all of the difficulties I identified with those objections in Sections 4.3 and 4.4. In addition, if the objection were construed in this way it would fail to apply to rape cases, and it is clear that the stranger versus offspring objection is meant to apply to such cases as well. As Schwarz puts it: "Suppose the woman has been raped. She still has a duty to sustain the life of the child. . . . The biological relation of mother to child is still there, unaffected by the circumstance of the rape" (1990: 119). But if the biological relation is not morally relevant in virtue of its relation to something that the woman did, then it is difficult to understand how it can be morally relevant to what the woman is now obligated to do.[58]

In addition, the claim that it is the biological difference that makes the difference in terms of permissibility in the case of Laverne and Shirley produces extremely counterintuitive results if we consider variations on the violinist and pregnancy cases that differ from the original cases in terms of biological relatedness only. Consider first the following case: You are about to unplug yourself from the stranger-violinist, as Thomson's critic concedes you are permitted to do. At the last moment, a DNA test reveals that the violinist is actually a son of yours who you never knew existed. Many years ago you had contributed to a study in which people donated sperm and egg samples for fertility research, and without your knowledge and against your expressed wishes someone had stolen some of what you had donated and created a zygote *in vitro*, which was then implanted in a woman, the result of which now lies on the bed next to you. If one objects to Thomson's violinist analogy on the grounds that it ignores the morally relevant distinction between biological relatedness and biological nonrelatedness, then one will have to insist that in this modified case, it would be morally impermissible for you to unplug yourself from the violinist. But this is likely to strike most people as highly implausible. It is not difficult to imagine that this discovery would have some effect on you. Even though you have had no personal relationship or interaction with the violinist, the fact that he is your biological offspring might well make it more difficult for you to decide to unplug yourself. And it is not difficult to imagine that others might criticize you for deciding to unplug yourself in a way that they

---

[58] Lee (1996: 122) suggests that "the biological relationship [between pregnant woman and unborn child] itself does have moral significance" because the "relationship is one of physical continuity or prolongation.... The mother and the father are in a certain sense prolonged or continued in their progeny." Lee concedes that this point is "difficult to articulate" and as a result it is also difficult to argue against. But even if it is accepted, it does nothing to justify the claim that the relation imposes special moral duties on the pregnant woman. It justifies the claim that a woman who destroys her own fetus destroys something that is in some sense a part of her or a future continuation of her, but we then need a reason to believe that it is impermissible for people to destroy what is in this sense a part or future continuation of themselves. And it is by no means clear that this is so. Indeed, to the extent that Lee is correct to characterize a woman's choice to abort as the choice of "an action against herself, against herself because she exists in a way in her child," it would if anything seem that her act is *easier* to justify than if this claim were not true. In general, after all, it is easier to justify the permissibility of acts that harm ourselves than of acts that harm others.

would not have done had the violinist been biologically unrelated to you.[59] Still, it is extremely difficult to believe that while you have the right to unplug yourself from the violinist in Thomson's version you do not have such a right in this version.

Perhaps some critics of abortion will be willing to bite the bullet at this point and maintain that unplugging yourself in this version of the story would be morally impermissible. This would permit them to remain consistent with their other beliefs. But it would also dramatically reduce the force of their argument, since most people who do not already share their belief will be unlikely to accept this judgment of the case. And, in any event, there is a second way of testing the moral relevance of biological relatedness that produces results that the critic of abortion in particular will almost certainly be unwilling to accept. For just as we can modify the violinist story so that you are biologically related to the violinist, so can we modify the pregnant woman story so that she is *not* biologically related to the fetus she is carrying. Consider the case of what is commonly referred to as a gestational surrogate mother, a woman who has an embryo implanted in her that is the product of the conception of another couple's sperm and egg. In this case, the embryo is biologically unrelated to the woman who is pregnant, just as the violinist is biologically unrelated to you in Thomson's version of the story. In typical cases, of course, the woman has the embryo implanted voluntarily, and this would make the case relevantly different from the violinist story. But suppose instead that she simply wakes up one morning in the hospital and discovers that she has had the embryo implanted in her. Perhaps she had checked into the hospital to have some other procedure performed and due to some administrative mix-up she has instead had this biologically unrelated embryo implanted in her. The embryo has been implanted, and there is no way to remove it now without causing its death. If one maintains that the good samaritan argument would succeed were it not for the morally relevant distinction between biological relatedness and biological nonrelatedness, then one will be forced

[59] It may even be plausible to suppose that you would have the duty to incur some relatively small cost on his behalf that you would not have to incur on behalf of one not related to you, though even this judgment is difficult to make sense of given that the moral salience of merely genetic facts is obscure. But even if we accept such a claim, it does little to undermine the good samaritan argument. The burdens imposed by an unwanted pregnancy are substantially greater than the burdens you would be obligated to incur on behalf of a stranger, and not just marginally greater.

to agree that the argument does succeed in the case of this unwanted pregnancy. One will have to say that it would be morally impermissible for a woman who is raped to have an abortion, because the product of the rape contains some of her DNA, but morally permissible for a woman who has an embryo implanted in her against her will to have an abortion, provided that the egg with which the embryo was created came from someone else. It is extremely difficult to imagine that any critic of abortion (let alone a defender) would be willing to accept this differential judgment, to agree that whether or not abortion violates the fetus's right to life depends on whether or not the egg whose fertilization resulted in the fetus originated in the pregnant woman's body. But if critics of abortion are not willing to accept this claim, then they cannot maintain that biological relatedness makes the difference between the permissibility of unplugging yourself from Thomson's violinist and the impermissibility of abortion.

Mere facts about biological relatedness, then, seem to be poor candidates for accounting for the difference in our assessments of Laverne and Shirley. Their moral salience is obscure at best, and insisting on their moral relevance produces results that virtually everyone, including virtually every critic of abortion, will find unacceptable. Still, if this is the only explanation for our judgment that is available, it may be good enough. Difficult as it may be to believe that this is what makes the difference in the case, and difficult as it may be to accept the implications that this would have for the two variant cases I have just described, it may be less difficult than abandoning the claim that what Laverne does is impermissible while what Shirley does is not. But abandoning this claim is not necessary. There is a different and more satisfying explanation that can be given for that judgment: A woman has a stronger duty to assist her son or daughter than to assist a stranger not because she is the child's biological parent, but because she is the child's *guardian*.

This explanation is preferable for several reasons. First, to be a guardian for someone is to occupy a certain kind of social role, and the moral salience of such a relation is significantly less problematic than is the salience of purely biological relations. It is generally accepted that people can have special duties to their friends, their neighbors, and so on, and on this account, the moral relevance of parenthood coheres naturally with these other judgments that we are inclined to make. Second, this explanation avoids the problems of the two variant cases discussed previously. For as I argued in Section 4.4, it seems plausible to suppose that when a woman (or man) takes a newborn child home with her from the hospital, she tacitly accepts the role of guardian for the child.[60] Nothing that was said against the tacit consent objection in Section 4.3 counts against this claim, since such a woman voluntarily brings about a state of affairs in which there is now a child under her care, while a woman who engages in intercourse voluntarily brings about a state of affairs in which there is now a man having intercourse with her foreseeing that this may give rise to a further state of affairs.[61] And this account enables us to make sense of the two pairs of cases that undermine the biological relatedness account. You are not the violinist's guardian in either version of the story, and this accounts for why you may permissibly unplug yourself in either version. And neither the woman who is raped nor the woman who has an unrelated embryo unwillingly implanted in her are guardians of the fetuses they carry, and this explains why abortion will either be permissible in both cases or impermissible in both cases. Finally, this analysis enables us to account for judgments that we would naturally make in variant cases of the story of Laverne and Shirley. Suppose, for example, that Laverne's daughter is adopted. Does this make any difference to your assessment? I suspect that it does

[60] It is also worth reiterating another point I made in that context: To say that parents have a *special* duty to assist their children in virtue of the role they have voluntarily assumed does not entail that a woman who gives birth to a child and declines to assume that role has *no duty* to assist the child at all. It would entail this only if it insisted that there are no general positive duties to assist others, and the good samaritan argument does not require that there be no such duties. It requires only that whatever duty there is to assist others in general is not so strong as to require you to remain plugged into the violinist. Overlooking this point can make Thomson's argument seem to be vulnerable in a way that it is not. Lee, for example, objects that Thomson's argument would lead us to condone such acts as those of people who "have left their newborn child in a garbage dumpster" (1996: 110). But it has no such implication. A woman who leaves a newborn child in a garbage dumpster when she could instead leave it at a hospital or police station does something reprehensible, but this is true even if the newborn is not hers, but one that is left on her doorstep.

[61] It might be objected that we can find ourselves occupying social roles without ever voluntarily agreeing to do so. And this seems to be true. You may find that you have become someone's friend without ever intending to, and this may lead you to have special obligations to him. But this poses no problem for Thomson's argument either. One could say, as Schwarz does, that the special relation between pregnant woman and the unborn child is one in which "the child is entrusted to her" (1990: 120), but then there is no reason not to also say that Thomson's scenario is one in which the violinist has been entrusted to you. If anything, there is more reason to say this in the violinist case, since in that case there is literally a group of people who have done the entrusting while there is no one who has done so in the pregnancy case.

not. It would be difficult to deny that adoptive parents have all of the duties to the three-year-old children they have adopted that biological parents have to the three-year-old children they have raised from birth.

That parents have special obligations to their own children is a claim that is likely to be accepted by both sides of the abortion debate. But it will count against the good samaritan argument only if these obligations are generated by the mere fact of the biological relation between them. There is no good reason to accept this account of these obligations and good reason not to. And so there is no good reason to accept the stranger versus offspring objection and good reason not to.

4.8. THE ADULT VERSUS INFANT OBJECTION

Another potential problem with the good samaritan argument arises from the following consideration: The individual whose life is dependent on you in the violinist story is a fully developed adult while the individual whose life is dependent on the woman in the case of an unwanted pregnancy is an underdeveloped infant. This difference is significant because it is plausible to suppose that infants have a stronger right to assistance from others than do adults. And if this is so, then the permissibility of declining to assist a fully developed adult will fail to establish the permissibility of declining to assist a developing infant in relevantly similar circumstances. This consideration has not been widely marshalled as an objection to the good samaritan argument in particular, but the comparison between the responsibility a pregnant woman has to support the fetus she carries and the responsibility she has to care for an abandoned baby left outside her door is one that arises frequently in the literature against abortion independent of discussions of the argument (e.g., McFadden 1996: 116), and it is at times used in the context of defending other objections to the argument (e.g., Beckwith 1992: 116, in his defense of the killing versus letting die objection).

It might be objected that the difference cited by this objection cannot pose a problem for the good samaritan argument because that argument is limited to the claim that the impermissibility of abortion does not follow from the claim that the fetus has the same right to life as you and I. And even if we agree that infants have greater rights to *assistance* than do adults, we will surely not insist that they have a greater right to life. But this observation alone is insufficient to vindicate the argument. On Thomson's account, at least, the right to life is the right not to be killed unjustly. When you unplug yourself from the violinist, you do not violate his right to life because you kill him by depriving him of something to which he has no right. But if you kill someone by depriving him of something to which he does have a right, say, by taking away some of his legitimately acquired property, then you do violate his right to life. And the claim that infants have a greater right to assistance than do adults entails that it is possible that aborting the fetus kills it by depriving it of assistance to which it does have a right, even though unplugging yourself from the violinist kills him by depriving him of assistance to which he does not have a right. As a result, more must be said to overturn the adult versus infant objection.

And more can be said. The first thing that can be said is that we need some account of the source of the greater right to assistance that infants have. It is difficult to imagine that this account will succeed unless it turns on the claim that infants are more in need of assistance than adults. And if this is how the account works, then it is difficult to see how it will avoid the implication that even though violinists in general lack so strong a right, this violinist in particular has it. This particular violinist, after all, is every bit as helpless as a newborn infant.

But suppose that this response is unsatisfying. In that case, we can simply modify Thomson's analogy. Suppose that the violinist you find yourself plugged into is a three-year-old prodigy. Assuming that we agree that children have a greater right to assistance than do adults, then even if we believe that the adult violinist has a weaker right to assistance than do small children, we won't believe that of this particular violinist. Yet if you agree that it would be morally permissible for you to unplug yourself from the adult violinist, it is difficult to believe that you would find it impermissible for you to unplug yourself from the three-year-old. Emotionally, you may well find that unplugging yourself from a child is more difficult than unplugging yourself from an adult, and it might be argued that unplugging yourself from a child would involve a kind of coldheartedness that would not have to be involved in Thomson's violinist case. But even if we were to agree with all of this, this would still fail to undermine the good samaritan argument. The argument, as I have stressed before, does not insist that a woman who has an abortion is not a worse person than you are if you unplug yourself from the violinist. It maintains only that if your act is morally permissible, then so is hers. And so the infant's stronger right to assistance is insufficient to undermine the good samaritan argument.

Indeed, we can modify the violinist analogy still further and make this conclusion even stronger. Suppose that the violinist you find yourself plugged into is a female violinist in an *irreversible* coma. No matter what you do, she will never regain consciousness. However, this violinist is pregnant. If you remain plugged into her for the remainder of her pregnancy, she will remain alive and the fetus she is carrying will continue to develop and will successfully be brought to term. If you unplug yourself, she will die now and the fetus will die as a result. It is difficult to imagine that even the strongest critics of abortion would insist that it would be impermissible for you to unplug yourself in this case. They will, of course, maintain that there are a number of relevant differences between this case and that of a pregnant woman having an abortion. But that is not the issue here. So long as they agree that it would be permissible for you to unplug yourself in this case, then they must agree that the difference between the rights of infants and the rights of adults does not explain why it is permissible for you to unplug yourself in Thomson's original story. And that is all that one must accept in order to agree that the adult versus infant objection must be rejected.

4.9. THE DIFFERENT BURDENS OBJECTION

Another difference between the two cases is fairly straightforward: In Thomson's story, you must remain bedridden for nine months in order for the violinist to survive, but this is not so in a typical case of pregnancy. There are numerous burdens imposed on a woman who is pregnant, of course, as there are burdens imposed on you in Thomson's story, but the burdens are not the same. Does this difference weaken the good samaritan argument?

John Martin Fischer has presented an argument that attempts to demonstrate that it does, by appealing to the following variant on Thomson's case.[62] Suppose you are already in a hospital room recovering from major surgery and will have to remain in bed for nine months in order to recuperate. A great violinist is then brought into your room, and everything proceeds as in the original story. Fischer urges that in this "surgery case" it would be impermissible for you to unplug yourself from the violinist. And yet, he points out, the violinist would be making use of your body here in precisely the same way as he would in Thomson's version. Fischer concludes from this that it is not "the right to decide what happens in and to one's body" that drives our

---

[62] The objection is also pressed by a number of other writers including Nathanson (1979: 220–1) and Lee (1996: 128).

intuitions in Thomson's original example. Rather, it is the extent to which your being forced to remain attached to the violinist is disruptive of your various plans and projects, hinders what he refers to as your self-determination. In Thomson's example, this disruption is great; in Fischer's variant, it is marginal (Fischer 1991: 7–8). And so, in Thomson's example you are permitted to unplug yourself, while in Fischer's you are not. This creates a problem for Thomson's analogy, Fischer then argues, because "it is not evident that pregnancy is properly treated as relevantly similar to [Thomson's] violinist case rather than the surgery [variant]" when we compare the cases in terms of their hindering the agent's self-determination. And indeed, he suggests that it is "not unreasonable" to suppose that typical pregnancies are "much more" like his version than they are like Thomson's (Fischer 1991: 10). If this is so, then concluding that we may unplug ourselves from Thomson's violinist provides very weak support for the claim that in typical cases a woman may seek an abortion.

Fischer's objection consists of three claims: that unplugging yourself is permissible in Thomson's story but not in the surgery variant; that this is best explained by appealing to the difference in the level of threat to self-determination in the two cases; and that, judged by this criterion, typical pregnancies are in fact substantially more like the surgery variant than like Thomson's example. There may be some room to question the third claim, and it is not clear that Thomson herself would accept the first (since she might argue that in this case it would be indecent of you not to help the violinist, but not a violation of his rights), but I will assume, at least for the sake of the argument, that Fischer is correct about these and focus here on the second.

So let us suppose that we agree with Fischer that it would be morally impermissible for you to unplug yourself in the surgery variant. Why should this be so? Presumably, Fischer is right that this must be because the cost to you is so minimal in the surgery variant and so great in Thomson's story. But I do not see why the only sort of cost that can be invoked to explain the distinction must be cashed out, as Fischer does, in terms of self-determination. For suppose Fischer is right to limit the relevant considerations in this way, and then consider the following further variation: You are already in a hospital room recovering from major surgery and will have to remain in bed for a week in order to recuperate when the famous violinist is brought in and is plugged into you for a week. So the procedure imposes no cost on you in terms of self-determination. However, your recovery was expected to be completely painless, and if you don't unplug yourself soon the procedure will cause you a great deal of physical pain over the next seven days. Call this the "painful" variant. I suspect that most of us do not believe that you violate the violinist's right to life by unplugging yourself in this case. We do not, for example, think that it is morally impermissible for a person to refuse to undergo the very painful procedure involved in removing some bone marrow, even if he is already in the hospital anyway and could prevent someone else, even a famous violinist, from dying by doing so. Yet on Fischer's account, we would be forced to agree that the violinist has a right to your bone marrow since you have to be in the hospital anyway even if extracting it will cause you great pain.

I conclude from this that the more reasonable explanation of our differential responses to Thomson's story and Fischer's variant, assuming that we have a differential response, involves appealing to the *total* cost to you in each case and not just to the cost in terms of restricting your self-determination. And once we accept this, we can make Thomson's story sufficiently like a typical case of pregnancy without losing the intuitive response to it on which the good samaritan argument depends.

Indeed, there is a simple, if somewhat contrived, way to make the story sufficiently like a typical case of pregnancy. Suppose (to offer one final variation) you wake up in the morning and find that you have had implanted in you what I will call a "pseudo-zygote." A pseudo-zygote behaves in exactly the same way that a zygote does: If left in your body, it will develop into a pseudo-embryo and then pseudo-fetus, and will continue to grow for approximately nine months, having all of the same effects on your body as a genuine fetus would have before it finally induces contractions and is delivered in an equally painful manner. The only difference between a zygote and a pseudo-zygote is that the pseudo-zygote is a purely artificial device: It is not living, it is not conscious, it has no moral standing. So under ordinary circumstances, you would have no qualms whatsoever about having it removed from you even if doing so meant destroying it in the process. But when you wake up in the morning, you find that the circumstances are not ordinary. For it turns out that there is a famous violinist somewhere who is dying of a rare disease. And it also turns out that the only way for him to be cured is for him to receive an injection of a very rare synthetic serum. It turns out, in addition, that the only way to generate the serum is to allow a pseudo-zygote to develop to term and then to extract the serum from the pseudo-fetus (pseudo-infant?) after it is "born." Finally, and unfortunately for you, it also turns out that you are the only person whose body is capable of keeping the pseudo-fetus "alive" for the requisite nine months of development. So either you bring the pseudo-fetus to term and give "birth" to it and the violinist lives, or you remove the pseudo-fetus and the violinist dies. The pseudo-fetus itself, remember, has no moral standing. The only issue is whether you are obligated to incur the cost of carrying it to term where removing it prematurely effectively kills the violinist and bringing it to term amounts to saving the violinist. Acknowledging that you would have such a duty unless there was some nontrivial cost to you, you ask the doctor what you can expect to happen over the next nine months. You are told that it is reasonable to expect the following to occur in typical cases[63]:

Physical Costs: You will almost certainly suffer at least some of the following common symptoms over the next nine months: fatigue, nausea, vomiting, frequent urination, excessive salivation, heartburn, indigestion, flatulence, bloating, constipation, headaches, faintness or dizziness, food aversions and cravings, varicose veins, cramps, body aches, hemorrhoids, bleeding gums, backache, skin blotching, swelling especially of ankles and feet, itchy abdomen, shortness of breath, difficulty sleeping, clumsiness, nosebleeds.

In addition, you will certainly gain weight over nine months to the point where you will experience discomfort and difficulty moving; you will also have to endure the process of losing the weight afterwards or suffer long-term health consequences. Also, you will find that you will be very restricted in the medications you will be permitted to take; if you suffer from allergies, for example, you may well find that you'll just have to live with the symptoms, as well as many of the symptoms already described. Finally, there will be a period of at least a few hours and quite possibly many more than this during which you will experience physical contractions about which nearly every other person who has undergone this procedure has said, "It was the most excruciating pain I have felt in my entire life." There will then be a slow process of recuperation during which you will at the least be exhausted and sore, and may also have to recover from some minor incisions that are routinely done to facilitate the procedure.

Autonomy Costs: You will only have to spend the very end of these nine months in a hospital bed (or equivalent); still, there are a number of other restrictions on your self-determination you should be aware of. You won't be allowed to smoke or use recreational drugs and will be allowed to drink only moderately. You may well find this to be a substantial curtailment of your freedom. You will also find that during the last month or so airlines may prevent you from flying

---

[63] Much of the following is taken from Eisenberg, Murkoff, and Hathaway (1991).

and your health plan (assuming you have one) may forbid you from being more than a certain distance from its favored hospital.

Financial Costs: We'll assume that your medical coverage is pretty good. Still, there are some things you'll have to pay for out of your own pocket. For one thing, those clothes of yours aren't going to fit much longer. You'll have to buy some that will only fit you for a short while and that tend to be rather expensive. You may also lose at least some wages.

Psychological Costs: We should also let you know that there will be a number of hormone changes during this period. So expect that at one point or another you will experience at least some of the following: irritability, mood swings, weepiness, difficulty concentrating and remembering things, anxiousness, boredom, weariness, impatience. It is also extremely likely that you will experience substantial changes in your sexual appetite, and it is not unusual to suffer a period of depression or let down after the procedure has been completed.

I then ask: Do you really believe that it would be morally impermissible for you to remove and destroy the pseudo-fetus? I do not know how to go about arguing the point, so I will merely state my suspicion that most people who agree that you may unplug yourself in Thomson's original story will also agree that you may "unplug" yourself here. If so, then the differences between the costs involved in a typical pregnancy and the costs involved in Thomson's version of the story do not, contrary to Fischer's claim, make a difference to the strength of the good samaritan argument.[64]

There is, however, one final twist that might be added to the objection. Although I have not seen the point explicitly raised in the context of the good samaritan argument in particular, it is a common theme of much recent writing against abortion that having an abortion is itself both psychologically and physically unhealthy for the pregnant woman. Reardon, for example, refers to research reporting evidence linking abortion to such stress-related consequences as "sexual dysfunction, depression, flashbacks, sleep disorders, anxiety attacks, eating disorders, impacted grieving, a diminished capacity for bonding with later children, increased tendency toward violent outbursts, chronic problems in maintaining intimate relationships, difficulty concentrating, and a loss

---

[64] For a useful survey of court decisions holding that the harms of a typical pregnancy constitute serious bodily injury under the law, see McDonagh (1996: 84–91).

of pleasure in previously enjoyed activities and people" (1996: 142; see also Reardon 1987: chap. 4).[65] And packets of information prepared by organizations opposed to abortion often include pamphlets and booklets with such titles as "How to Survive Your Abortion" and "Psychological Complications of Abortion" and references to books with such titles as "Every Woman Has a Right to Know the Dangers of Legal Abortion" (McKinney et al. undated; LeBow 1986; Saltenberger 1982). In addition, abortion even at early stages of pregnancy is a surgical procedure and thus poses attendant medical risks, which cannot in fairness be ignored. A booklet prepared by the Lousiana Department of Health and Hospitals, for example, cites such risks as pelvic infection, blood clots in the uterus, heavy bleeding, cut or torn cervix, perforation of the uterus wall, and anesthesia-related complications (1995: 16–17; see also Reardon 1987: chap. 3). It also refers to studies providing evidence that having an abortion increases a woman's risk of devloping breast cancer (1995: 17), a claim also made in pamphlets typically enclosed with materials provided by organizations opposed to abortion (e.g., Willke 1994; Brown 1995).[66] To set the analogy straight, then, we must specify that the process of unplugging yourself from the violinist also imposes a variety of costs or risks of costs, and of comparable magnitude.

This modification seems to me worth including, but it does not seem to undermine the strength of the good samaritan argument. It may have some bearing on whether or not women (or some women) would be wise to have an abortion, but if it would be permissible to unplug yourself painlessly, it is difficult to see why it would not also be permissible to unplug yourself at some cost to yourself in order to avoid the substantially greater cost of not unplugging yourself.

---

[65] The psychological impact of abortion is also acknowledged and explored by defenders of abortion, including most notably Francke (1978).

[66] The claim that abortions increase the risk of breast cancer is one of the most controversial in the literature on the consequences of abortion. According to Recer, at least five studies have found that abortion increases the risk of breast cancer, six have found that it does not, and one has found that it lowers the risk. The wide disparity of results may in part be explained by a yet further study, reported by Recer upon its publication in the *Journal of the National Cancer Institute*. According to that study, previous studies may have been skewed by the simple fact that women do not always tell the truth about whether or not they have had an abortion, and may be less inclined to do so in areas where it is less socially acceptable (Recer 1996: A-11).

4.10. THE ORGAN OWNERSHIP OBJECTION

One of the most interesting and least discussed objections to the good samaritan argument begins with the following suggestion: In the case of you and the violinist, the claim that the kidneys that lie beneath your skin belong to you is essentially uncontroversial. But on the assumption that the fetus has a right to life, it is perhaps not obvious that the organs that lie beneath the skin of a pregnant woman and whose functioning is needed to keep the fetus alive belong exclusively to her.[67] This objection has been pressed by Wicclair (1981) and Stone (1983) and has rarely been treated in the subsequent literature.[68]

Both Wicclair and Stone attempt to establish the plausibility of this suggestion by asking us to consider the case of a species of rational beings (and thus, individuals with the same right to life as you or I) whose natural means of reproduction in one way or another involves the life of one individual being temporarily dependent on the use of an organ or set of organs contained in another. I will follow Stone's example here, though the considerations involved would apply equally to Wicclair's.

So consider a species of such beings who reproduce in the following way (Stone 1983: 82): upon reaching the age of 70, each individual X divides into two distinct, full-sized individuals, Y and Z, who inherit none of X's memories or acquired traits; X in effect ceases to exist at this point and is replaced by Y and Z who are distinct, rational beings with a right to life from the moment of fissioning on. As an evolutionary response to certain primordial environmental conditions, the new individuals are always formed in the following manner: Y's body contains a full set of

---

[67] Or if they do belong to her it is only, as Stone puts it, in a technical sense that does not imply the right to exclusive use of it (1983: 83). The objection can be spelled out either by denying that the organs are the woman's or by denying that their being hers grants her the right to control them; the choice makes no difference in terms of the objection's merits.

[68] The suggestion that a problem for Thomson arises from the thought that "perhaps even some of the organs of the fetus are either shared with the mother or are to be located in the body of the mother" is also found in Margolis (1973: 58), though it is not aimed at the violinist case in particular and is not given an explicit defense. And Beckwith can be understood as making the same objection in terms of the claim that the fetus's need for the pregnant woman's support is the natural condition for a member of its species at this stage of its development (1992: 113; 1994: 165–6). For a brief discussion of an historical antecedent to this view, see Connery (1977: 298–9). The only explicit response to this objection of which I am aware is found in Kamm (1992: 99–101), though she does not specifically address the arguments given by Wicclair and Stone.

functioning organs while some of the vital organs in Z's body take nine months to develop, and a band of flesh connects the two through which a common bloodstream enables Z to use the organs contained in Y's body. After nine months, when the organs inside Z's body are able to function on their own, the band naturally dissolves and Y and Z go off on their separate ways.

Stone now asks us to suppose that we have just emerged as the Y in one such fissioning and propose to sever our body from our partner, George, because we don't wish to shoulder the burden of being hooked up to him for nine months and never consented to giving him the use of, say, the liver in our body, in the first place.

Am I entitled to "unplug" George? Surely not. For in this case it seems plain that George has a claim on the continued use of my liver. From whence is this claim derived? I submit that George is entitled to the continued use of my liver because (1) this use is necessary to sustain his life, and (2) my liver is part of the biological equipment the use of which George acquired through the normal process of his biological creation, a process typical to his species.... we both acquired its use through a normal instance of the process of biological creation typical to members of our species, a process which functions to provide us both with its use. For both George and myself, this organ is part of the biological life-support system bequeathed us by nature through the process of our own creation. (Stone 1983: 82–3)

And since these two conditions both obtain in the case of the woman and the fetus, but the second does not in the case of you and the violinist, it follows that you may unplug yourself from the violinist but the pregnant woman may not unplug herself from the fetus.

The crucial step in the argument is clearly the claim that condition (2) makes the difference between having a just claim to the use of an organ and not having such a claim. It therefore merits closer scrutiny. Condition (2) makes two distinct claims: (i) that what George has acquired through this natural process is the use of the liver, and (ii) that the fact that the use of the liver was acquired naturally as a part of the normal means of reproduction for his species makes his claim to it legitimate. Both claims should be rejected.

Let me begin with claim (i), and by noting the distinction between the following two claims:

(a) Z acquired the use of a particular organ through a particular process.
(b) Z acquired something, which requires the use of a particular organ, through a particular process.

These two claims are not identical, nor does (a) follow from (b). For consider the following example: Adam and Eve, through some unspecified process, each acquire the use of adjoining plots of land in a very hot climate. Adam's plot contains a tall, leafy tree, which produces shade over much of Eve's plot of land. As a result, the plot of land acquired by Eve is cool and its remaining cool requires the use of the tree on Adam's plot of land. But this does not mean that Eve has acquired the use of the tree. Only Adam has acquired that. As a result, what Eve has acquired through the process in question does not justify a claim against Adam if Adam decides to chop down the tree. Suppose that keeping the tree alive is a substantial burden to Adam; it would make life much easier for him to kill it or to remove it and let it die. But Eve will die from exposure to the sunlight unless Adam waits nine months, after which Eve will have developed sufficient resistance to the sun. The fact that Eve has acquired the right to her plot of land, the fact that the land she has acquired the right to is currently cool, and the fact that her land's remaining cool requires the use of Adam's tree does not justify the claim that she has acquired the right to the use of Adam's tree. Similarly, it does not follow from the facts that through some process George has naturally acquired a supply of blood (which is at present healthy) and that the use of the liver in your body is necessary for the blood to remain healthy, that George has acquired the right to the use of the liver in your body. The facts are equally consistent with saying that what he has acquired is healthy blood coursing through his veins, blood that will continue to be healthy just in case the band between you and George remains intact. And on this account, you are within your rights to withdraw George's use of your liver. This does not demonstrate that George has not acquired the right to the use of the liver. But it does show that the facts as described do not provide any particular support for the claim that he has.

But suppose that claim (i) is somehow vindicated. There remains the problem of claim (ii). Stone emphasizes that George acquires whatever it is that he acquires through a natural process that is a normal part of reproduction for his species. But why should this matter? Consider the following thought experiment. Every so often, as a result of a nonnormal, atypical mutation in the process of human reproduction, a pair of conjoined (Siamese) twins is born. Consider a set of such twins who stand in the same dependence relation to each other as do Y and Z. And suppose that you are the independent one. If we are accepting that you are permitted to unplug yourself from Thomson's violinist, then it is difficult to see how we can avoid also accepting that you are permitted to unplug yourself from your twin. Indeed, it seems likely that Stone has included the "normal" proviso precisely to accommodate such intuitions. But now suppose that environmental factors slowly begin to favor those who are disposed to produce conjoined twins. Over time, this will become normal. On Stone's account, it would follow that once such twinning became sufficiently normal, the independent member of each set of twins would have an obligation to support the dependent partner. But this seems extremely odd. Why should the fact that a dependence relation was produced by a natural regularity rather than by a natural mutation make any moral difference? I can think of only one possible answer, which is suggested by Stone's use of the expression "a process which *functions* to provide us both with its use" (emphasis added). If function is taken in a strongly teleological sense, one might think that in the alien case you have to share the liver in your body with George because that is what alien livers are *there for* in your species, while in the human case you don't have to share the liver in your body with your conjoined twin because that's not what human livers are there for. But if the objection to the good samaritan argument ultimately rests on the assumption that the woman's body is by nature there for the fetus to make use of, then it simply begs the question it is attempting to settle, since the question at issue here is precisely whether or not the fetus is entitled to make use of the woman's body.

I have argued here that the facts as Stone describes them provide no reason to conclude that it would be morally impermissible for you to unplug yourself from George. But it is also worth noting that even if I am wrong about this, Stone's argument is still subject to a further objection. For the case of you and George is in one important respect different from the case of a pregnant woman and fetus. In the case of you and George, both individuals come to be making use of the organs in your body at the same time; there is no prior ownership. In this respect, you and George are like two people who simultaneously arrive on some unclaimed land. But this is not so in the case of the pregnant woman.[69] The organs inside her body were provided to her by nature well before the fetus began to make use of them, just as the organs inside your body in Thomson's story were provided to you by nature well before the violinist began to make use of them. This seems to provide the pregnant woman with a further reason for holding that the organs inside her body are hers that

---

[69] Kamm makes this point (1992: 101).

does not apply to Stone's case of you and George.[70] And thus even if we were to agree with Stone that it would be morally impermissible for you to disconnect yourself from George, this would still fail to undermine the good samaritan argument.

4.11. THE CHILD SUPPORT OBJECTION

There is yet another difference. In the case of you and the violinist, you are the only person who is being asked to suffer a burden on the violinist's behalf. If you agree to remain plugged in for nine months and the violinist recovers, then he is off and on his way and the story is over. But in the case of the pregnant woman and the fetus, there is someone else who may be called upon to make a sacrifice if the woman agrees to bring the fetus to term: the baby's father. The role of the father is conspicuously absent from Thomson's story, and this threatens to create a problem for the good samaritan argument for the following reason: If there is a sense in which the father's position is symmetric with the mother's, and if we agree that the father has a duty to make sacrifices on behalf of the child, then there is an equally strong reason for thinking that the woman has a duty to make a sacrifice for the fetus, a reason that will go unnoticed in the violinist case. And this, in turn, might justify the claim that you are entitled to unplug yourself from the violinist while the woman is not entitled to have an abortion.

This objection has been pressed by Beckwith, among others, who argues as follows:[71] consider a man who has a brief sexual encounter with a woman. Since he does not wish to become a father, he insists that they use contraception, but the woman becomes pregnant despite their having taken every reasonable precaution. Although the man remains unaware of this fact, the woman decides to bring the pregnancy to term. After the baby is born, she tracks the man down and pleads for child support. He refuses. After all, he says, even though he is partly responsible for the child's existence, the fact that he used contraception shows

[70] A defender of the organ ownership objection, of course, could deny that initial possession of property entitles one to continued possession of it if someone later comes along who needs it in order to go on living. This position would enable such a critic to maintain that the difference between the case of the pregnant woman and Stone's case of you and George is not morally relevant. But it would equally imply in Thomson's case of you and the violinist that even though you owned your kidneys first, they are now equally the property of the violinist since he now needs the use of them in order to go on living.

[71] See also Beckwith (1992: 111), Pavlischek (1993), Lee (1996: 120).

that he did not wish to accept the responsibilities of being a father. As a result of his refusal, the woman takes legal action against him.

As Beckwith points out, "according to nearly all child-support laws in the United States he would still be obligated to pay support *precisely because* of his relationship to this child" (1994: 164).[72] The relationship that underwrites this obligation, Beckwith emphasizes, is not the mere fact that he is the biological father of the child. That would imply that sperm donors are also "morally responsible" for children conceived with their semen, and Beckwith takes it that this is plainly implausible. Rather, "the father's responsibility for his offspring stems from the fact that he engaged in an act, sexual intercourse, that he fully realized could result in the creation of another human being, although he took every precaution to avoid such a result" (1994: 164). This is precisely the same relation to which the pregnant woman stands to the fetus, and so if it is sufficient to generate an obligation in the father, it must be equally sufficient to generate an obligation in the mother. There seems, then, to be good reason to insist that the woman has a duty to the fetus, a reason whose presence is masked by the absence of a figure comparable to the father in the case of you and the violinist.

There are several problems with this objection based on the obligation to pay child support. The first is that it conflates moral obligations with legal obligations. It is clear from Beckwith's comment about the sperm donor case that when he says the father has an obligation in his example, he means a moral obligation and not merely a legal one.[73] And since the good samaritan argument is an argument about whether abortion is morally impermissible, and not about whether it would be morally permissible to make abortion illegal even if it is not morally impermissible, this is what he must mean if his objection is to have any chance of succeeding. But the only support Beckwith provides for this claim is the observation that there are many laws that would require the man to pay child support. And it simply does not follow from this fact that the man stands under a moral obligation to pay such support.

Now this observation may at first seem to do little damage to Beckwith's position for two reasons. The first is that we surely have

---

[72] The same issue is raised in Shostak and McLouth (1990: chap. 12).

[73] This is also clear from the fact that the objection falls under the heading "*Ethical Problems with Thomson's Argument*" rather than the heading he later uses to discuss "Legal Problems with Thomson's Argument" (1994: 163 [emphasis added], 168).

a negative moral response to fathers who pay no child support independent of the existence of laws requiring them to do so. So it may seem that the appeal to such laws is not necessary to Beckwith's position. But while it is clear that we will find what such men do to be morally criticizable, it may seem less clear that what they do is literally impermissible. If the man took reasonable precautions and made clear to the woman that he was unwilling to become a father, then while we may still be justified in saying that he is now behaving selfishly and callously, it may seem less clear that we would be justified in saying that he is violating the moral rights of the child or of the woman. As in the case of a man who has given a child up for adoption, we may feel that it would be bad of him to shun the child if the child should later seek him out and wish to establish some sort of relationship with him, but, again as with that case, we may nonetheless feel that he is not obligated to support the child.

The second reason that might be given for discounting the significance of the argument's conflation of moral and legal obligation is this. We are all familiar with the fact that we cannot read sound moral principles directly off of the existence of legal statutes. Slavery was once legal but that doesn't (and didn't) make it morally permissible. But Beckwith's example is clearly very different. Although some might attempt to mount a challenge to laws requiring reluctant fathers to pay child support, most will think them to be perfectly appropriate, and any defense of the moral permissibility of abortion that rested on the claim that child support laws are morally impermissible would be shaky at best, and unlikely to prove successful on the abortion critic's own terms.

But the first objection I raised against the child support objection has no such implication. Even if we agree that laws requiring such men to pay child support are morally proper, it still does not follow that such men stand under any moral obligation to pay such support that is independent of their obligation to obey the law generally. Consider, for example, a law requiring citizens to serve on juries. Such a law can impose a significant burden on people (even when the slight compensation they are offered for their time is taken into account), but most people accept such laws as morally permissible, and often as morally superior to the alternatives. But it clearly does not follow from the fact that a statute creating a legal obligation for people to serve on juries is morally permissible that in the absence of such a law people stand under a moral obligation to serve on juries. And the same holds for Beckwith's example. The claim that child-support laws are morally proper is perfectly consistent with the claim that there is no independent moral obligation for such men to pay child support. And so one might attempt to defend the good samaritan argument from the child support objection by agreeing that laws requiring child support are morally proper and by agreeing that reluctant fathers who decline to pay such support do something morally objectionable, but by nonetheless insisting that what they do is nonetheless morally permissible.

But let us nonetheless suppose, at least for the sake of the argument, that the man in Beckwith's example does have a genuine moral obligation to pay child support to the mother of the child he did not wish to have. Given this assumption, the proponent of the child support objection maintains that it is inconsistent for the defender of the good samaritan argument to then appeal to the fact that the pregnant woman does not wish to have the child. As Pavlischek puts the claim, defenders of abortion as a legal right must "either surrender the defense of abortion on demand and allow for the passage of laws restricting abortion, or surrender the advocacy of paternal responsibility for children of mothers who choose to forego an abortion" (1993: 342).

But the appearance of inconsistency here is misleading. It does not follow from the claim that the man has a moral obligation to provide financial support for the child that the woman has a moral obligation to provide bodily support for the fetus. For the nature of the burdens involved in providing support in the two cases is fundamentally different.[74] And if the example is changed so that the difference is eliminated, the paternal obligation objection is clearly undermined: It becomes plain that considerations that could warrant imposing one sort of burden on a person would not be sufficient to warrant imposing the other sort of burden. Suppose, for example, that in order for the child to survive, the father must go through the procedure I described in Section 4.9 in response to the different burdens objection: He must have a pseudo-zygote implanted in him and let it develop into a pseudo-embryo and then pseudo-fetus before giving "birth" to it in a manner that parallels the nature of childbirth as closely as is anatomically possible so that a life-saving synthetic drug may then be extracted from it and given to the child. It goes without saying that no court would order him to undergo such a procedure.

[74] Pavlischek seems to treat them as on a par: "If such a minimal life-sustaining sacrifice cannot be required of the mother before birth, how could even minimal child support be required of the father after birth?" (1993: 348). But picturing the burdens of pregnancy as being of the same sort as those involved in making minimal child support payments is extremely implausible.

Or suppose instead, more mundanely, that in order for the child to survive, the father would have to undergo a painful series of bone marrow transplants, or have one of his kidneys removed. Again, the law would surely not compel him to undergo such procedures. In the case of *McFall v. Shimp* (1978), for example, in which a man sued his cousin for refusing to provide him with the bone marrow he needed in order to survive, the United States Supreme Court wrote as follows: "For a society which respects the rights of *one* individual, to sink its teeth into the jugular vein or neck of one of its members and suck from it sustenance for *another* member, is revolting to our hard-wrought concepts of jurisprudence. Forcible extraction of living body tissue causes revulsion to the judicial mind. Such would raise the spectra of the swastika and the Inquisition, reminiscent of the horrors this portends."[75] If the law did require such bodily sacrifices on the part of reluctant fathers, and did so consistently, and if it also then refrained from requiring women with undesired pregnancies to make comparable bodily sacrifices on behalf of their unborn children, then the charge of inconsistency here would be prima facie quite powerful (assuming, of course, that the law purported to treat the fetus as an individual with the same right to life as you or I, which it plainly does not). But given that the law does not impose such burdens on unwilling fathers, and given that virtually everyone would regard it as outrageous if it did, the charge of inconsistency must be dismissed even granting the assumption that the fetus has a right to life.

A proponent of the child support objection might attempt to respond to this argument in two ways. One would be to appeal to the claim that there is an important difference in probabilities: It is relatively rare that a man's engaging in intercourse leads to its being the case that there is a child who stands in need of some of his bone marrow, but relatively common that a woman's engaging in intercourse leads to its being the case that there is a fetus who stands in need of the use of her body. So it might be argued that the child does not have a right to the father's

---

[75] Cited by Calabresi (1991: 5n). Calabresi notes that anti-abortion laws require women to be good samaritans in the sense that the law did not require Shimp to be one, and so suggests although does not explicitly argue that the two should stand or fall together (1991: 6–7). In his response to Calabresi, Murray suggests that: "Under certain circumstances we may have moral obligations to give body parts or products to another" (1991: 20), but even he limits this to cases where the burdens involved would be extremely small and hardly comparable even to relatively burden-free pregnancies.

bone marrow because the probabilities involved were so small, while the fetus does have a right to the use of the woman's body because the probabilities involved were relatively larger. But this response is unacceptable on the abortion critic's own terms: It would commit the critic to saying that whether or not the fetus has a right to the use of the woman's body depends on how likely it was that she would become pregnant at the time she had intercourse, that whether or not abortion is morally permissible depends on the level of fertility of the pregnant woman. And this is a concession that critics of abortion are unwilling to make.

Beckwith offers what might be seen as a second attempt to respond to this dissolution of the child support objection by quoting with approval the following claim by Michael Levin: "All child-support laws make the parental body an indirect resource for the child. If the father is a construction worker, the state will intervene unless some of the calories he expends lifting equipment go to providing food for his children" (Levin 1986: 51, cited by Beckwith 1994: 164). The claim that such laws use the man's body as an indirect resource is a plausible one, but it does nothing to answer the argument against the child-support objection because it simply assumes that there is no morally significant difference between the state's using your body directly and its using your body indirectly. And this assumption is unwarranted. In the first case, the state allows you to do anything you want with your body, and then takes some of the money you receive in compensation for doing something productive with it and spends the money to accomplish a particular task. In the second case, it forces you to use your body to accomplish a particular task. Even if the tasks in the two cases are equally legitimate and worthy, it hardly follows that if it is unobjectionable for the state to do one then it is unobjectionable for the state to do the other. If the state determined that it would be in the public interest to build a new highway, for example, it would hardly follow from the claim that it would be morally permissible for the state to take some of the money that workers earn to help pay for the highway that it would also be morally permissible for the state to force such workers to help to build the highway. And if a particular construction worker's negligence were found to be responsible for a particular house's being destroyed, it would hardly follow from the claim that it would be morally permissible for the state to take some of the money that he earns as a construction worker to help the victim rebuild the house that it would also be morally permissible for the state to force the worker to rebuild it himself. The state's taking control over

251

a person's body is fundamentally different from the state's taking control over some of the money that a person earns while freely controlling that body. This is a claim that critics and defenders of abortion both accept.

Indeed, the force of this difference can be brought out even more clearly by attending to a case that is even closer to those involving abortion: cases where child support is paid by a woman. Suppose that a man and a woman have a child together, and that after a period of time, the woman decides to leave the family. There are expenses involved in raising and caring for the child, and so the man sues for, and is awarded, child support from the woman. Assume that the child has some significant medical needs, so that all of the woman's money is, in effect, going toward keeping the child healthy. This is a clear instance of the sort of case about which most people will agree that it is morally proper to impose such an obligation on the mother. But now suppose that instead of needing money to pay the medical bills, what the child needs is a new kidney, or a bone marrow transplant. Again, the law clearly does not and clearly would not require a woman under such circumstances to make such a sacrifice and, again, virtually everyone would regard it as outrageous if it did. And imagine, finally, that the mother herself could not provide, say, the needed bone marrow, but that if she were to conceive and bring to term a second child, the second child's bone marrow would be suitable for saving the life of the first child. There are, of course, a number of distinct and thorny ethical problems that are raised by the prospect of a woman deliberately conceiving one child to use as a means for saving a second. But even if we bracket these concerns off and assume that it would be perfectly *permissible* for a woman to conceive and carry a child to term for such purposes, it is still clear that the law would never *require* her do so if she did not want to because of the nature of the burden to her that would be involved. But this is just to say that even if the law would require a woman to make significant financial sacrifices on behalf of her born child, it would not require her to undergo the burdens of a typical unwanted pregnancy on behalf of that child. And so, once again, the existence and presumed legitimacy of child support laws, even if they are construed as evidence of an underlying moral obligation to provide such support, does nothing to undermine the good samaritan argument. There is no inconsistency in holding both that reluctant fathers (and mothers) should have a legal obligation to provide financial support for their offspring and that pregnant women should have no legal obligation to carry their pregnancies to term. And there is therefore no inconsistency in holding both that that reluctant fathers (and mothers) have a moral obligation to provide financial support for their offspring and that pregnant women have no moral obligation to carry their pregnancies to term.

In a postscript to a revised version of his 1993 article, Pavlischek responds to a 1997 article of mine in which I presented an earlier version of my responses to the tacit consent and responsibility objections and in which I briefly replied in a footnote to Pavlishchek's and Beckwith's defenses of the child support objection along the same general lines I have offered here (Pavlishchek 1998: 189–92). Pavlishchek's primary criticism of the position I have taken, in this section in particular and in this chapter in general, is that my account leaves him "entirely perplexed" as to how the difference between the "distinctly intimate and personal" nature of the physical burden on the mother and the purely financial nature of the burden on the father can make a difference in whether or not the voluntariness of their initial actions can suffice to generate an obligation on their part to undergo the burden in question (1998: 190). And this seems to be so for Pavlishchek, at least in part, because even if there is a noticeable difference in the *nature* of the burdens involved, there may be relatively little difference in how *onerous* the burdens are to to the individuals who would be compelled to suffer them. As Pavlishchek puts the point, "one would hardly be thought irrational to think that forced appropriation of the father's time and labor over almost two decades counts for less than the physical burden of pregnancy for a mere nine months" (1998: 190).

Pavlishchek is correct in stating that I have provided no account of how this difference in burdens accounts for the difference in obligations. And I am inclined to believe that he is also correct in viewing the project of providing such an account as a difficult if not perplexing one. But Pavlishchek is nonetheless mistaken in maintaining that the burden is on the defender of the good samaritan argument to provide it. It is true that in defending the good samaritan argument I have in part relied on the claim that a difference in the nature of a particular burden can make a difference in whether or not we are entitled to impose that burden upon people as a result of their voluntary actions. But it is equally true that any critic of the good samaritan argument will also have to accept this claim if he is to avoid the unacceptable implications I have noted in this section. Unless Pavlishchek is willing to endorse laws compelling people to donate needed bone marrow or organs to their children, for example, he must also agree that the legitimacy of laws imposing financial burdens on unwilling parents provides no support for the legitimacy of laws imposing physical burdens on unwilling parents that would violate their bodily autonomy. And the fact (if it is a fact) that the severity of the father's burden is no less than the severity of the mother's does nothing to advance Pavlishchek's case. Most people, for example, would find spending five years in prison more onerous than suffering one moderately painful whipping, but while we are willing to accept that certain crimes are such that they entitle the state to imprison someone for five years, we do not think that the state would be entitled to impose even a moderately painful whipping on someone convicted of precisely the same crime. Indeed, consider an even more extreme case. Virtually every woman would agree that spending the rest of her life in prison would be a much worse fate than being required to conceive and bring an unwanted pregnancy to term. But while most people would agree that in, say, committing first-degree murder, the woman had forfeited her right to live freely in society, surely no one would insist that she had thereby forfeited her right not to be impregnated against her will. The claim that the difference between the nature of the bodily burdens imposed on an unwilling pregnant woman and the nature of the financial burdens imposed on an unwilling father is a morally relevant difference, therefore, is common ground between defenders of the good samaritan argument and its critics. Indeed, as with the other claims I have attempted to argue from in this book, it is common ground, more generally, between defenders of abortion and its critics. And as a result, there is no need for the defender of the good samaritan argument, in particular, or of the moral permissibility of abortion in general, to provide a justification for it.

4.12. THE EXTRACTION VERSUS ABORTION OBJECTION

One difference between the violinist case and the unwanted pregnancy case is sometimes cited as a way of generating an objection from what would at first seem instead to be a great virtue of the good samaritan argument. The virtue is that it makes sense of a strong intuition that many have but find difficult to justify: They believe that aborting a viable fetus is morally worse than aborting a nonviable one, but find it difficult to accept the claim that the fetus acquires a right to life at that point. Whether or not a fetus is viable seems to be more a fact about its environment and the existing state of technology than about its own nature, and so it is difficult to see how its being viable could make the difference between its having a right to life and its not having a right to life. But on the account provided by the good samaritan argument, the moral relevance of viability becomes clear and in a way that is consistent with believing that one's viability does not determine whether or not one has a right to life. For on that account, the right the pregnant woman has is not the right to kill the fetus but the right to unburden herself of it, even if this must involve its death. If the fetus is viable, and thus can be safely removed, then the woman has the right only to have it removed, not to have it killed. That aborting a viable fetus is impermissible while aborting an unviable fetus is permissible, therefore, is consistent with the assumption that the fetus acquires a right to life at some point before viability, including the moment of its conception.

This virtue of the position generated by the good samaritan argument is sometimes identified as an objection in the following manner. Since it is at least imaginable that technology might one day produce either an artificial womb capable of sustaining fetal life from conception onward or a procedure by which a fetus could safely be removed from one woman and reimplanted in another, it would follow from what has been said that under such circumstances women would never have a right to kill their fetuses but only to have them removed alive. As one such critic has put it, "Thomson's argument is not really a defence of *abortion*, it is a defence of *extraction*" (Levin 1985: 125).[76] Now abortion as a medical procedure is typically defined in terms of the expulsion and not the death of the fetus, and so in this sense the distinction between abortion and extraction is empty. But the force of the objection is nonetheless clear: To the extent that women who currently seek abortions want the fetus that they are carrying to die and not merely to be extracted and then raised by others, it would follow that the good samaritan argument does not establish the moral permissibility of what they wish to do. This objection, if it is to be accepted as such, makes three distinct claims: that it is possible for such technology to become available; that if it becomes available, its availability will prevent the argument from justifying the permissibility of a woman's ensuring the death of her fetus and not merely its removal; and that this result counts as a reason to be dissatisfied with the argument. I will respond to these points in reverse order.

So far as I can see, the third claim should simply be rejected. As one writer has put it, "There is no reason to think of the death of the fetus as

---

[76] See also Ross (1982: 237) and Overall (1985: 281).

something the [defender of the permissibility of abortion] passionately wants so much as something, given what he does want, he is prepared to accept" (Ross 1982: 233).[77] This is clearly Thomson's view: Your right to unplug yourself from the violinist, she emphasizes, does not entail that if by some miracle he survives the procedure you may then go ahead and slit his throat. And similarly, "The desire for the child's death is not one which anybody may gratify, should it turn out to be possible to detach the child alive" (1971: 126).[78] Indeed, even if we do not assume that the fetus has the same right to life as you or I, it may still seem reasonable to believe that it would be wrong to kill a viable fetus when it could instead be removed and cared for by someone who is willing to care for it. Most people do not think that kittens have the same right to life as you or I, after all, but many would still think it wrong for you to kill a kitten that you did not wish to care for when others were willing to relieve you of the burden of caring for it (though not as wrong as killing an unwanted infant would be).[79]

How might a proponent of the abortion versus extraction objection respond? In order for the objection to retain its force, we must believe that when a woman is in a position to have her fetus removed either dead or alive, and when someone else will care for the child if it is removed, she has the right to have the fetus removed dead. I can imagine only one kind of consideration that might seem to support this contention. One could appeal to the claim that the woman has a right to kill the viable fetus she is carrying because if she does not do so, she will then suffer the mental distress of having an offspring of hers out in the world that she is not caring for. But if women have a right to kill a viable fetus to prevent themselves from future psychological or moral demands, then surely men must have this right as well. And this in turn would imply that the father's right to avoid such distress would be violated when women chose to have their viable fetuses removed alive rather than dead. This is not to say that a father's right to avoid such distress would grant him the right to force a woman to abort a fetus that she intended to carry to term. That would plainly constitute an unreasonable infringement on her bodily integrity. But the case pointed to by the

---

77 The same point is recognized by Knight and Callahan (1989: 214), and defended by Gert (1995: 122) and Overall (1987: 71ff.).

78 This is also the position taken by the protagonist of Koman's provocative fictional treatment of the social implications of such technology (1989: 225).

79 Though see Ross (1982: 238) for the claim that respecting the woman's desire not to be a parent may be permissible even granting the fetus some moral standing.

objection under consideration here is crucially different in this respect. In this case, the woman is going to have the fetus removed either way, and it is only a question of whether the fetus will be removed dead or alive. Given this scenario, it is difficult to see why her preferences should override those of the father. Indeed, as Overall has pointed out (1987: 73), the claim that the woman has such a right would entail that if the baby survived an attempted abortion, or was born prematurely, before the woman had an opportunity to have the abortion performed, then she would still have the right to have it killed. And this is plainly unacceptable. It may well be true that many women who seek abortions do so because they want the fetus that they are carrying to be killed. And such women will to that extent be dissatisfied with a position on which it is morally permissible for them to have their viable fetuses extracted but not killed. But in the absence of an independent reason to think that they are entitled to have the fetus die when it is already viable, this seems to count more as a criticism of their desires than as an objection to the good samaritan argument.

The argument's critic has one further response available at this point that merits consideration. Mackenzie develops a variation on the objection I have been arguing against that is grounded in "a phenomenological account of pregnant embodiment" on which "the experience of pregnancy, particularly in the early stages" is such that "[f]rom the perspective of the pregnant woman" the fetus is "a being whose separateness is not fully realized as such by her" (1992: 186–7). On this account, "[w]hat the abortion decision involves is a decision that this part of herself should not *become* a being in relation to whom such questions of parental responsibility and emotional attachment arise. In other words, abortion is not a matter of wanting to kill *this particular being*, which is, after all, as yet indistinguishable from oneself. It is rather a matter of not wanting there to *be* a future child, so intimately related to oneself, for which one either has to take responsibility or give up to another" (1992: 190). On this account, there is a morally relevant difference, from the point of view of the woman actually experiencing the pregnancy, between having the fetus removed alive and having it removed dead. If it is removed dead, then this "part of herself" will never "become" a distinct being making emotional and moral claims on her. There will never be such an individual. If it is removed alive and then kept alive, however, it will later become such a being, and the woman will then have to suffer the psychological consequences. In this respect, choosing to abort a fetus, again at least in the early stages of pregnancy, might be seen as on a par with choosing not to have a part of oneself cloned into a separate person.

It is not at all clear how one is to go about assessing Mackenzie's phenomenology of pregnancy. She is careful to emphasize that "this phenomenological description is not a description of the subjective feelings of individual women" or "an empirical description of the way in which all women experience or feel about their pregnancies." It had better not be, in any event, since presumably many women begin to experience the conceptus as a separate individual making emotional and moral demands on them as soon as they learn that they are pregnant. They may immediately make changes in their diet, for example, such as eliminating or greatly reducing their consumption of alcohol, caffeine, and so on, and they do this not because they think that they owe it to themselves, but because they experience themselves as already being in a parental relation to another distinct individual. But then what is the phenomenological account an account *of*? Mackenzie describes it as "a normative and reflective apprehension of the way in which conscious experience is structured by our (bodily) situations, perspectives and modes of perception" (1992: 186). If it is supposed to be an account of the way in which experience *is* so structured, then it is difficult to see this as anything other than the false empirical claim that Mackenzie seeks to distance herself from. But if it is a *normative* claim, then it is a claim about how our experiences *should* be so structured, and it then stands in need of support. Mackenzie plainly concedes, for example, that the fetus is a biologically distinct individual, and one could as easily argue that normatively a pregnant woman who experiences the fetus as merely a part of her body that will later become distinct from her should reflect on her situation and apprehend things differently. After all, a white person may find that his conscious experience of black people is such that he does not really experience them as distinct individuals, but reflection on his situation should nonetheless lead him to experience them as such.

But let us suppose that we accept Mackenzie's account as a normative one. We agree that in some robust sense, it is natural or appropriate for women to experience the fetus as merely a part of themselves, at least during the early stages of their pregnancies. What follows from this? Presumably, Mackenzie is correct to say that it follows that the desire that women who seek abortions in such circumstances are acting on is "not a matter of wanting to kill *this particular being*, which is, after all, as yet indistinguishable from oneself." But this establishes only that the motive of a woman who experiences pregnancy in the appropriate way is not a morally criticizable motive. And this does nothing to show that the act itself is morally permissible. The particular being, after all, is in fact distinguishable from the pregnant woman even if it is appropriate for her to experience things otherwise. I conclude that it is not a problem for the good samaritan argument if it entails that abortion is impermissible when the fetus is viable.

But let us suppose that I have been mistaken, and that we should accept the third claim made by the extraction versus abortion objection, the claim that a defense of abortion is inadequate if it justifies the permissibility of a woman's securing the removal, but not the death, of the fetuses they carry in those cases where the fetus is viable. This will still pose a problem for the good samaritan argument only if we also accept the first and second claims. And serious doubts can be raised about both. Consider first the second claim. Suppose that the imagined artificial life-support system has been invented and that keeping a fetus on such artificial life-support for nine months is quite expensive. Now consider a woman who has her unwanted fetus merely extracted (but not killed) under such circumstances. What will happen to the fetus? The fetus will still die unless someone is willing to take on the great burden of supporting it for nine months. The mere availability of the technology itself, after all, does not entail that the fetus will survive the extraction process. Of course, one might argue that someone has an obligation to shoulder the burden of keeping the fetus alive if the technology exists, so that the fetus will in fact survive. But who would that be? Suppose one says it is the woman who had the fetus removed. That would be like saying that you may unplug yourself from the violinist only if you then shoulder the burden of keeping an artificial kidney machine running for nine months even though the machine could be kept running by anyone willing to shoulder the burden. And I strongly suspect that if you think you may remove yourself from the violinist in the first place you will also think that you may do so without having to keep the machine running. One might instead say that society as a whole has such an obligation. But notice that this is to add a much stronger assumption than the mere assumption that the technology becomes available. Indeed, one would have to assume not only that society does have such an obligation but that it will in fact recognize and live up to it. And the plausibility of that assumption is not well grounded if present attitudes are any indication. Rightly or wrongly, we allow plenty of people to die who could have been saved if the most advanced technology available had been given to them for as long as they needed it. And the number of unwanted fetuses in a given year would be far greater than the number of people currently in need of such support. Under such circumstances, a woman who has an unwanted fetus extracted could, for all intents and purposes, be confident that the fetus would eventually die.

Finally, it is worth raising a brief skeptical question about the objection's first claim. As Morowitz and Trefil point out (1992: 132ff.), there are two fundamentally different ways in which our ability to keep premature babies alive can improve: We can increase the percentage who survive from a given stage in pregnancy and we can decrease the level of gestation at which it is possible for at least some to survive. Impressive, even breathtaking improvements of the first sort provide no real evidence of the feasibility of the second. And, indeed, almost all of the recent improvements in the survivability of premature infants has been of the first sort. In particular, the sharp rise in survivability at 25 weeks of gestation has not been accompanied by a significant decrease in the level of gestational development at which survivability outside the womb is possible. None of this, of course, shows such technology to be literally impossible. But it should at least give pause to those who imagine that a technological resolution to the abortion controversy will be available at any point in the near future. For the foreseeable future, at least, it seems reasonable to suppose that the permissibility of extracting the fetus will continue to mean the permissibility of performing an act that results in the fetus's death. Thus, even if one thinks that a woman should be entitled to secure the death of a viable fetus and not merely its removal (again, an assumption that is extremely questionable at best), the good samaritan argument seems to provide a justification for that for the foreseeable future as well.

4.13. THE THIRD-PARTY OBJECTION

Here is a further difference between the case of a woman with an unwanted pregnancy and Thomson's case of you and the violinist: What you assent to in the violinist example, assuming that you do assent to it, is that it is morally permissible for *you* to unplug yourself from the famous violinist. But strictly speaking, what a defender of abortion seeks to establish is not that it is morally permissible for a woman to perform an abortion on herself, but rather that it is morally permissible for a third party to abort the fetus on her behalf. It does not always follow from the fact that it is permissible for you to do an act for your own benefit that it is also permissible for a third party to do the same act on your behalf. If you and a stranger are trapped in a life boat that will only support one of you, for example, we might agree that it is permissible for you to place your interests ahead of his without agreeing that a third party would be entitled to place your interests ahead of his. And so, once again, we are in a position to agree that unplugging yourself from the violinist is permissible while denying that this implies that abortion (when performed by a third party) is similarly permissible.

I am not aware of any writer who has pressed this concern as an objection to the good samaritan argument in particular, but it is sometimes raised as an objection to the related argument that abortion is permissible as a form of self-defense. Here the argument in defense of the moral permissibility of abortion rests on the claim that the fetus should be understood as an innocent threat, on a par with a hypnotized knife attacker, and the objection maintains that even if it would be permissible for you to place your life ahead of that of your attacker, a third party would have to view this as a conflict between innocents and remain neutral.[80] Even if the third-party objection to the self-defense argument has not been explicitly extended to the case of the good samaritan argument, however, it is clear that it can be so extended. It is therefore worth asking how the third-party objection, understood as an objection to the good samaritan argument, fares.

The answer is that it fares poorly. The first problem is simply that the violinist story can easily be modified to eliminate the distinction between the first- and third-party without losing any of its intuitive force. For suppose you wake up in the hospital in precisely the same situation as in the original story, except that the plug that needs to be pulled in order for you to be unplugged from the violinist is just out of your reach. A doctor, who could easily pull the plug, walks by, and you ask him to do so. He replies by saying, "I'm sorry; it would be perfectly permissible for you to unplug yourself if you could reach the plug, but it would be impermissible for me to pull the plug on your behalf, because that would require me to take sides in a conflict between innocent persons. And in such conflicts, I am morally required to remain neutral." This response by the doctor seems hardly less implausible than the claim that you are not permitted to unplug yourself in the first place. Moreover, the implausibility of this claim can be accounted

---

[80] For defenses of the self-defense argument, see, for example, English (1975) and McDonagh (1996). The third party objection to the self-defense argument is pressed forcefully by Davis (1984).

for in a manner that is perfectly consistent with the genuine insight that underlies the third-party objection. For it does seem reasonable to suppose that in a life boat dilemma each person is entitled to give preference to his own interests without this entailing that a third party could permissibly intervene on behalf of one over the other. But this is so only because in such cases neither person has a more legitimate claim to any of the resources available than does the other. And in the violinist case, things are importantly different: You do have a more legitimate claim to the use of your kidneys than does the violinist. That is why it is permissible for you to unplug yourself in the first place. And that is why the permissibility of your unplugging yourself does imply the permissibility of a third party's doing the unplugging on your behalf. Since it is permissible for a third party to unplug you from the violinist, the third party objection must be rejected.

4.14. THE FEMINIST OBJECTION

There is a final difference between the violinist case and the fetus case that arises for some readers but not for others. I am one of the readers for whom the difference does arise. For when the "you" in Thomson's story refers to me, the person plugged into the violinist is a man, while the person who is pregnant is a woman. Of course, even if Thomson's reader is a woman, there is still a difference between the two cases: She can see that there was nothing about her being a woman rather than a man that made it any more likely that she would end up being plugged into a famous violinist, while there is something about her being a woman rather than a man that makes it more likely that she will end up being pregnant. Thomson's analogy, then, overlooks the fact that only women become pregnant. Does this make a difference?

In one sense, perhaps it does. To the extent that one accepts the claim that women constitute an oppressed group, and to the extent that one accepts the claim that it is prima facie wrong to impose burdens on members of an oppressed group when those burdens are likely to perpetuate their oppression, then one may have grounds for thinking that the good samaritan argument is actually *stronger* than Thomson's analogy suggests. Suppose, after all, that violinists contract this kidney ailment on a fairly regular basis, and that you are a member of an oppressed race of people who are the only ones with kidneys capable of sustaining the lives of others. Only members of your race can ever find themselves plugged into violinists, and this has in part contributed to the oppression historically suffered by your race. This might make it seem even more unfair to say that you must remain plugged into the violinist than it would be in Thomson's case. Forcing you to make sacrifices on behalf of the violinist, after all, might make it even more difficult for you to overcome the already unfair disadvantages you suffer as a member of an oppressed group, and contribute to the harmful stereotype of your race as more "caring" and "nurturing" than others, thus perpetuating this oppression still further. And if this variation more closely captures the facts about women's social situation than does Thomson's, then this would show that the good samaritan argument is even stronger than Thomson herself makes it out to be.

4.14.1. The Ignoring Patriarchy Version

Some feminists, however, have treated this omission in Thomson's presentation of the good samaritan argument as a reason to reject the argument itself. Sally Markowitz, for example, appeals to the feminist belief that "our failure to face the scope and depth of [women's] oppression does much to maintain it" (1990: 374). On this account, an argument in defense of abortion that encourages us to understand the practice independently of the patriarchical context in which it takes place actually serves to reinforce the values that perpetuate patriarchical oppression. And since reinforcing the oppression of women is plainly objectionable, it follows that an argument in defense of abortion whose propagation affects such reinforcement is objectionable as well. As Markowitz puts it, arguments such as the good samaritan argument violate feminist standards because they "manage to skirt the issue of women's status, as a group, in a sexist society" and "obscure the relation of reproductive practices to women's oppression" (1990: 375). And so, on this account, the right to abortion must be grounded in considerations of the role that access to abortion can play in reducing inequalities between the sexes. Critics of abortion, of course, can take little comfort from this objection to the good samaritan argument, since it amounts to the claim that the argument should be rejected because it obscures the real reason that abortion is defensible. Still, it is worth considering the objection on its own terms. And understood in this way, there are several reasons to reject it.

The first is that it simply does not follow from the fact that a given argument makes no reference to the oppression of women that accepting or defending it encourages us to overlook the evidence or seriousness of such oppression. Suppose, for example, that one were asked to justify the claim that a person has a right to kill a rapist in self-defense. And suppose that in response, one argued that rape is a serious violation of bodily autonomy and that persons have the right to kill their attackers in order to avoid such serious violations. Such an argument would seem perfectly reasonable. But surely one can accept and defend such an argument without obscuring the fact that rape is overwhelmingly a crime committed by men against women, and that its persistence contributes to inequalities between men and women generally, even though the argument itself makes no reference to such facts. They are omitted not because they are unimportant, but because they are not necessary. And the same is true of the good samaritan argument.

A second problem with the objection is this. The objection requires that an acceptable argument for the moral permissibility of abortion must include as one of its premises the claim that we live in a society in which women are oppressed by men. The claim that "[w]omen's reproductive freedom ... should never be discussed as if it were isolated from all the conditions that women's equality depends on" is frequently put forward by feminists independently of concerns about the good samaritan argument in particular (Gillespie 1997: 1). And Markowitz herself is explicit in emphasizing that the argument she proposes as superior to the good samaritan argument is one that attempts to "justify abortion on demand for women *because they live in a sexist society* (1990: 379, emphasis in the original). But this means that the argument's conclusion is substantively much weaker than is the conclusion of the good samaritan argument. It is the conclusion that it is permissible for women to have abortions so long as they live in a sexist society. If social arrangements improved, on this account, abortion would then become impermissible. Or if it became possible for men to become pregnant, then it would be permissible for women to have abortions but not for men to have abortions, since men would not be members of an oppressed group. The good samaritan argument avoids such implications, and the objection that urges us to reject it cannot.

Finally, even if one accepts the claim that a defense of abortion must include reference to facts about women's oppression, this shows only that one should supplement Thomson's presentation of the good samaritan argument, not that one should reject the argument itself. If we change the story so that you are a member of the oppressed race of kidney-support providers described above, then telling the story and basing the good samaritan argument on it rather than on Thomson's story will serve as a reminder that this is the situation in which women with unwanted pregnancies find themselves.

4.14.2. *The Selfishness Version*

Markowitz offers one further reason for feminists to be dissatisfied with the good samaritan argument.[81] Such arguments, she writes, "allow, indeed invite, the charge that the choice to abort is selfish," and she notes that Thomson herself accepts that abortion may in many cases be selfish or "indecent," even though not morally impermissible. On the defense of abortion provided by the good samaritan argument, that is, "feminists are reduced to claiming a right to be as selfish as men are,"[82] whereas on Markowtiz's alternative account, the right to abortion is grounded in less self-centered considerations about group oppression. There are two problems with this argument. The first is that it is not at all clear that there is anything wrong with saying that abortion is sometimes, or even often, a selfish act. To say that an act is selfish is simply to say that it arises from an agent's putting her own interests

---

[81] Actually, she offers three further reasons in addition to the one I discuss in the text. Two of these amount to the concern that the good samaritan argument is vulnerable to objections treated elsewhere in this chapter (the responsibility objection and the compensation objection) and so require no further comment here. The third involves the claim that the right to autonomy upon which Thomson's argument is based "seems to be in tension with a demand for state-funded abortions, especially since not everyone supports abortion. At any rate, we will need another argument to justify the funding of abortion for poor women" (1990: 380).
   But the question of whether abortion is morally permissible and the question of whether the state should fund abortions are two distinct questions. It is no objection to an argument defending an answer to one that it does not provide an answer to the other. Indeed, it is if anything an advantage of a defense of a positive answer to the first question that one can accept it without being forced to accept a particular answer to the second question, given that the second question is itself so controversial. Finally, it is not at all obvious that the good samaritan argument could not be used to ground a defense of state-funded abortions for poor women. Although I do not wish to press the claim here, it seems at least plausible to suppose that if poor women frequently found themselves plugged into violinists and unable to afford the procedure needed to unplug themselves, then it would be appropriate for the government to pay for such procedures. And so a defense of state funding for abortions might well be developed along the same general lines as the good samaritan argument.

[82] It might be argued that this claim should be used as support not for the conclusion that feminists should defend abortion in a different way, but for the conclusion that they should oppose it. The argument that feminist principles support the position taken by the critic of abortion is addressed in Section 5.3.

ahead of those of others, and in many cases of abortion this may simply be true. It may be objected that it is easy for me to say this since I am a man and will never have to face the burden of an unwanted pregnancy. I find, on the contrary, that it is more difficult for me to say this precisely because I am acutely aware that I will never have to face such a dilemma, and so am passing judgment on others only. But such awareness cannot responsibly be invoked as an excuse to avoid judgment. I will never have to face the choices that many ordinary Germans had to face during Hitler's reign, but this cannot prevent me from acknowledging that many ordinary Germans behaved selfishly under their circumstances.

The second problem with what might be called the selfishness objection is that, if we do find it objectionable to picture abortion as a selfish act, then the objection will tell equally against Markowitz's defense of abortion. It is true that on Markowitz's account, the *right* to abortion is not grounded in self-centered considerations. But this says nothing about the reasons women might have for actually *exercizing* this right. Any reason for holding that a given abortion was a selfish act on the good samaritan account of why abortion is permissible will apply equally as a reason for thinking that it was a selfish act on Markowitz's analysis (or, indeed, on any analysis) of why abortion is permissible. This is, in any event, a debate between different ways of defending the moral permissibility of abortion. We should therefore return to those objections that a critic of abortion itself is in a position to aim at the good samaritan argument.

4.15. THE DUTY TO SAVE THE VIOLINIST OBJECTION

I have been assuming up to this point that you do agree that it would be morally permissible for you to unplug yourself from the violinist in Thomson's story. But while I am quite confident that this is your initial response to the example, I do not wish to rely on the claim that you will maintain this response with certainty. Perhaps a reason can be given for concluding that it is mistaken. Given that your initial impression that unplugging yourself is permissible is likely to be a very strong one, it will take quite a strong argument to overcome it. But perhaps such an argument can be made. And if we can be convinced that, initial responses notwithstanding, it would be morally impermissible for you to unplug yourself from the violinist, then even if the analogy is accepted (especially if it is accepted), the argument as a whole will still fail to justify the permissibility of abortion. On the whole, critics of the good samaritan argument have been far less likely to pursue this approach, but at least a few such objections have been defended, and they, too, merit consideration.

4.15.1. *The Conscription Version*

Two such arguments are found in Michaels (1984). The first is itself essentially an argument from analogy. The good samaritan argument depends on the assumption that once we agree to characterize carrying a pregnancy to term as a form of good samaritanism we will agree that we cannot say that a woman is morally required to do so. But if there are other instances in which we agree that it is impermissible to decline to be a good samaritan, then the argument will be deprived of its force. And Michaels suggests (1984: 217–19) that the general acceptance of the legitimacy of a military draft demonstrates that there are other such instances. If we may compel young men to incur great hardships in order to benefit others, why may we not compel pregnant women to do so as well?

There are several difficulties with the argument from conscription. First, as Michaels herself notes, there seems to be a difference between compelling someone to do something necessary for the public good and compelling them to do something necessary to help a particular individual. Michaels thinks the problem can be overcome by appealing to such examples as Gandhi and Martin Luther King, Jr., but even if we agree to call the sacrifices they made for the public good a form of good samaritanism in some sense, it is surely not a sense in which we will feel comfortable saying that it is impermissible to decline to make such sacrifices. Second, even if we accept Michaels's skepticism about the importance (or even conceptual clarity) of the distinction between helping private individuals and serving the public interest, the draft still seems to possess distinctive features that resist generalization. In particular, those who take it to be justified typically do so on the grounds that it is necessary to a country's national security, which is to say more than merely that it is in the public interest. Many other things could be uncontroversially thought to be in the public interest, such as making national parks and highways cleaner, but would not plausibly be taken to justify such compulsion. And it seems extremely implausible to think that preventing abortions is necessary to or even contributes to national security.[83] Finally, we must notice that the draft is not an example in which we think it morally impermissible for a person to decline to offer to make a great sacrifice for his country. It is an example in which we think it morally permissible for the state to require people to make such sacrifices even though they would not be morally required to make them independently of having been so selected. So at most, the analogy might establish that, under certain circumstances, it would be morally permissible for the state to require pregnant women (or some selected subset of them) to make substantial sacrifices for the good of their fetuses or for the good of others' fetuses or for the public good even though they would not be morally required to make such sacrifices independently of having been so selected. This shows only that laws restricting abortion might be permissible in some extreme circumstances even if abortion itself is not morally impermissible, and that is perfectly consistent with the claim made by the good samaritan argument that abortion is morally permissible.

4.15.2. The Involuntary Samaritan Version

Michaels's second argument is best put in the form of a question: "If we cannot require Good Samaritanism of the pregnant woman, then how can we require that the fetus terminate the course of its life in order that the woman may pursue uninterruptedly the course of hers?" (1984: 220). Even if we agree that carrying a pregnancy to term is a form of good samaritanism and that one cannot be morally required to be a good samaritan, that is, it still does not follow that we cannot forbid abortion since permitting abortion would be to force an even greater act of good samaritanism upon the fetus. Granted, Michaels admits, we are not requiring the fetus to *do* anything, but we are nonetheless requiring it to bear great costs so that the woman can avoid (presumably) lesser costs to herself. In this sense, Michaels suggests, the fetus is like a young child whose parents' inconsiderate move to the Amazon jungle "in order to pursue their passion for capturing poisonous snakes" would deprive

---

[83] Perhaps under some bizarre circumstances, such as those depicted in Margaret Atwood's *The Handmaiden's Tale*, in which the nation is threatened with a severe shortage of fertile women, things might be otherwise and perhaps in such cases Michaels's analogy would have to be accepted. But this is an extremely minor concession.

him of the safety and comfort of his life in Amherst. We would not call the parents good samaritans for forgoing the move out of concern for their son, so neither should we call the woman a good samaritan for forgoing the benefits that having an abortion would have afforded her.

This argument is defective for two reasons. In the first place, the analogy is too strained to be useful. Although Michaels offers a parenthetical assurance that if the story doesn't do, a more satisfactory one can always be constructed (1984: 221), there seems to be a problem with any such analogy: We still are asking the young child to *do* something, to play with bugs in the mud instead of his friends in the park in this case, while we are not asking the fetus to do anything. So Michaels still has not provided a convincing reason for supposing that the fetus's lack of agency is not relevant to our assessment of the situation. But more fundamentally, Michaels's approach here would, if accepted, undermine the notion of good samaritanship entirely. For consider any clearly paradigmatic instance of good samaritanship. A man volunteers to donate some of his bone marrow to a stranger who needs it, or gives the coat he is wearing to a homeless man on the street. If we accept Michaels's claim that allowing the woman to have an abortion is forcing the fetus to be a good samaritan, then we will also have to say that forbidding the patient to steal the bone marrow or the homeless man to steal the coat would be forcing them to be good samaritans. But this is plainly to stretch the notion of good samaritanism beyond recognition.

4.15.3. The Justification versus Excuse Version

One of the very few other explicit defenses of the claim that you are morally required to remain plugged into the violinst that I have been able to find is that of Humber (1975: 289–90).[84] Humber argues that if

---

[84] Jeff McMahan has pointed out to me that one could also defend such a duty along the following lines: Commonsense morality seems to acknowledge that there are cases in which, due to circumstances entirely beyond your control, you incur an obligation to assist others in need. If you are the first and only person who comes across a car wreck, for example, then you have a duty to provide aid to the victims that you would not have if you simply heard that there was a car wreck somewhere and that there were victims there in need of assistance. Your situation in Thomson's story might then be understood in the same way. The fact that you happen to be the only one with the appropriate blood type is like the fact that you happen to be the only one to come across the car wreck, and so you do incur an obligation to keep the violinist alive due entirely to circumstances beyond your control.

the reader is convinced that he may unplug himself from the violinist, this is only due to a failure to distinguish between acts that are justified and those that are merely excused. If a consideration *justifies* a person in performing a given action, then the consideration makes it the case that her doing the action is permissible. If a consideration *excuses* the act, it provides some reason to reduce or perhaps withhold entirely our criticism of the person who did the act, even though the act itself was impermissible. If an act is justified, it needs no excuse. If I kill you while under great duress, this may count as an excuse but not a justification; whereas if I kill you in self-defense, this will be a justification and not merely an excuse. Humber's claim is that when we meditate on the case of the violinist, what we should conclude is that if we unplug ourselves we have an excuse for our behavior, but do not have a justification. And if that is right, then even (especially) if we accept the violinist analogy, we should conclude that a woman who has an abortion does something that is morally impermissible even though she may often have an excuse that should mitigate our criticism of her for doing it.

The distinction between justification and excuse is perfectly legitimate. But why should we believe that we are only excused, and not justified, in unplugging ourselves from the violinist? Humber argues as follows: In Thomson's version of the violinist case, the cost to you of remaining plugged in is quite serious. In a variation on the case, however, such as Fischer's "surgery" variant (discussed in Section 4.9), the cost to you could be extremely trivial, and in such a case we may well think it impermissible for you to unplug yourself. If keeping the violinist alive would only require 10 more seconds of your time, then unplugging yourself would likely strike many of us as morally impermissible. But in both cases you do the same thing, namely, unplug yourself. The only difference is that in one case there is a great deal of pressure on you to unplug yourself and in the other there is not. And breaking under the sort of pressure that we take it a typical person could not withstand is a paradigmatic example of an excusing condition, not a justifying one. So

The problem with this approach is precisely that it does work from our commonsense response to cases. For part of the very same response it appeals to as support for the existence of such duties also acknowledges limits in the amount and nature of the burdens they can require us to bear. Suppose, for example, that you are the only one to come across a car wreck, and that you can save one of the victims only by having implanted in you the pseudo-zygote described in Section 6.9 and then bringing it to term. The common intuition appealed to here clearly allows you to refrain from bearing this sort of cost.

you are excused for unplugging yourself in Thomson's version of the story, but not justified.

The problem with this version of the objection is that it begs the question. For it simply assumes that if the violinist is entitled to your help in the no-burden case, then he is also entitled to your help in the serious-burden case. Only on this assumption does the added pressure amount to an excuse for your act, rather than a justification of it, since a consideration is an excuse only if the act is already conceded to be impermissible on independent grounds. After all, one could imagine yet another variation in which the violinist has, before lapsing into unconsciousness, explicitly given you permission to unplug yourself. In such a case you might well still believe that it would be a better thing to do to keep him alive, although it was not morally required of you, but you might eventually crack under the pressure of trying to do this and withdraw your support. The pressure on you would play just the same role as in Thomson's case, but here it is clear that it would not be an excuse, since what you do in this case is clearly permissible. This does not in itself show that it is permissible to un-plug yourself in Thomson's case, of course. But it does show that the fact that the level of burden makes a difference in our assessment of cases provides no particular support for the conclusion that we are ex-cused, as opposed to justified, in unplugging ourself from the violinist in Thomson's case.

4.15.4. *The Consequentialist Version*

There is one last, and more straightforward, way in which one might argue that it is morally impermissible for you to unplug yourself from the violinist. For surely the cost to you of remaining plugged into him for nine months is less than the cost to him of your refraining from doing so. The act of remaining plugged into the violinist, then, would contribute more to the total amount of happiness in the world than would the act of unplugging yourself. One could therefore appeal to a consequentialist standard of evaluation and insist that if the overall consequences of your unplugging yourself are worse from an impartial point of view than the overall consequences of remaining attached, then morality requires you to remain attached. So far as I have been able to determine, few if any writers have explicitly defended this objection to the good samaritan argument. Even Peter Singer, who is one of the most prominent utili-tarians writing on practical issues, says only that "a utilitarian . . . *would* reject Thomson's judgment in the case of the violinist" (1993: 148, emphasis added), without explicitly stating that he is willing to reject it himself. Still, utilitarianism in particular, and consequentialism in general, are powerful doctrines with many distinguished admirers, so it is important to consider the merits of the objection even if it has rarely been pressed explicitly.

One could respond to the objection, of course, by arguing against consequentialism as a moral theory. Or one might try to show that consequentialism does not really imply that you must remain plugged into the violinist. Perhaps there are unnoticed long-term costs or harmful side effects to a policy requiring people to remain plugged into violinists under such circumstances that outweigh the obvious benefits. But these approaches are not necessary. For suppose that we concede for the sake of the argument that consequentialism is true and that it entails that you are morally required to remain plugged into the violinist (indeed, presumably you would be morally required to volunteer to plug yourself into him in the first place). What follows from this about the moral permissibility of abortion?

It certainly does not follow that the good samaritan argument has been defeated. The good samaritan argument maintains that the impermissibility of abortion does not follow from the claim that the fetus has a right to life. The consequentialist objection does not undermine this claim because the consequentialist does not claim that the fetus, or anyone else, has a right to life. Indeed, the consequentialist claims precisely that they do not have such a right. More generally, it does not follow that the position maintained by the critic of abortion is vindicated. If consequentialism is true, then abortion will be permissible when it produces better overall consequences and impermissible when it does not. And, more importantly, there will be no significant moral difference among abortion, contraception, and abstaining from sexual intercourse. Whatever loss in terms of total happiness is produced when a woman aborts a fetus, after all, is equally produced when she prevents herself from conceiving during intercourse or refrains from having intercourse in the first place. It is true, of course, that from a consequentialist point of view contraception is preferable to abortion since it is less costly. But the defender of abortion need not deny this. His claim is merely that, if contraception is not used or fails, then having an abortion is morally permissible. For these reasons, the critic of abortion cannot appeal to consequentialism as a way of defeating the good samaritan argument.

4.16. THE COMPENSATION OBJECTION

If the choice is between incurring the costs of remaining plugged into the violinist for nine months or unplugging yourself from him, it is difficult to imagine much more that can be said in favor of the view that you are morally required to remain plugged in. But these need not be the only options. It is possible that someone might offer to compensate you for your remaining plugged in. In that case, the choice would be between two courses of action that would leave you equally well off in the end, but one of which would be much worse for the violinist. On the other hand, it is not possible for someone to offer to compensate the violinist for being unplugged from you, since in that case he will die. It may seem plausible to suppose that under such circumstances it would be impermissible for you to unplug yourself, and that this judgment would translate naturally to the case of the woman who seeks to end an unwanted pregnancy.[85]

There are several problems with appealing to the prospect of compensation as a way of raising an objection to the good samaritan argument. It is not clear that we can identify a way of fairly compensating you for your sacrifice, and even if there is, it is not clear that this would translate to the case of the pregnant woman. But suppose we agree upon a dollar amount that would fairly compensate the woman for the burden she had suffered. This seems improbable, but one could appeal to the fact that juries do this sort of thing all the time. If a worker loses her arm in an accident caused by the employer's negligence, the jury will try to determine a fair payment to compensate the worker for her injuries. In their deliberations, jurors might take into account such factors as whether the arm was especially valuable to the woman (did she enjoy playing the piano, was it necessary for her to perform her job, etc.) and in principle we could do the same in the case of the pregnant woman. If we accept this assumption, then we agree that there is a dollar amount that more or less restores the woman who carries an unwanted pregnancy to term to the level of well-being she would have enjoyed had she not done so.

But even if we accept this assumption, the compensation objection must still be rejected. The objection turns on the claim that if the pregnant woman is offered fair compensation for the burden that an unwanted pregnancy imposes, then it would be morally impermissible for her to

---

[85] Tooley presses this objection to Thomson's argument, although he applies the principle directly to the case of the pregnant woman rather than *via* the violinist analogy (1972: 50–1).

decline to accept the offer. And while this claim may be superficially appealing, it is ultimately unacceptable. For suppose that we decide on the dollar amount that would fairly compensate you if you were the one who lost an arm in the factory accident. Let's say that $10 million would do the trick. The claim needed in order to sustain the compensation objection would then entail that so long as someone is willing to pay you $10 million, it would be morally impermissible for you to refuse to save someone's life if doing so would cost you an arm. And that is very difficult to accept. The fact that we would fulfill all of our duties to you by giving you $10 million if you lost your arm in an accident does not entail that you would have a duty to sacrifice your arm in order to save someone's life if you knew ahead of time that we would compensate you for doing so with $10 million.

Finally, it is of course important to note that, as things stand, no one is offering to compensate women for carrying unwanted pregnancies to term, and there is no reason to expect things to change in this respect. And so long as things do not change, the compensation objection would provide no support for critics of the good samaritan argument even were it not subject to the difficulties I have identified here.

4.17. THE INCONSISTENCY OBJECTION

Almost every criticism of the good samaritan argument attacks the violinist analogy in one way or another, but Roger F. Gibson has leveled a much graver charge: that the argument as a whole is inconsistent. The account of someone's having a right to life on which the argument rests, Gibson rightly notes, is somewhat circular: To have a right to life is to have the right not to be killed *unjustly*, which means the right not to be killed in a way that violates some other right that one has. In the case of the fetus, this other right must refer to the right to the use of a woman's body. But, as Gibson also points out, Thomson argues that in many (if not most) cases the fetus does not have the right to the use of the woman's body since in many (if not most) cases the pregnant woman has not granted it such a right. It follows from this, Gibson argues, that in such cases the fetus has no right to life after all, and this flatly contradicts the central claim made by the good samaritan argument: that it accepts the assumption that every fetus has a right to life and demonstrates that abortion is morally permissible even granting this assumption. As Gibson puts it (1984: 136), the proponent of the good samaritan argument "seems committed to maintaining the truth of the following inconsistent set of statements:

S1: All fetuses have a right to life (i.e., a right not to be killed unjustly).
S2: No fetus can be aborted/killed unjustly unless it possesses a right to a woman's body.
S3: Some fetuses do not possess a right to a woman's body."

Gibson professes himself unable to find a satisfactory response to this objection, but I suggest that a rather simple one emerges when we begin by noting that the three statements attributed to the proponent of the argument are not, in fact, inconsistent. The conjunction of S2 and S3 entails that not all fetuses are the sort whose killing would be unjust; the killings of those who do not possess the right to a woman's body would not be unjust killings. But S1 does not insist that all fetuses are in fact the sorts whose killings would be unjust; it merely states that all fetuses have a right not to be killed unjustly, that is, a right not to be killed *if* their killing would be unjust. And this is perfectly consistent with the claim (entailed by S2 and S3) that not all fetuses are such that their killing would be unjust.[86]

The three statements Gibson identifies would be jointly inconsistent, then, only if S2 instead asserted what I will call

S2': No fetus can have a right to life unless it possesses a right to a woman's body,

since the conjunction of S3 and S2' entails that some fetuses do not have a right to life, which is inconsistent with S1.

But the good samaritan argument does not maintain that S2' is true, and indeed it seems plainly to be false. To have a right to life, the fetus need not currently have the right to a particular woman's body in just the same way that to have a right to spend one's money as one sees fit, one need not currently have any particular money. The moneyless still have their right to spend, and if they acquire some cash, it will for that reason be unjust to take their money from them. The unwelcome fetuses still have their right to life, and if they acquire the right to a woman's body, it will for that reason be unjust to deprive them of their use of that body while such use is needed in order for them to remain alive. There is thus no good reason to burden the proponent of the good

---

[86] This is also noted by Reeder (1996: 23n5).

samaritan argument with S2' and good reason not to, and so there is no good reason to accept Gibson's charge of inconsistency.

4.18. SOME PUZZLES RESOLVED

In Section 4.1, I presented a defense of the good samaritan argument. In the sections that followed, I attempted to show that none of the objections that have thus far been raised against the argument are powerful enough to warrant overturning it, and I attempted to establish this on terms that critics of abortion already accept. The result, if my arguments have been successful, is that the good samaritan argument should be accepted. Even if the typical human fetus does have a right to life, this does not suffice to establish that abortion in typical circumstances is morally impermissible. And if this is correct, then the rights-based argument against abortion must be rejected even if my arguments against its crucial first premise in Chapters 2 and 3 are unsuccessful.

Let us now suppose that we do accept the good samaritan argument. I want to conclude this long chapter by identifying a few implications this acceptance will have. The implications are diverse, but they have a common feature: In each case, they show how acceptance of the good samaritan argument's analysis of abortion can account for what might otherwise seem to be a puzzling point of convergence in which many defenders and critics of abortion are likely to agree about a variety of related questions. That the analysis provided by the good samaritan argument has this feature can in part be viewed simply as an added bonus that comes with accepting the argument. In this sense, it is nice that the argument has these implications, but the argument would be no worse if it didn't. And the fact that the argument provides a way to make sense of these various points of general agreement need not be taken as a reason to conclude that appealing to the good samaritan argument is the only satisfactory means of defending abortion. There may well be other ways for defenders of abortion to respond to these various issues. Still, the fact that the argument's analysis has these implications should nonetheless be viewed in part as providing further supplemental support for the argument itself. The fact that the argument's analysis provides illuminating solutions to these further puzzles, that is, provides further reason to believe that the analysis itself is correct.

One such puzzle has already been discussed in Section 4.12. On the one hand, there seems to many people to be a morally relevant difference between abortion prior to the point at which the fetus becomes viable and abortion after that point. Many defenders of abortion in general are at least more hesitant to support abortion after viability and some are inclined to oppose it. And critics who oppose abortion prior to viability often believe that there is something especially objectionable about abortion after viability. Indeed, if there is anything at all resembling a common or middle ground in the abortion debate, it consists in the claim that there is a morally relevant difference of some sort between early abortions and late-term abortions on viable fetuses. Yet on the other hand, there seems to be no morally relevant difference in the moral status of the fetus itself between the last moment when it is not viable and the first moment when it is viable. Critics of abortion, of course, deny that there is such a difference, since they maintain that the fetus has the same right to life as you and I well before this point. But defenders of abortion, too, find it difficult to affirm that there is such a difference, since it is difficult to discern any relevant change in the nature of the fetus itself at this stage in its development.

But the analysis of abortion provided by the good samaritan argument enables us to resolve this puzzle.[87] There is a morally relevant difference between causing the death of the fetus before and after viability not because there is a morally relevant difference between the *fetus* before and after viability, but rather because there is a morally relevant difference between the fetus–woman relation before and after viability. In the violinist story, for example, it is clear why there is a morally relevant difference between the relation between you and the violinist before and after the point at which the violinist becomes "viable." Prior to the point at which he recovers from his kidney ailment, he cannot survive without being plugged into you. After that point, he can. The claim that you have a right to unplug yourself from him at any point in time, therefore, entails that you have the right to do an act that will result in his death only prior to the point at which he can survive without the use of your body. Once he is cured, you can of course still choose to unplug yourself from him. But you cannot choose to kill him before or in the process of doing so. And so if we accept the good samaritan argument's analysis of abortion, it becomes clear why the common view that there is something distinctively problematic about abortions on viable fetuses is well grounded. The claim that a pregnant woman has the right to withdraw the needed life support that she is providing for the fetus, after all, will entail that she has the right to do an act that will

---

[87] This feature of the argument is also noted by Overall (1987: 82–3).

result in the death of the fetus only prior to the point at which the fetus can survive without the use of her body.

A second and related problem arises from the fact that the moment at which the unborn fetus becomes a newborn infant, like the moment at which the nonviable fetus becomes a viable fetus, marks no significant change in the nature of the individual involved. Virtually every defender of abortion is, at the very least, reluctant to have the permissibility of abortion stand or fall with the permissibility of killing a newborn human infant, but it can again seem very difficult to see how this linkage can be avoided. If it is permissible to abort a late-term fetus, and a late-term fetus is not significantly different from a newborn (especially a prematurely born) infant, then how could it be impermissible to kill a newborn infant? Here, again, the good samaritan analysis provides a simple answer. The fact that it is permissible for you to unplug yourself from the violinist, after all, does not imply that if you agree to remain plugged into him for nine months, you may then kill him after he has been successfully unplugged. And so on the good samaritan account, it is easy to see why the permissibility of abortion does not imply the permissibility of killing newborn babies.

A further puzzle arises from a relatively uncontroversial legal practice. If an attacker assaults a pregnant woman and kills the fetus she is carrying, he can be charged with a serious offense because of the death he has caused. Critics of abortion often point to this as evidence of inconsistency or hypocrisy on the part of defenders of abortion. As one pro-life activist has put it, "If a pregnant woman is murdered, we [society] want to bring the perpetrator up on double-homicide charges. However, if that same woman was to abort she would be invoking her freedom of choice. It's almost as if it's not really a baby unless you want it to be. And that, of course, is ridiculous" (Dinah Monahan, quoted in Allen 1995: 12). The implication that whether or not the fetus is a baby depends on whether the woman wants it to be a baby is, clearly, unacceptable, as is the implication that this is true of the question of whether or not it has the same right to life as you or I. We cannot justify the practice of punishing the attacker but not the woman by saying that whether or not the fetus has a right to life depends on whether or not the woman wants it to have a right to life. If the permissibility of abortion is defended by insisting that the fetus is just a blob of tissue, however, then it may indeed prove difficult to justify the practice of charging the attacker with a second serious offense. Destroying a blob of tissue, after all, is not generally a serious crime.

But on the analysis provided by the good samaritan argument, the coherence of this practice, too, is clearly illuminated without raising problems for the claim that abortion is morally permissible. If you do choose to allow the violinist to use your kidneys in Thomson's example, after all, the fact that you could also have chosen not to do so does not give someone else the right to unplug the violinist from you against your will. If I murder you in your bed, causing the violinist to be deprived of the use of the kidneys that you have agreed to let him use, then I am guilty of unjustly killing you and of unjustly killing the violinist by depriving him of life support that he had acquired the right to use. In this respect, it is no different from a case in which I kill a violinist by destroying a life support machine to which he was attached and which he had acquired the right to use. If you choose to unplug yourself from the violinist, on the other hand, causing the violinist to be deprived of the use of your kidneys, you are not guilty of such an unjust killing, since in that case you do not deprive the violinist of something to which he was entitled.

There are some cases of abortion that raise serious concerns for even the most resolute defender of the practice, and these can seem to pose yet a further difficulty. Virtually everyone agrees that there is something objectionable about abortion for sex selection, for example, but it can seem difficult to determine how to render this judgment consistent with the claim that abortion in general is permissible. The good samaritan analysis provides an illuminating framework for resolving this potential difficulty as well. Suppose that you are in the hospital bed next to mine, and that I am the one who wakes up plugged into the violinist. After giving my situation some careful thought, I decide that I am willing to make the necessary sacrifices, and you find yourself thinking highly of me. The violinist is separated from me by a screen, and after remaining plugged into him for a few weeks, I discover one day that he is black. I decide to unplug myself, because while I am willing to remain plugged in to keep a white violinist alive, I am not willing to make such a sacrifice for a black violinist. Surely it is plausible to suppose that you have good reason to think me a reprehensible person, even while conceding that what I do in unplugging myself is morally permissible. And so the same can be said for cases of abortion where the motive involved is, for one reason or another, subject to legitimate moral criticism.

It is sometimes argued that a defender of abortion cannot make sense of the genuine experience of grief that is felt by a woman who suffers a miscarriage. If abortion is permissible because the fetus is just a clump of cells after all, then a woman who miscarries should feel no worse than a woman who fails to get pregnant, or who discovers that although she believed she was pregnant she really wasn't. The good samaritan analysis permits the defender of abortion to avoid this problem as well.[88] If you care enough about the violinist to remain plugged into him, and he nonetheless dies, it will surely be appropriate for you to grieve in a way that it would not be if it simply turned out that there had been no violinist plugged into you in the first place.[89]

Finally, critics of abortion often complain that there is something hypocritical about the credo often invoked by its defenders, at least within the political arena, that abortion should be "safe, legal, and rare." It is sometimes said that if there is anything at all that the two sides can agree about it is that it we should try to reduce the number of abortions that take place, but, the critic of abortion seems to be in a position to ask, if there is nothing wrong with abortion, then what difference does it make how often it occurs? Defenders of abortion, of course, could try to answer this question by pointing out that abortion is a more expensive and invasive way of preventing unwanted children from being born than is the use of contraception. But this seems less than fully convincing. The appeal of the thought that abortion should be rare lies in more than the thought that it is inefficient. It appeals to the idea that abortion involves a kind of loss that contraception does not. And once again, the good samaritan analysis renders the dissolution of this problem a simple matter. For surely it is clear that while we would want to be allowed to unplug ourselves from stricken violinists, we would also want

---

[88] This feature of the argument is also noted by Overall (1987: 79–80).

[89] It might be objected that the good samaritan argument that I have defended in this chapter permits us to account for this phenomenon only if we reject the arguments that I have made in the previous chapters. The good samaritan argument permits us to reconcile the appropriate grieving that often accompanies miscarriage with the claim that abortion is morally permissible, that is, only if we conjoin the argument with the claim that the fetus truly is an individual with the same right to life as you or I, a claim that I argued against in Chapters 2 and 3. Indeed, it might be objected, more generally, that *all* of the positive implications of the good samaritan argument that I have noted in this section depend on the contention that the fetus has a right to life. But such an objection is misguided. I have argued that the fetus is not an individual with the same right to life as you or I, but none of the arguments that I have advanced in defense of this claim entail that the fetus is of no value at all, or that it is not of sufficient value to warrant, for example, grieving over its loss. The fact that the fetus is in the process of developing into someone like you or me may well warrant viewing the loss of a fetus as a loss of something of value even if it is not the loss of something that has the same right to life as you or I.

to minimize the number of instances in which violinists find themselves dependent upon individuals who are unwilling to assist them.

I began this chapter by noting that the good samaritan argument has at times been compared to Anselm's ontological proof of the existence of God and to Zeno's paradoxes of motion: People are generally confident that there is something wrong with the argument, but disagree about what, precisely, the problem is. I conclude by suggesting that these comparisons get things backwards. The good samaritan argument does not generate new puzzles. Rather, it resolves existing ones. And critics of the argument have failed to uncover a crucial flaw in it not because the argument is as clever as those of Anselm and Zeno, but because it is less clever. It is merely sound.

Chapter 5

Non-Rights-Based Arguments

5.0. OVERVIEW

In Section 1.3, I drew a distinction between two different kinds of argument that critics of abortion appeal to in attempting to defend the thesis that abortion, at least in typical cases, is morally impermissible. One kind of argument I called the rights-based argument. This argument turns on two claims: The claim that the fetus (at least in typical cases of abortion) has a right to life, and the claim that if the fetus has a right to life, then abortion (at least in typical circumstances) is morally impermissible. I have now completed my case against the rights-based argument, arguing against the argument's first claim in Chapters 2 and 3 and against the second in Chapter 4. If my arguments against either or both of these claims have been successful, then I have established that the rights–based argument against abortion must be rejected on grounds that the critic of abortion can and does accept. But it remains to consider those arguments against the moral permissibility of abortion that do not commit the critic of abortion to either of these two claims. Such non-rights-based arguments are not affected by anything that has been said in Chapters 2–4 and thus require separate consideration. Arguments against abortion that do not rest on the claim that the fetus has a right to life are not as frequently raised in the philosophical or scholarly literature on abortion, but they have clearly been raised by critics of abortion nonetheless. It is the goal of this final chapter to identify them and to establish that they, too, should be rejected, and on grounds that the critic of abortion already accepts.

5.1. THE GOLDEN RULE ARGUMENT

In Chapter 2, I considered a number of arguments in defense of the claim that the fetus acquires a right to life at the moment of its conception. Each argument turned on the fact you and I stand in a certain relation to the fetus from the moment of its conception and attempted to show that this entailed that if you and I have this right, then so does the fetus. I argued that none of these arguments were successful. But there is a further relation that obtains between you and me on the one hand and zygotes on the other, which I overlooked in that chapter: A zygote is something that you and I once were. Now, saying that you and I were once zygotes might at first seem to be merely another way of saying that every zygote has the potential to develop into a mature human being like you and me. And I did consider and argue against those arguments that claim to show that a zygote has a right to life in virtue of this relation. But to say that you and I were once zygotes is to say more than that every zygote has the potential to become a mature human being. It is to say that *only* zygotes have the potential to become mature human beings. This latter claim may also be true, but it is neither identical with, nor does it follow from, the former claim. Human reproduction, after all, might have evolved in such a way that people were sometimes produced by parthenogenesis, developing spontaneously from an unfertilized egg, or sometimes by some sort of metamorphosis in which they arose from some other set of cells. If that were the case, and you had arisen through one of these alternative routes, then it would not be true that you were once a zygote. But human reproduction did not evolve in that way, so I can say with confidence that you were once a zygote. And this extra fact may be of significance for the following reason: One might argue that if you are glad that the zygote from which you developed was not aborted at any point in its development, and if you adhere to the principle of fairness embodied in the golden rule, then you must conclude that other (or at least other relevantly similar) fetuses should not be aborted at any point in their development from their zygotic origins either. In short, one could argue that abortion is morally wrong because it violates the golden rule.

This is perhaps not the most straightforward argument against the moral permissibility of abortion, but it is also not an uncommon one, especially in the public debate over the issue. Those active in the movement opposed to abortion, for example, often cite as a part of the motivation for their activism the recognition that, under certain circumstances, they themselves might have been aborted (Luker 1984: esp. 132–3), and speakers who argue in defense of abortion report that they are often asked how they would feel about the prospect of their mother's having had an abortion when pregnant with them. In addition, rallies organized by opponents of abortion often include such chants as: "Rejoice, rejoice, rejoice, our moms were not pro-choice!" and feature bumper stickers and T-shirts with such slogans as, "As a Former Fetus I Oppose Abortion!", "Favor Abortion? Someone could have told *your* Mom!", and "Choose Life: Your Mom Did!" The golden rule argument, moreover, provides a way to argue against the moral permissibility of abortion without first having to defend the claim that the fetus has the same right to life as you and I. At least two philosophers have gone on record in defense of such a position[1], and their arguments merit scrutiny.

5.1.1. Hare's Version

Hare (1975: 153–4ff) puts his version of the argument as follows. Suppose we accept the principle that "we should do to others as we wish them to do to us." Then by "a logical extension" of this principle, we should also accept the injunction that "we should do to others what we are glad was done to us." But assuming that we are glad that others refrained from terminating the pregnancy that resulted in our birth, it follows that "we are enjoined not, *ceteris paribus*, to terminate any pregnancy which will result in the birth of a person having a life like ours." We can put the argument as follows:

P1: We should, *ceteris paribus*, do to others as we wish them to do to us.

C1: We should, *ceteris paribus*, do to others what we are glad was done to us.

P2: We are glad that others refrained from terminating the pregnancy that resulted in our birth.

C2: We should, *ceteris paribus*, refrain from terminating those pregnancies that would result in the birth of others (relevantly like us).

Hare concedes that this argument does not justify the strong conclusion that abortion is always morally wrong, but he does claim that it warrants the conclusion that abortion "is prima facie and in general wrong

---

[1] See also Nathanson (1979: 227–9). And although he declined to reveal his views on abortion during his Supreme Court confirmation hearings, Clarence Thomas had apparently also endorsed this sort of argument: His mother recalls him telling her that he opposed abortion on demand because "If you had had one, where would I be?" (Mayer and Abramson (1994: 67)).

in default of sufficient countervailing reasons." And although he admits that such reasons "are not too hard to find in many cases," I take it that the argument as a whole nonetheless purports to show that, special considerations aside, there is something morally wrong about abortion per se (1975: 166). Indeed, in the more recent of his two presentations of what is essentially the same argument, Hare characterizes the argument's conclusion as implying that "taking all pregnancies together as a class, abortion would be wrong in the vast majority of them" (1989: 179). What should a defender of abortion say about this argument?

Let me begin by asking why we should accept P1. Hare offers two suggestions. One is simply that the principle is firmly grounded in the Christian tradition, and that the abortion debate often takes place in this context. But since Hare himself peppers his paper with complaints about appeals to those intuitions that are merely the result of contingent facts about our uprbringing, and since whether or not one was raised as a Christian is precisely one such fact, he can hardly expect this to count as a justification for P1. The second claim is that this type of argument is the "formal basis" of such diverse moral theories as "the Kantian Categorical Imperative, the ideal observer theory, the rational contractor theory, various kinds of utilitarianism" as well as his own "universal prescriptivism" (1975: 153). This strategy seems more promising as a route toward justification. Since most philosophers will think there is reason to accept one or the other (or some combination) of these views, if all of them are formally founded on this principle, then most will think there is reason to accept this principle. Hare is not explicit here about his reasons for this claim, but from the context the idea surely has something to do with a commitment to universality or impartiality: I can't call a principle a moral principle unless I am willing to have it govern both others' conduct and my own. In any event, taking something like this to be what Hare has in mind, there seems to be sufficient reason to respond to Hare's version of the golden rule argument simply by rejecting P1.

First, notice that the principle is not symmetric: It asserts that we *should* do to others as we *wish* them to do to us. But what I wish you to do and what I think you should do are two different things, so that if the principle is meant to rest on the sort of formal impartiality that all these theories have in common, it should instead read

P1': We should do to others as we think they should do to us.

Indeed, not only does P1's lack of symmetry deprive it of the sort of support Hare claims for it, but it seems also to generate unreasonable implications as well. I may well wish others to shower me with lavish presents without thinking that such gift giving is something that (they or) I should do.[2] It is perfectly coherent for me to say that I wish that others would do more for me than merely what they should do for me, but it is incoherent for me to say that I should do more for others than merely what I should do for them. Indeed, it seems perfectly coherent for me to say that I wish that others would do for me things that they *shouldn't do* for me, but incoherent for me to say that I should do for others what I should not to.

A second problem with P1 is that it treats all moral shoulds equally, whereas many of the theories Hare appeals to for support would insist, at the least, on distinguishing between what I should be morally required to do, what I should be morally permitted to do, and what I should be morally praised for doing. So while P1′ represents an improvement over P1, even it does not suffice if it is to stand on the sort of support Hare is appealing to. Instead, we would have to say something like

P1″: We are (a) required to do to others what we think they are required to do to us, (b) permitted to do to others what we think they are permitted to do to us, (c) forbidden to do to others what we think they are forbidden to do to us, and (d) entitled to praise for doing to others what we think they are entitled to praise for doing to us.

I suspect that most people initially drawn to P1 will find P1″ to reflect their considered view more accurately.

If I am right about this, then Hare's argument collapses. The conclusion that others are required to refrain from terminating pregnancies that would result in the birth of others relevantly like us would follow from P1″ only if we also accepted what I will call

P2′: We think others were required to refrain from terminating the pregnancy that resulted in our birth.

And insisting on the truth of P2′ would clearly beg the question, since the whole point of the argument is to try to determine whether or not terminating such pregnancies is permissible in the first place. From P1″ and P2 we can conclude only that a woman who believes that her mother deserves praise for refraining from terminating the pregnancy that resulted in her birth should in turn believe that she is entitled to praise if

---

[2] Bayles makes this point about Hare's argument (1976: 299).

she refrains from terminating a pregnancy that would result in the birth of another relevantly like her. But this constitutes no serious challenge to the practice of abortion. It is merely to say, what I expect any defender of the permissibility of abortion would happily acknowledge, that a child should be grateful to his or her mother for the burdens she incurred in carrying her child to term. In this sense, the more well-founded of the various signs carried by those protesting abortion is the one that reads "If My Mom Didn't Care/ I Might Not Be Here/ Thanks, Mom!" (cited in Schaeffer and Koop 1979: 53), which suggests not that the mother who carried her pregnancy to term did something she was morally obligated to do, but rather that she did something worthy of praise and gratitude. Indeed, in an ironic twist to the case of *Doe v. Bolton*, the lesser-known decision handed down at the same time as *Roe v. Wade*, the woman who unsuccessfully attempted to obtain an abortion has since become an opponent of abortion, while the daughter she subsequently gave birth to now says of her mother that "If she'd had an abortion she would have had her right" (quoted in Tribe 1992: 6). In short: P1 of Hare's version of the golden rule argument is unacceptable, and the only acceptable revision of it renders Hare's argument itself invalid.

Let us suppose, however, that despite these considerations we find ourselves nonetheless enamored of P1 as Hare has presented it. There remains the question of P2. Hare sketches a defense of P2 by urging us to meditate on those things that make us glad that we were born, which he in turn seems to equate with our being glad to be alive. As I understand it, then, the argument in defense of P2 that each of us is to address to ourself is this: I am glad to be alive; therefore, I am glad that I was born; therefore, I am glad that nobody terminated the pregnancy that resulted in my birth. But this argument is highly suspect. Consider, for example, the case of a woman whose pregnancy is life-threatening but who is prevented from having an abortion and dies during delivery. The child who is born may well go on to have a well-lived life. So he may truthfully say, "I am glad to be alive." Still, it would be grotesque to insist that this commits him to being glad that people refused to provide his mother with an abortion.[3] The unjustifiable gulf between being glad to be alive

---

[3] The gap in the argument is also overlooked by, for example, Bagley, who suggests that we consider how we would respond if told that our mothers had been prevented from aborting us: "Do you regret her failure? In other words, are you glad that you have life?" (1990: 97). But these are two importantly distinct questions and answering the latter affirmatively is consistent with answering the former negatively.

and being glad that the events necessary to your being born occurred can be made even more clear by appealing to other sorts of examples. A person who was conceived as a result of rape surely need not be glad that his mother was raped. And a person whose parents met as refugees from Nazi Germany can be certain that he would not have been born had the Holocaust never occurred, but that cannot make him glad that it did.

Now, it might be objected that these attempted counterexamples ignore Hare's *ceteris paribus* clause. If a person can be glad to be alive and yet not glad that his mother refrained from having an abortion only in those cases in which not having an abortion caused her very serious or lethal harm, then the *ceteris paribus* clause might be invoked to justify the claim that abortion is impermissible except in those severe cases. And of course that result might well be welcomed by those who wish to (or are at least willing to) allow for abortions but only in such cases. But once we agree to sever the link between one's being glad to be alive and one's being glad that no one terminated the pregnancy that resulted in one's birth, there is no principled way to draw this line, certainly none that is provided by appealing to the golden rule. Anyone whose mother did not want to be pregnant could feel both sorrow that his mother suffered an unwanted burden and happiness that he is alive as a result. And thus one could accept P1 of the golden rule argument and also be glad that one is alive, and still consistently maintain that it is morally permissible for any woman who does not wish to be pregnant to have an abortion.

Finally, Hare's argument is subject to a powerful *reductio ad absurdum*: If it shows abortion to be wrong, then it also shows contraception to be equally wrong and for the same reason. After all, if I am glad that my mother did not have an abortion while pregnant with me and if this suffices to commit me to the view that abortion is wrong, then since I must also be glad (and equally glad) that she was not using contraception at the time I was conceived, this must equally commit me to the view that contraception is wrong and equally wrong. But this implication is unacceptable. And so, therefore, is Hare's argument.

Hare's response to this significant difficulty is essentially to concede it (1989: 182–3). He suggests that there may be some reasons to distinguish the practices, such as the fact that abortion is a more complex medical procedure and that it involves killing someone the woman may feel affection for, but it is not at all clear how these considerations can legitimately enter the picture on a golden rule account: If it makes no difference to me whether I was born because my mother was prevented from using contraception or because she was prevented from having an abortion, then if the argument shows I should refrain from endorsing abortion, it seems equally to show that I should refrain from endorsing contraception. And even if these considerations are admitted, they seem only to show that a woman may have a self-interested reason to use contraception rather than abortion if she is going to use one or the other, not that she has a moral reason to think that one is permissible even if the other is not. And even if it did establish that she had a moral reason to prefer contraception to abortion, this would do nothing to show that it would be immoral for her to have an abortion if she had (wrongly?) neglected to use contraception in the first place or if the contraception she had used had failed. There seems, then, to be no way for Hare's argument to avoid entailing this unacceptable conclusion.

A defender of Hare's position here might complain that in characterizing this implication as unacceptable, I am counting on the reader's sharing the belief that contraception is morally permissible. And if I am doing this, then I am violating the fundamental principle this book has set out to follow, to attempt to defend abortion while appealing to claims that critics of abortion generally accept. For, it might be pointed out at this point, many people who oppose abortion also oppose contraception. This is true. But it does not diminish the force of this objection to Hare's argument. What is unacceptable about Hare's argument is not merely that it entails that contraception is immoral (though for many people, this implication alone suffices to render the argument objectionable), but that it entails that contraception is morally on a par with abortion. Many critics of abortion do not oppose contraception, but even those critics of abortion who do oppose both contraception and abortion do not accept that they are equally wrong and for the same reason. In addition, if Hare's argument entails that contraception is immoral, then it also entails that abstaining from intercourse altogether is also immoral, since I must be just as glad that my parents did not abstain from intercourse as I am that they did not use contraception and that my mother did not have an abortion. But surely every critic of abortion agrees that it is not immoral to abstain from having sexual intercourse. And so one can appeal to this *reductio ad aburdum* objection to Hare's argument as a further reason to reject it while still engaging critics of abortion on their own terms.

5.1.2. Gensler's Version

The fact that Hare's version of the golden rule argument is unacceptable does not mean that every version of the argument is. Gensler has attempted to defend a version of the argument that recognizes that "Hare's formulation of the golden rule . . . is defective" and that attempts to avoid the fatal asymmetry between *ought* and *glad* noted previously (1986: 318n.5). Gensler's version of the argument consists of a defense of his version of the golden rule and an attempt to apply it to the case of abortion, and I will treat each in turn.

Gensler begins with two principles, the universalizability principle and the prescriptivity principle. The universalizability principle "demands that we make similar ethical judgments about the same sort of situation." In particular, if all of the circumstances are identical in two cases, one cannot endorse non-identical moral judgments just because one of the cases involves you and the other doesn't. If the universalizability principle is true, it follows that "If you are consistent and think that it would be all right for someone *to do A to X*, then you will think that it would be all right for someone *to do A to you* in similar circumstances" (1986: 311). The prescriptivity principle "demands that we keep our ethical beliefs in harmony with the rest of our lives (our actions, intentions, desires, and so forth)." In particular, if the prescriptivity principle is true, it follows that "If you are consistent and think that it would be *all right* for someone to do *A* to you in similar circumstances, then you will *consent* to the idea of someone doing *A* to you in similar circumstances" (1986: 311). With these two premises, Gensler is able to justify his version of the golden rule:

P1: If you are consistent and think that it would be all right for someone *to do A to X*, then you will think that it would be all right for someone *to do A to you* in similar circumstances (from the universalizability principle).

P2: If you are consistent and think that it would be *all right* for someone to do *A* to you in similar circumstances, then you will *consent* to the idea of someone doing *A* to you in similar circumstances (from the prescriptivity principle).

C: If you are consistent and think that it would be *all right to do A to X*, then you will *consent* to the idea of someone *doing A to you* in similar circumstances (Gensler's version of the golden rule).

Gensler then provides as an example of how this version of the golden rule is meant to operate, an argument based on the assumption that "you do not consent to the idea of people stealing from you in normal circumstances." If this is true, and if Gensler's version of the golden rule is correct, then you cannot consistently believe that stealing is permissible in normal circumstances. The golden rule, he then clarifies, governs your *"present reaction* toward a hypothetical case" and not your actual response if you were in the situation. So in asking how the principle would treat the action of robbing someone while he was asleep, the "Right Question" is "Do I now consent to the idea of my being robbed while asleep?" rather than "If I were robbed while I was asleep would I then (while asleep) consent to this action?" (1986: 312). And assuming that you do not now consent to that act either, you also cannot consistently deny that robbing people in their sleep in normal circumstances is morally impermissible.

Finally, Gensler attempts to motivate the claim he needs you to assent to in order for his argument to yield a negative judgment of abortion, namely, that "You do not consent to the idea of your having been aborted in normal circumstances" (1986: 314). He does this by means of the following example:

Suppose that you had a sadistic mother who, while pregnant with you, contemplated injecting herself with a blindness-drug which would have no effect on her but which would cause the fetus (you) to be born blind and remain blind all its (your) life. Your mother could have done this to you. Do you think this would have been all right – and do you consent to the idea of her having done this? (1986: 313)

Gensler takes it that you will clearly answer no, and regardless of what stage the pregnancy has reached. But to apply his version of the golden rule to the case of abortion, he then argues, "We need only switch from a blindness-drug (which blinds the fetus) to a death-drug (which kills the fetus)" (1986: 314). And surely if you didn't consent to the blindness-drug you won't consent to the death-drug. We can view this as a continuation of the argument begun previously, where C2 is simply a particular instantiation of the version of the golden rule that constitutes that argument's conclusion:

C2: If you are consistent and think that *abortion is normally permissible*, then you will consent to the idea of *your having been aborted* in normal circumstances.

P3: You do not consent to the idea of your having been aborted in normal circumstances.

C3: Therefore, if you are consistent, then you will not think that abortion is normally permissible.

There is basically one problem with this argument, but it is a big enough problem to warrant rejecting it. The problem lies in Gensler's use of the word *consent*. What does he mean by it? Presumably we are not meant to take the expression literally, since one cannot literally consent to having something happen in the past.[4] Gensler emphasizes that his version of the golden rule "has to do with my *present reaction* toward a hypothetical case in which I may imagine myself as asleep or dead or even a fetus," but my present reaction cannot be one of agreeing to let something happen in the past, even the hypothetical past. At several points, Gensler equates the idea of consenting to a given act with the idea of approving of it: "If I think it would be all right to rob Jones but yet I don't consent to (or approve of) the idea of someone robbing me in similar circumstances, then I violate [the golden rule] and am inconsistent" (1986: 311; see also two instances of this on p. 314). And this seems to make more sense: I can express approval or disapproval of events in the past, whether they involve me or not. But now the question is: what, specifically, does Gensler mean by "approve of"? There seem to be three possibilities.

The first is that to approve of an action is to think favorably of it, to endorse it, to think it the right thing to do. This, I take it, is the ordinary meaning of the term. It would seem very strange to say "I approve of her doing it, but don't think she should be doing it."[5] But if this is what Gensler means by consenting to an action, then P2 (which Gensler derives from the prescriptivity principle) is simply false. You can think it morally permissible[6] for someone to circulate stories about your lurid past without having to think that circulating such stories is the right thing for them to do. Gensler says that "if I think an act would be all right but I don't consent to it being done, then I . . . am inconsistent" (1986: 311), but there is nothing at all inconsistent about agreeing that lurid

---

4 Wilson presses this point in some detail (1988: 123–5).

5 In this sense, to approve *of* an action is to do more than merely to approve it; a senate committee might approve a bill without approving of it (say as part of a bargain to get other bills passed).

6 I am assuming that by "all right" Gensler means "morally permissible" since this is the way he characterizes the golden rule in the specific instantiation dealing with abortion. It is true that "all right" might also be taken to mean "morally obligatory," and in this sense P2 would avoid the objection raised here, but as Wilson has pointed out, this would reduce the argument's conclusion to the claim that abortion is not normally obligatory, a claim that can be readily endorsed by all sides (1988: 120–1).

gossip is morally permissible while refusing to approve of it in this sense. For there is simply nothing inconsistent or hypocritical about thinking that someone has made a morally criticizable choice even though they have made a morally permissible choice. This would be inconsistent only if you also held the view that the only grounds for morally disapproving of what a person does is that the action is impermissible, and this is an extremely implausible view and one that Gensler has provided no reason for accepting. So Gensler's version of the golden rule argument will fail if this is what is meant by consent.

A second and weaker sense of approval, however, would seem to rescue Gensler from this difficulty. This is the sense in which to approve of something is simply to accept it as permissible. The role of the approver, on this account, is simply to determine whether or not the proposed action in question is consistent with the appropriate requirements and then to give or withhold her approval accordingly. In this sense, P2 is certainly plausible. It would be hypocritical for you to maintain that gossiping is morally permissible in general and then to refuse to acknowledge that those who are gossiping about you are doing something permissible. Strictly speaking, it need not be *inconsistent* for you to do this. It would be inconsistent for you positively to assert that what they do is impermissible, since this would contradict your general claim, which entails that what they do is permissible. But by refraining from consenting to their actions, you need not be denying that what they do is permissible. You are merely declining to affirm it. Still, Gensler would be right to say that there is an important sense in which this would fail to keep your moral beliefs "in harmony" with the rest of your life. So there is an important sense in which, if to approve of something is simply to accept it as permissible, then P2 is true.

If we defend P2 in this way, however, the problem is simply shifted to P3. For saying that P3 is true in this sense will simply beg the question that Gensler is trying to answer. That is, in order to say that P3 is true, we will now have to say "I do not think it would have been morally permissible for my mother to have had an abortion when she was pregnant with me." And whether it would have been permissible for her to do so is precisely the question at issue.

There is a third possibility. When Gensler introduces the application of his version of the golden rule to the case of stealing, he characterizes the assumption that you do not consent to the idea of people stealing from you as "an empirical premise about your *desires*" (1986: 311, emphasis added). Similarly, he characterizes the argument as a whole as showing what follows given that somone has "a certain *desire*," and he notes that he will "generally assume that the reader *desires* not to be robbed or blinded or killed" (1986: 312, emphasis added). And he responds to the prospect of a person who might consent to the death-drug but not to the blindness-drug by saying that "Such a person could be consistent, but only with bizarre *desires* about how he himself is to be treated" (1986: 315, emphasis added). So perhaps Gensler should simply be understood as saying that to consent to or approve of an act is to desire that it be done.

In many respects, this does indeed seem to be the most straightforward interpretation of the text, and it does put P3 back on firmer ground. I have refrained from attributing it to Gensler as the primary reading, however, because if this is what he does mean, then his formulation of the golden rule has precisely the same defect that he explicitly recognizes in Hare's version. And since he claims that the purpose of his argument is to defend a version of the golden rule that is immune to this objection, it seems uncharitable to attribute this version of the rule to him unless no other cogent interpretation is forthcoming. Since I have argued that the other interpretations fail to yield a convincing argument, however, we must finally consider that this may be what Gensler means. Near the end of his paper, for example, Gensler at one point characterizes his argument as follows: "I claim that most of the times the pro-abortionist will find that he is indeed inconsistent – he is supporting certain moral principles about the treatment of others that he would not wish to have followed in their actions toward him" (1986: 316). Strictly speaking, Gensler here seems to be saying of the defender of abortion that he would not wish his mother to have acted on the principle that abortion is morally permissible when she was pregnant with him. But there is no reason to think that this is so: The defender of abortion may not wish that his mother had had an abortion, but he need not wish that she acted on a principle that made her having an abortion impermissible. But Gensler can also be taken to mean that the defender of abortion would not wish his mother to have had an abortion. This much may certainly be true, but now we really are back to Hare's version of the argument and thus to Hare's fallacy: It simply does not matter what I would *like* other people to do or refrain from doing to me because it does not follow from the fact that I desire that they not do something to me that I must think it impermissible for them to do it to me (or, therefore, for me to do it to them). Again, I may well desire that they not tell stories about my lurid past without thinking that it is impermissible for me to tell stories about their lurid pasts. So if we construe consent in this way, then P2 (and C1) turn out to be false. There seems, then, to be no consistent meaning of consent on which all of the premises of Gensler's argument are true.

This objection seems to me sufficient to warrant rejecting Gensler's version of the golden rule argument, but it is worth noting a few additional difficulties. One concerns his attempt to justify P3 by appealing to the example of the blindness-drug. Gensler argues that it would be bizarre to refuse to consent to the blindness-drug case but to consent to the death-drug case and that not consenting to the death-drug case amounts to accepting P3. But both of these claims are subject to serious objection.

The first claim can be challenged on the grounds that it neglects the distinction between potential people and future people. When the pregnant woman takes the blindness-drug, a defender of abortion can plausibly argue, there is a future person she is harming, namely the one who will later be born blind. He is worse off than he would have been had she not taken the drug. When she takes the death-drug, however, there is no such person who is made worse off than he would otherwise have been. The killing-drug does not harm anyone's interests because it does not result in a person who is worse off than he would have been had the drug not been taken, since it does not result in any person at all.[7] A critic of abortion, of course, could respond to this rebuttal by arguing that the fetus is already a person. But it would seem that in order to do so, he would then be abandoning what is distinctive about the golden rule argument, that it is supposed to be able to show that abortion is immoral without having to rely on such claims.

The second claim Gensler uses to support P3 maintains that if you do not consent in the death-drug case, then you do not consent to the idea of your having been aborted in normal circumstances. But there is an important difference between the two cases, which Gensler neglects entirely. In the case of the blindness-drug, Gensler explicitly stipulates that taking it will have "no effect" (1986: 313) on the pregnant woman. She takes it not to relieve herself of some substantial burden, but merely in order to satisfy her sadistic desire to cause some suffering in somone else. But this means that if we agree that we do not consent to this

---

[7] For more on this point see Steinbock (1992); see also Dworkin (1993: 19).

(on any account of what "consent" means) and then substitute a death-drug for a blindness-drug, we are committed only to the claim that we do not consent to the idea of our mother having an abortion when doing so would do nothing to relieve her of any burden but would cause suffering in someone else, which would in turn give her pleasure. It is difficult to imagine what such a case would look like, since an abortion will by definition relieve her of the burdens of pregnancy, whereas the blindness-drug relieves her of nothing. But I suppose we might picture a case where for some reason the abortion will cause just as much physical pain and inconvenience to her as pregnancy and childbirth would, and where she has the abortion only because this will cause someone else, let us suppose the father of the child who wants very much for her to continue the pregnancy, to suffer. We can certainly agree that we do not consent to the idea of her doing this, in any of the senses of consent noted above. But this is hardly tantamount to agreeing that we do not consent to abortion under normal circumstances.

Finally, it is important to note that Gensler, too, fails to overcome the objection that his argument, if accepted, would also entail that the use of contraceptives and even abstinence is impermissible, and equally so. After all, if I don't consent to or approve of abortion because it would have caused me not to have been born, then it would seem I must also disapprove of abstinence and contraception on the same grounds.

Gensler's response to this objection is to concede its initial force but to say that there is a difference between abortion and contraception which is brought out by focusing on the universalization requirement implicit in P1:

> If I hold "It is wrong to have an abortion in this (my) case," then I have to make the same judgment in all similar cases; but I can easily hold (consistently) that it is in general wrong to have an abortion. But if I hold "It is wrong to prevent conception . . . in this (my) case," then I again have to make the same judgment in all similar cases; but I cannot hold (consistently) that it is in general wrong to prevent conception – since this would commit me to desiring a policy which would bring about a greatly overpopulated world of starving people at a very low level of human life." (1986: 317)

And so as a result, Gensler says he comes "though with hesitation" to consent to his parents' having not conceived him, though not to consent to their having aborted him (1986: 317).

There are a few problems with this response. First, notice that Gensler again slips into grounding his argument on what I would call "desire." And as we have already seen, what I would desire is not the issue. But there is a more important problem here. Gensler maintains that if you hold that it is wrong to prevent conception in your case, then you will also have to hold that "it is in general wrong to prevent conception." But this is not so. You will have only to hold that preventing conception is wrong in circumstances similar to those under which you were conceived. And everything turns on what makes such cases similar. Consider, for example, a newly married, financially secure couple who desire and plan to have two children and who could easily support one child right away. They prefer to wait a few years before starting a family, but prefer not to wait a few years before having sexual intercourse. So they use contraception. Suppose your parents did not use contraception and conceived you shortly after they were married, even though they, too, were hoping to wait a few years before starting a family. On Gensler's account, you will initially be inclined not to consent to the idea of their having used contraception, but will eventually be persuaded to consent to it because refusing to consent to it would commit you to approving of a policy that would lead to devastating overpopulation. But refusing to approve of your parents using contraception in this case commits you only to the view that it is wrong to use contraception under similar circumstances. And nothing about accepting this rule would commit you to producing an overcrowded world of starving people. The rule applies only to people who have no children, who can easily support one, and who want and plan to have children anyway. It would not increase the population because it would not force anyone to have a child who did not want to have a child, nor would it force anyone to have more children than they wanted to have, nor would it force anyone to have a child they could not support. So Gensler has no grounds for rebutting the claim that if his argument shows that abortion is immoral, it shows that it is equally immoral, and for the same reason, for people in such circumstances to use contraception. And surely that result is unacceptable to critics and defenders of abortion alike.

I conclude that both Hare and Gensler have failed to offer an adequate defense of the golden rule argument against abortion and suggest that the analyses that render their failures clear provide strong reason to doubt that any other defense of the argument would prove to be more successful.

5.2. THE CULTURE OF DEATH ARGUMENT

A second non-rights-based argument against abortion turns on the claim that a permissive attitude toward abortion contributes to what is often referred to as a "culture of death" (e.g., Pope John Paul II 1995: 17), in which attitudes become more permissive toward killing in general. Thus, even if the fetus itself does not have the same right to life as you and I, or even if its having such a right does not suffice to make abortion impermissible, abortion must still be opposed as a means of avoiding other killings that are uncontroversially impermissible, such as the killing of infants or the elderly. This argument, like the golden rule argument, is not generally represented in the academic literature on abortion, but, again like the golden rule argument, it is widely defended in more popular works opposed to abortion.

There are three reasons to reject this culture of death argument. The first is that there is insufficient statistical evidence to warrant the claim that infanticide rates are higher now than they were generally when abortion was illegal. In fact, according to Everett Lee, a demographer who has analyzed decades worth of such statistics, precisely the opposite is the case: The deliberate killing of newborns was more common 30 years ago than it is today, although today individual cases are more likely to receive national attention. Moreover, there is a sensible explanation for why this would be the case: "There's no question that abortion prevents, or substitutes for, a lot of these infanticides" (Lee, quoted in Kantrowitz 1997: A-24). Indeed, as a recent unpublished paper by John Donohue of Stanford University Law School and economist Steven Levitt of the University of Chicago argues, the decriminalization of abortion throughout the United States in 1973 has likely been responsible for the significant *decrease* in overall crime that occurred during the late 1990s. As Donohue and Levitt point out in the abstract of their paper, three strands of relatively uncontroversial empirical evidence support this thesis (1999: abstract): First, the significant decline in the crime rate in the United States began to occur just as the first generation of Americans to have been born after *Roe v. Wade* began to reach the peak ages of criminal activity. Second, the few states that decriminalized abortion a few years prior to 1973 were the first to experience a decreasing crime rate. Third, the states with the highest abortion rates have seen a greater decrease in crime. In addition, as Donohue and Levitt also point out, there is a natural explanation for why liberal access to abortion would eventually lead to a decrease rather than an increase in crime. Abortion, after all, is not randomly distributed throughout the population. A disproportionate number of abortions are performed on women who are, on average, at a higher risk of having children who would go on to engage in criminal activity. According to Donohue and Levitt's statistical study, then, legalized abortion in the United States "can explain about half of the recent fall in crime." None of this is to say, of course, that the resulting decrease in crime counts as a good argument in favor of abortion (and neither Donohue nor Levitt claim that it is). Rather, it is to say that it presents a decisive consideration against the empirical assumption underlying the culture of death argument against abortion.

The second reason to reject that argument is that even if we assume for the sake of the argument that there has been an increase in infanticide in particular, or of crime in general, it does not follow that the decriminalization of abortion in the United States in 1973 played an actual causal role in the (assumed) subsequent increase in criminal activity. There are many other possible explanations as well. And a general survey of existing attitudes toward abortion suggests that the claim is implausible. In contemporary Japan, for example, abortion is treated as the primary method of birth control, and there is no evidence that this has fostered a more general culture of death in that country.[8] Indeed, if anything, it is a common lament that violent crime is far more pervasive in the United States than in Japan.

But let us suppose that both the empirical claim underlying the culture of death argument and the hypothesis it proposes to account for it are correct. Let us suppose that a society that adopts a permissive attitude toward abortion can reasonably expect to see an increase in infanticide and just plain old murder. Even if we assume all of this, the argument's conclusion still does not follow. For at this point, a distinction long appealed to by critics of abortion comes back to haunt them: the distinction between intending harm and merely foreseeing it. An example that is commonly used to illustrate the moral relevance of this distinction turns on the apparently well-established claim that when societies increase their spending on education, the rate of suicide goes up. But surely this fact does not establish that increasing spending on education is morally impermissible. In increasing such spending, one intends to benefit those who will benefit and merely foresees that some

---

[8] The example of Japan is cited in this context by Hadley (1996: 68–9).

additional suicides will occur as a result. And the same would have to be true in this case as well: In supporting the liberalization of attitudes toward abortion, one would intend to benefit those women who would be relieved of the burdens of their unwanted pregnancy and would merely foresee that some additional murders will occur as well. There are, of course, many reasons that could be given for holding that liberalizing attitudes toward abortion is relevantly different from increasing spending on education, but then one would have to provide direct reasons for holding that abortion is morally impermissible. The culture of death argument attempts to avoid doing this, hoping that the impermissibility of other practices will somehow rub off on it. But it cannot successfully do so.

5.3. THE PRO-LIFE FEMINIST ARGUMENT

None of the arguments advanced in this book turn on claims that are in any particular sense feminist in nature. I have not appealed, for example, to the claim that sexual inequalities within society foster an environment in which women do not feel free to say no to sex, or to the claim that access to abortion is necessary in order for women to achieve sexual, economic, or political equality with men. None of the arguments in this book would lose their force if it turned out that social arrangements between the sexes were perfectly equal, or that both men and women were capable of becoming pregnant. Nonetheless, the position in defense of which these arguments have been presented, the position that abortion, at least in typical cases, is morally permissible, is itself often characterized as a feminist one. It therefore comes as a surprise to many people to learn that there is a body of writings, both historical and contemporary, whose present-day proponents characterize their position as pro-life feminism.

Some of the claims that are made in the recent literature by feminist critics of abortion raise no issues beyond those that have already been addressed in this book. One of the central concerns of such writers, for example, has been to establish that many early leaders of the women's rights movement in the United States, including such prominent figures as Susan B. Anthony and Elizabeth Cady Stanton, were morally opposed to abortion (e.g., 1869: 60–3; 1868: 44). This much can surely be conceded, since there need be no presumption that agreement with a person's views on suffrage implies agreement with her views on abortion. And, indeed, when one examines the writings of these historical figures, the arguments they present typically turn out to be some version of the rights-based argument against abortion already addressed in this work. It is salutory to acknowledge that a number of feminist writers have defended the argument that the fetus is a human being and that abortion is therefore wrong because it is murder, but the fact that this argument has been defended by feminists as well as nonfeminists does nothing to free the argument itself of the numerous difficulties I have identified with it in the preceding chapters.[9]

While some of the arguments defended by feminist critics of abortion are simply traditional arguments against abortion endorsed by untraditional figures, however, other arguments are not. The arguments that are distinctive of what its proponents call the pro-life feminist position attempt to sidestep the issue of fetal rights altogether and instead try to show that the immorality of abortion follows from the ideals of feminism. The result is a position that combines opposition to abortion with (typically) opposition to such other practices as euthanasia, capital punishment, nuclear proliferation and (sometimes) the exploitation of nonhuman animals and the environment. Pro-life feminism thus constitutes what is sometimes referred to as a "consistent ethic of life" (or, at least, of human life), one that is immune to the objections that I have aimed at the rights-based argument and that thus merits separate consideration as an independent and distinctive strand of thought within the anti-abortion movement. It is possible, of course, to disarm any argument that seeks to ground opposition to abortion in the ideals of feminism simply by arguing against feminism. And since many critics of abortion are also critics of feminism, this may provide one way to rebut the pro-life feminist position on terms that many critics of abortion accept. But rejecting feminism is likely to seem an unattractive option for many people, and I will argue here that it is, in any event, unnecessary. Arguments of the sort identified with pro-life feminism may

---

[9] Early feminist critics of abortion who explicitly rest their case against the practice on the claim that abortion is murder include, in addition to Stanton (1868: 44) and Anthony (1869: 60), such figures as Davis (1870: 25), Norton (1870: 87), Woodhull and Claflin (1874a: 94; 1874b: 97), Oreman (1901: 124), and Melendy (1911: 126). The rights-based argument against abortion is also clearly invoked even when the term *murder* is not used by such early feminists as Duffey (1876: 82) and Smith (1873: 110). And particular versions of the argument treated in Chapter 2 can be found in this early literature as well, such as the potentiality argument (e.g., Blackwell (1852: 28–9); Woodhull and Claflin (1874b: 96–7)), the essential property argument (e.g., Densmore (1868: 33)), and the slippery slope argument (Stockham (1887: 37)).

provide reason to believe that abortion is undesirable, and even that it is morally criticizable, but they fail to justify the claim that abortion is morally impermissible.[10]

The most prominent arguments in the pro-life feminist literature have a common structure. They begin with the claim that feminism involves a commitment to some particular value, and then argue that abortion violates that value. One such argument focuses on the value of nurturing or caring. In her influential book, *In a Different Voice*, Carol Gilligan argued that there are distinctively male and female ways of thinking about moral problems, and that while the male perspective typically focuses on the impersonal application of impartial rules to adjudicate disputes between competing individuals, the female perspective characteristically attends to the importance of preserving the interconnectedness between ourselves and others, and promotes the value of the caring for others that this entails. A number of feminist writers following Gilligan have attempted to clarify and promote this "feminine voice" in ethics, and this has largely become a defense of what (also following Gilligan) is now commonly referred to as an "ethics of care" (Gilligan 1982: e.g., 63). But as a number of critics of abortion have argued, this seems to pose a problem for any feminist who wishes to defend the practice of abortion. As Wolf-Devine has put it, there is "a prima facie inconsistency between an ethics of care and abortion. Quite simply, abortion is a failure to care for one living being who exists in a particularly intimate relationship to oneself. If empathy, nurturance, and taking responsibility for caring for others are characteristic of the feminine voice, then abortion does not appear to be a feminine response to an unwanted pregnancy" (1989: 87).[11]

---

[10] In fairness to the figures to be discussed in this section, it should be noted that it is not always entirely clear that feminist critics of abortion mean to be defending the strong claim that abortion is impermissible, as opposed to the much weaker claim that it would be better if fewer abortions took place. The comparison of abortion to such practices as euthanasia and capital punishment certainly suggests that the claim is meant to be that abortion is impermissible, however, and to the extent that such figures align themselves with the wider pro-life movement, they seem to embrace it. In any event, it is only as an argument for the claim that abortion is morally impermissible that the claims of the pro-life feminist literature count as a challenge to the thesis defended in this book, so it is in this way that the arguments will be construed.

[11] A similar position is taken by Kopaczynski (1995: chap. 6). See also Gomberg's characterization of abortion as "a violation of nurturing duties" (1991: 518), and Fox-Genovese's concern that "abortion challenges feminists to come to terms with

The claim that abortion is not a caring response to an unwanted pregnancy, of course, may be difficult to sustain in some cases. A woman who has an abortion out of the concern that she already has as many children as she can care for may see herself as choosing the option most consistent with the value of caring. And the claim that a feminist should endorse the value of caring may also be subject to dispute. A feminist might object that the claim that nurturing is a distinctively female value perpetuates precisely the sort of harmful stereotypes that feminism is committed to eradicating. But let us go ahead and suppose that both claims are correct. What follows from them? It follows that a woman who has an abortion acts uncaringly, and that a feminist is entitled to criticize her morally on these grounds. But it does not follow that a feminist should conclude that a woman who has an abortion does something that is morally impermissible. Many acts that are criticizable as uncaring are nonetheless morally permissible. The claim that I have been defending in this book is the claim that abortion is typically permissible, not that it is typically uncriticizable. And the argument from the value of caring does nothing to undermine this claim even if it is accepted.

It may be objected that this response to the argument misses its point. The point, it may be said, is not that feminists want to add the feminine categories of virtuous and vicious to the masculine categories of permissible and impermissible, but rather that they want to replace the latter entirely. On this account, all that there is to moral judgment is the judgment about whether or not it would be caring or virtuous to do something. And, according to this argument, it turns out that abortion fails the only test that morality has to offer.

I am dubious of the prospects for a plausible feminism that eliminates the categories of permissibility and impermissibility from our moral thinking entirely. It seems insufficient, for example, to say of the rapist only that he fails to display the virtue of caring toward his victim. And it is far from clear that this is what Gilligan's followers, let alone Gilligan herself, intend to be doing. But even if such a version of feminism is vindicated, the central claim of this book will still remain unaffected.

the contradictions in their own thought, notably the contradiction between the commitment to community and nurture and the commitment to individual right" (1991: 83). The concern that feminism is inconsistent with traditional defenses of abortion has also led other feminists to conclude not that feminists should oppose abortion, but that feminists should support abortion for different reasons (e.g., Rudy 1996: chap. 5).

If no acts are morally impermissible, after all, then acts of abortion, in particular, are not morally impermissible.

When feminism promotes positive values such as those of caring, love, and nurturing, it does not commit itself to the claim that acts which fail to exemplify these virtues are morally impermissible. This is why feminism's embrace of such values cannot be used to show that feminists should reject abortion as impermissible. But feminism can also be understood as rejecting certain kinds of behavior as impermissible. And if abortion can be shown to be an instance of such a kind of behavior, then the strategy of deriving the impermissibility of abortion from the values of feminism will succeed.

One version of this sort of argument appeals to the claim that feminism is committed to opposing violence. Abortion by any means is clearly a violent act in at least some sense, and this again suggests that a defender of feminism should be an opponent of abortion. As one such writer has put it, "Why should women's traditional (and quite wise) abhorrence of violence stop at the threshold of their own bodies?" (Maloney 1995: 269).[12] But this argument is implausible. Feminism is not committed to opposing violence per se. It does not insist, for example, that it is morally impermissible for a woman to attack a rapist violently in self-defense. Rather, feminism is committed to opposing *unjustified* violence. Moreover, feminism is not committed to the view that violence against any living thing is unjustified. Chemotherapy violently destroys living cancer cells, for example, and no feminist would say that this is morally wrong. There are, of course, any number of important differences between a cancer cell and a human fetus that a critic of abortion might point to. It certainly does not follow from the fact that destroying cancer cells is morally permissible that destroying human fetuses is as well. But in order to justify this distinction, the critic of abortion would then have to explain *why* the human fetus is different, why it is reasonable to suppose that the fetus has a right not to be treated in this way whereas cancer cells do not. But to do this is simply to revert to the rights-based argument, which I have already rejected in the previous chapters. Relying on the traditional rights-based argument against abortion is precisely what those arguments that are distinctive of the pro-life feminist literature seek to avoid having to do. But without doing so, its appeal to the wrongness of violence is simply implausible.

---

[12] The same argument is also made by, e.g., Crossed (1995: 278), Castonguay (1995: 283), Beckwith (1994: 171–2), and Wolf-Devine (1989: 414).

A second version of this sort of argument appeals instead to feminism's traditional opposition to the exploitation or oppression of the powerless by the powerful. But this argument simply begs the question. To say that an act of harming an individual is an act of exploitation or oppression is already to say that the act is unjust, and the question at issue here is precisely whether abortion is unjust in this sense. That such an appeal is ultimately circular is usually made clear when the argument is explicitly spelled out. As one feminist critic of abortion has put it, for example, "[t]he basic ideal of feminism is a society in which the powerful do not deny the weak their rights, yet abortion is truly patriarchal because it is a prime example of the powerful (women) depriving the weak (unborn children) of their rights, to the point of killing them" (Bailey 1995: 163).[13] But if abortion violates the rights of the fetus, then there is no need to invoke feminism as a basis for opposing it; it will be impermissible simply because it violates the rights of the fetus, and we will again be back to the traditional rights-based argument against abortion, which I have already considered in great detail.

An additional argument that is also frequently made by feminist critics of abortion is consequentialist in nature. The claim is that a social policy that allows easy access to abortion makes it impossible for a number of other feminist goals to be successfully achieved. Most feminists, for example, would endorse such goals as "fairness in hiring, more flex-time, part-time, and home-commute jobs, better access to prenatal and obstetric care, attractive adoption opportunities . . . and help with child care and parenting when we choose to keep our babies." Yet Frederica Mathewes-Green maintains that "these changes will never come as long as we're lying down on abortion tables 1,600,000 times a year to ensure the status quo" (1995a: 182). Anne M. Maloney provides a similar list of desirable changes that virtually any feminist would endorse, and argues that they "will occur only when we insist upon them" and that "abortion on demand precludes such insistence. When abortion is easily accessible, society no longer has to take pregnancy seriously" (1995: 271).[14]

There are two problems with this argument. The first is that it is simply not clear why a society cannot have both liberal access to abortion

---

[13] The same argument is made by Maloney (1995: 270), Callahan (1993: 233), Davis (1995: 225).

[14] The same argument is also made by de Jong (1995b: 173), Bottcher (1995: 177), and Callahan (1993: 232, 236).

and progressive policies regarding work, child care, health care, and so forth. Some countries seem already to be able to accomplish this, and the historical record provides little reason to believe that family-related policies were more progressive when abortion was less easily available in such countries as the United States. The claim that access to abortion prevents such other reforms from occurring is an empirical claim, and a very sweeping empirical claim. And while it is often asserted by feminist critics of abortion, it does not seem to have been given a convincing empirical defense. It is as if someone were to assert without evidence that automobile safety advocates should abandon their demand for liberal access to air bags in all automobiles, on the grounds that society would stop taking automobile accidents seriously and would never be willing to adopt more enlightened measures to prevent them and to treat victims when they occurred. There is, it should be noted, one sense in which it does seem quite plausible to say that liberal access to abortion prevents feminists from achieving other important goals: because there is a substantial amount of support for the movement to restrict such access, feminist defenders of abortion are forced to commit a great deal of resources to lobbying for abortion rights that they would otherwise have used to lobby for better day care, work benefits, and so forth. But this suggests that a concern for better day care and so forth should motivate opponents of abortion to stop using their resources to oppose abortion, rather than that it should motivate defenders of abortion to stop using their resources to defend it.

But let us suppose for the sake of the argument that we are convinced of the truth of the empirical claim about the effects of easy access to abortion. It still does not follow that abortion is morally impermissible, any more than it would follow that equipping automobiles with air bags would be morally impermissible if doing so diminished the support for other safety measures. In each case, it would follow only that the gaining of one important benefit could come only at the expense of another. And that is a far weaker claim. Indeed, one could as easily argue, if the empirical claim is true, that feminists should stop demanding better day care, and so forth, on the grounds that meeting such demands would require them to abdicate their rights to abort unwanted preganancies.

Another common argument raised by feminist critics of abortion is that "abortion perpetuates the image of women as reusable sex objects" (Bailey 1995: 163). If men knew that every time they had intercourse with a woman there was a chance that they would become a father, that there would be no way to prevent an unwanted pregnancy from being brought to term should one occur, then they would be far less likely to have sex outside of serious, caring relationships. The easy availability of abortion, on the other hand, enables them to pursue sexual gratification with little concern for the future, and thus with little concern for their partners. This argument is frequently driven home with the observation that the Playboy Foundation gives generously to organizations that lobby in favor of liberal access to abortion (e.g., Bailey 1995: 163; de Jong 1995b: 173).

There is nothing unreasonable about the suspicion that the Playboy Foundation's motives in funding abortion rights groups are less than noble, though little of significance follows from this. It seems equally reasonable to suspect that its support of groups opposed to censorship is ultimately self-serving as well, but this does little to cast doubt on the worthiness of opposing censorship. And there are, in any event, more serious problems with this argument. The first is that it applies equally, indeed more strongly, to contraception. It must be admitted that it seems plausible to suppose that some men who engage in casual sex where abortion is easily available would not do so if abortion were not available, but it seems even more plausible to suppose that many more men who would still be willing to take their chances without abortion as a back-up so long as effective contraception were available would be unwilling to do so if there were no contraception. If we look at things from the promiscuous male's point of view, as the argument encourages us to do, the increased security that contraception adds to sex without contraception is substantially greater than the increased security that contraception plus abortion as a back-up adds to contraception without such a back-up, especially since whether or not a woman will abort the product of a one-night stand is largely beyond the man's control even if abortion is widely available. So if we really want to stop men from taking sex so lightly, we should deem contraception off limits as well. But feminist critics of abortion, like critics of abortion in general, are unwilling to rest the case against abortion on a position that entails that contraception is (at least) as great an evil. There are, of course, many potentially relevant differences between contraception and abortion that a critic of abortion might appeal to, most obviously that abortion involves killing a human fetus while contraception involves preventing a human fetus from coming into existence. But if the critic of abortion is forced to appeal to such distinctions, she will again have to go ahead and defend the claim that the human fetus has a right to life that sperm and eggs lack, and that will again be to abandon the distinctively feminist approach to the issue in favor of the rights-based argument that has already been rejected in this work.

But let us suppose that this objection can be overcome. There is a further problem. For the fact that a form of behavior contributes to the objectification of women cannot in itself plausibly be held to show that the act is morally impermissible. Wearing certain kinds of makeup, dressing in provocative clothing, affecting certain manners of speech and comportment – all of these can plausibly be said to contribute to an environment in which women are viewed by men primarily as objects of sexual desire. If they do contribute to such objectification, then this fact can plausibly be appealed to as a justification for criticizing women who behave in these ways. But it is difficult to imagine that they would warrant the conclusion that women do not have the moral right to behave in these ways. As with the case of contraception, there are again any number of features that might be pointed to in distinguishing abortion from, say, wearing revealing clothing, but this would again require the feminist critic of abortion to make good the sorts of claims that I have already argued against in the previous chapters.

A further argument against abortion that has been raised by some feminist critics of the practice turns on the claim that there is an important parallel between the way in which defenders of abortion justify their claim that the fetus has less moral standing than you and I have, and the way in which defenders of patriarchical institutions have traditionally justified their claim that women have less moral standing than men have. Surely if anything is definitive of feminism it is the rejection of the claim that women have less moral standing than men, and if this rejection is inconsistent with such defenses of abortion, then a feminist should be committed to rejecting such defenses of abortion as well.

The central observation underlying this argument is that, in both cases, defenders of differential moral standing appeal to biological considerations. Defenders of male superiority have appealed to various claims about the physical differences between men and women, ranging from claims about their reproductive systems to claims about their brains, and yet those who defend abortion on the grounds that the fetus, although a human being, is not yet a person with the same right to life as you or I, seem to be doing precisely the same thing. As one proponent of this argument has put it, "In denying the personhood of the unborn child, feminists have borrowed the very same justifications that the patriarchs have used so successfully throughout history to deny full recognition as persons to women" (Bottcher 1995: 177).[15]

Such writers have correctly identified a parallel between the two cases. And there is nothing amiss in noting its irony. But whether the parallel should actually be a source of concern to the feminist defender of abortion depends entirely on what is taken to be wrong with the argument for male superiority in the first place. If the feminist rejects this argument by maintaining that biological differences are never morally relevant, then it will surely be inconsistent for her to appeal to such differences in denying equal rights to the fetus. But the claim that biological differences are never morally relevant is on the face of it implausible. If it were true, we would have to attribute equal moral rights to (at least) all biological organisms. Moreover, such a claim is not necessary in order to undermine the various arguments for male superiority that have been advanced throughout the ages. One can deny that the difference between having a penis and having a vagina is morally relevant without insisting that biological differences are never morally relevant.

Finally, feminist critics of abortion often argue that the demand for a permissive attitude toward abortion represents a capitulation to the distinctively antifeminist view that what is male is the norm for human behavior. Men are by their nature more free to combine sexual activity with career advancement than are women, for example, because sexual activity cannot cause them to incur the burdens of an unwanted pregnancy. One way to promote sexual equality in this respect would be to provide pregnant women with more resources to assist them in their pregnancies. This approach would treat the fact that women can become pregnant as just as normal as the fact that men cannot. The other way to provide an equal playing field would be to ensure that women could abort their pregancies if they wanted to. But this approach would reflect the presumption that the male way of combining sexual freedom with economic autonomy is the normal or appropriate way. And this is not the way that a feminist should attempt to respond to such concerns. As one such critic has put it, "[i]f women must submit to abortion to preserve their lifestyle or career, their economic or social status, they are pandering to a system devised and run by men for male convenience" (de Jong 1995b: 172).[16]

---

[15] The same sort of argument is also made by de Jong (1995a: 168–9), Maloney (1995: 269–70), Mathewes-Green (1995a: 183; 1995b: 185), and Callahan (1993: 234).
[16] See also Davis (1995: 225–6).

Like many of the observations contained in the writings of feminists opposed to abortion, there is much to agree with here. But, again as with many of the other statements to be found in the literature, this claim does not support the conclusion that abortion is morally impermissible. One can surely denounce an environment in which many women have no attractive alternatives to abortion without maintaining that women who see no such alternatives do something morally impermissible when they choose to abort their pregnancies. While the feminist critique of abortion raises serious concerns about the complacent attitude that one might take in viewing abortion as a painless solution to the problem of unwanted pregnancies, therefore, it fails to provide support for the claim that abortion is morally impermissible. And that is the claim I have been concerned to argue against in this work.

5.4. THE UNCERTAINTY ARGUMENT

Let me suppose that you have now read carefully through all of the arguments I have advanced in this book and have subjected them all to critical scrutiny. And let me suppose, somewhat optimistically, that on the whole you have been convinced. When confronted with the choice between the view that abortion is generally impermissible and the view that it is generally permissible, you are inclined to side with the view that it is generally permissible, and are inclined to do so on grounds that critics of abortion can and do generally accept. Still, optimistic as I might be about the persuasiveness of the arguments I have presented, I could hardly suppose that they will have led you to accept this view with certainty. They certainly have not led me to do so. I am acutely aware of the possibility that I have underestimated the strength of the objections that can be raised against the position I have defended, or have overestimated the strength of the objections I have raised against the position I have opposed. I believe that abortion is generally morally permissible, and I believe that my belief rests on sound, well-considered reasons, but I am uncertain nonetheless.

This uncertainty about the permissibility of abortion is sometimes appealed to as a reason to conclude that abortion is morally impermissible after all. As one writer has put it, "The very fact that the status of the fetus is controversial ought to count for something in our moral deliberations concerning abortion. Specifically, it seems morally questionable to condone a practice of killing something whose status is still in controversy" (Lindsay 1974: 32).[17] The attempt to argue against abortion by appealing to our uncertainty about it has received less attention in the philosophical literature than have the more familiar arguments, but it has nonetheless made its way into the academic and popular debate on the subject. In addition, the argument from uncertainty represents a theological position that has long been maintained by the Catholic Church. Pope John Paul II puts the point as follows: "What is at stake is so important that, from the standpoint of moral obligation, the mere probability[18] that a human person is involved would suffice to justify an absolutely clear prohibition of any intervention aimed at killing a human embryo" (1995: 108). And Grisez has put the argument this way: "*To be willing to kill what for all we know could be a person is to be willing to kill it if it is a person.* And since we cannot absolutely settle if it is a person except by a metaphysical postulate, for all practical purposes we must hold that to be willing to kill the embryo is to be willing to kill a person" (1970: 306, emphasis in original).[19]

The basic structure of the argument from uncertainty is clear. The argument conjoins the claim that we are uncertain about the moral status of abortion with a principle designed to govern moral choices made under such conditions of uncertainty. What is less clear, however, is just what, precisely, the principle appealed to is meant to say. There are at least three distinct principles for governing moral choice in conditions of uncertainty that proponents of the appeal to uncertainty appear at times to have in mind. Each of these principles closely parallels a relatively uncontroversial principle designed to govern rational choice under certain conditions of uncertainty. There thus seem to be at least three distinct versions of the argument from uncertainty, each of which can plausibly be viewed as arising from a relatively secure foundation. I will begin by identifying all three versions of the argument and will then argue that none of them should be accepted.

---

[17] See also, for example, Boss (1993: 143): "we are more likely to avoid moral tragedy if we ... give the fetus the benefit of the doubt until we can prove beyond a reasonable doubt that he or she is not a person." For other versions of this argument, see Schwarz (1994), Gordon (1994a: 3), and Nathanson (1979: 259–60).

[18] In the Catholic moral tradition, to say that a given claim is "probable" is not to say that it is "more likely true than not," but merely that there is some, even if relatively small, chance that it is true.

[19] See also Lee (1996: 6n4).

5.4.1. *Three Versions of the Argument*

Perhaps the simplest version of the argument from uncertainty rests on the claim that it would be so terrible to accept the belief that abortion is permissible if this belief turned out to be mistaken, that even the most remote chance that the belief is mistaken is enough to render the risk involved in accepting the belief itself unacceptable. This version of the argument conjoins the claim that mistakenly accepting the permissibility of abortion would be so terrible with a principle designed to govern our choices under such circumstances that parallels the disaster-avoidance principle of rational choice. Suppose that one ball is about to be drawn from an enormous jar containing a number of black and white balls. You must place a bet on whether the selected ball will be black or white. If you bet on white and are correct, you will win ten dollars. If you bet on black and are correct, you will win a hundred dollars. If you bet on black and are incorrect, you will lose ten dollars. If you bet on white and are incorrect, you will be tortured to death in the most horrible manner imaginable. In this sort of case, there is really no need to count the balls in the jar and determine precisely what the odds are that the selected ball will be black. Even if you were all but certain that the selected ball would be white, the result of betting on white and being mistaken would be so terrible that even the slightest uncertainty about whether it would be white would surely be enough to warrant your refusal to bet on white. And so, on this version of the argument, even the slightest uncertainty about whether abortion is really permissible is enough to warrant your refusal to accept the belief that it is permissible.

A second version of the argument from uncertainty does not depend on the claim that mistakenly accepting the belief that abortion is permissible would be so catastrophic. Instead, it rests on the weaker claim that accepting the belief that abortion is permissible if that belief turns out to be false would be worse than accepting the belief that abortion is impermissible if that belief turns out to be false. This claim can be defended as follows: Suppose that you accept the claim that abortion is morally permissible and that belief turns out to be mistaken. In that case, you will have mistakenly accepted the permissibility of mass murder. Suppose, on the other hand, that you accept the claim that abortion is morally impermissible and that belief turns out to be mistaken. In that case, you will have mistakenly accepted the permissibility of needlessly imposing significant burdens on a great number of pregnant women. But as morally serious as this wrong would be if it turned out that abortion is morally permissible, the claim maintains, it would not be as serious as the wrong that accepting the permissibility of abortion would be if abortion turned out to be morally on a par with mass murder.

The version of the argument from uncertainty that appeals to this relatively weaker claim must then conjoin the claim with a different principle for governing our moral choices under conditions of uncertainty, namely: When choosing under conditions of uncertainty between one of two moral beliefs to accept, one should make the choice with the best worse-case outcome. This principle also has a relatively uncontroversial counterpart in the domain of rational choice theory: The maximin principle on which it is rational, given certain conditions, to make the choice that maximizes the minimum. Suppose, for example, that a ball is about to be drawn from the enormous jar, and you are again forced to choose between betting that it will be black or white. If you bet on white and the ball is white, you win $10. If you bet on white and the ball is black, you lose $50. If you bet on black and the ball is black, you win $5. If you bet on black and the ball is white, you lose $25. Which bet should you make? If you knew what color the ball would be, of course, you would know which bet to make. But given that you don't know, it seems reasonable to conclude that you should at least make sure that you don't lose the $50, and should thus bet on black. Similarly, on this version of the argument, if you knew the answer to the question of whether or not abortion is morally permissible, then you'd know which answer to accept, but given that you don't know the answer with certainty, you should at least make sure that you don't accept the moral permissibility of mass murder, and should thus choose to accept the claim that abortion is morally impermissible.

A final version of the argument from uncertainty rests on a principle that runs parallel to the principle of expected utility. Suppose, for example, that you do know how many black balls and how many white balls are in the jar from which you are to select a ball. And suppose that you also know the prospective costs and benefits to you of guessing correctly or incorrectly in either case. In that case, you can decide which bet is the more rational to make by calculating the expected utility to you of either choice. For each bet, you multiply the probability of guessing correctly by the payoff for guessing correctly and add this to the product of multiplying the probability of guessing incorrectly by the payoff for guessing incorrectly. The rational bet is then the one on which your expected payoff is greater. Suppose, for example, that there are six times as many white balls as black ones, that the benefits for betting correctly are the same in either case, but that the cost to you of betting on white if the ball turns out to be black is 10 times greater than the cost to you of betting on black if the ball turns out to be white. In that case, even though you think it more likely that the ball selected will be white, the rational thing for you to do is to bet on black.

Similarly, on this version of the argument from uncertainty, you should reason as follows: Suppose that you feel quite confident that abortion is, in fact, morally permissible. Perhaps you are so confident that you think that it is six times more likely that it is permissible than that it is not. Still, you must concede that mistakenly accepting the belief that abortion is permissible if that belief turns out to be false is more than six times worse than mistakenly accepting the belief that abortion is impermissible if that belief turns out to be false. And so, once again, when you make your decision according to the most appropriate decision procedure given your uncertainty about the permissibility of abortion, you find that the right thing for you to do is to accept the claim that abortion is morally impermissible.

5.4.2. Three Objections

There are three reasons to reject the argument from uncertainty. The objections are perhaps most easily aimed at the simplest, disaster-avoidance version of the argument, but in the end they are successful when aimed at any version of it. The first reason to reject the argument is that, regardless of how it is formulated, the argument produces implications that virtually everyone, including virtually every critic of abortion, must reject as unacceptable. The disaster-avoidance version of the argument, for example, depends on the claim that as long as we are not literally certain that an act is morally permissible, we must accept the claim that it is morally impermissible. But there are, to put it mildly, many acts about which we are not literally certain that they are morally permissible. Numerous arguments, for example, have been offered in defense of the claim that nonhuman animals, and even plants or ecosystems, have the same right to life that you and I have. But critics of abortion will surely reject the view that we must accept the claim that plants and animals have a right to life merely because we cannot be certain that they do not. It may well be true, of course, that cogent and persuasive objections can be raised against those arguments that purport to demonstrate that such individuals have a right to life. It may even be true that many of these arguments are relatively weak to begin with. But even if all of this is so, we can still hardly say that the weaknesses of the arguments are so great as to make us literally certain that these individuals do not have a right to life. The disaster-avoidance version of the argument from uncertainty therefore implies that we must accept the belief that (at the least) all plants and animals have a right to life. And surely the critic of abortion will reject this as an unacceptable implication.

It might at first be thought that some other version of the argument from uncertainty could avoid this objection. But this is not the case. It would be worse, for example, to mistakenly accept the belief that mowing your lawn is not on a par with mass murder if it turns out that mowing your lawn really is on a par with mass murder, than to mistakenly accept the belief that mowing your lawn is on a par with mass murder if it turns out that it really isn't. So the maximin version of the argument will produce the same unacceptably strong results. And there is no reason to believe that the expected utility version of the argument will fare any better. It is difficult to know precisely how you are supposed to determine the probability that your belief that abortion is permissible is mistaken in the first place, but it is even more difficult still to see why that probability should be significantly higher than the probability that your belief that killing plants and animals is permissible is mistaken. And even if we accept the claim that the probability that we are mistaken about plants is much smaller than the probability that we are mistaken about fetuses, this is still not enough to sustain the argument from uncertainty. For suppose you feel that it is, say, 6 times more likely that abortion is permissible than that it is not, but you feel confident that it is a full 100 times more likely that mowing your lawn is permissible than that it is impermissible. Even if this is so, it seems clear that mistakenly accepting the belief that mowing your lawn is permissible should it turn out not to be would be even more than 100 times worse than mistakenly accepting the belief that mowing your lawn is impermissible should it turn out not to be. As great as the gap may seem between the liklihood that mowing your lawn is permissible and the liklihood that it is not, the gap seems even bigger between the horror of committing mass murder for the most trivial of reasons and the inconvenience of living with an unruly lawn or simply doing without a lawn altogether. There is no good reason, then, to think that an expected utility calculation would not produce the same unacceptable results as do the other versions of the argument.

I believe that I have already said enough to warrant accepting this *reductio ad aburdum* objection to the argument from uncertainty. But some critics of abortion might be tempted to respond at this point by simply maintaining that we can indeed be certain enough about our other moral beliefs. The moral status of grass, they might object, is far less controversial than the moral status of the fetus. It is therefore worth pursuing in a bit more detail two more specific cases in which the claim that we can be certain enough about the permissibility of a given action to avoid the reductio objection is even more plainly implausible.[20] For in responding to defenses of the conception criterion based on considerations about the zygote's potential to develop into a mature, adult human being, many defenders of abortion have argued that if zygotes have a right to life, then so do individual human cells and unfertilized eggs. Critics of abortion have raised powerful objections to these arguments, and I am inclined to believe that these objections may well be successful. But even if critics of abortion believe that these objections are quite strong, they cannot honestly maintain that they can endorse them with a sufficient degree of certainty to avoid the result that the argument from uncertainty would entail that we must accept the belief that individual human cells and unfertilized eggs have the same right to life that you and I have.

---

[20] One further case may also merit attention in this context. Many philosophers have argued that letting an innocent person die is morally on a par with killing an innocent person. And many of the arguments they have offered in defense of this thesis are prima facie quite strong, even compelling. If this thesis is true, then we would seem forced to conclude that, for example, going to a movie is morally on a par with murder, since the money one spends on a movie could instead be used to save the life of a person who is threatened by a temporary food shortage (e.g., Kagan 1989: 1). The critic of abortion will surely reject the arguments in favor of this position, and I am again inclined to believe that they can do so successfully. But the arguments involved in doing so are again so subtle and difficult that it would simply be dishonest for a critic of abortion to claim to be sufficiently certain that this claim is mistaken. I doubt that anyone who has carefully read Kagan's book, *The Limits of Morality*, for example, could honestly state that he is more than 99 percent confident that Kagan's position is mistaken. And yet surely it would be more than 100 times worse to accept the belief that going to a movie is not on a par with murder if that belief turns out to be mistaken than to accept the belief that it is on a par with murder if that belief turns out to be mistaken. So any version of the argument from uncertainty will also entail that we must accept the belief that going to a movie rather than spending the money on famine relief is morally on a par with murder. And this, too, is a result that critics of abortion will reject as unacceptable.

Consider, for example, the argument for attributing such a right to individual cells in the human body. The argument turns on the claim that cloning human beings is, at least in principle, possible. Given the possibility of cloning, on this account, it turns out that any cell in your body also has the potential to become an individual like you and I. I am not myself sufficiently convinced by arguments of this sort, and none of the objections that I raised against the conception criterion in Chapter 2 made any appeal to implications of the possibility of cloning. I believe that the critic of abortion may well be able to block the assimilation of the zygote case with the human cell case by appealing to a distinction between different kinds of potentiality and by arguing that the difference between the two is a morally relevant one. But even if I am right about this, surely the critic of abortion must concede that the considerations involved in mounting such a rebuttal are subtle and contentious at best. He must concede, that is, that even if we find the response to the cloning argument to be successful, we must nonetheless wind up significantly short of being certain that the cloning argument fails, even if we feel fairly confident that it does. And this concession would be enough to undermine the argument from uncertainty even on the expected utility version. Even if the critic of abortion can claim that it is 50 times more likely that cutting your hair is not on a par with mass murder than that it is, he would have to concede that the horror of such mass murder, if mass murder it turns out to be, is much more than 50 times worse than the inconvenience of going without a haircut. If the argument from uncertainty entails that we must accept the belief that abortion is morally impermissible, therefore, it must also entail that we must accept the belief that cutting your hair is morally impermissible. Since this implication is plainly unacceptable to critics and defenders of abortion alike, so too is the argument that entails it.

The argument for attributing a right to life to unfertilized eggs turns on the possibility of parthenogenesis, the process by which a viable fetus emerges from an unfertilized egg without any contribution from, or interaction with, a sperm. If an unfertilized egg has the ability to develop, under certain conditions, into a full fledged adult human being, then it can again seem very difficult to justify attributing rights to zygotes that we do not then attribute to such eggs. Indeed, Morowitz and Trefil cite parthenogenesis as the "strongest" argument against the view that there is a morally relevant difference between an unfertilized egg and a fertilized one (1992: 44, 52). As with the case of the argument from cloning, I believe that there is substantial room within which the critic of abortion may be able to develop a convincing response to this argument. While parthenogenic reproduction of adults from unfertilized eggs can now be routinely produced in reptiles, amphibians, and birds, for example, no such experiments have been successfully duplicated in the case of mammals, let alone the case of humans.[21] If parthenogenesis were a natural method of reproduction for human beings, then the argument from parthenogenesis would be stronger and perhaps even decisive, but since it has never occurred either in nature or in the laboratory, it may seem plausible for the critic of abortion to reject it on these grounds.

But although I am not genuinely convinced by the argument from parthenogenesis, I am firmly convinced that it cannot be dismissed just that easily. There seem to be specific reasons that parthenogenesis does not occur in human beings, and once those reasons are understood, the moral significance of the fact that it does not occur can become substantially less clear. The problem, apparently, lies in the unique role that the placenta plays in mammalian fetal development. In particular, it seems that most of the instructions for the development of the placenta are carried by the sperm and unavailable in the egg. As a result, while a mammalian egg may be able to begin dividing by itself – and indeed cases of human unfertilized ova that have undergone spontaneous cleavage have been reported (see, e.g., Howesipian 1992: 499–500) – it is unable to provide itself with the full placenta it will need to survive. And it is not at all clear that a critic of abortion can appeal to this fortuitous fact about placental development to demonstrate with certainty that the unfertilized egg has less moral standing as a zygote. For suppose we accept what seems to be true: that an unfertilized human egg does in fact have the potential by itself to begin dividing, but that the dividing entitity will never develop into a child because of the absence of instructions for generating a placenta. If we appeal to this as a reason to deny a right to life to the unfertilized egg, then it would seem we would also have to deny a right to life to a zygote with a genetic defect that would prevent it from successfully implanting or developing past a certain stage. But a proponent of the conception criterion will surely deny this.

In addition, even though a zygote, but not an egg, contains all the *information* needed for generating the placenta, it does not contain all of the *material* necessary. Consider this description of an early conceptus

---

[21] Though there have been reports of parthenogenically produced rabbits (Beck et al. 1985: 67).

at the blastocyst stage as looking in cross section like a class ring with a heavy stone on top: "The stone contains the cells that will eventually develop into the embryo, and the sphere contains cells that will eventually develop, *along with material from the mother*, into the placenta" (Morowitz and Trefil 1992: 46, emphasis added). But if the unfertilized egg's inability to generate the placenta without the help of the sperm is sufficient to justify saying that it lacks a right to life because even though by itself it can *begin* to become a child by initiating cell division, it cannot complete the task, then the early conceptus's inability to generate the placenta without the added help of the mother's body should be sufficient to justify saying that the early conceptus also lacks a right to life because even though by itself it can continue to develop by continuing cell division it cannot complete the task without the aid of the mother's body. And, again, the proponent of the conception criterion must deny this claim.

And there is more. For while the unfertilized human egg does not by itself have the necessary information *available* to it, this is not to say that it does not *contain* the information. In the terminology of current theory, both the sperm and the egg contain the necessary information about placental development, but in the egg DNA the information is "switched off," or "imprinted." As Morowitz and Treil point out, this is significant for the following reason:

We routinely manipulate DNA in our laboratiories. Before long, researchers will have worked out the nature of the off-on sequence that governs the development of the placenta. Removing and inserting methyl groups into the DNA [in effect, switching a gene on or off] is a relatively straightforward operation. It is only a matter of time, then, before someone stimulates an unfertilized egg, lets it divide, removes the DNA from one cell, and resets the off-on sequence that allows development to go forward. When this happens – and we have little doubt that it will happen – we will have true parthenogenesis. We will be able to produce an adult human being from a single unfertilized egg (1992: 55).

All of this can make it seem that the difference between a fertilized egg and an unfertilized egg is not morally significant enough to warrant the conclusion that the zygote has the same right to life as you or I while the unfertilized egg does not. Again, as with the case of cloning, I do not want to insist that the argument from parthenogensis is decisive, or even to claim that it is more reasonable to accept it than to reject it. My point is simply that the argument from parthenogenesis is strong enough, and the considerations invoked in rebutting it subtle enough, that the critic of abortion cannot honestly say that he is sufficiently certain that it is mistaken, even if he is quite confident that it is. And, as in the case of the argument from cloning, this concession is enough to demonstrate that if the argument from uncertainty entails that we must accept the belief that abortion is morally impermissible, then it also entails that we must accept the belief that unfertilized eggs have the same right to life as you or I. Since critics of abortion consistently reject this latter claim, they must reject the argument that entails it.

I am inclined to believe that this *reductio ad absurdum* objection to the argument from uncertainty is decisive. But it is worth noticing two further problems that arise, even if the critic of abortion decides that he is willing to live with the argument's highly counterintuitive implications. The first problem concerns the argument's conclusion. The problem is that even if the argument's conclusion is accepted, it is not strong enough to establish the claim that the critic of abortion wishes to establish. That this is so can best be seen by comparing the case of abortion with the various cases involving the black and white balls. What those cases establish is that there are various conditions under which your uncertainty about which ball will be selected can make it rational for you to bet that the ball will be black, and that this can be so even in cases where you correctly believe that it is much more likely than not that the ball will be white. But this does absolutely nothing to show that it would be rational for you to *believe* that the ball will be black. Whatever reasons you have for believing that it will be white remain good reasons to believe that it will be white despite the application of these principles. What the application of these principles can establish is, at most, that there are conditions under which it would be rational for you to act *as if* you believe that the ball will be black.[22] And that is a very different matter.

Similarly, then, even if the counterintuitive implications of the argument from uncertainty did not provide a sufficient justification for

---

[22] I say "at most" because it is not at all clear that the argument establishes even this much. In the expected utility version, for example, where you know that there are more white balls then black ones, it is rational for you to bet on black, but it is hardly clear that this amounts to acting as if you believe that the ball will be white. It can as easily be characterized as acting as if you believe that the ball is black and also believe that the cost of being wrong about this are so great that you believe it makes more sense to place a bet against what you believe in. For purposes of the discussion here, though, I will grant that the argument establishes at least this much.

rejecting it, the argument would still fail to provide any reason to believe that abortion is morally impermissible. At most, it would provide
reason to believe that it would be moral for you to act as if you believe
it. Yet the claim made by critics of abortion is not the claim that belief
in the impermissibility of abortion is something that should be acted on
despite the fact that it is more likely false than true. Rather, it is the claim
that abortion is, in fact, morally impermissible. The thesis of this book
is that the arguments that have been offered in defense of this claim can
be shown to be mistaken on the critic of abortion's own terms. And the
argument from uncertainty provides no reason to doubt this thesis, let
alone to deny it, even if the argument is accepted. At most, it provides
a reason to act as if there is reason to deny it.

But let us go ahead and ask whether the argument succeeds even
in this more limited sense. It must be conceded, after all, that it would
still be an important conclusion to believe that one should act as if one
believed that abortion is impermissible in practice, even if the argument
given for this conclusion provided no reason actually to believe that
abortion is impermissible in principle. We must therefore ask the crucial
question: Does the cogency of the various principles of rational choice
I have referred to provide sufficient support for the parallel principles
of moral choice upon which the argument from uncertainty depends?
The answer to this question, presumably, depends on why we find the
principles of rational choice plausible in the first place. I want to suggest
that on what seems to be the most plausible account of why they are,
they fail to provide support for the parallel moral principles. If that is
so, then not only does the argument from uncertainty produce unacceptably counterintuitive implications, and not only is its conclusion
importantly weaker than the conclusion the critic of abortion aims to
defend, but the argument fails to justify even this weaker conclusion.

I will put the problem in terms of the expected utility version of the
argument, and in terms of the example where it is rational for you to
bet on black because even though the ball is more likely to be white
than black, the cost to you of mistakenly betting on white if it turns out
to be black is far greater than the cost to you of mistakenly betting on
black if it turns out to be white. But what I say should hold for any
version of the argument. So why is it reasonable to accept the principle
of expected utility in such a case? The basic idea would seem to be this:
In assessing the two possible negative outcomes that could arise from
betting incorrectly on the black or white ball, the only considerations
that seem to be relevant from the prudential point of view are how

bad the consequences would be. The nature of the route by which the consequences would be reached does not itself seem relevant from the prudential point of view. In particular, it does not seem at all relevant prudentially that in incurring the relatively smaller cost you would be incurring a cost as a result of betting on a claim that you did not, in fact, believe to be true, while in incurring the relatively larger cost, you would be incurring a cost as a result of betting on a claim that you did, in fact, believe to be true. These considerations do not affect your prudential assessment of the outcomes, and so expected utility, as a principle of rational choice, is entitled to ignore them.

But now consider the attempt to extend this kind of reasoning to the area of moral choice. In order to provide a comparable defense of the parallel moral principle and its application by the argument from uncertainty, we would have to say something like this:

In assessing the two possible negative outcomes – (1) supporting the unjust burdening of women with unwanted pregnancies if you act as if you believe that abortion is impermissible, and that belief turns out to be mistaken; and (2) permitting the unjust killing of innocent fetuses if you act as if you believe that abortion is permissible, and that belief turns out to be mistaken – the only considerations that seem to be relevant from the moral point of view are how bad the consequences are, that is, how much harm will occur. The nature of the route by which the consequences are reached does not itself seem morally relevant. In particular, it does not seem at all morally relevant that in supporting the unjust burdening of women you would be doing something you strongly believe to be wrong, while in permitting the unjust killing of innocent fetuses you would be doing something you strongly believe not to be wrong.

An assumption of this sort is needed in order to justify the move from the rational principle to the moral principle. Defenders of the argument from uncertainty have provided no defense of this assumption. Indeed, they have not recognized it as an assumption required by their position. And there are strong reasons to think it a dubious assumption at best. It asserts that there is no morally relevant difference between doing what you strongly believe to be right with the recognition that unjust harm might thereby result if you turn out to be mistaken, and doing what you strongly believe to be wrong with the recognition that unjust harm might thereby be avoided if you turn out to be mistaken. If consequences were all that mattered from the moral point of view, then this would indeed prove an irrelevant distinction. But the claim that consequences are all that matter from the moral point of view is itself subject to serious objection and is in any event consistently rejected by those who oppose abortion. If consequences are all that matter from the moral point of view, after all, then abortion will be right when it produces better consequences than the alternatives, and wrong when it does not. But when you make a moral decision, you are not merely choosing between two different possible states of affairs. You are also deciding what will be brought into the world as a result of your intention and what will be brought into it despite your intention. This seems to matter morally. This is not to say that this is an overriding consideration. If you are only 51 percent convinced that abortion is morally permissible, then this extra consideration may be enough to tip the balance in favor of opposing the practice. After all, in this case you are only being asked to do something you think slightly more likely than not to be wrong. But it is nonetheless a legitimate and substantial consideration that must be taken into account. If you have not yet been convinced by arguments in favor of the claim that abortion is morally impermissible and have been substantially swayed by some of the objections to them, then the moral principle being appealed to here would be asking you deliberately to impose what you strongly believe to be significant and wrongful harms on women in order to prevent what you strongly believe not to be greater wrongs against fetuses. In short, it would be asking you to act against your conscience.

This feature of this particular version of the argument from uncertainty seems in the end to uncover a more general reason for rejecting any such argument. For any argument from uncertainty must operate, at least in part, by urging you to ignore the distinction between those arguments that you find persuasive and those that you do not. It must insist that the mere fact that an argument for one conclusion convinces you while arguments for a contrary conclusion do not is not in itself a good reason for you to act on that conclusion. By requiring you to give equal weight to those considerations that you believe to be compelling and those that you do not, it therefore requires you to sacrifice your integrity, to abdicate your responsibility for making up your own mind about what principles you should act on. This is something that a morally responsible person cannot do, and it is difficult to imagine that a critic of abortion would be willing to deny this.

This does not mean, of course, that if you find yourself on the whole to be in agreement with the arguments defended in this work you should therefore let your inquiry into the subject of abortion end as this book draws to a close. Rather, it suggests that what you should do when you finish reading this book is precisely what I have attempted to do while writing it: to consider the claim that abortion is generally morally permissible with the seriousness and rigor that it deserves, to subject the claim to critical scrutiny, to treat with care and respect those arguments against the claim that have been advanced by others, but nonetheless to maintain and to publicly defend the thesis that, at least until further and better reasons come along, the most reasonable belief to hold is that the claim is true.

Bibliography

Note: in cases where I cite articles as they appear reprinted in anthologies, I refer to the article by the date of its original publication, but cite the page numbers from the anthology identified here (e.g., Thomson (1971) refers to the pagination in Pojman and Beckwith's 1994 anthology *The Abortion Controversy* of Judith Thomson's article, "A Defense of Abortion," which was first published in 1971). I have done this so that the order in which various contributions to a particular line of argument have been made is preserved in the presentation in the text (e.g., so that it is clear that Thomson's "Rights and Deaths" (referred to as Thomson (1973) was written after, and not before, "A Defense of Abortion").

Ajzenstat, Samuel. 1990. "The Liberal Crisis: Feminists on Abortion." In Ian Gentles, ed. *A Time to Choose Life: Women, Abortion, and Human Rights*. Toronto: Stoddart Publishing Co., 1990, pp. 234–6.

Algeo, Donald. 1981. "Abortion, Personhood, and Moral Rights." *The Monist*, Vol. 64, No. 4 (October), pp. 543–9.

Allen, Floyd. 1995. "Dinah Monahan: Passing on the Heritage of Life." *Celebrate Life*, Vol. 17, No. 6, pp. 12–13.

American Life League, Inc. (no author listed). 1995. "Abortion – Not Even When the Pregnancy Threatens the Life of the Mother?" (pamphlet).

Anthony, Susan B. 1869. "Marriage and Maternity." In Mary Krane Derr, Linda Naranjo-Huebl, and Rachel MacNair, eds. *Prolife Feminism: Yesterday & Today*. New York: Sulzburger & Graham Publishing, Ltd., 1995, pp. 60–3.

Audi, Robert. 1996. "Intuitionism, Pluralism, and the Foundations of Ethics." In Walter Sinnott-Armstrong and Mark Timmons, eds. *Moral Knowledge?: New Readings in Moral Epistemology*. Oxford: Oxford University Press, 1996, pp. 101–36.

"Audience Discussion." 1983. In Margery W. Shaw and A. Edward Doudera, eds. *Defining Human Life: Medical, Legal, and Ethical Implications*. Ann Arbor, MI and Washington, DC: AUPHA Press, 1983, pp. 23–30.

Baddeley, Alan. 1987. "Amnesia." In Richard L. Gregory, ed. *The Oxford Companion to the Mind*. Oxford: Oxford University Press, 1987, pp. 20–2.

Bagley, Chris. 1990. "Social Service and Abortion Policy." In Ian Gentles, ed. *A Time to Choose Life: Women, Abortion, and Human Rights*. Toronto: Stoddart Publishing Co., 1990. pp. 95–106.

Bailey, Jane Thomas. 1995. "Feminism 101: A Primer For Prolife Persons." In Mary Krane Derr, et al., eds. *Prolife Feminism: Yesterday & Today*. New York: Sulzburger & Graham Publishing, Ltd., 1995, pp. 159–64.

Bayles, Michael D. 1976. "Harm to the Unconceived." *Philosophy and Public Affairs*, Vol. 5, No. 3 (Spring), pp. 292–304.

Beck, F., D. P. Davies, and D. B. Moffat. 1985. *Human Embryology*, 2nd ed. Oxford: Blackwell Scientific Publications.

Becker, E. Lovell, ed. 1986. *International Dictionary of Medicine and Biology*. New York: John Wiley & Sons.

Becker, Lawrence C. 1975. "Human Being: The Boundaries of the Concept." In Michael F. Goodman, ed. *What Is a Person?* Clifton, NJ: Humana Press, 1988, pp. 57–81.

Beckwith, Francis J. 1992. "Personal Bodily Rights, Abortion, and Unplugging the Violinist." *International Philosophical Quarterly*, Vol. XXXII, No. 1 (March), pp. 105–18.

———. 1993. *Politically Correct Death: Answering Arguments for Abortion Rights*. Grand Rapids, MI: Baker Books.

———. 1994. "Arguments from Bodily Rights: A Critical Analysis." In Louis P. Pojman and Francis J. Beckwith, eds. *The Abortion Controversy*. Boston: Jones and Bartlett Publishers, 1994, pp. 155–75.

———. 1996. "Ignorance of Fetal Status as a Justification of Abortion: A Critical Analysis." In Brad Stetson, ed. *The Silent Subject: Reflections on the Unborn in American Culture*. Westport, CT: Praeger Publishers, 1996, pp. 33–42.

Benson, Iain T. 1990. "What's Wrong With 'Choice'." In Ian Gentles, ed. *A Time to Choose Life: Women Abortion, and Human Rights*. Toronto: Stoddart Publishing Co., 1990, pp. 24–46.

Berkow, Robert, M.D., ed. 1992. *The Merck Manual*, 16th ed. Rahway, NJ: Merck Research Laboratories.

Bethell, Tom. 1980. "The Family Conference." *Human Life Review*, Vol. VI, No. 3 (Summer), pp. 7–18.

Blackwell, Dr. Elizabeth. 1852. "Look at the First Faint Gleam of Life..." In Mary Krane Derr, et al., eds. *Prolife Feminism: Yesterday & Today*. New York: Sulzburger & Graham Publishing, Ltd., 1995, pp. 28–9.

Blumenfeld, Jean Beer. 1977. "Abortion and the Human Brain." *Philosophical Studies*, Vol. 32, No. 3 (October), pp. 251–68.

Bok, Sissela. 1988. "Who Shall Count as a Human Being?: A Treacherous Question in the Abortion Discussion." In Michael F. Goodman, ed. *What is a Person?* Clifton, NJ: Humana Press, 1988, pp. 213–28.

Bolton, Martha Brandt. 1979. "Responsible Women and Abortion Decisions." In Onora O'Neill and William Ruddick, eds. *Having Children: Philosophical and Legal Reflections on Parenthood*. New York: Oxford University Press, 1979, pp. 39–51.

Boonin, David. 1997. "A Defense of 'A Defense of Abortion': On the Responsibility Objection to Thomson's Argument." *Ethics*, Vol. 107 (January), pp. 286–313.

Boss, Judith A. 1993. *The Birth Lottery: Prenatal Diagnosis and Selective Abortion.* Chicago: Loyola University Press.

Bottcher, Rosemary. 1995. "Abortion Threatens Women's Equality." In Mary Krane Derr, et al., eds. *Prolife Feminism: Yesterday & Today.* New York: Sulzburger & Graham Publishing, Ltd., 1995, pp. 175–78.

Brandt, R. B. 1972. "The Morality of Abortion." *The Monist*, Vol. 56, pp. 503–26.

Braude, Peter, et al. 1986. "Status of the Pre-embryo (general discussion). In Gregory Bock and Maeve O'Connor, eds. *Human Embryo Research: Yes or No?* London and New York: Tavistock Publications, 1986, pp. 141–51.

Brody, Baruch. 1971a. "Abortion and the Law." *Journal of Philosophy*, Vol. 68, No. 12 (June 17), pp. 357–69.

———. 1971b. "Thomson on Abortion." *Philosophy and Public Affairs*, Vol. 1, No. 3 (Spring), pp. 335–40.

———. 1974. "On the Humanity of the Foetus." In Tom L. Beauchamp and LeRoy Walters, eds. *Contemporary Issues in Bioethics.* Belmont, CA: Wadsworth Publishing Company, Inc., 1978, pp. 229–40.

———. 1975. *Abortion and the Sanctity of Human Life: A Philosophical View.* Cambridge, MA: The MIT Press.

Brody, Jane E. 1995. "2-drug Mix Effective in Abortion." *New Orleans Times-Picayune*, August 31, p. 1, [reprinted from *New York Times*].

Brown, Judie. 1995. "Abortion: Your Risks" (pamphlet). Stafford, VA: American Life League, Inc.

Brown, Judie and Brian Young. 1994. "Exceptions: Abandoning 'The Least of These My Brethren': Why Pro-Life Legislation Should Not Contradict Pro-Life Principle" (booklet). Stafford, VA: American Life League, Inc.

Buckle, Stephen. 1988. "Arguing from Potential." *Bioethics*, Vol. 2, No. 3, pp. 227–53.

Burgess, J. A., and S. A. Tawia. 1996. "When Did You First Begin to Feel It? – Locating the Beginning of Human Consciousness." *Bioethics*, Vol. 10, No. 1, pp. 1–26.

Burtchaell, James Tunstead. 1982a. "Die Buben sind unser Ungluck!: The Holocaust and Abortion." In James Tunstead Burtchaell, *Rachel Weeping and Other Essays on Abortion.* Kansas City, MO: Andrews and McMeel, Inc., 1882, pp. 141–238.

———. 1982b. "Very Small Fry: Arguments for Abortion." In James Tunstead Burtchaell, *Rachel Weeping and Other Essays on Abortion.* Kansas City, MO: Andrews and McMeel, Inc., date, pp. 61–140.

Byrn, Robert M. 1980. "Manipulating the Terms of Life." *Human Life Review*, Vol. VI, No. 2 (Spring), pp. 59–70.

Calabresi, Guido. 1991. "Do We Own Our Bodies?" *Health Matrix*, Vol. 1, No. 1, pp. 5–18.

Callahan, Joan C. 1993. "The Fetus and Fundamental Rights." In Robert M. Baird & Stuart E. Rosenbaum, eds. *The Ethics of Abortion: Pro-Life vs. Pro-Choice*, rev. ed. Buffalo, NY: Prometheus Books, 1993, pp. 249–62.

Carrier, L. S. 1975. "Abortion and the Right to Life." *Social Theory and Practice*, Vol. 3, No. 4, pp. 381–401.

Carroll, Charles. 1972. "Abortion Without Ethics." In Thomas W. Hilgers and Dennis J. Horan, eds. *Abortion and Social Justice*. Kansas City, MO: Sheed & Ward, Inc., 1972, pp. 249–66.

Carruthers, Peter. 1992. *The Animals Issue: Moral Theory in Practice*. Cambridge: Cambridge University Press.

Castonguay, Kay. 1995. "Enough Violence, Enough Hatred, Enough Injustice." In Mary Krane Derr, et al., eds. *Prolife Feminism: Yesterday & Today*. New York: Sulzburger & Graham Publishing, Ltd., 1995, pp. 282–3.

Chalmers, David J. 1996. *The Conscious Mind: In Search of a Fundamental Theory*. Oxford: Oxford University Press.

Colliton, William F., M. D. undated. "How Are Abortions Performed?" (pamphlet). Stafford, VA: American Life League, Inc.

Condit, Celeste Michelle. 1990. *Decoding Abortion Rhetoric: Communicating Social Change*. Urbana and Chicago: University of Illinois Press.

Connery, John, S.J. 1977. *Abortion: The Development of the Roman Catholic Perspective*. Chicago: Loyola University Press.

Cooney, William. 1991. "The Fallacy of All Person-denying Arguments for Abortion." *Journal of Applied Philosophy*, Vol. 8, No. 2, pp. 161–5.

Coughlin, Michael J. 1988. "'From the Moment of Conception . . .': The Vatican Instruction on Artificial Procreation Techniques." *Bioethics*, Vol. 2, No. 4, pp. 294–316.

———. 1989. "Review of Norman Ford's, *When Did I Begin?*" *Bioethics*, Vol. 3, No. 4, pp. 333–41.

Crighton, Michael [writing as Jeffery Hudson]. 1968. *A Case of Need*. New York: Signet Books.

Critchley, Macdonald, ed. 1978. *Butterworths Medical Dictionary*, 2nd ed. London: Butterworths.

Crossed, Carol Nan Feldman. 1995. "FFL Chapter Declines to be Silenced." In Mary Krane Derr, et al., eds. *Prolife Feminism: Yesterday & Today*. New York: Sulzburger & Graham Publishing, Ltd., 1995, pp. 278–80.

Crum, Gary. 1992. "Pro-Life." In Gary Crum and Thelma McCormack, *Abortion: Pro-Choice or Pro-Life?* Washington, DC: The American University Press, 1992, pp. 3–65.

Cudd, Ann E. 1990. "Sensationalized Philosophy: A Reply to Marquis's 'Why Abortion Is Immoral.'" *The Journal of Philosophy*, Vol. 87, No. 5 (May), pp. 262–4.

Curran, Charles E. "Abortion: Its Moral Aspects." In Edward Batchelor, Jr., ed. *Abortion: The Moral Issues*. New York: The Pilgrim Press, 1982, pp. 115–28.

Daniels, Charles B. 1992. "Having a Future." *Dialogue*, Vol. XXXI, pp. 661–5.

Davis, Alison. 1995. "Women With Disabilities: Abortion and Liberation." In Mary Kane Derr, et al., eds. *Prolife Feminism: Yesterday & Today*. New York: Sulzburger & Graham Publishing, Ltd., 1995, pp. 219–26.

Bibliography

Davis, Michael. 1983. "Foetuses, Famous Violinists, and the Right to Continued Aid." *The Philosophical Quarterly*, Vol. 33, No. 132 (July), pp. 259–78.

Davis, Nancy. 1984. "Abortion and Self-Defense." In Jay L. Garfield and Patricia Hennessey, eds. *Abortion: Moral and Legal Perspectives*. Amherst: The University of Massachusetts Press, 1984, pp. 186–210.

Davis, Pauline Wright. 1870. "A True Woman." In Mary Kane Derr, et al., eds. *Prolife Feminism: Yesterday & Today*. New York: Sulzburger & Graham Publishing, Ltd., 1995, pp. 24–5.

Dawson, Karen. 1988. "Segmentation and Moral Status *in vivo* and *in vitro*: A Scientific Perspective." *Bioethics*, Vol. 2, No. 1, pp. 1–14.

de Jong, Daphne Clair. 1995a. "Feminism and Abortion: The Great Inconsistency." In Mary Kane Derr, et al., eds. *Prolife Feminism: Yesterday & Today*. New York: Sulzburger & Graham Publishing, Ltd., 1995, pp. 168–71.

———. 1995b. "The Feminist Sell-Out." In Mary Kane Derr, et al., eds. *Prolife Feminism: Yesterday & Today*. New York: Sulzburger & Graham Publishing, Ltd., 1995, pp. 171–4.

Dennett, Daniel C. 1987. "Consciousness." In Richard L. Gregory, *The Oxford Companion to the Mind*. Oxford: Oxford University Press, pp. 160–4.

Densmore, Dr. Anna. 1868. "Lectures of Dr. Anna Densmore." In Derr, et al., eds. *Prolife Feminism*, pp. 31–4.

"Depo-Provera: Contraceptive Injection." 1995. Advertisement in *Parents* magazine, Vol. 70, No. 11 (November), pp. 153–4.

Derbyshire, Stuart W. G. 1999. "Locating the Beginnings of Pain." *Bioethics*, Vol. 13, No. 1, pp. 1–31.

Devine, Philip E. 1990. *Ethics of Homicide*. Notre Dame: University of Notre Dame Press.

Diagram Group, The. 1987. *The Brain: A User's Manual*. New York: G. P. Putnam.

Donagan, Alan. 1977. *The Theory of Morality*. Chicago: University of Chicago Press.

Donceel, Joseph. F. "Abortion: Mediate vs. Immediate Animation." In Edward Batchelor, Jr., ed. *Abortion: The Moral Issues*. New York: The Pilgrim Press, 1982, pp. 110–114.

Donohue, John J., and Steven D. Levitt. 1999. "Legalized Abortion and Crime" (unpublished paper).

Dore, Clement. 1989. "Abortion, Some Slippery Slope Arguments and Identity Over Time." *Philosophical Studies*, Vol. 55, No. 3 (March), pp. 279–91.

Duffey, Eliza Bisbee. 1876. "The Limitation of Offspring." In Mary Kane Derr, et al., eds. *Prolife Feminism: Yesterday & Today*. New York: Sulzburger & Graham Publishing, Ltd., 1995, pp. 77–83.

Dunstan, G. R. 1984. "The Moral Status of the Human Embryo: A Tradition Recalled." *Journal of Medical Ethics*, Vol. 10, No. 1, pp. 38–44.

Dworkin, Ronald. 1993. *Life's Dominion: An Argument about Abortion, Euthanasia, and Individual Freedom*. New York: Alfred A. Knopf.

Eidsmoe, John A. 1984. "A Biblical View of Abortion." In Leonard J. Nelson, ed. *The Death Decision*. Ann Arbor, MI: Servant Books, 1984, pp. 17–28.

Eisenberg, Arlene, Heidi E. Murkoff, and Sandee E. Hathaway. 1991. *What to Expect When You're Expecting*, 2nd ed. New York: Workman Publishing.

Engelhardt, H. Tristram, Jr. 1974. "The Ontology of Abortion." *Ethics*, Vol. 84, No. 3, pp. 217–34.

English, Jane. 1975. "Abortion and the Concept of a Person." In Lewis M. Schwartz, ed. *Arguing About Abortion*. Belmont, CA: Wadsworth, 1993, pp. 159–68.

Feezell, Randolph M. 1987. "Potentiality, Death, and Abortion." *Southern Journal of Philosophy*, Vol. XXV, No. 1 (Spring), pp. 39–48.

Feinberg, Paul D. 1978. "The Morality of Abortion." In Richard L. Ganz, ed. *Thou Shalt Not Kill: The Christian Case against Abortion*. New Rochelle, NY: Arlington House Publishers, 1978, pp. 127–49.

Finnis, John. 1973. "The Rights and Wrongs of Abortion: A Reply to Judith Thomson." *Philosophy and Public Affairs*, Vol. 2 (Winter), pp. 117–45.

Fischer, John Martin. 1991. "Abortion and Self-Determination." *Journal of Social Philosophy*, Vol. XXII, No. 2 (Fall), pp. 5–13.

Foot, Philippa. 1984. "Killing and Letting Die." In Bonnie Steinbock and Alastair Norcross, eds. *Killing and Letting Die*, 2nd ed. New York: Fordham University Press, 1994, pp. 280–9.

Ford, Norman M. 1988. *When Did I Begin?: Conception of the Human Individual in History, Philosophy and Science*. Cambridge: Cambridge University Press.

———. 1989. "A Reply to Michael Coughlan." *Bioethics*, Vol. 3, No. 3, pp. 342–5.

Fox-Genovese, Elizabeth. 1991. *Feminism without Illusions: A Critique of Individualism*. Chapel Hill: The University of North Carolina Press.

Frame, John M. 1978. "Abortion from a Biblical Perspective." In Richard L. Ganz, ed. *Thou Shalt Not Kill: The Christian Case against Abortion*. New Rochelle, NY: Arlington House Publishers, pp. 43–75.

Francke, Linda Bird. 1978. *The Ambivalence of Abortion*. New York: Random House.

Friel, John P., ed. 1981. *Dorland's Illustrated Medical Dictionary*, 26th ed. Philadelphia: W. B. Saunders Co.

Galvin, Richard Francis. 1988. "Noonan's Argument against Abortion: Probability, Possibility, and Potential." *Journal of Social Philosophy*, Vol. XIX, No. 2 (Summer), pp. 80–9.

Gennaro, Alfonso R., ed. 1979. *Blakiston's Gould Medical Dictionary*, 4th ed. New York: McGraw-Hill.

Gensler, Harry J. 1986. "The Golden Rule Argument Against Abortion." In Louis P. Pojman and Francis J. Beckwith, eds. *The Abortion Controversy: A Reader*. Boston: Jones and Bartlett, 1994, pp. 305–19.

Gert, Heather J. 1995. "Viability." In Susan Dwyer and Joel Feinberg, eds. *The Problem of Abortion*, 3rd ed. Belmont, CA: Wadsworth Publishing Co., 1993, pp. 118–26.

Gibson, Roger F. 1984. "On An Inconsistency in Thomson's Abortion Argument." *Philosophical Studies* 46, pp. 131–9.

Gillespie, Norman C. 1977. "Abortion and Human Rights." In Lewis M. Schwartz, ed. *Arguing about Abortion*. Belmont, CA: Wadsworth, 1993, pp. 149–55.

Gilligan, Carol. 1982. *In A Different Voice*. Cambridge, MA: Harvard University Press.

Goldenring, John M. 1982. "Development of the Fetal Brain" [letter]. *New England Journal of Medicine.* August 26, p. 307.

———. 1985. "The Brain-life Theory: Towards a Consistent Biological Definition of Humanness." *Journal of Medical Ethics*, Vol. 11, pp. 198–204.

Goldstein, Robert D. 1988. *Mother-Love and Abortion: A Legal Interpretation.* Berkeley: University of California Press.

Gomberg, Paul. 1991. "Abortion and the Morality of Nurturance." *Canadian Journal of Philosophy*, Vol. 21, No. 4, pp. 513–24.

Gordon, Doris. 1993. "Abortion and Thomson's Violinist: Unplugging a Bad Analogy" (pamphlet). Wheaton, MD: Libertarians for Life.

———. 1994a. "Abortion, Choice, and Libertarian Principles." Wheaton, MD: Libertarians for Life (pamphlet).

———. 1994b. "Why Abortion Violates Rights" (pamphlet) Wheaton, MD: Libertarians for Life.

———. 1995. "Abortion and Rights: Applying Libertarian Principles Correctly." *Studies in Prolife Feminism*, Vol. 1, No. 2, pp. 121–40.

Gowans, Christopher. 1994. *Innocence Lost: An Examination of Inescapable Moral Wrongdoing.* Oxford: Oxford University Press.

Grant, George. 1990. "The Triumph of the Will." In Ian Gentles, ed., *A Time to Choose Life: Women, Abortion, and Human Rights.* Toronto: Stoddart Publishing Co., 1990, pp. 9–18.

Griffith, Stephen. 1995. "Fetal Death, Fetal Pain, and the Moral Standing of a Fetus." *Public Affairs Quarterly*, Vol. 9, No. 2 (April), pp. 115–26.

Grisez, Germain. 1970. *Abortion: The Myths, the Realities, and the Arguments.* New York: Corpus Books.

Grobstein, Clifford. 1983. "A Biological Perspective on the Origin of Human Life and Personhood." Margery W. Shaw and A. Edward Doudera, eds. *Defining Human Life: Medical, Legal, and Ethical Implications.* Ann Arbor, MI and Washington, DC: AUPHA Press, 1983, pp. 3–11.

———. 1988. *Science and the Unborn: Choosing Human Futures.* New York: Basic Books.

Hadley, Janet. 1996. *Abortion: Between Freedom and Necessity.* Philadelphia: Temple University Press.

Hare, R. M. 1975. "Abortion and the Golden Rule." In R. M. Hare, *Essays on Bioethics.* Oxford: Clarendon Press, 1993, pp. 147–67.

———. 1989. "A Kantian Approach to Abortion." (revised version) In R. M. Hare, *Essays on Bioethics.* Oxford: Clarendon Press, 1993, pp. 168–84.

———. 1996. "Foundationalism and Coherentism in Ethics." In Walter Sinnott-Armstrong and Mark Timmons, eds. *Moral Knowledge?: New Readings in Moral Epistemology.* Oxford: Oxford University Press, pp. 190–9.

Harrison, Beverly. 1983. *Our Right to Choose.* Boston: Beacon Press.

Healy, Edwin F. 1956. *Medical Ethics.* Chicago: Loyola University Press.

Hellegers, Andre E. 1970. "Fetal Development." In Tom L. Beauchamp and Le Roy Walters, eds. *Contemporary Issues in Bioethics.* Belmont, CA: Wadsworth Publishing Company, Inc., 1978, pp. 194–8.

Hensyl, William R. 1990. *Stedman's Medical Dictionary*, 25th ed. Baltimore: Williams and Wilkins.

Bibliography

Hochderffer, Kathy. 1994. "Fight For Life: A Pro-Life Student's Abortion Debate Guide" (booklet). Los Angeles: International Life Services, Inc.

Holland, Alan. 1990. "A Fortnight of My Life is Missing: A Discussion of the Status of the Human 'Pre-embryo'." *Journal of Applied Philosophy*, Vol. 7, No. 1, pp. 25–37.

Horan, Dennis J., and Thomas J. Balch. 1987. "*Roe v. Wade*: No Basis in Law, Logic, or History." In Louis P. Pojman and Francis J. Beckwith eds. *The Abortion Controversy*. Boston: Jones and Bartlett Publishers, 1994, pp. 86–108.

Howsepian, A. A. 1992. "Who or What Are We?" *Review of Metaphysics*, Vol. 45, No. 3 (March), pp. 483–502.

Huffman, Tom L. 1993. "Abortion, Moral Responsibility, and Self-Defense." *Public Affairs Quarterly*, Vol. 7, No. 4 (October), pp. 287–302.

Humber, James M. 1975. "Abortion: The Avoidable Moral Dilemma." *The Journal of Value Inquiry*, Vol. 9, No. 4 (Winter), pp. 282–302.

Hurka, Thomas. 1994. "Review of F. M. Kamm's *Creation and Abortion*." *Journal of Medical Ethics*, Vol. 20, No. 2, pp. 121–2.

Hursthouse, Rosalind. 1991. "Virtue Theory and Abortion." *Philosophy and Public Affairs*, Vol. 20, No. 3 (Summer), pp. 223–46.

Irving, Dianne N. 1993a. "The Impact of 'Scientific Misinformation' on Other Fields: Philosophy, Theology, Biomedical Ethics, Public Policy." In C. Ward Kischer and Dianne N. Irving, *The Human Development Hoax: Time to Tell the Truth!* Clinton Township, MI: Gold Leaf Press, 1995, pp. 77–109.

———. 1993b. "Scientific and Philosophical Expertise: An Evaluation of the Argument of 'Personhood'." In C. Ward Kischer and Dianne N. Irving, *The Human Development Hoax: Time to Tell the Truth!* Clinton Township, MI: Gold Leaf Press, 1995, pp. 110–38.

———. 1994. "'New Age' Embryology Text Books: Implications for Fetal Research." In C. Ward Kischer and Dianne N. Irving, *The Human Development Hoax: Time to Tell the Truth!* Clinton Township, MI: Gold Leaf Press, 1995, pp. 19–39.

———. 1995. "Post-Abortion Trauma: Bring on the Facts." In Kischer and Irving, *Human Development Hoax: Time to Tell the Truth!* Clinton Township, MI: Gold Leaf Press, 1995, pp. 40–4.

Jacobovits, Immanuel. 1965. "Jewish Views on Abortion." In Fred Rosner and J. David Bleich, eds. *Jewish Bioethics*. Brooklyn: Hebrew Publishing Company, 1979, pp. 118–33.

Jokic, Aleksandar. "Why Potentiality Cannot Matter." *Journal of Social Philosophy*, Vol. XXIV, No. 3 (Winter), pp. 177–93.

Joyce, Robert E. 1981. "When Does a Person Begin?" In Thomas W. Hilgers, Dennis J. Horan, and David Mall, eds. *New Perspectives on Human Abortion*. Frederick, Maryland: University Publications of America, Inc., 1981, pp. 345–56.

Kagan, Shelly. 1989. *The Limits of Morality*. Oxford: Clarendon Press.

Kamm, Frances Myrna. 1992. *Creation and Abortion*. Oxford: Oxford University Press.

Kantrowitz, Barbara. 1997. "Despite Recent Spate of Baby Killings, Cases Still Rare." *New Orleans Times-Picayune*, Sunday, July 13, p. A-24 (reprinted from *Newsweek*).

Kaplan, Lawrence J., and Rosemarie Tong. 1994. *Controlling Our Reproductive Destiny: A Technological and Philosophical Perspective*. Cambridge, MA: MIT Press.

Knight, James W., and Joan C. Callahan. 1989. *Preventing Birth: Contemporary Methods and Related Moral Controversies*. Salt Lake City: University of Utah Press.

Koman, Victor. 1989. *Solomon's Knife*. New York: Franklin Watts.

Koop, C. Everett, M.D. 1978. "A Physician Looks at Abortion." In Richard L. Ganz, ed. *Thou Shalt Not Kill: The Christian Case against Abortion*. New Rochelle, NY: Arlington House Publishers, 1978, pp. 8–25.

Kopaczynski, Germain. 1995. *No Higher Court: Contemporary Feminism and the Right to Abortion*. Scranton, PA: University of Scranton Press.

Kuhse, Helga. 1987. *The Sanctity-of-Life Doctrine in Medicine*. Oxford: Clarendon Press.

———. 1988. "A Report From Australia: When A Human Life Has Not yet Begun – According to the Law." *Bioethics*, Vol. 2, No. 4, pp. 334–42.

Kuhse, Helga, and Peter Singer. 1990. "Individuals, Humans and Persons: The Issue of Moral Status." In Peter Singer, Helga Kuhse, Stephen Buckle, Karen Dawson, Pascal Kasimba, eds. *Embryo Experimentation*. Cambridge: Cambridge University Press, 1990, pp. 65–75.

Langer, Richard. 1992. "Abortion and the Right to Privacy." *Journal of Social Philosophy*, Vol. 23, No. 2 (Fall), pp. 23–51.

———. 1993. "Silverstein and the 'Responsibility Objection.'" *Social Theory and Practice*, Vol. 19, No. 3 (Fall), pp. 345–58.

Larmer, Robert. 1995. "Abortion, Personhood, and the Potential for Consciousness." *Journal of Applied Philosophy*, Vol. 12, No. 3, pp. 241–51.

Laurance, Jeremy. 1997. "MPs Say Foetus Responds at Ten Weeks." Undated article from *London Times* posted at www.prolife.org/ultimate/fact3.html.

LeBow, Barbara. 1986. "Psychological Complications of Abortion" (booklet). Stafford, VA: American Life League.

Lee, Patrick. 1996. *Abortion and Unborn Human Life*. Washington, DC: The Catholic University of America Press.

Levi, Don S. 1987. "Hypothetical Cases and Abortion." *Social Theory and Practice*, Vol. 13, No. 1, pp. 17–48.

Levin, David S. 1985. "Thomson and the Current State of the Abortion Controversy." *Journal of Applied Philosophy*, Vol. 2, No. 1, pp. 121–5.

Levin, Michael. 1986. "Review of Robert Wennberg's, *Life in the Balance*." *Constitutional Commentary* 3.

Lewin, Tamar. 1997. "A New Procedure Makes Abortions Possible Earlier." *New York Times*, Sunday, December 21, pp. 1, 18 [section 1].

Li, Chenyang. 1992. "The Fallacy of the Slippery Slope Argument on Abortion." *Journal of Applied Philosophy*, Vol. 9, No. 2, pp. 233–7.

Liley, Albert W. 1972. "The Foetus in Control of His Environment." In Thomas W. Hilgers and Dennis J. Horan, eds. *Abortion and Social Justice*. Kansas City, MO: Sheed & Ward, Inc., 1972, pp. 27–36.

Lindsay, Anne. 1974. "On the Slippery Slope Again." *Analysis*, Vol. 34, No. 4 (April), p. 32.

Lockwood, Michael. 1985a. "The Warnock Report: A Philosophical Appraisal." In Michael Lockwood, ed. *Moral Dilemmas in Modern Medicine*. Oxford: Oxford University Press, 1985, pp. 155–86.

———. 1985b. "When Does a Life Begin?" In Michael Lockwood, ed. *Moral Dilemmas in Modern Medicine*. Oxford: Oxford University Press, pp. 9–31.

Long, Roderick T. 1993. "Abortion, Abandonment, and Postitive Rights: The Limits of Compulsory Altruism." *Social Philosophy and Policy*, Vol. 10, No. 1, pp. 166–91.

Louisiana Department of Health and Hospitals. 1995. "Abortion: Making a Decision." Baton Rouge, LA.

Luker, Kristin. 1984. *Abortion and the Politics of Motherhood*. Berkeley: University of California Press.

Mackenzie, Catriona. 1992. "Abortion and Embodiment." In Susan Dwyer and Joel Feinberg, eds. *The Problem of Abortion*, 3rd ed. Belmont, CA: Wadsworth Publishing Co., pp. 175–93.

MacKinnon, Catharine. 1984. "*Roe v. Wade*: A Study in Male Ideology." In Lewis M. Schwartz, ed. *Arguing about Abortion*. Belmont, CA: Wadsworth, 1993, pp. 218–26.

Maloney, Anne M. 1995. "Cassandra's Fate: Why Feminists Ought to be Prolife." In Mary Krane Derr, et al., eds. *Prolife Feminism: Yesterday & Today*. New York: Sulzburger & Graham Publishing, Ltd., 1995, pp. 267–71.

Margolis, Joseph. 1973. "Abortion." *Ethics*, Vol. 84, No. 1, pp. 51–61.

Markowitz, Sally. 1990. "A Feminist Defense of Abortion." In Louis P. Pojman and Francis J. Beckwith, eds. *The Abortion Controversy*. Boston: Jones and Bartlett Publishers, 1994, pp. 373–83.

Marquis, Donald. 1989. "Why Abortion is Immoral." In Louis P. Pojman and Francis J. Beckwith, eds. *The Abortion Controversy*. Boston: Jones and Bartlett Publishers, 1994, pp. 320–37.

———. 1994. "A Future Like Ours and the Concept of Person: A Reply to McInerney and Paske." In Louis P. Pojman and Francis J. Beckwith, eds. *The Abortion Controversy*. Boston: Jones and Bartlett Publishers, 1994, pp. 354–69.

———. 1995. "Fetuses, Futures, and Values: A Reply to Shirley." *Southwest Philosophy Review*, Vol. 6, No. 2, pp. 263–5.

Mathewes-Green, Frederica. 1995a. "The Bitter Price of 'Choice'." In Mary Krane Derr, et al., eds., *Prolife Feminism: Yesterday & Today*. New York: Sulzburger & Graham Publishing, Ltd., 1995, pp. 181–4.

———. 1995b. "Designated Unperson." In Mary Krane Derr, et al., eds. *Prolife Feminism: Yesterday & Today*. New York: Sulzburger & Graham Publishing, Ltd., 1995, pp. 184–7.

Bibliography

Matthews, Gareth B. 1979. "Life and Death as the Arrival and Departure of the Psyche." *American Philosophical Quarterly*, Vol. 16, No. 2, pp. 151–7.

Mayer, Jane, and Jill Abramson. 1994. *Strange Justice: The Selling of Clarence Thomas*. Boston and New York: Houghton Mifflin Co.

McConnell, Terrance C. 1978. "Moral Dilemmas and Consistency in Ethics." In Christopher W. Gowans, ed. *Moral Dilemmas*. Oxford: Oxford University Press, 1987, pp. 154–73.

McDonagh, Eileen L. 1996. *Breaking the Abortion Deadlock: From Choice to Consent.* Oxford: Oxford University Press.

McFadden, Maria. 1996. "Motherhood in the 90s: To Have or Have Not." In Brad Stetson, ed. *The Silent Subject: Reflections on the Unborn in American Culture.* Westport, CT: Praeger Publishers, 1996, pp. 115–22.

McInerney, Peter K. 1990. "Does a Fetus Already Have a Future-Like-Ours?" *The Journal of Philosophy*, Vol. 87 (May), pp. 264–8.

McKenna, George. 1995. "On Abortion: A Lincolnian Position." *The Atlantic Monthly*, Vol. 276, No. 3 (September), pp. 51–68.

McKinney, Patty, undated. "How to Survive Your Abortion" (pamphlet). Snowflake, AZ: The Precious Feet People.

McLaren, A[nne]. 1986. "Prelude to Embryogenesis." In Gregory Bock and Maeve O'Connor, eds., *Human Embryo Research*, pp. 17–23.

McMahan, Jeff. 1993. "Killing, Letting Die, and Withdrawing Aid." In Bonnie Steinbock and Alastair Norcross, eds. *Killing and Letting Die*, 2nd ed. New York: Fordham University Press, 1994, pp. 383–420.

———. 1994. "Self-Defense and the Problem of the Innocent Attacker." *Ethics* 104, pp. 252–90.

Melendy, Dr. Mary Ries. 1911. "No Apology For Abortion." In Mary Krane Derr, et al., eds. *Prolife Feminism: Yesterday & Today*. New York: Sulzburger & Graham Publishing, Ltd., 1995, pp. 126–7.

Michaels, Meredith W. 1984. "Abortion and the Claims of Samaritanism." In Jay L. Garfield and Patricia Hennessey, eds. *Abortion: Moral and Legal Perspectives.* Amherst: The University of Massachusetts Press, 1984, pp. 213–26.

Mitchell, John A. and Scott B. Rae. 1996. "The Moral Status of Fetuses and Embryos." In Brad Stetson, ed. *The Silent Subject: Reflections on the Unborn in American Culture*. Westport, CT: Praeger Publishers, 1996, pp. 19–32.

Mohr, James C. 1978. *Abortion in America: The Origin and Evolution of National Policy, 1800–1900*. New York: Oxford University Press.

Moore, Keith L. 1988. *Essentials of Human Embryology*. Toronto: B. C. Decker, Inc.

Moore, Keith L., and T. V. N. Persaud. 1993. *Before We Are Born: Essentials of Embryology and Birth Defects*, 4th ed. Philadelphia: W. B. Saunders Co.

Morowitz, Harold J., and James S. Trefil. 1992. *The Facts of Life: Science and the Abortion Controversy.* Oxford: Oxford University Press.

Morris, William, ed. 1973. *The American Heritage Dictionary of the English Language*. Boston: American Heritage Publishing Co., Inc. and Houghton Mifflin Company.

Moussa, Mario, and Thomas A. Shannon. 1985. "The Search for the New Pineal Gland: Brain Life and Personhood." *Hastings Center Report*, Vol. 22, No. 3, pp. 30–7.

Murray, Thomas H. 1991. "Are We Morally Obligated to Make Gifts of Our Bodies?" *Health Matrix*, Vol. 1, No. 1.

Nagel, Thomas. 1970. "Death." In Thomas Nagel, *Mortal Questions*. Cambridge: Cambridge University Press, 1979, pp. 1–10.

———. 1974. "What Is It Like To Be a Bat?" In Thomas Nagel, *Mortal Questions*. Cambridge: Cambridge University Press, 1979, pp. 165–80.

Narveson, Jan. 1975. "Semantics, Future Generations, and the Abortion Problem: Comments on a Fallacious Case Against the Morality of Abortion." *Social Theory and Practice*, Vol. 3, No. 4, pp. 461–85.

Nathanson, Bernard N., M.D. 1979. *Aborting America*. Garden City, NY: Doubleday & Company, Inc.

Neff, Christyne L. 1991. "Woman, Womb, and Bodily Integrity." *Yale Journal of Law and Feminism*. Vol. 5, pp. 327–53.

Newton, Lisa H. 1978. "The Irrelevance of Religion in the Abortion Debate." In Edward Batchelor, Jr., ed. *Abortion: The Moral Issues*. New York: The Pilgrim Press, 1982, pp. 3–6.

Nicholson, Linda. 1981. "Abortion: What Kind of Moral Issue?" *The Journal of Value Inquiry*, Vol. 15, No. 3, pp. 235–41.

Noonan, Harold W. 1989. *Personal Identity*. London: Routledge.

Noonan, John T., Jr. 1970. "An Almost Absolute Value in History." In Lewis M. Schwartz, ed. *Arguing about Abortion*. Belmont, CA: Wadsworth, 1993, pp. 55–61.

———. 1979. *A Private Choice: Abortion in America in the Seventies*. New York: The Free Press.

———. 1984. "Christian Tradition and the Control of Human Reproduction." In Leonard J. Nelson, ed. *The Death Decision*. Ann Arbor, MI: Servant Books, 1984, pp. 1–15.

Norcross, Alastair. 1990. "Killing, Abortion, and Contraception: A Reply to Marquis." *The Journal of Philosophy*, Vol. 87, No. 5 (May), pp. 268–77.

Norton, David F. 1996. "A Letter from David F. Nolan" in "An Exchange Between David F. Nolan and Doris Gordon On Abortion and the Libertarian Party Platform." Wheaton, MD: Libertarians For Life, pp. 1–2.

Norton, Sarah F. 1870. "Tragedy – Social and Domestic." In Mary Kane Derr, et al., eds. *Prolife Feminism: Yesterday & Today*. New York: Sulzburger & Graham Publishing, Ltd., 1995, pp. 85–9.

Oreman, Dr. Jennie G. 1901. "The Medical Woman's Temptation and How to Meet It." In Mary Kane Derr, et al., eds. *Prolife Feminism: Yesterday & Today*. New York: Sulzburger & Graham Publishing, Ltd., 1995, pp. 123–4.

Ornstein, Robert, and Richard F. Thompson. 1984. *The Amazing Brain*. Boston: Houghton Mifflin Company.

Otsuka, Michael. 1994. "Killing the Innocent in Self-Defense." *Philosophy and Public Affairs*, Vol. 23, No. 1, pp. 74–94.

Overall, Christine. 1985. "New Reproductive Technology: Some Implications for the Abortion Issue." *The Journal of Value Inquiry*, Vol. 19, No. 4, pp. 279–92.

————. 1987. *Ethics and Human Reproduction: A Feminist Analysis*. Boston: Allen & Unwin.

Parent, William. 1986. Editor's introduction. In Judith Jarvis Thomson, *Rights, Restitution, and Risk*. Cambridge, MA: Harvard University Press, pp. vii–x.

Parfit, Derek. 1971. "Personal Identity." In John Perry, ed. *Personal Identity*. Berkeley: University of California Press, 1975, pp. 199–223.

Paul, Ellen Frankel, and Jeffery Paul. 1979. "Self-Ownership, Abortion and Infanticide." *Journal of Medical Ethics*, Vol. 5, No. 3, pp. 133–6.

Pavlischek, Keith J. 1993. "Abortion Logic and Paternal Responsibility: One More Look at Judith Thomson's 'A Defense of Abortion'." *Public Affairs Quarterly*, Vol. 7, No. 4 (October), pp. 341–61.

————. 1998. "Abortion Logic and Paternal Responsibility: One More Look at Judith Thomson's Argument and a Critique of David Boonin-Vail's Defense of It" (revised version of Pavlischek 1993). In Louis P. Pojman and Francis J. Beckwith, eds. *The Abortion Controversy: 25 Years after Roe v. Wade: A Reader*, 2nd ed. Belmont, CA: Wadsworth, 1998, pp. 176–98.

Pluhar, Werner S. 1977. "Abortion and Simple Consciousness." *Journal of Philosophy*, Vol. LXXIV, No. 3 (March), pp. 159–72.

Pojman, Louis P., and Francis J. Beckwith, eds. 1994. *The Abortion Controversy: A Reader*. Boston: Jones and Bartlett.

Pope John Paul II. 1995. *The Gospel of Life* [Evangelium Vitae]. New York: Random House.

Poundstone, Tom. 1996. "The Catholic Debate on the Moral Status of the Embryo." In Brad Stetson, ed. *The Silent Subject: Reflections on the Unborn in American Culture*. Westport, CT: Praeger Publishers, 1996, pp. 169–75.

Powell, Eileen Alt. 1995. "Americans Given Eight Years in Iraqui Jail." New Orleans *Times-Picayune*, Sunday, March 26, p. A-3.

Powell, John. *Abortion: The Silent Holocaust*. 1981. Allen, Texas: Argus Communications.

Precious Foot People Catalog. 1995. Snowflake, AZ: Heritage House '76, Inc.

Procter, Paul, ed. 1995. *Cambridge International Dictionary of English*. Cambridge: Cambridge University Press.

Quinn, Warren. 1984. "Abortion: Identity and Loss." In Warren Quinn, *Morality and Action*. Cambridge: Cambridge University Press, 1993, pp. 20–51.

————. 1989. "Actions, Intentions, and Consequences: The Doctrine of Double Effect." In Warren Quinn, *Morality and Action*. Cambridge: Cambridge University Press, 1993, pp. 175–93.

Rachels, James. 1994. "Review of Ronald Dworkin's, *Life's Dominion*." *Bioethics*, Vol. 8, No. 3, pp. 268–72.

Ramsey, Paul. 1968. "The Morality of Abortion." In Edward Batchelor, Jr., ed., *Abortion: The Moral Issues*. New York: The Pilgrim Press, 1982, pp. 73–91.

————. 1970. "Points in Deciding about Abortion." In John T. Noonan, Jr., ed. *The Morality of Abortion: Legal and Historical Perspectives*. Cambridge: Harvard University Press, 1970, pp. 60–100.

Ratner, Herbert. 1989–90. "The Pre-Embryo." *Child and Family*, Vol. 21, No. 1.

Rawls, John. 1971. *A Theory of Justice*. Cambridge, MA: Harvard University Press.

Reagan, Leslie J. 1997. *When Abortion Was a Crime: Women, Medicine, and Law in the United States, 1867–1973*. Berkeley: University of California Press.

Reardon, David C. 1987. *Aborted Women: Silent No More*. Chicago: Loyola University Press.

———. 1996. "Women Who Abort: Their Reflections on the Unborn." In Brad Stetson, ed. *The Silent Subject: Reflections on the Unborn in American Culture*. Westport, CT: Praeger Publishers, 1996, pp. 135–47.

Recer, Paul. 1996. "Abortion, Cancer Link Disputed." New Orleans *Times-Picayune*, Wednesday, December 4, p. A-11.

Reeder, John P., Jr. 1996. *Killing and Saving: Abortion, Hunger, and War*. University Park, PA: The Pennsylvania State University Press.

Regan, Tom. 1983. *The Case for Animal Rights*. Berkeley, CA: University of California Press.

Reiman, Jeffrey H. "The Impotency of the Potentiality Argument for Fetal Rights: Reply to Wilkens." *Journal of Social Philosophy*, Vol. 24, No. 3, pp. 170–6.

Restak, Richard M., M.D. 1979. *The Brain: The Last Frontier*. New York: Warner Books.

Rice, Charles E. 1986. "The Human Life Amendment." Stafford, VA: American Life League, Inc. [booklet]

Riddle, John M. 1992. *Contraception and Abortion from the Ancient World to the Renaissance*. Cambridge, MA: Harvard University Press.

Rogers, Katherin A. 1992. "Personhood, Potentiality, and the Temporarily Comatose Patient." *Public Affairs Quarterly*, Vol. 6, No. 2 (April), pp. 245–54.

Rosenblatt, Roger. 1992. *Life Itself: Abortion in the American Mind*. New York: Random House.

Ross, Steven L. 1982. "Abortion and the Death of the Fetus." *Philosophy and Public Affairs*, Vol. 11, No. 3 (Summer), pp. 232–45.

Rothbard, Murray N. 1973. *For A New Liberty*. New York: The Macmillan Co.

———. 1982. *The Ethics of Liberty*. Atlantic Highlands, NJ: Humanities Press.

Rudinow, Joel. 1975. "Further in the Modest Defense." *Analysis*, Vol. 35, No. 3 (January), pp. 91–2.

Rudy, Kathy. 1996. *Beyond Pro-Life and Pro-Choice: Moral Diversity in the Abortion Debate*. Boston: Beacon Press.

Ryan, George M., Jr. 1983. "Medical Implications of Bestowing Personhood on the Unborn." In Margery W. Shaw and A. Edward Doudera, eds. *Defining Human Life: Medical, Legal, and Ethical Implications*. Ann Arbor: MI and Washington, DC: AUPHA Press, 1983, pp. 84–9.

Saltenberger, Ann. 1982. *Every Woman Has a Right to Know The Dangers of Legal Abortion*. Glassboro, NJ: Air-Plus Enterprises.

Schaeffer, Francis A., and C. Everett Koop, M.D. 1979. *Whatever Happened to the Human Race?* Old Tappan, NJ: Fleming H. Revell, Co.

Schwarz, Catherine, ed. 1993. *The Chambers Dictionary*. Edinburgh: Chambers Harrap Publishers Ltd.

Schwarz, Stephen. 1990. *The Moral Question of Abortion*. Chicago: Loyola University Press.

———. 1994. "America's Hidden Citizens." Stafford, VA: American Life League, Inc. [pamphlet].

Bibliography

Schwarz, Stephen D., And R. K. Tacelli. 1989. "Abortion and Some Philosophers: A Critical Examination." *Public Affairs Quarterly*, Vol. 3, No. 2 (April), pp. 81–98.

Seller, Mary J. 1993. "The Human Embryo: A Scientist's Point of View." *Bioethics*, Vol. 7, Nos. 2/3, pp. 135–40.

Shaw, Margery W. 1983. "The Destiny of the Fetus." In William B. Bondeson, H. Tristam Engelhardt, Jr., Stuart F. Spicker, and Daniel H. Winship, eds. *Abortion and the Status of the Fetus*. Dordrecht: D. Reidel Publishing Company, 1983, pp. 273–9.

Shirley, Edward S. 1995. "Marquis' Argument against Abortion: A Critique." *Southwest Philosophy Review*, Vol. 6, No. 1, pp. 79–89.

Shostak, Arthur B., and Gary McLouth (with Lynn Seng). 1990. *Men and Abortion: Lessons, Losses, and Love*. New York: Praeger Publishers.

Silverstein, Harry S. 1987. "On a Woman's 'Responsibility' for the Fetus." *Social Theory and Practice*, Vol. 13, No. 1 (Spring), pp. 103–19.

———. 1993. "Reply to Langer." *Social Theory and Practice*, Vol. 19, No. 3 (Fall), pp. 359–67.

Simmons, Paul D. 1982. "A Theological Response to Fundamentalism on the Abortion Issue." In Edward Batchelor, Jr., ed. *Abortion: The Moral Issues*. New York: The Pilgrim Press, 1982, pp. 175–87.

Simpson, J. A., and E. S. C. Weiner, eds. 1989. *The Oxford English Dictionary*, 2nd ed. Oxford: The Clarendon Press.

Singer, Peter. 1993. *Practical Ethics*, 2nd ed. Cambridge: Cambridge University Press.

Singer, Peter, and Karen Dawson. 1988. "IVF Technology and the Argument from Potential." *Philosophy and Public Affairs*, Vol. 17, No. 2, pp. 87–104.

Smith, Anthony. 1984. *The Mind*. New York: Viking Press.

Smith, Holly M. 1983. "Intercourse and Moral Responsibility for the Fetus." In Bondeson et al., eds. *Abortion and the Status of the Fetus*. Dordrecht: D. Reidel Publishing Company, 1983, pp. 229–45.

Smith, Laura Cuppy. 1873. "How One Woman Entered the Ranks of Social Reform, or, A Mother's Story." In Mary Kane Derr, et al., eds. *Prolife Feminism: Yesterday & Today*. New York: Sulzburger & Graham Publishing, Ltd., 1995, pp. 108–12.

Soukhanov, Anne H., ed. 1992. *The American Heritage Dictionary of the English Language*, 3rd ed.

Stanton, Elizabeth Cady. 1868. "Child Murder." In Mary Kane Derr, et al., eds. *Prolife Feminism: Yesterday & Today*. New York: Sulzburger & Graham Publishing, Ltd., 1995, p. 44.

"Statement of Position and Agenda." Undated. Brooklyn, NY: Jewish Anti-Abortion League.

Steinbock, Bonnie. 1992. *Life Before Birth: The Moral and Legal Status of Embryos and Fetuses*. Oxford: Oxford University Press.

Stetson, Brad. 1996. "Introduction: The Silent Subject." In Brad Stetson, ed. *The Silent Subject: Reflections on the Unborn in American Culture*. Westport, CT: Praeger Publishers, 1996, pp. 1–15.

Stockham, Dr. Alice Bunker. 1887. "Feticide." In Mary Kane Derr, et al., eds. *Prolife Feminism: Yesterday & Today.* New York: Sulzburger & Graham Publishing, Ltd., 1995, pp. 36–40.

Stone, Jim. 1983. "Abortion and the Control of Human Bodies." *Journal of Value Inquiry,* Vol. 17, No. 1, pp. 77–85.

———. 1987. "Why Potentiality Matters." *Canadian Journal of Philosophy,* Vol. 17, No. 4 (December), pp. 815–30.

———. 1994. "Why Potentiality Still Matters." *Canadian Journal of Philosophy,* Vol. 24, No. 2 (June), pp. 281–94.

———. 1995. "Abortion as Murder?: A Response." *Journal of Social Philosophy,* Vol. 26, No. 1 (Spring), pp. 129–46.

Strasser, Mark. 1987. "Noonan on Contraception and Abortion." *Bioethics,* Vol. 1, No. 2, pp. 199–205.

Strong, Carson, and Garland Anderson. "The Moral Status of the Near-Term Fetus." 1989. *Journal of Medical Ethics,* Vol. 15, No. 1, pp. 25–7.

Sumner, L. W. 1981. *Abortion and Moral Theory.* Princeton: Princeton University Press.

Swensen, Daniel. 1991. *Abortion: Thinking Clearly versus Feeling Strongly.* Dallas: Monument Press.

Thomson, Judith Jarvis. 1971. "A Defense of Abortion." Reprinted in Louis P. Pojman and Francis J. Beckwith, eds. *The Abortion Controversy: A Reader.* Boston: Jones and Bartlett, 1994, pp. 113–27.

———. 1973. "Rights and Deaths." *Philosophy and Public Affairs,* Vol. 2 (Winter), pp. 146–59.

Thurnham, Peter M. P., and Sarah Thurnham. 1986. *When Nature Fails – Why Handicap?: The Case for Legalising Pre-embryo Research into Congenital Handicap.* London: Conservative Political Centre.

Tindale, Christopher W. 1994. "Totipotency and the Value of Embryonic Cells." *Journal of Value Inquiry,* Vol. 28, No. 4 (December), pp. 519–28.

Tooley, Michael. 1972. "Abortion and Infanticide." In Susan Dwyer and Joel Feinberg, eds. *The Problem of Abortion,* 3rd ed. Belmont, CA: Wadsworth Publishing Co., 1996, pp. 40–58.

———. 1983. *Abortion and Infanticide.* Oxford: Clarendon Press.

Trevarthen, Colwyn. 1987. "Brain Development." In Richard Gregory, ed. *The Oxford Companion to the Mind.* Oxford: Oxford University Press, pp. 101–10.

Tribe, Laurence. H. 1992. *Abortion: The Clash of Absolutes* (new edition). New York: W. W. Norton & Company.

van Inwagen, Peter. 1990. *Material Beings.* Ithaca and London: Cornell University Press.

Veatch, Robert M. 1983. "Definitions of Life and Death: Should There Be Consistency?" In Margery W. Shaw and A. Edward Doudera, eds. *Defining Human Life: Medical, Legal, and Ethical Implications.* Ann Arbor MI and Washington, DC: AUPHA Press, 1983, pp. 99–118.

"Victory Won." 1995. Advertisement in *National Right to Life News,* Vol. 22, No. 15 (Nov 13), p. 19.

Vieira, Dr. Edwin, Jr. 1978. "The 'Right' of Abortion: A Dogma in Search of a Rationale" [pamphlet]. Wheaton, MD: Libertarians for Life.

Bibliography

————. Undated a. "A False Assumption" (pamphlet). Wheaton, MD: Libertarians for Life.

————. Undated b. "If the Unborn Child is a Person Entitled to Rights, Abortion is Aggression" (pamphlet). Wheaton, MD: Libertarians for Life.

Walen, Alec. 1997. "Consensual Sex without Assuming the Risk of Carrying an Unwanted Fetus; Another Foundation for the Right to an Abortion." *Brooklyn Law Review*, Vol. 63, No. 4 (Winter), pp. 1051–40.

Walker, John. Undated a. "Abortion and the Question of the Person" (pamphlet). Wheaton, MD: Libertarians for Life.

————. Undated b. "Why Parental Obligation?" (pamphlet). Wheaton, MD: Libertarians for Life.

Walker, John, and Doris Gordon. 1993. "Abortion and Libertarianism's First Principles." *LFL Reports: The Newsletter of Libertarians for Life*, No. 9, p. 7.

Waller, Bruce N. 1995. "Abortion and In Vitro Fertilization." *Journal of Social Philosophy*, Vol. XXVI, No. 1 (Spring), pp. 119–28.

Walsh, James L., and Moira M. McQueen. 1993. "The Morality of Induced Delivery of the Anencephalic Fetus Prior to Viability." *Kennedy Institute of Ethics Journal*, Vol. 3, No. 4, pp. 357–69.

Warnock, Mary. 1985. *A Question of Life: The Warnock Report on Human Fertilisation and Embryology*. Oxford: Basil Blackwell.

————. 1987. "Do Human Cells Have Rights?" *Bioethics*, Vol. 1, No. 1 (January), pp. 1–14.

Warren, Mary Anne. 1973. "On the Moral and Legal Status of Abortion." In Lewis M. Schwartz, ed. *Arguing About Abortion*. Belmont, CA: Wadsworth, 1993, pp. 227–42.

Wennberg, Robert N. 1985. *Life in the Balance: Exploring the Abortion Controversy*. Grand Rapids, MI: William B. Eerdmans Publishing Co.

Werner, Richard. 1976. "Hare on Abortion." *Analysis*, Vol. 36, No. 4 (June), pp. 177–81.

Wertheimer, Roger. 1971. "Understanding the Abortion Argument." In Marshall Cohen, Thomas Nagel, and Thomas Scanlon, eds. *The Rights and Wrongs of Abortion*. Princeton: Princeton University Press, 1974, pp. 23–51.

Weston, Anthony. 1984. "Drawing Lines: The Abortion Perplex and the Presuppositions of Applied Ethics." *The Monist*, Vol. 67, No. 4 (October), pp. 589–603.

Whitbeck, Caroline. 1983. "The Moral Implications of Regarding Women as People: New Perspectives on Pregnancy and Personhood." In Bondeson, et al., eds. *Abortion and the Status of the Fetus*. Dordrecht: D. Reidel Publishing Company, 1983, pp. 247–72.

Wicclair, Mark R. 1981. "The Abortion Controversy and the Claim That This Body is Mine." *Social Theory and Practice*, Vol. 7, No. 3 (Fall), pp. 337–46.

Wikler, Daniel. "Concepts of Personhood: A Philosophical Perspective." In Margery W. Shaw and A. Edward Doudera, eds. *Defining Human Life: Medical, Legal, and Ethical Implications*. Ann Arbor, MI and Washington, DC: AUPHA Press, 1983, pp. 12–23.

Wilcox, John T. 1989. "Nature as Demonic in Thomson's Defense of Abortion." In Robert M. Baird and Stuart E. Rosenbaum, eds. *The Ethics of Abortion: Pro-Life vs. Pro-Choice*, rev. ed. Buffalo, NY: Pranetheus Books, 1993, pp. 212–25.

Wiley, Juli Loesch. 1995. "Toward a Holistic Ethic of Life." In Mary Kane Derr, et al., eds. *Prolife Feminism: Yesterday & Today*. New York: Sulzburger & Graham Publishing, Ltd., 1995, pp. 192–5.

Wilkins, Burleigh T. 1993. "Does the Fetus Have a Right to Life?" *Journal of Social Philosophy*, Vol. XXIV, No. 1 (Spring), pp. 123–37.

Williams, Bernard. 1970. "The Self and the Future." In John Perry, ed. *Personal Identity*. Berkeley: University of California Press, 1975, pp. 179–98.

———. 1973. "Ethical Consistency." In Christopher W. Gowans, ed. Oxford: Oxford University Press, 1987. *Moral Dilemmas*, pp. 115–37.

———. 1985. "Which Slopes Are Slippery?" In Michael Lockwood, ed. *Moral Dilemmas in Modern Medicine*. Oxford: Oxford University Press, 1985, pp. 126–37.

———. 1986. "Types of Moral Argument against Embryo Research." In Gregory Bock and Maeve O'Connor, eds. *Human Embryo Research: Yes or No? London and New York: Tavistock Publications*, 1986, pp. 185–212.

Williams, George H. 1972. "Forward: The Democratization of a Near Constant in History." In Thomas W. Hilgers and Dennis J. Horan, eds. *Abortion and Social Justice*. Kansas City, MO: Sheed & Ward, Inc., 1972, pp. ix–xix.

Williams, Glanville. 1957. *The Sanctity of Life and the Criminal Law*. New York: Alfred A. Knopf.

Willke, Dr., and Mrs. J. C. 1975. *Handbook on Abortion*. Cincinnati, OH: Hayes Publishing Co. Inc.

Willke, J. C. 1994. "The Deadly After-Effect of Abortion: Breast Cancer" [pamphlet]. Cincinnati: Hayes Publishing Co. Inc.

Wilson, Bryan. 1988. "On a Kantian Argument against Abortion." *Philosophical Studies*, Vol. 53, No. 1 (January), pp. 119–30.

Wilson, Ellen. 1980. "Looking Glass Logic." *Human Life Review*, Vol. VI, No. 2 (Spring), pp. 5–15.

Winkler, Earl R. 1984. "Abortion and Victimisability." *Journal of Applied Philosophy*, Vol. 1, No. 2, pp. 305–18.

Wolf-Devine, Celia. 1989. "Abortion and the 'Feminine Voice'." In Louis P. Pojman and Francis J. Beckwith, eds. *The Abortion Controversy*. Boston: Jones and Bartlett Publishers, 1994, pp. 408–24.

Wolpert, Lewis. 1991. *The Triumph of the Embryo*. Oxford: Oxford University Press.

Woodhull, Victoria, and Tennessee Claflin. 1874a. "What Will Become of the Children?" In Mary Kane Derr, et al., eds. *Prolife Feminism: Yesterday & Today*. New York: Sulzburger & Graham Publishing, Ltd., 1995, pp. 94–5.

———. 1874b. "The Slaughter of the Innocents." In Mary Kane Derr, et al., eds. *Prolife Feminism: Yesterday & Today*. New York: Sulzburger & Graham Publishing, Ltd., 1995, pp. 95–7.

Wreen, Michael J. 1986. "The Power of Potentiality." *Theoria*, Vol. LII, Parts 1–2, pp. 16–40.

"Young One" (advertisement) 1995. *National Right to Life News*, Vol. 22, No. 13 (September 7), p. 9

Zaitchik, Alan. 1981. "Viability and the Morality of Abortion." *Philosophy and Public Affairs*, Vol. 10, No. 1 (winter), pp. 18–26.

Index

Printed in the United States
49179LVS00004B/142